Nordic Childhoods 17.. 19..

This volume strengthens interest and research in the fields of both Childhood Studies and Nordic Studies by exploring conceptions of children and childhood in the Nordic countries (Denmark, Finland, Iceland, Norway, and Sweden). Although some books have been written on the history of childhood in these countries, few are multidisciplinary, focus on this region as a whole, or are available in English. This volume contains essays by scholars from the fields of literature, history, theology, religious studies, intellectual history, cultural studies, Scandinavian studies, education, music, and art history. Contributors study the history of childhood in a wide variety of sources, such as folk and fairy tales, legal codes, religious texts, essays on education, letters, sermons, speeches, hymns, paintings, novels, and school essays written by children. They also examine texts intended specifically for children, including text books, catechisms, newspapers, songbooks, and children's literature. By bringing together scholars from multiple disciplines who raise distinctive questions about childhood and take into account a wide range of sources, the book offers a fresh and substantive contribution to the history of childhood in the Nordic countries between 1700 and 1960. The volume also helps readers trace the historical roots of the internationally recognized practices and policies regarding child welfare within the Nordic countries today and prompts readers from any country to reflect on their own conceptions of and commitments to children.

Reidar Aasgaard is Professor of History of Ideas at the University of Oslo, Norway.

Marcia J. Bunge is Professor of Religion and the Bernhardson Distinguished Chair at Gustavus Adolphus College, USA.

Merethe Roos is Professor of History at the University College of Southeast Norway.

Ashgate Studies in Childhood, 1700 to the Present

This series recognizes and supports innovative work on the child and on literature for children and adolescents that informs teaching and engages with current and emerging debates in the field. Proposals are welcome for interdisciplinary and comparative studies by humanities scholars working in a variety of fields, including literature; book history, periodicals history, print culture, and the sociology of texts; theater, film, musicology, and performance studies; history, including the history of education; gender studies; art history and visual culture; cultural studies; and theology and religion.

Recent titles in this series:
Space and Place in Children's Literature, 1789 to the Present
By Maria Sachiko Cecire, Hannah Field, Malini Roy

Ethics and Children's Literature
By Claudia Mills

The Child Savage, 1890-2010: From Comics to Games
Edited by Elisabeth Wesseling

British Hymn Books for Children, 1800-1900
By Alisa Clapp-Itnyre

Nordic Childhoods 1700–1960
From Folk Beliefs to Pippi Longstocking

Edited by Reidar Aasgaard, Marcia J. Bunge, and Merethe Roos

Routledge
Taylor & Francis Group

LONDON AND NEW YORK

First published 2018 by Routledge

2 Park Square, Milton Park, Abingdon, Oxfordshire OX14 4RN
52 Vanderbilt Avenue, New York, NY 10017

Routledge is an imprint of the Taylor & Francis Group, an informa business

First issued in paperback 2019

Library of Congress Cataloging in Publication Data
A catalog record for this title has been requested

ISBN: 978-1-138-29422-6 (hbk)
ISBN: 978-0-367-88627-1 (pbk)

Typeset in Sabon
by Deanta Global Publishing Services, Chennai, India

Contents

List of Figures   viii
Biographical Notes   x
Acknowledgments   xv

1   Introduction   1
     REIDAR AASGAARD AND MARCIA J. BUNGE

PART I
Spheres of Life: Home, Church, and Society   15

2   The Child in Norwegian and Scandinavian Folk Beliefs   17
     ØRNULF A. HODNE

3   The Household Code: Protestant Upbringing in
     Denmark–Norway from the Reformation
     to the Enlightenment   40
     INGRID MARKUSSEN

4   "Let the Little Children Come to Me": Representations of
     Children in the Confessional Culture of Lutheran Scandinavia   58
     KRISTIN B. AAVITSLAND

5   Education of Children in Rural Finland: The Roles
     of Homes, Churches, and Manor Houses   76
     ANU LAHTINEN

6   Children's Rights and Duties: Snapshots into the History
     of Education and Child Protection in Denmark
     (ca. 1700–1900)   91
     ANETTE FAYE JACOBSEN

PART II
Children's Development: Formation, Education, and Work   109

 7 "A Plain and Cheerful, Active Life on Earth": Children,
    Education, and Faith in the Works of N. F. S. Grundtvig
    (1783–1872, Denmark)   111
    MARCIA J. BUNGE

 8 "Educating Poor, Rich, and Dangerous Children":
    The Birth of a Segregated School System in Nineteenth-
    Century Sweden   131
    BENGT SANDIN

 9 The Child in the Early Nineteenth-Century Norwegian
    School System   147
    THOR INGE RØRVIK

10 Negotiating Family, Education, and Labor: Working-Class
    Children in Finland in the Nineteenth and
    Twentieth Centuries   163
    PIRJO MARKKOLA

11 Sheep, Fish, and School: Conflicting Arenas of Childhood
    in the Lives of Icelandic Children, 1900–1970   175
    ÓLÖF GARÐARSDÓTTIR

12 Educational Policy and Boarding Schools for Indigenous
    Sami Children in Norway from 1700 to the Present   188
    KETIL LENERT HANSEN

13 Children and Their Stories of World War II: A Study of
    Essays by Norwegian School Children from 1946   205
    ELLEN SCHRUMPF

14 "In Song We Meet on Common Ground": Conceptions
    of Children in Songbooks for Norwegian Schools
    (1914–1964)   220
    EILIV O. OLSEN

PART III
Literature: Children's Books, Fairy Tales, and Novels   239

15 Children, Dying, and Death: Views from an
    Eighteenth-Century Periodical for Children   241
    MERETHE ROOS

16 Incandescent Objects and Pictures of Misery: Hans Christian
Andersen's Fairy Tales for Children   254
MARIA TATAR

17 Inventing Subjectivity and the Rights of the Child
in Nineteenth-Century Nordic Children's Literature   265
OLLE WIDHE

18 Competent Children: Childhood in Nordic Children's
Literature from 1850 to 1960   283
ÅSE MARIE OMMUNDSEN

19 The Small People in the Big Picture: Children in Swedish
Working-Class Novels of the 1930s   303
KARIN NYKVIST

Select Bibliography   319
References   321
Index   352

Figures

2.1 The parents tried to influence the child's destiny while it lay in the cradle 22

2.2 The mother was a vital provider of care for the child in the cradle—especially for the unbaptized child 24

2.3 *The Woman Who Murdered Her Child*: a painting by Eyolf Soot (1859–1928) 30

2.4 Box for a miscarried fetus in Voss church 31

2.5 The attempt was made by means of "creeping" to cure children who suffered from epilepsy, hernia, or rickets 34

2.6 *The Woman Who Told Adventure Stories*: a drawing by Adolph Tidemand (1814–1876) 37

3.1 Epitaph from Køge Church, showing the Dean Christen Lauritsen Glob (1581–1633) 42

4.1 "Suffer little children to come unto me", ca. 1550. Larvik Church, southern Norway 60

4.2 Christen Svenningsen and his family commemorative portrait, 1664, Søndeled Church, southern Norway 63

4.3 Elias Figenschou: Peder Gabelsen Krag and his Family 67

4.4 The deceased children of Enevold Skaktavl. Detail of commemorative portrait, 1700 68

4.5 Commemorative portrait of the Hjortberg family. Släps Church, southwestern Sweden 68

4.6 Commemorative portrait of Thomas Uro and his family. Ulvik Church, western Norway 69

4.7 C. W. Eckersberg: Portrait of C. F. Holm's children, 1832 71

4.8 Children portrait of unknown provenience, 1690 73

11.1 Population in towns and villages with 200 inhabitants or more. Iceland 1901–1970 (%) 177

11.2 Distribution of school children by type of school 1908–1970 (%) 179

11.3 Feeding the animals. Dýrafjörður in the Vestfjords,
       North-Western Iceland 1962   180
11.4 Women and teenaged girls working side by side in the
       Herring Industry. Seyðisfjörður, East Iceland 1963   183
11.5 Dock work. Thirteen-year-old boys working in the
       Reykjavík Harbor in 1964   184
11.6 Summer jobs of Reykjavík youth by sex and
       age 1962 (%)   185
12.1 Map of the area of the Sami (called Sápmi)   189
12.2 Sami children were sent to boarding schools where
       they spoke only Norwegian   194
18.1 Elling Holst: *Norsk billedbog for børn* (1888)   284
18.2 The Beheaded Doll. Jørgen Moe: *I brønden og
       i tjærnet* (1877)   288
18.3 Viggo. Henrik Sørensen. Illustration from the book
       I brønden og i tjærnet by Jørgen Moe (1928, 1939,
       1963, 1972, 1987)   291
18.4 Jørgen Moe: *I brønden og i tjærnet* (1898)   292
18.5 Inger Johanne (Dikken Zwilgmeyer). *Vi børn* (1890)   295
18.6 Elsa Beskow: *Dugtiga Annika* (1941)   298

Biographical Notes

Aasgaard, Reidar (Oslo, Norway) Aasgaard is Professor of Intellectual History/History of Ideas at the University of Oslo. He has published books, chapters, and articles in English and in Norwegian on the New Testament, Early Christianity, Christian Apocrypha, Augustine, and children and family relations in antiquity, and also teaches courses on the history of childhood. He was director of the research project "Tiny Voices from the Past: New Perspectives on Childhood in Early Europe" (2013–2017), funded by the Norwegian Research Council and the University of Oslo.

Aavitsland, Kristin B. (Oslo, Norway) Aavitsland is Professor of Medieval Culture and Church History at MF Norwegian School of Theology in Oslo, where she teaches and researches medieval and early modern cultural history, and leads the research project "Tracing the Jerusalem Code: Christian Cultures in Scandinavia." She is the author of *Imagining the Human Condition in Medieval Rome* (2012). Recent articles include "Visualizing the Art of Dying in Early Protestant Scandinavia: A Reading of a Late Sixteenth-Century Tapestry from Leksvik, Norway" in the *Journal of Early Modern Christianity* (2014); and "Remembering Death in Denmark–Norway during the Period of Lutheran Orthodoxy" in *Preparing for Death – Remembering the Dead* (Vandenhoeck and Ruprecht, 2015).

Bunge, Marcia J. (Minnesota, USA) Bunge is Professor of Religion and the Bernhardson Distinguished Chair at Gustavus Adolphus College (USA), and Extraordinary Professor at NW University (South Africa). She is the translator of J. G. Herder, *Against Pure Reason* (Fortress, 1993), and she has edited and contributed to several works on religious understandings of children, including *The Child in Christian Thought* (Eerdmans, 2001); *Children and Childhood in World Religions: Primary Sources and Texts* (Rutgers, 2009); *The Child in Christian Thought* (Eerdmans, 2001); and *Children, Adults, and Shared Responsibilities: Jewish, Christian, and Muslim Perspectives* (Cambridge University, 2012).

Faye Jacobson, Anette (Copenhagen, Denmark) Jacobsen is Senior Researcher at the Danish Institute for Human Rights. Recent writings include "Children's Rights in the European Court of Human Rights – An Emerging Power Structure," *International Journal of Children's Rights* 24, (2016): 549–574. She is also co-author of *Da skolen blev sin egen* [*When school was his own*] (Aarhus Universitetsforlag, 2014); co-author of *Da skolen blev sat i system* [*When Education Became Systematically Organised*] (Aarhus Universitetsforlag 2014) and *Husbondret. Rettighedskulturer i Danmark, 1750–1920* [*Household. Rights Cultures in Denmark*] (Museum Tusculanum, 2008).

Garðarsdóttir, Ólöf (Reykjavík, Iceland) Garðarsdóttir is Professor in Social History, School of Education at the University of Iceland. She is author of several books and articles on historical demography and the history of childhood and of the family, including *Barnen och välfärdspolitiken. Nordiska barndomar 1900–2000* [Children and Welfare Policy. Nordic Childhoods 1900–2000] (Dialogos, 2011).

Hansen, Ketil Lenert (Tromsø, Norway) Hansen is Associate Professor at the Regional Centre for Child and Youth Mental Health and Child Welfare North (RKBU Nord), the Arctic University of Norway. He is author of several articles on bullying, discrimination, violence, and health among the Sami population in the arctic region in Norway, including: "Ethnic discrimination and health: the relationship between experienced ethnic discrimination and multiple health domains in Norway's rural Sami population" (*International Journal of Circumpolar Health*, 2015); "Ethnic Discrimination and Psychological Distress: A Study of Sami and Non-Sami Populations in Norway" (*Transcultural Psychiatry*, 2012); and co-author of "Childhood Violence and Adult Chronic Pain among Indigenous Sami and Non-Sami Populations in Norway: A SAMINOR 2 Questionnaire Study" (*International Journal of Circumpolar Health*, 2016).

Hodne, Ørnulf A. (Oslo, Norway) Hodne is Reader Emeritus of Cultural Studies and Researcher and Lecturer at the Department of Culture Studies and Oriental Languages, University of Oslo. He has published extensively on Norwegian cultural history, especially folklore and folk poetry, and on children's upbringing, including: *Jørgen Moe og folkeeventyrene. Informanter og utgivelsesprinsipper* [*Jørgen Moe and Folktales. Informants and Publication Policies*] (Universitetsforlaget, 1979); *Norsk folketro* [*Norwegian Folklore*] (J. W. Cappelens forlag, 1999); and *Trolldom i Norge. Hekser og trollmenn i folketro og lokaltradisjon* [Witchcraft in Norway. Witches and Wizards in Folklore and Local Traditions] (Cappelen Damm, 2008).

Lahtinen, Anu (Turku, Finland) Lahtinen is Professor of Finnish and Nordic History at the University of Helsinki. She is author of five monographs and numerous articles, including a chapter (100 pages) on education in medieval and early modern Finland, in *Kasvatus ja koulutus Suomessa keskiajalta 1860-luvulle* [Education in Finland from the Middle Ages to the 1860s] (co-written with Jussi Hanska, Finnish Literature Society, 2010).

Markkola, Pirjo (Tampere, Finland) Markkola is Professor of History at the Faculty of Social Sciences, University of Tampere. She is the co-editor of *Education, State and Citizenship* (NordWel, 2013) and a special issue of the *Journal of Church and State* on "Lutheranism and the Nordic Welfare States" (2014). She is co-author of *Barnen och välfärdspolitiken. Nordiska barndomar 1900–2000* [Children and Welfare Policies. Nordic Childhoods 1900–2000] (Dialogos, 2011) and the Finnish inquiry on child abuse and neglect in child protection institutions and foster homes in Finland, 1937–1983 (2016). She is the author of several books and articles.

Markussen, Ingrid (Oslo, Norway; Denmark) Markussen is Professor Emerita of History of Ideas, Faculty of Humanities (IFIKK), University of Oslo, and Researcher at The Royal Danish School of Education (Denmark). She is author of *Visdommens lænker* [The Shackles of Wisdom] (Landbohistorisk Selskab, 1988); *Til Skaberens Ære, Statens Tjeneste og Vor Egen Nytte* [To the Creator's Glory, State Department and our Own Gain] (Odense University Studies, 1995); and "The Role of Schools and Education from the 16th to the end of the 18th Century" in *The Nordic languages* (2005).

Nykvist, Karin (Lund, Sweden) Nykvist is Associate Professor of Comparative Literature, Centre of Languages and Literature, Lund University. She is the author of several articles on the construction of childhood in fiction and film, including: "In the Kingdom of Cancer: Dying Children Living Their Own Lives in the Contemporary YA novel" in *Child Autonomy and Child Governance in Children's Literature* (Routledge, 2017); "Through the Eyes of a Child: Childhood and Mass Dictatorship in Modern European Literature" in *Imagining Mass Dictatorships. The Individual and the Masses in Literature and Cinema* (Palgrave Macmillian, 2013); and "Remembering and Recreating Childhood in the Works of Ingmar Bergman and August Strindberg" in *Negotiating Childhoods* (Inter-Disciplinary Press, 2010).

Olsen, Eiliv O. (Bergen, Norway) Olsen is Associate Professor Emeritus of Music Education at the Department of Teacher Education, Bergen University College (Norway). He is co-editor of *Musikk – mulighetenes fag* [*Music – a School Subject with Possibilities*] (Fagbokforlaget, 2007) and *Med sang! Perspektiver på norske skolesangbøker etter 1814* [*With Song! Perspectives upon Norwegian Compulsory School Songbooks after 1814*] (Novus, 2014).

Ommundsen, Åse Marie (Oslo, Norway) Ommundsen is Professor of Literature at Faculty of Education, Oslo and Akershus University College of Applied Sciences and Professor II at the Nord University, Bodø (Norway). She is the author of *Litterære grenseoverskridelser. Når grensene mellom barne- og voksenlitteraturen viskes ut* [*Literary Boundary Crossings. Erasing the borders between literature for children and adults*] (2010) and *Djevelfrø og englebarn. Synet på barn i kristne barneblader i perioden 1875 til 1910* [*Devil Seeds and Little Angels: The View upon Children in Religious Magazines for Children from 1875 to 1910*] (1998). Recent articles include "Children's Rule in Comic Strips and TV Series" (Routledge, 2017) and "Norwegian Children's Literature in the Aftermath of 22nd July: Collective Memory and Trauma Relief" (Cambridge Scholars Publishing, 2017).

Roos, Merethe (Notodden, Norway) Roos is Professor of History in the Department of Culture, Religion and Social Studies at the University College of Southeast Norway. She is the author on a number of books and articles on the eighteenth and nineteenth century, including: *Enlightened Preaching. Balthasar Münter's Authorship 1772–1793* (Brill, 2013); *Poverty, Charity, and the Risk of Eternal Damnation: Balthasar Münter's Clerical Risk Communication in late 18th Century Copenhagen* (Waxmann, 2012); *Struensee in Britain. The Reception of the Struensee Affair in British Periodicals 1772* (Brill, 2015); and *Kraften i allmenn dannelse. Skolen som formidler av humaniora. Bidrag til en historisk lesning* (Portal, 2016).

Rørvik, Thor Inge (Oslo, Norway) Rørvik is Lecturer of History of Ideas, Faculty of Humanities (IFIKK), at the University of Oslo. He is co-author of *Universitetet i Oslo 1870–1911: Vitenskapenes universitet*, bind 2 [The University of Oslo 1870–1911: University of the Sciences] (Unipub, 2011), and author of several articles on Norwegian history of ideas in the eighteenth and nineteenth century, e.g. "The Generation of 1814. Aspects on an Extinct Paradigm of Breeding" in *Scandinavian Studies in Rhetoric. Rethorica Scandinavica 1997–2010* (Retorikförlaget, 2011).

Sandin, Bengt (Linköping, Sweden) Sandin is Professor of Child Studies, Department of Thematic Studies/Child Studies, University of Linköping. He is author of *Situating Child Consumption, Rethinking Values and Notions of Children, Childhood and Consumption* (Nordic Academic Press Falun, 2012); "Swedish Childhoods from the Era of Great Power to the Welfare State" in *Swedish Wooden Toys* (Yale University Press, 2014); and "Children and the Swedish Welfare State: From Different to Similar" in *Reinventing Childhood After World War II* (University of Pennsylvania Press, 2012).

Schrumpf, Ellen (Bø, Norway) Schrumpf is Professor of History in the Department of Culture, Religion, and Social Studies at the University

College of Southeast Norway, where she teaches childhood history. She is the author of *Barnearbeid: plikt eller privilegium? Barnearbeid og oppvekst i to norske industrisamfunn i perioden 1850–1910* [Child Work: Duty of Privilege? Working Children in Two Industrial Communities in Norway 1850–1910] (Høyskoleforlaget, 1997); *Barndomshistorie* [Childhood History] (Det Norske Samlaget, 2007); and she is co-editor of *Industrious Children. Work and Childhood in the Nordic Countries 1850–1990* (Odense University Press 1997).

Tatar, Maria (Harvard, USA) Tatar is the John L. Loeb Professor of Folklore and Mythology and Germanic Languages and Literatures, Harvard University (USA). She is the author of *The Hard Facts of the Grimms' Fairy Tales* (Princeton University Press, 1987); *The Annotated Hans Christian Andersen* (W. W. Norton & Co, 2007); *Classic Fairy Tales* (W. W. Norton & Co, 1999); and *The Annotated Brothers Grimm* (W. W. Norton & Co, 2004), among other volumes. She is a frequent contributor to National Public Radio in the USA, the *New York Times*, *The New Yorker*, and other media outlets.

Widhe, Olle (Gothenburg, Sweden) Widhe is Associate Professor and Coordinator of Graduate Studies at the Department of Literature, History of Ideas, and Religion at the University of Gothenburg where he teaches the history of children's literature and the use of children's literature in the classroom. He is the author of *Dö din Hund!: krig, lek och läsning i svensk barnboksutgivning under 200 år* [*Die You Dog! War, Play and Reading in Swedish Children's Literature 1789–1989*] (Ellerströms, 2015) and several articles about children's literature and children's rights.

Acknowledgments

A great number of people have been involved in producing this interdisciplinary volume on Nordic Childhoods. The book is one of the outcomes of a larger project entitled "Tiny Voices from the Past: New Perspectives on Childhood in Early Europe" (2013–2017). The project was funded by the Research Council of Norway and hosted by the History of Ideas (Intellectual History) section, which is located in the Department of Philosophy, Classics, History of Art, and Ideas (IFIKK) at the University of Oslo.

As co-editors, we have many people to thank for helping us to complete the publication of this volume.

We are indebted to The Research Council of Norway and IFIKK for providing the funding and other resources necessary for contributors to meet together in Oslo to exchange ideas and respond in person to drafts of one another's work.

We also want to thank the contributors for their stimulating and collegial discussions during our consultations and for their insightful and perceptive chapters. Contributors came from various disciplines and countries and worked together in a genuine spirit of collaboration.

We wish to thank all the local and international core group members of the "Tiny Voices from the Past" Thanks also go to Oana Maria Cojocaru, who served as editorial secretary for the volume, and the research assistants, Camilla Christensen, Rakel Diesen, Lars Fredrik Janby, Cecilie Krohn, and Camilla Roll.

A special thanks goes to Brian McNeil for proofreading the volume and for his skillful translations of four chapters: Ketil Lenert Hansen and Ørnulf Hodne from Norwegian, Ingrid Markussen from Danish, and Olle Widhe from Swedish.

Thanks also are due to the colleagues in the History of Ideas section for their hospitality to all the contributors and to core members of the project during the process of finishing this book and the project as a whole.

Finally, we are grateful to the editors and staff at Routledge/Taylor & Francis for including this book in their series on "Studies in Childhood: 1700 to the Present" and for their support and flexibility during the publishing process.

1 Introduction

Reidar Aasgaard and Marcia J. Bunge

Today, Nordic countries and the "Nordic models" are receiving growing attention around the world. The five countries that are called "Nordic"— Denmark, Finland, Iceland, Norway, and Sweden—are often hot topics in the news and international debates because they rank so highly in many measures of well-being. For example, they are ranked among the top countries in the world for economic success, political stability, and quality of life. The Nordic countries also earn top scores in studies of global happiness. They are often referred to as "welfare states" because they provide many services to the entire population, have a marked involvement of the state in the lives of its citizens, and nurture a strong sense of shared civic responsibility. They have universal health care, low poverty rates, small income gaps, well-developed social networks, and a high level of trust among the people and between the people and the civil authorities. Gender equality has also been given high priority. In 1906, Finland was the first European country to give women the right to vote, and many women have top positions within political, economic, and cultural life. Thus, the "Nordic model" and the "Nordic welfare states" are in many contexts referred to as "ideal," "exceptional," or even "nearly perfect."[1] Of course, these countries are far from perfect, but they are nonetheless in many respects flourishing and well functioning. Thus, other countries are taking notice and paying attention to various Nordic "models," as they seek to strengthen their own social, economic, and political life.

Along with these and other dimensions of "the Nordic," these five countries are also internationally recognized for their long-standing commitments to child protection, child welfare, and children's rights. The Nordic countries have a long history of providing health care to all children and are ranked highly in all categories of child well-being. They provide extensive prenatal care, social services, and generous paid leaves for new parents. Denmark, for example, allows parents to take nearly a year of paid leave to care for their newborns. Since the 1930s, the Finnish government has been sending all expectant mothers a maternity package with clothes and baby goods. Sweden was the first country to outlaw physical punishment of children. And Norway was the first country globally to appoint a national, state-funded ombudsman or public advocate charged with representing the interests of children. The Nordic countries have also been important supporters of not-for-profit agencies that provide for the needs and rights of children around the world, such as the United Nations Children's Fund (UNICEF), Save the Children, and SOS Children's Villages.

The Nordic countries also capture international attention because they are among the top in the world in terms of literacy and education. Literacy rates stand at 100 percent, and the countries' educational systems score very highly in terms of quality and equal access. Finland, for example, has been ranked among the top five in global educational assessments of fifteen year olds, and the other Nordic countries are not much further down the list.[2] Primary and secondary educations are free of charge and open to all. Basically, all children attend the same common schools and those with special needs, such as disabilities, are given additional support. The educational opportunities are equal for girls and boys, the school system is similar both in urban and rural areas, and all schools use a common curriculum. Equal numbers of boys and girls enter college, and college students, regardless of class or gender, pay nothing for tuition. Although historically the countries have been relatively poor, they have had a long-standing commitment to education, which is reflected in the history of their legislation. Norway had its first educational act in 1739 as part of Denmark. Denmark introduced universal education for all children in 1814, Sweden in 1842, Finland in 1866, and Iceland followed in 1907.

Related perhaps to their high literacy rates and strong educational systems, the Nordic countries have a rich history of literature for and about children. This literature includes fairy tales of oral as well as literary origin, children's songs in a variety of genres, and poems and stories written for children. Reading is regarded an important part of good childhood, and book stores cater to both adults and children. In central parts of this varied body of children's books, children—both girls and boys—have been depicted as active and in control of their own lives; a significant example in this literature is the famous Pippi Longstocking. The Nordic countries are also well known for children's books of high aesthetic quality, produced by prominent artists.

Research on the History of Children and Childhood in the Nordic Countries

In spite of the long-lasting commitments of Nordic countries to children and child well-being, limited attention has been given to the history behind these matters and to the history of childhood itself. Contemporary commitments to children in the Nordic countries did not emerge in a vacuum or arrive on the scene "full blown." Nordic policies and practices regarding child protection and education arose out of long and sometimes bitter debates and power-struggles. Nordic literature for and about children took different forms over the centuries, reflecting shifting perceptions of boys and girls. Furthermore, even though the countries share many common features and perhaps from an international perspective appear to be quite similar, they are each distinctive. They have unique and complex characteristics, policies, and histories. For example, Norway was not even an independent country until 1905; it was once part of Denmark and later Sweden. For a long time, particularly in the eighteenth and nineteenth centuries, Sweden and Denmark were rivals, and even enemies. Parts of present-day Finland were at points under the control of Russia or Sweden. Iceland was under the rule of Norwegian and then Danish kings until 1944.

The complex histories and distinctive features of the Nordic countries are reflected in several excellent recent studies of the history of children and childhood. However, most of these studies are highly specialized, tend to focus on one place or historical period alone, and deal with individual countries. Furthermore, very few are available in English. As for research on historical periods, for example, more attention has been given to the Protestant Reformation in the sixteenth century or to the explosion of children's literature in the late twentieth century than to the period between 1700 and the early twentieth century. Of the studies that do examine the eighteenth, nineteenth, or early twentieth centuries, most focus on a particular figure or country and draw few comparisons among the Nordic countries. These studies, too, are often addressed to experts in a specific field, and thus are less accessible to scholars in other fields, or to others who are interested in children and the history of childhood. Some substantive studies by Nordic scholars, including many in this volume, are addressed to a broader audience but are published in Nordic languages. The select bibliography at the end of this volume includes many of these scholarly works. Although a number of works in English can be found in the bibliography, particularly some articles and book chapters, research literature on Nordic childhoods in English is still quite limited.[3] Finally, very few texts in the field of Nordic studies or childhood studies are multi-disciplinary—although this has been changing over the last few years—and the range of sources they explore is thus often limited.

Aim and Guiding Questions of This Volume

The aim of this volume is to address this gap in the literature and to strengthen research in the fields of both childhood studies and Nordic studies by offering a book in English that explores Nordic perspectives on children between 1700 and c.1960 from a variety of sources and disciplines. The volume contains essays from scholars in diverse fields, including social sciences, literature, history, religious studies, cultural studies, Scandinavian studies, music, art history and intellectual history. Since these scholars come from various disciplines, they also examine the history of childhood from a wide variety of sources, such as folk tales, legal codes, speeches, hymns, poems, paintings, novels, and school essays written by children themselves. The contributors also examine a variety of texts aimed specifically at children, including text books, catechisms, newspapers, journals, songbooks, and novels for children.

Building on these varied kinds of sources and employing their own disciplinary methods, the authors of this volume seek to address the following overarching questions:

1   What do their sources reveal about conceptions of the nature, role, or status of children and about issues of gender, race, socio-economic status, minority status, or religious identity?
2   How do the sources speak about the treatment of children, individual and communal obligations to children, and children's own agency and responsibilities?
3   What are some of the questions, figures, and themes regarding children that are significant in each author's particular discipline?
4   What clues, if any, do the sources give about the historical background for present-day commitments to child welfare and advocacy?
5   In what ways, if any, can the book challenge readers—regardless of country—to explore contemporary understandings of children, children's rights and responsibilities, and human dignity and worth?

Although it was of course not possible for each and every author to address all of these questions, they helped guide the common work of the volume even as they enabled all authors to sharpen the focus of their particular area of research.

By bringing together scholars from multiple disciplines to address these and other questions about the history of childhood in the Nordic countries, the volume offers a substantive and distinctive contribution to research within this field. Furthermore, with its combination of childhood studies and Nordic studies, the volume may also inspire other scholars to incorporate research on childhood into the studies of other regions or cultures, such as African studies or Latin-American studies. And since conceptions of children and of human nature are closely interwoven, the volume can also spark further reflection on child well-being and human dignity in other parts of the world, whether these regions and cultures have much in common with the Nordic countries or differ in most respects.

Title and Period Studied

The book is entitled *"Nordic Childhoods"* to highlight some of the commonalities and differences within the history of childhood in the Nordic countries. On the one hand, the histories of childhood in these countries necessarily share some similarities because there are several factors that bind the Nordic countries together. For example, they all became Lutheran in the early sixteenth century, and their populations in the past have been, and still are today, predominantly Lutheran. Thus, many common values, beliefs, and practices shaped their histories and conceptions of children, including a high regard for education and literacy. Furthermore, traditionally, agriculture, fishery, and hunting have been very important, with life in many areas often being conditioned by a demanding climate.

Common linguistic roots have also played a central role in forming similar perspectives on children in the Nordic countries. The languages in Denmark, Norway, and Sweden are variants of Scandinavian and are easily understood across the countries. In Finland, the majority language is Finnish, which is linguistically very different from Scandinavian; but a significant minority speaks Swedish, and all children in Finland also learn some Swedish at school. In Iceland, the language is Icelandic, which is close to Old Norse, but which differs considerably from the other modern Scandinavian languages; however, many Icelanders speak or understand Danish. Thus, a common religious and linguistic heritage has been, and still is, an element that links the Nordic countries to each other.

On the other hand, one cannot speak of childhood as one uniform matter in the area and the period under consideration here. In spite of the many common conditions that have shaped children's lives and adult views of childhood in the Nordic countries, there are also marked differences. Each has a particular history with varied economic and political circumstances, social and cultural tensions, religious developments, and ideas about gender and class. Even in terms of size and geographical features, the Nordic countries differ. Sweden is the largest, with over 9 million people. Norway, Denmark, and Finland are all around 5 million. With only about 330,000 people, Iceland is the smallest. Topographically, they are also different: Norway is well known for its fjords and mountains. Denmark has long beaches and is generally flat. Finland is almost all forest and lakes and primarily rural. Sweden is a mixture of flat, cultivated areas and lakes in the south, and forests, hills, and sparsely populated areas in the north. Iceland, the most northern country, has less than 2 percent forest, active volcanoes, and more sheep than people. In various ways in these countries, nature has been a source of income, a place for leisure, and a dangerous force.

Thus, whereas one can speak of something as being "Nordic," including experiences of and ideas about childhood, the title of the book includes the plural word, "Childhoods," and its contents honor the fact that the word, "Nordic," should be used with caution. Indeed, one aim of the volume is to highlight the great variety in historical constructions of childhood in the Nordic countries.

The chronological limits set for this book are 1700–1960. Although such limits are of course artificial and approximate, they mark significant shifts in conceptions of childhood. The eighteenth century in the Nordic countries, as also in other regions, was a time of change, with growing attention to new ideas about the nation, human rights, individual responsibility and autonomy, and education and pedagogy. Enlightenment and Pietism, and later Romanticism, were among the influential movements that shaped many areas of life also in this part of northern Europe, including childhood.

The other end of the time span, 1960, indicates that the volume primarily deals with historical childhood. Furthermore, by this time, ideas about the "welfare state" were well established in the Nordic countries. Even though the chapters focus primarily on the period between 1700 and 1960, several of them also explore ideas and practices that shaped this period, rooted particularly in ancient folk beliefs and the Lutheran Reformation, while other chapters deal with matters that anticipate contemporary notions and concerns.

By exploring the period 1700–1960, an era often termed "Late Modernity," the volume contributes to the history of childhood in these countries as well as the broader history of these relatively young nations. The history of childhood is a prerequisite for understanding the current attitudes to children and childhood in the Nordic countries. But since children are a significant part of any community, the history of childhood of this period can also serve to shed light on central elements in the development of this region as a whole.

Structure and Scope of the Volume

The chapters of the volume are divided into three main parts. The parts are structured around three main thematic areas, which are quite distinct yet necessarily overlap in some respects.

The first area explores the three social spheres, or institutions, to which children in the Nordic countries belonged, and which strongly shaped their ideas and experiences. These spheres include: (1) the home, which was the basic unit for children and adults alike, whether it is denoted family, household, or other; (2) the Lutheran church, which was the predominant religious institution throughout the Nordic countries and which shaped their values, beliefs, and practices; and (3) society, which for children would have included the local community, sometimes the school, and the state or nation.

The second thematic area deals with children's development. It explores several factors that in crucial ways shaped children from infancy, such as: (1) formation, which would have mainly taken place in the home or church and was closely related to Lutheranism; (2) education at school, which would often have been adapted to the needs and concerns of different classes or levels of society; and (3) children's work, which for many communities and families was pursued out of necessity but which, in many cases, also served to make children able to master their own lives as future adults.

The third and final thematic area focuses on a more limited field: literature. Given the longstanding emphasis on literacy in the Nordic countries, literature is a significant source for Nordic histories of childhood. The chapters in this section deal with a variety of genres, such as: (1) novels written for adults that describe children on their way to adulthood; (2) fairy tales intended for adults and children alike; and (3) stories explicitly written for children, and even with the intention of seeing the world from children's own perspective.

Even though all chapters address different thematic areas and sources, they situate their topic and material within a larger cultural and social context, whether within the history of childhood or the history of the Nordic countries, and thus provide readers with an overview of the field and the period of concern. In a few instances, different chapters also touch on some of the same central figures but from different perspectives; or they deal with similar phenomena, for example education, but in different countries. In this way, the book offers readers the ability to go into more detail in specific areas, to make comparisons among countries, and to reflect on their own conceptions of and commitments to children.

The time period and the geographical areas examined in this book are of course far too long and broad to be covered in detail. The volume seeks to offer, however, both a certain overview of the history of childhood in the Nordic countries and to make a few specialized and substantive explorations into childhood in several particular fields and disciplines. Emphasis is on Denmark, Sweden, and Norway, while Finland and Iceland have two and one contributions respectively.[4] Within a volume like this, such lopsidedness is unavoidable, but each chapter also aims at taking side glances to the other countries.

Some of the material in the following chapters has not been studied at all, such as the Norwegian school essays written in 1946 by children about their war experiences (see Chapter 13 by Schrumpf). Other sources have been studied extensively, but—surprisingly–almost not at all with attention to children and childhood, such as the works of N. F. S. Grundtvig, the great nineteenth-century Danish poet (Bunge). Individually, but also together, these very diverse case studies are intended to serve as an impetus for further reading, study, and research on various sources that deal with the history of children and childhood within a Nordic setting.

Although the scope of the volume is broad, it cannot be exhaustive and therefore contains a number of omissions. For example, much could have been said about children's leisure activities or about the many movements and organizations for children, whether in sports, labor movements, scouting, or other. Furthermore, we have very little on children in minority groups except on childhood within a Sami context, a significant ethnic culture that includes the northern parts of Norway, Sweden, and Finland (Hansen). Given these and other omissions, the volume can hopefully spark further research and international publications in the history of childhood in the Nordic countries.

Central Themes and Findings

From the chapters in this volume there emerge several important themes and specific findings that contribute to an understanding of the history of children and childhood in the Nordic countries. Even though each chapter takes its point of departure in the special material and area of competence of the authors, they still converge on many points across differences in disciplines and approaches, some of which will be touched on here.

Central Place of the Family

The family had a crucial place in the lives of children in the Nordic countries, whether socially, culturally, religiously, or otherwise. In various ways, the theme of family is central in all of the sources studied for this volume, including the visual arts, with its representations of family ideals (Aavitsland). If we are to have an adequate understanding of the shape of Nordic childhood(s) from the eighteenth century onwards, then the Protestant Reformation is an inevitable presupposition: Martin Luther (1483–1546) and his Nordic successors lifted up the importance of the family and saw having children as an important calling or vocation (Aavitsland, Markussen, and Rørvik).

Household codes

Conceptions of the family were understood in close alignment with Luther's household codes. These codes, based on biblical texts, were expressed in several of Luther's writings, including in his *Small Catechism* and *Large Catechism*, and in their Nordic follow-ups, such as the catechism of Erik Pontoppidan (1698–1764). Household codes provide instructions for domestic and civic life and outline various duties of children, parents, the church, and the state. Duties to children, indeed to all those in need, expressed in these codes were based on the biblical idea that all people are made in the image of God and on the commands to teach children and to love and serve the neighbor, including the poor and orphans. Several chapters in this volume highlight the importance of the household codes and the Lutheran Church for children's well-being, education, and shared obligations to children. The codes also outlined children's own responsibilities to others and to God (Bunge, Jacobsen, Markussen, and Rørvik). Folk beliefs also reflected a strong concern for the interests and well-being of children, particularly in their earliest stages of life (Hodne).

Tensions Regarding Authority

Although these codes helped encourage a sense of obligation to nurture and educate all children, this model was hierarchical, and Lutheranism itself has never been monolithic. Thus, in the history of childhood in the Nordic countries we also find tensions between the state and the family, parents and children, or religious authorities and the people regarding obligations to and authority over children (Markussen). Furthermore, even though the Nordic countries have been and continue to be predominantly

Lutheran, this Lutheranism is complex, and many movements, religious thinkers, and factions have played a role in the history of childhood, such as Lutheran orthodox thinkers, pietists, and rationalists. Strands within the church were at times in conflict, and some religious leaders were jailed or censored. Several chapters address such conflicts, which both reflected social tensions between the agricultural population and local superiors, and ideological differences between the common believers and the ecclesiastical elite about what practices best served children's interests (Hodne, Sandin).

Children's Rights

Despite such tensions, basic commitments to child protection found in folk beliefs and Lutheranism played a role in shaping attention in the Nordic countries to children's rights. Conceptions of duties and obligations expressed in the household codes helped set the stage for later landmark laws regarding child protection and children's rights in all five countries. Even though approaches to children's rights differed greatly over time in the Nordic countries, focus was all along very much on the best interest of the children (Jacobsen).

Social Ranking

Even though equality of human worth shaped Nordic conceptions of children and children's rights, several chapters also highlight elements in the history of the Nordic countries that served to "rank" children with regard to gender, class, and geographic location. There were marked differences between girls and boys, and clear gender distinctions affected social roles and educational and occupational possibilities. In everyday life, however, gender roles could also be more fluid, depending on practical needs and the social level of the children. Class and class identity also played a considerable role in shaping ideas of childhood and the lives of children during this period (Markkola, Ommundsen, Sandin, Widhe). In addition, children served as symbols of the working class in literature that addressed tensions and changes in society, with the children paradoxically being depicted both as victims and as resourceful agents (Nykvist). Differences in living conditions between rural areas and cities also greatly affected children's lives, as did the growing urbanization and industrialization of the nineteenth century and the early twentieth century (Garðarsdóttir, Lahtinen, Markkola, Sandin).

Education

As regards formation and education in the Nordic countries, teaching children to read and write was part of Lutheran heritage. Thus, religious movements and the church have a central place in this history, since education initially was seen as the duty of parents and the church (Markussen, Rørvik). Some religious movements, such as Pietism, played a positive role in helping to establish schools and advocated for equal education for all (Jacobsen). The actions of individuals and aristocratic families also played a central role in starting schools (Lahtinen, Markussen). In many cases, children also worked to help support their families, and they and their families struggled to balance responsibilities of work and education (Lahtinen, Markkola). Work was—also according to Lutheran ideas of "vocation"—regarded as valuable in itself, serving to build self-confidence and self-reliance in children and to prepare them for adult life (Garðarsdóttir, Hansen, Rørvik).

Literacy

Related to education, the Nordic countries also have a long history of literacy and advanced reading cultures (Markussen, Roos). The centrality of literacy for both boys and girls is closely connected to Lutheran notions of "the priesthood of all believers" and of "vocation." The priesthood of all believers claims that all are equally united to Christ and, thus, everyone should be able to read and interpret the Bible. The notion of vocation holds that all people have gifts and talents to love and serve others, thereby contributing to the common good. The emphasis on literacy is seen in early family portraits and their notion of the ideal parents (Aavitsland). Thus, the focus on literacy across class and gender lines was established soon after the arrival of Lutheranism in the sixteenth century (Bunge, Jacobsen) and was not something that emerged only out of the Enlightenment. Although reading was a required part of confirmation, levels of literacy in several areas were at times very low nonetheless (Lahtinen).

Struggles Leading to Common Schools

Literacy and education are deeply rooted in the Lutheran tradition. Nevertheless, contemporary Nordic commitments to equal access to education and to common schools for all children were established only after long struggles (Jacobsen, Lahtinen, Sandin). The path to equal education and one common school system was not the same in the Nordic countries and each has a complex history. As clearly demonstrated in many of the chapters, education was very often unequal and clouded by conflicting interests among parents, religious leaders, and political authorities as well as by issues of class, gender, and demography.

Songs and Hymns

Throughout the history of the Nordic countries, singing songs and hymns, and music generally, have been a central part of children's lives. Singing was part of formation in the home, experiences at church, and community life. The Nordic prominence of music stemmed, in part, from Luther's emphasis on the power of music and the long tradition of hymn writing in the Lutheran church, but also from the popular song and dance traditions of the Middle Ages. Several Nordic poets and educational and religious leaders wrote hymns and songs for and about children (Bunge, Olsen). Music was seen as an important part of formation and education, whether social or religious. In the visual arts, too, children were depicted as singing with their families and communities, whether at home, in church, or on the streets.

Intimate Relationship to Nature

When studying Nordic song and hymn books, conceptions of children also become apparent: In these books, children are often presented in close and intimate relationship to the natural world, not least to various animals, and children are also frequently depicted as playing outdoors, skiing, and enjoying the natural world (Olsen, Ommundsen, Widhe). Many images from nature are also used to describe children, such as "growing flowers" or delicate little "birds" (Bunge, Roos, Tatar). This emphasis on children's closeness to nature has not only Romanticism as its source, but also Nordic mythology, Christian ideas of the goodness of creation, and the dramatic landscapes and diverse flora and fauna of these countries.

Children as Competent

In the literature of the Nordic countries, children have often been depicted as active and confident, while at the same time being regarded as vulnerable and dependent, whether on parents, adults, or others (Roos, Widhe). In contemporary Nordic children's literature, "the competent child" who is responsible and independent is a common theme, such as in Astrid Lindgren's stories about Pippi Longstocking. We see in this history of Nordic childhood, however, that the notion of the competent child is much older than twentieth-century children's literature (Ommundsen, Widhe). Competence was, however, defined differently according to class or gender (Nykvist, Ommundsen, Sandin). The notion of the competent child was also often linked with conceptions of the nation (Nykvist, Olsen).

Children's Agency

We also see that pedagogical aims of the school system included helping children become responsible and self-sufficient. For example, the nineteenth-century Norwegian and Danish schools aimed to make "common" children able to master their lives at their social level (Rørvik). The theme of competence was expressed in a number of ways and in various contexts so that children could be depicted as more competent than adults (Roos), as competent in times of war (Schrumpf), and as competent in terms of being creative and imaginative (Garðarsdóttir, Ommundsen, Widhe).

Children's Development and Voice

The history of childhood in the Nordic countries also reveals adult efforts to accommodate children's level of understanding as well as to acknowledge their own voice and perspective. Although honoring the child's voice and perspective is often thought to have emerged only in the twentieth century, it is also found in mid-nineteenth-century children's literature, fairy tales, and educational ideas (Bunge, Tatar, Widhe).

Significance of the Volume for Further Interdisciplinary and International Research

By disclosing these and other findings, the volume contributes in a variety of ways to Nordic studies, childhood studies, and broader discussions about children today, and helps to highlight the need for further interdisciplinary research on childhood in the Nordic countries and other parts of the world.

Nordic Studies

By having a close look at childhood, the volume provides glimpses into central ideas and values that underlie contemporary commitments to child protection, well-being, and children's rights in these countries. Furthermore, it offers insights into core values of these societies as a whole. The book is able to provide a fresh examination of these core values, particularly by focusing on childhood and building on a broad variety of sources, ranging from socio-historical material and legal documents to art and children's own writings—and there are many more kinds of sources that can be explored further. The strong traditions of singing and hymn writing in these countries, as well as Lutheranism, seem to be particularly fruitful yet sometimes neglected sources for Nordic studies. The same is also likely to be the case with material created by children themselves, whether in the form of writings, songs, or works of art.

Childhood Studies

This volume inspires further work in regional studies within this "world" of studies. By combining childhood and Nordic studies, it illustrates the value of integrating research on childhood into the study of any culture or region. And again, the book also shows the importance—and need—for paying attention to a diversity of material to explore the history of children and childhood in all its breadth. From the varied history of Nordic childhoods, we are made aware that reducing particular views of children to one or two types of sources fails to take into account many significant elements of a region's history, social and religious heritage, culture, and even geography.

The book also reveals that many lines of division in conceptions of children, such as class, gender, ethnic identity, religious affiliation, and geographic location, must be taken into serious consideration, while, at the same time, pointing out that such lines are not always rigid. For example, even though gender roles were often strictly defined in Nordic religious or legal sources, the responsibilities of boys and girls varied, depending on family needs or particular economic situations. In the same way, rural and urban divisions were often stark, yet at other times highly fluid.

The book also reminds those interested in the history of childhood of the complex place of religion in shaping conceptions of and commitments to children. Over 80 percent of human beings today self-affiliate with one form of religion or another, and across time and cultures and in diverse ways religion is a fact and factor in most people's lives, including children's lives. Nevertheless, studies of childhood sometimes ignore its role or limit it to one positive or negative dimension alone. The study of the Nordic countries with their strong and complex Lutheran heritage can prompt further investigation in other contexts of the role that religious beliefs, practices, leaders, and communities often play in the history of childhood experiences and well-being of children.

Contemporary Reflection on Children

The book illustrates the fact that the current approach in the Nordic countries to protection, health care, and education for all children took many years and much effort to develop. It can also prompt readers to reflect on the sources and grounds for common conceptions of children and childhood found in their own contexts. In the Nordic sources, children are often depicted as competent, creative, and social agents, and any history of childhood should include a reflection on children's own actions, ideas, rights, responsibilities, and contributions to communities.

The history of education in the Nordic countries can also help readers explore questions about the intricate relationships that influence public discourses and to reflect seriously on notions of children that shape present-day educational policies in their own contexts. Readers might ponder, for example: What arguments, if any, are given for providing all children with equal educational opportunities? What might my country learn from the history of education and from today's school systems in the Nordic countries?

The history of the Nordic countries can also stimulate discussion on the notion of child equality. In any geographic context, we can raise a number of questions that the study of Nordic childhoods prompts, such as: Do we see children as equals? In what ways do we consciously or unconsciously rank them according to various categories, such as gender, class, race, religion, appearance, neighborhood, ability or disability? And what perceptions and ideas about children as human beings do we hold? How might attention to children help us to think more seriously about how we live and organize our societies? Even though constructions of children and children's own experiences vary greatly across time and cultures—as they do in the Nordic countries too—we hope that the history of childhood in these countries can challenge readers to reflect on their understanding of the needs, rights, and potential of children, and on their own obligations to children in their midst and around the world.

Notes

1 See for example the humorous but also insightful book by Booth 2014.
2 See reports of The Programme for International Student Assessment, known as PISA (www.oecd.org/pisa/).
3 Some central and fairly comprehensive studies are Coninck-Smith, Sandin, and Schrumpf 1997; Brembeck, Johannson, and Kampmann 2004; and Einarsdottir and Wagner 2006.
4 As we have noted, Norway was in union with Denmark until 1814 and with Sweden until 1905, and thus has significant parts of its history in common with them.

Part I
Spheres of Life
Home, Church, and Society

2 The Child in Norwegian and Scandinavian Folk Beliefs

Ørnulf A. Hodne

The term "folk beliefs" (*folketro*) is used here to denote magical and mythical ideas about supernatural powers and forces that are distinct from what is generally accepted in religion and science. Folk beliefs encompass every existential sphere in human life from the cradle to the grave: celebrations of yearly recurrences and of highpoints in life (birth, christening, wedding, burial, Christmas, Easter, Pentecost, Midsummer), people's work (agriculture, hunting, and fishing), weather conditions, and other natural phenomena. In the case of children, who are in a highly vulnerable phase of human life—often dying in infancy—the most prominent aspect of folk beliefs was a series of apotropaic magical devices that were intended to protect children against dangers. Such dangers were understood to come either from invisible spirits and beings (such as trolls, nymphs, or other creatures from the underworld) that were always close at hand and that threatened children's life and health or from human beings who (for various reasons) wanted to harm them. Folk beliefs also laid down rules of conduct for the mother during pregnancy. They stated how weak and sick children could be strengthened and healed by magical means, and they declared what signs and omens contained messages about the child's destiny. There is also evidence that many perceptions based on folk beliefs intervened in children's upbringing via popular verse, frightening warnings that regulated their behavior, and admonitory examples that showed the fatal consequences that a failure to look after children could have.

A comprehensive collection of popular traditions, including folk beliefs about children, was undertaken in Norway in the nineteenth century. Among the most important works are Andraeas Faye's *Norske Sagn* (1833), Peder Christen Asbjørnsen's *Norske huldreeventyr og folkesagn* (1845; 1847), and Magnus B. Landstad's *Norske folkeviser* (1853).[1] Similar projects were undertaken in the other Scandinavian countries, such as the Swedish collections by Eva Wigström (1832–1901) and in Evald Tang Kristensen's *Jydske Folkeminder* (1871–1897) from Denmark.[2] Many of the pioneer collectors were also able scholars, but this research truly came into its own only in the early twentieth century, when there was a sufficient basis of material to provide employment for students of folklore, ethnologists, and historians of culture. Folk beliefs were no exception since they affected every sphere of life, and children were one of the most important concerns of these beliefs. Indeed, it was impossible to conduct research into children and childcare in earlier times without encountering magic and "superstition" in one form or another. But this is seldom the principal interest of the scholars; it forms only a small part of a larger investigation.[3] The most comprehensive account in Norway of children in Norwegian folk culture is by the ethnologist, Lily Weiser-Aall, in *Svangerskap og fødsel i nyere norsk tradisjon. En kildekritisk studie* (*Pregnancy and Birth in Recent Norwegian Tradition. A Source-Critical Study*, 1968).

This chapter concentrates exclusively on practices and beliefs concerning children from a holistic perspective: it will bring together the apparently contradictory ideas in an overarching shared, values-based function, namely, *care* for children. My investigation is based on older and more recent sources, both written and oral; some of this material is little known. I show how folk beliefs became a topic of conflict between the common people and their superiors, and I explore the circumstances that gradually led to a shift from models of care based primarily on folk beliefs to those based on new scientific knowledge and on Lutheran beliefs and practices.

Protection of the Unborn Child

It was customary among the people to believe that if a pregnant woman touched or saw something ugly, repulsive, and frightening that evoked terror or agitation in her, these impressions would leave a physical mark on the child. It was particularly dangerous to stare at certain animals. To see a bear could mean that a child would be shaggy and hairy all over his body, a glutton, or deformed. A man who people called "Bear's Paw" was born with a clubfoot because his mother was frightened by a bear while he was in her womb. If the mother saw a snake, the child might get restless eyes, a cleft tongue, or the skin of a snake. It was said in Vik in Sogn (in western Norway) that if a child was born with curly hair, but the hair was smooth on the front of its head—a so-called "cow's lick"—this was because a cow had licked the mother.[4]

This was why it was held that pregnant women ought not to go fishing with the menfolk. For if they saw a sea wolf, an anglerfish, or a flounder, the child could have an equally ugly jaw, a prominent lower jaw, hideous teeth, or a "fish's gum" (an open palate). Other defects might be caused by the mother staring at certain birds. For this reason, hunters usually ripped open the webs of ducks and other swimming birds, so that the child would not get webbed toes and fingers.

If the child was born with red or blue-red marks on its face, the mother was thought to have seen a conflagration; or else blood had spattered on her while she was pregnant. This is why she must not see animals being slaughtered. If one drop of blood landed on her, the child would have a red mole at the same place. If she even touched blood, the unborn child would have a bloodstain. We hear from Søgne (in southern Norway) about a pregnant woman who was present at a slaughter. She jumped when she saw the gash in the throat of the sheep she had just killed, and the daughter who was born immediately after this had a mark on her throat like the gash made by a knife.[5] One way to ward off the consequences was to say a prayer, or to touch her back, for in this way, she "moved" the mark to a place on the child's body where it was less visible and embarrassing.[6] In the mid-nineteenth century, this was still a counsel that invited a commentary from a medical official:

> One should be very careful not to play jokes on pregnant women, nor to throw anything at them, show them frightening things, and things of this sort, since there are many examples of children whose bodies have been marked afterwards; if this happens, I find the old advice useful, namely, that the woman should immediately touch herself on the back.[7]

By following certain cautionary rules during pregnancy, it was also possible to prevent the child from being born with serious illnesses. To see slaughtered animals die or to hear their dying scream gave the child an illness (epilepsy) with the corresponding name: calf's fall, cow's fall, pig's fall, goat's fall, and fish's fall. The child's illness took the same form as the animal's agony agony: It shook the child, which shuddered and uttered animal sounds. Like the other apotropaic devices, this practice too is well represented in Danish and Swedish folklore collections. Evald Tang Kristensen writes in *Jydske Folkeminder*:

> A pregnant woman must not walk over a place where an eel has lain and writhed, because the child can thereby catch an illness called 'eel's writhing.' She must not walk over a place where a sheep has lain while it was being slaughtered, in order that the child may not have a stroke. She must not sit down on the graves of the dead, because this could mean that the fetus would have a stroke.[8]

We find similar examples from Sweden in Eva Wigström's *Folktro og sägner,* which also tells us that there were remedies for the sickness:

> If a boy gets epilepsy because his mother saw hens being slaughtered during the pregnancy, the remedy for the sickness is to slaughter a hen and make the sick child imbibe two drops of blood from the cut-off head and one drop from the body ... If the stroke occurred while the moon was waning, this means is employed twice while it is waxing and once while it is waning. If the stroke occurred while the moon was waxing, the opposite applies. If it is a girl who has this kind of stroke, a rooster is slaughtered instead of a hen.[9]

But the apotropaic devices were not only prohibitions against wrong behavior. The future mother would have happy and beautiful children if she herself was happy and not troubled by despondency and depression—for it was believed that her mood was inheritable. She ought, therefore, to see and surround herself with beautiful things and have good and joyful experiences. But we also find examples of how the things may go wrong: "A young wife decked herself with curls of hair on her forehead. The child had two small horns" (Hordabø, western Norway). According to Lily Weiser-Aall, the idea that the mother's vanity would incur punishment was due to a religious and, in particular, a pietistic worldview that can be found in popular belief both in Scandinavia and in Germany.[10]

Predictions about the Unborn Child

Concern about the unborn child may also have inspired the search for knowledge about the child with the aid of signs and omens. According to popular belief, a pregnant woman could have recourse to a number of these signs when she wanted to know the child's sex—knowledge that could be of practical use both to her and to her family. If she carried the unborn child high up, or her "stomach was broad," it would be a boy; if she carried it "low" and her stomach projected greatly and was "sharp," it would be a girl. "If there were two children, the boy lay on the bottom."[11] "If the unborn child kicked a lot, it was a boy," and that made the mother more cheerful and healthier, with a ruddier face.[12] Popular beliefs about birth were similar in Scandinavia. It was customarily believed:

> [B]oys lay on the right side in the mother's womb, and that girls lay on the left side. This is mentioned already by Hippocrates, who held that the right side was the warmer, and therefore offered better conditions for the development of the so-called stronger sex. In order to have a son, therefore, it was recommended that a woman should lie on her right side.[13]

Other prophecies were so-called "random oracles" where the pregnant woman was often passive. If one took the breast cartilage from a newly slaughtered animal, spat on it, and threw it against a wall while one thought hard of the woman, she would bear a boy if it stuck to the wall—otherwise, she would bear a girl. She could also have a helper "ride the weaving shuttles" for her. The helper took the weaving shuttles out of a finished woven fabric and rode with them three times counterclockwise around the house with closed eyes, saying: "I am riding the weaving shuttles for N. N." If the first person the helper then set eyes on was a woman, a girl would be born; if it was a man, this prophesied a boy.[14]

On other occasions, it was fear for the child's future that found expression in superstition. If the unborn child wept in the mother's womb, this signified a bad destiny. "It was a terribly bad sign when the child wept in the mother's womb," we hear from Elverum (in the eastern part of southern

Norway). "The speaker could recall several cases where people said about someone who had had particularly bad misfortune: 'You can't expect anything else with someone who wept before he was born'."[15] And in another source: "Jacob and Esau cried out in their mother's womb, it is said, as did Gjest Bårdsen and Christian II.[16] The latter was born with a hand full of blood."[17] Ola Sevle from Nore in Numedal, who killed "Sølv-Tølløv" in Upper Sigdal (in central southern Norway) and was beheaded for his deed, is also said to have cried out before his birth. He also had a red ring around his neck when he was born: "They were marks of the executioner's sword, the one used to decapitate people." It was said that it was possible to avert the crime that was prophesied, if one brought the child to the executioner immediately after its birth: "When he swings the sword three times over the child, it is prevented from carrying out the evil deed."[18]

A Darling of Fortune (Literally: "A Child of Luck")

As soon as the child was born, it was important for the family to try to find out what destiny awaited it: whether or not it was chosen to be a so-called "child of luck." They found the signs of luck on the newborn child itself and in the time at which it was born. These express a strong desire that all would go well with the boy or girl in the course of its life. In Norwegian and Scandinavian popular tradition, it is consistently a positive sign to be born with the "victory hat" (beautiful hat, victory crown, emperor's hat), that is to say, with hat-like remnants of the fetal membrane on one's head. Such children would have luck on their side throughout life, and would prosper greatly.

The "victory hat" also equipped them with supernatural abilities to protect both themselves and others against life-threatening harm and danger. With this in his possession, the soldier need have no fear when he went to war, since neither sword blows nor bullets hit him; he was invulnerable. The result was the same when a girl gave her own "victory hat" to her brother when he went into battle. And the numerous precautionary rules were not necessary for them in their childhood. We are told, with the same claim to credibility, that such persons were always lucky when they went hunting, that they were never lost at sea, and that they could halt floods and fires. This presupposed that they took good care of their "hat" so that it could follow its owner throughout life. "They were eager to take hold of this membrane and to take good care of it." Some therefore had the "hat" fastened to the breast of the child, or on its neck or armpit, while others dried it and hid it in a safe place until he or she could personally take charge of it and wear it as a kind of amulet. Finally, "it is laid in the coffin at one's death." Similar customs are known from several of the other Scandinavian countries. Its Icelandic name is *sigurkufl*.[19]

Great importance prophesizing the child's future was attributed to the time of birth (Figure 2.1). Some days were identified as particularly

Figure 2.1 The parents tried to influence the child's destiny while it lay in the cradle. It was believed that children who were rocked hard and long would get their sea legs. An old drawing by an unknown artist.

favorable: "Children born on feast days were lucky children," and "Sunday children are blessed children," we are told. "Sunday children have a fine character. There is always something good and attractive about them."[20] Such children "were better protected against evil powers than other children." But children who were born on Christmas Eve itself had the greatest honor and good fortune: "Christmas children were born to something great. And they would not commit great sins, because they were born on the same day as the child Jesus" (Trondenes, northern Norway). However, Good Friday and Friday the thirteenth were associated with troll powers, suffering, and bad fortune. Nor was it seen as good to be born on a Wednesday. The well-known Swedish folklore researcher, Louise Hagberg, (1868–1944) writes as follows:

> "Children born on a Wednesday never know rest," says a Norwegian adage. But "a child that is born on some great feast day such as New Year, Easter, Pentecost, or Midsummer Day, is regarded, according to Swedish popular belief in Finland, as 'set apart,' that is to say, one who receives great gifts and will become a prominent person. Similarly, we are told in Denmark that those who are born on the eve of some great feast day, such as Christmas, Easter, and Pentecost, can see everything in a supernatural manner."[21]

Even wind and weather had an influence on the newborn and helped to predetermine the course of its life and destiny. Children born in the springtime were cheerful, whereas children born in December encountered many storms in their life. A waxing moon meant big children: "Happy the one who is born when the moon is new."[22]

At the same time, however, the tradition emphasizes that the parents themselves could intervene actively, with immediate magical means that would promote the children's good; they should not leave everything in the hands of the powers that determine human destiny. If they wanted to ensure a safe outcome, the father put a tool in the child's hand or in the cradle, as soon as it saw the light of day. This tool symbolized the profession the child would have as an adult. For instance, a knife signified a carpenter, a fish line a fisher, and a measuring tape a horse dealer. Anders Åsen from Eidfjord (in western Norway) lived in the eighteenth century and was a skillful hunter. While his wife was giving birth, he ran to fetch his powder horn, intending to hang it around the neck of the newborn, since this would make him a great hunter.[23]

Some people planted a lucky tree for the child at its birth. If the tree grew and flourished, the child did likewise. We hear about this custom in the Swedish collection of Wigström:

> In Norrland (in the northern part of Sweden), we plant a sapling or a twig at the birth of a child, and we call this tree the tree of life. We get premonitions from it about the child's life. I knew a young girl who had a very promising tree of life. But it suddenly began to wither in its crown. 'Well, now it is suffering for me too,' said the girl. And it is certain that she and her tree of life died at the same time.[24]

Crisis Protection of the Child in the Cradle

Above all, the parents were responsible for giving the child in the cradle the best possible protection against harmful spirits and powers, such as trolls, that threatened it in the critical phase between birth and baptism in church. This entailed a very special surveillance, as we see clearly from the numerous protective devices that were available (Figure 2.2). No other phase in human life was as tightly filled with such magical aids as these days and weeks.

The greatest fear was that the child might be stolen by the wood nymphs, who would leave a changeling in its place. The wreakers of harm sought to afflict both mother and child, and this is why many protective devices envisaged both of them. The mother must not go out before the child had been baptized; she had to stay at home and look after it. A well-known adage in many places affirmed that: "The mother of a pagan should never go to the farmyard." The child must never lie alone and in the dark. There should ideally be lamps burning in the house, but the light in the oven could be enough. People outside the family should neither see nor touch an unbaptized child, since they could harm it with their evil eyes and hands. If they were admitted to the house, the floor must be swept after them when they

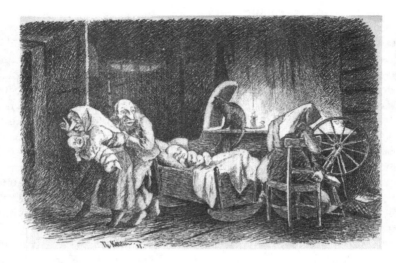

Figure 2.2 The mother was a vital provider of care for the child in the cradle—especially for the unbaptized child. One unguarded moment was enough to give invisible powers the opportunity to harm it or exchange it. In this drawing by Theodor Kittelsen (1857–1914), the woman at the spinning wheel has fallen asleep.

left. "The first water that a child is washed in should be blessed by means of an ember ('light a fire in it'). And one should throw the water out against the wall of the room and say: 'The name of Jesus.' The child would then not be wild, but would be quiet,"[25] and no goblins or other evils would "get power over it through water."[26] If they threw the water away outside, this must under no circumstances be done after seven o'clock in the evening.

Besides this, people had several holy and powerful things that were placed directly in the cradle and the child's clothes to give the newborn extra protection against the powers of the underworld. These safety devices were basically identical throughout Scandinavia, and they can be summed up as follows: an article of silver (a needle, a ring) or of steel (scissors, knife, ax, or military steel in the form of a sword or a gun) should lie in the cradle:

> It was a general practice in Scandinavia that unbaptized children should have something of steel in the cradle. In Denmark, this is known as 'putting steel in front of the troll,' when one makes a cut in the air with scissors above a newborn child's bed to prevent it from being stolen away and exchanged; this is also done in Norway. In Hällestad (in south-eastern Sweden), steel is placed on the threshold and scissors are hung on the lock of the door. In order to protect the newborn child, it was customary among the Swedes in Finland to hang two knives in the form of a cross over the entrance.[27]

A book with God's Word, or pages of such a book, had the same protective effect. A hymnbook was the most useful of all. "When one took a page of a hymnbook on which our Savior's name was written, and laid it on a child as soon as it was born, it would not be stolen and a changeling left in its place" (Jylland in Denmark). They sewed a silver coin or a silver button, buckle, or ring into a long, woven band of cloth; in some places, they sewed a piece of crisp bread into the cloth, "because bread is the wages God gives." They then read the Lord's Prayer over the child, made the sign of the cross over it in Jesus' name, and "made a blessing over it with burnt bread." Nonetheless, it happened that someone suddenly discovered that there was no longer a fine human child in the cradle, but the ugly and deformed child of a nymph.

The descriptions state with absolute certainty that these changelings (*vixlingr/skiptingr* in Old Norse or *skifting* in Danish) were mentally retarded, sick (e.g., Down syndrome, rickets, and hepatitis), and deformed children. They had huge heads, yellow and sallow skin, "old men's faces," protuberant eyes, long hands and short feet, pointy teeth, and weak and wobbly legs. A changeling was ravenously hungry like a village dog, and screamed by day and night; it was troublesome and stubborn, half-witted and stupid. It took a long time before it began to walk, it never learned to read, and it either could not or would not talk. The desire to get rid of such a wretched child must have been widespread, since there was no lack of suitable advice; the most common was to torment and ill-treat him or her so forcefully that the nymph mother would feel sorry for her child, and would return and reverse the exchange. We are told that the changeling was whipped, naked with birch twigs on a dung heap on three successive Thursday evenings. Its nose was pinched with glowing tongs. They made as if to throw it into the fire in their house or into the baker's oven and burn it alive, and they pushed it through a cleft rowan tree.

On the other hand, there are also stories of parents who were frightened by the underground beings into letting the child be at peace, or even into taking good care of it. This led to happiness and prosperity, we are told, whereas those who were bad could be afflicted with unhappiness and disasters. One Danish variant relates that the blessing lasted only as long as the changeling lived:

> The trolls were supposed to be both good towards the children they themselves took, and grateful when their own children were treated well … A fisher and his wife on Fur in the nineteenth century treated a changeling with love. And this was rewarded, because unbroken good fortune accompanied them as long as it lived. It was indeed a cross in their home—eighteen years old and fully adult, and yet at the same time a little child that wanted to lie in the cradle, a terrible monster in human form. But as soon as it died, the good fortune abandoned them. Their farm burned down twice, their own children died, and finally, others took over the farm.[28]

The tradition about changelings contains a great deal of compassion and suffering, but also fear, despair, and aggression. In the Norwegian material, however, I have not found any trace of the grotesque and inhuman burial practices for changelings that we find in Eva Wigström's Swedish collections, in a story that sounds like a legend:

> In the past, much more generally than nowadays, deaf and dumb or deformed children were thought to have been exchanged by trolls. For this reason, when they left this world, they were not allowed to lie in the church cemetery. They were buried in the border territory (which ran between the plots of ground) and a stake was driven through their body. But it happened, one springtime, that leaves of lily of the valley grew on such a grave, and these words were written on one of these leaves: 'Thanks be to God that I was given food and thanks be to God that I had enough to eat! And that person is blessed.' This became known, and this led to the abolition of the custom of burying changelings in unconsecrated ground and fastening them down with a stake through the body.[29]

Bestowal of a Name and Baptism

The church's baptism was the most important protective ritual available for an infant, and this made it vital to bring the newborn to the church as soon as possible and to ensure that the christening took place without any frightening deviations from the ritual. First, however, the child must receive a name, with all that this entailed. The fundamental rule for the bestowal of a name was to choose a name within the family and clan. The first boy was called after his paternal grandfather, the first girl after the maternal grandmother, and the second girl after the paternal grandmother. If the marriage produced more children, they were given the names of other relatives, such as deceased siblings. The name was to follow the family and create membership of the clan.

Complications arose when the person after whom the child was to be called had been a bad person or a poor example, for the child might resemble him or her and have the same fate. "He will be just like the one he is called after" (Setesdal, southern Norway).[30] The risk was that the one who was rejected would come back as a ghost and wreak revenge on the child and its parents. There is a well-known story of a woman who arrived too early at the morning service and found the church full of dead persons, including her grandfather and sister, who warned her: "We are ghosts. You must run now, for see how angry your grandfather is, because you have not bestowed his name. He will kill you." The woman fled, but she died two days later of the pinching and beating he had given her on her way home.[31]

If the mother dreamt of a dead person during the pregnancy, this tended to be interpreted to mean that the dead person "was looking for its name," and this desire was so strong that she had to gratify it for the sake of the child's well-being. "If she does not do so, one will be afflicted by him in dreams for a long time, and the woman will know no rest until she has promised to bestow the name of the dead person, the next time she has a child."[32] It is said that there are many old altarpieces in Nordland with letters from names carved or written on the back. These are names of dead persons; although their names had not been bestowed on newborn children, it was believed that they were satisfied with being remembered in this way.

In keeping with ancient law and the Christian faith, the child must not lie unbaptized for longer than one week without being brought to the church and receiving the baptism required by law. But there were some who interpreted this precept more strictly, and rushed head over heels from the farmstead out of fear of all the bad things that could happen to the unbaptized. On Sperstad farm (in Skjåk in central Norway), "a girl was born on Christmas Eve. They organized everything and took her to the church on Christmas Day and had her christened."[33]

If the child was sick at its birth, the way to the church was long, or it was in the middle of winter, a home baptism was not a rare event. The child was subsequently brought to the church, where the priest ratified the baptism. But this was not always the case. Village traditions in Norway have many tales of dramatic christening journeys, which in the worst instance had a tragic outcome for the child. Parish ministers around the country knew how badly things could go. Hans Strøm, pastor in Volda, relates that thirty of the children who were christened had lost their lives in the harsh winter of 1755. Early in the nineteenth century, the minister in Saltdal (northern Norway), Kr. Sommerfeldt, wrote: "Another factor that fills up the lists of deaths is the early baptism, which will surely not be abandoned here before an explicit order to this effect is issued; although it is not quite as bad now as it was in the past." As late as in the 1850s, the sociologist, Eilert Sundt, heard a pastor in Nordfjord (in western Norway) complain that the high rate of infant mortality most often was due to the "haste with which they seek to have them baptized," heedless of winter and storm.[34]

Then as now, a certain number of godparents were present at the baptism. There were usually five or six, all of them "honest people of good reputation," who were to be witnesses of the christening and assist the parents in the Christian education of the children; where necessary, they were expected to provide support in various ways. A typical group of godparents consisted of relatives and good neighbors of both sexes, both older and younger persons. The most honorable task was to hold the child during the baptism ceremony itself; this tended to be reserved for one of the grandmothers, while the girl who was a godmother removed the baby's hat.[35] In what follows, I will discuss briefly controversial customs based on folk beliefs that in some places could create conflict between the pastor and the parish.

The most tenacious custom was to hang onto the child while the words of baptism were being read. The idea may have been that the godparents too thereby received a share in the power from the holy text, and that they could communicate this to their godchild by touching it, thus strengthening it in faith. As late as in the last century, old villagers could remember that the expression "to hold by the foot" was used as a synonym of being a godparent. And in Lesja (central inland, southern Norway), the parents used this "invitation formula" when they were looking for a godparent: "If you have nothing special to do, could you come with us to church next Sunday and hold the foot of our little boy?"[36]

It was also customary in many places for the godparent who held the child to read the words of baptism after the pastor, for then the child would like books and be a good reader—otherwise, the little one will never learn to read well. The same ritual was used by the common people in Sweden: "In order that the child shall have a good memory and a good intelligence, according to ancient custom the godparents should read in a low voice after the pastor. In Denmark, they say the words after him, once he has said 'Amen'."[37] In addition, the woman who held the child should touch the font with the baby's head during the act of baptism, for then it would be talented. But if the priest should lose the place and read the wrong words or stammer, the child would not be a good learner, and would be a poor reader: "All that was needed was for the pastor to cough during the act of baptism, or to stumble in the words. In that case, the child would never come to be healthy, old, or happy."[38]

Many practices connected with baptism were based on the fear that such unforeseen events and deviations could entail long-term harm for the child and reduce the positive influence of the christening. This was why the godparents bore a great responsibility when they carried out their duties. The least slip could have catastrophic consequences. We hear from Eikebygd in Vest-Agder (the southernmost part of Norway) that when they removed the baptismal hat from the child, they did not do so carefully and respectfully, but merely shoved it backwards. The woman who held the child dropped it onto the floor and said: "This one will be a devil!" But the pastor said: "Take the child up again, madam. It can still become a child of God."[39] The child became butterfingered when the godparents lost the collection money on the floor, and became forgetful when they carelessly left something behind in the church.

Evald Tang Kristensen speaks of several such "superstitious beliefs and counsels" from Jylland (Denmark): "When the one who holds the child drags the christening robe over the chairs in the church, this is said to mean that the child will later come to wear out many garments." In some places in Denmark godmothers were advised to take the pacifier away from the child to be baptized:

> When the child enters the church, the pacifier should be lost on the floor of the church, for otherwise, it will be hard for the child to get its first teeth. This is why one hears older women say to the godmother, when

she brings the child to the church: 'See to it that you get rid of the pacifier,' and this is why, in some places, a great many pacifiers are found in
the rubbish when the church is swept.[40]

A well-used and beautiful christening robe was a powerful garment that had a
positive effect on the child who wore it. "The more often a robe has been used at
baptism, the stronger are the powers that dwell in it" (North Gudbrandsdalen,
in central southern Norway). This may explain the custom throughout the
whole country of putting the newly baptized child to sleep in its christening
clothes after they came home from the church: this led to good-natured, tran-
quil, healthy, and happy children. And if all the children in a family over several
generations were baptized in the same christening robe, there would always be
peace and harmony among them as long as this custom endured.

Failures of Care and the Loss of Children

Through baptism in the church, the christened child was finally and fully
integrated into the clan and into society in the most solicitous way that the
parents could offer. But as we have seen in the discussion of changelings,
not all newborn children were equally loved and welcomed. Some were met
with dislike, aversion, and a lack of love from the very outset, and they were
exposed to inhuman abuse and a lack of care. There are a number of statements, stories about nymphs, and legends in our collections of traditions
that speak about this dark side of children's history. The most terrifying
representative of this bloody violence and child abuse is the victim, when he
or she appears as an *utburd,* that is to say, as the ghost of an infant that was
killed by its mother immediately after birth. But the intention of the legends
about such ghosts goes much further than simply to tell a story: at the same
time, they want to be spokespersons for the unhappy child, and they function in the tradition as a frightening warning. To kill one's own child was
an action with consequences that went beyond this earthly life both for the
murderer and for the victim (Figure 2.3).

In Norse times, an *utburd* was a newborn boy or girl who was exposed in
the woods or the open fields and left to die, because the parents, for various
reasons, wanted to get rid of the child. In more recent Norwegian tradition,
the *utburd (ubbur, utbor, ropar)* signifies "children who are born in secret
and then killed, without being buried in the church cemetery. They cried
out and wailed to be baptized."[41] This belief finds expression in a number
of similar legends. "There was a girl in Tuftaden who gave birth in secret,
killed the child, and buried it in the Tufta hollow. They often heard it wail-
ing and behaving just like a young boy. A man they called Gamle-Tuften
went down and baptized it Ola, and since then, there has been peace."[42]

In particular, people heard gasping, weeping, and cries when the milk-
maids had children and got rid of them on the summer mountain farms so
that no one knew anything about it.

Figure 2.3 An *utburd* was the ghost of a newborn child whose mother had killed it and hidden it in the outlying fields, where it was compelled to lead a restless life until someone heard its cries of lament and gave it a Christian baptism. *The Woman Who Murdered Her Child*: a painting by Eyolf Soot (1859–1928).

Photo: Jacques Lathion. The National Museum of Art, Architecture and Design, Oslo.

In Swedish tradition, the *utburd* is called *myrdingen, mylingen*, or *utbørdingen*. In Iceland, it is called *útburdur*, and *nida(n)grisur* in the Faeroe Islands. In Denmark, where these ideas were less widespread, it was called *gloso* or *gravso*:

> There is a big pit on Vidstrup Field called Podøj, and it is said that a child was once killed in it. Many people are said to have heard it wailing and lamenting down there, and my sister, who was a seamstress and had something of the second sight, has assured me that one evening in Christmastime, as she passed by there, she heard the child weeping. The pit was near my parents' home, and she was absolutely convinced of this matter.[43]

The *utburd* usually manifested itself as a small, naked child. It always remained at the place where the crime had been committed, and it was dangerous and oppressive to meet as long as it was unredeemed, that is to say, unbaptized. If one did not know the child's gender, a mediaeval baptismal formula with two names, one for girls and one for boys, tended to be used: "I baptize you either Guro (Gudrun) or Jon!" Using Jon (John) and Gudrun/Guro synonymously with NN (*nescio nomen*, "I do not know the name") was an inheritance from the old tradition of the continental church, in Old

Norse: *Ek skirir dig Jon eda Gudrun edr hvossu du nefnir* ("I baptize you Jon or Gudrun or whatever your name is"). Anyone at all could perform an emergency baptism in the outfields, but most people preferred that this should be done by the pastor, who had the greatest power to bind and loose spirits that knew no peace.

The baptism of an *utburd* involved taking water in one's hand and throwing it behind oneself while one said the words of baptism and the Lord's Prayer backwards. According to popular beliefs, everything was back to front in the other world, and if one wanted to get into contact with the powers there, the rituals had to be carried out in this way, if they were to have any effect. The legend relates that one *utburd* from Sykkylven (western Norway) was so happy when he heard the words of baptism that he sprang up and cried out: "The man christened me Jo!" (Jo is short for Jon.) After this, nothing more was heard from him. They found his corpse and took it to the church cemetery, where it was buried.

Abortion was seen as a crime on a par with infanticide, and popular tradition speaks of it in roughly the same manner. This respect for the child in its mother's womb can also be seen in the treatment of a miscarriage. Such "mishaps" and "discards" were to be treated like a normal corpse. They were placed in small caskets and round containers and laid to rest in the cemetery in the grave of a relative or in crevices in the church wall, preferably as near to the altar as possible (Figure 2.4). The Norwegian folklorist Olav Bø wrote: "The burial of miscarried fetuses was the expression of a pious and moving wish to make available consecrated ground and peace for the small unborn children who had not been able to live," and it was a strong and convincing testimony to the respect for life.[44]

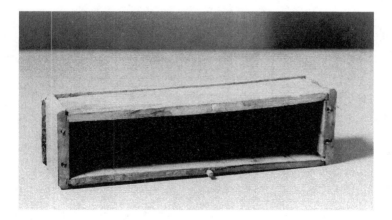

Figure 2.4 Box for a miscarried fetus in Voss church. Placing a miscarried fetus in such boxes was the expression of a pious wish to obtain consecrated earth and peace for the little ones who had not made it to birth. Gjøsteins Foto, Voss. Archive photograph in the Norsk Folkeminnesamling, IKOS, University of Oslo.

Even a minor negligence could have momentous consequences for the child's well-being, as we see in the tradition about kidnapping by a supernatural power. Both children and adults were exposed to this danger, but as long as the children were small, the parents had the grave obligation of taking extra good care of them, so that the spirits would not carry them off and entice them onto wrong paths, imprisoning them in their underworld. It was believed that church bells could ring and free those who had been kidnapped—the bells broke the magic. But this did not always succeed, and we hear of many attempts that failed.

On October 5, 1775, two small boys aged five and six disappeared from a farm in Hof parish in Solør (central southern Norway). The villagers searched in vain for them for many days. Finally, they asked the pastor, Søren Lemmich, to allow them to bring one of the church bells out into the wood and ring it to call the boys, who must surely have been kidnapped by underworld spirits. Their father, Bård Halvorsen Melsnes, went twice to the pastor, who refused to help. On October 27, however, the local assembly gave him permission to use the smallest of the bells in Åsnes chapel of ease. It was taken to the wood and rung unceasingly, day and night, for three days—but the children did not come back. The pastor was so annoyed by the bell ringing that he complained to the bishop and demanded that a fence be set up around the church, so that "every superstitious and ungodly person may be prevented from stealing with his own hand from the house of God, and still less from employing the church's ornaments to call upon spirits and perform magical practices." He wanted Bård Melsnes to be "punished as he deserves." When they wrote a report to the chancellery in Copenhagen, however, the diocesan official and the bishop took a milder tone, and suggested that Bård should be punished for his superstitious behavior by "making public confession and asking the parish for forgiveness for the scandal he had given." Each of those who had consented to the deed should pay a fine of one riksdaler (a silver coin, of ca. 25g) to the poor of the parish. The department presented its decision on August 17, 1776. The pastor was to make known from the pulpit that His Majesty, out of compassion with Bård and his "praiseworthy grief," had remitted all penalties for him and his accomplices! Now it was the pastor's task to speak with them and convince them of the superstitious nature of what they had done. As for the children, they must either have been "carried off by ravenous animals or kidnapped by wicked persons."[45]

Fighting Folk Beliefs and "Superstition"

The legal case in Solør in 1775–1776, is only one of several known instances in which a village pastor made use of the Danish-Norwegian legal system to put an end to "superstition" among the people and to the godless use of God's house and name. This must be understood as one important instrument in the Enlightenment campaign against pagan and "papistical" (Catholic) folk beliefs that the authorities of the state launched already in the sixteenth and seventeenth centuries, and that was given its theoretical justification in a number of theological and cultural-philosophical dissertations in the wake of the Reformation. Examples include Nils Hemmingsen's *Advarsel om at undgaa Overtro paa Troldom* (*Warning to Avoid Superstitious Belief in Magic*, 1575), Jens Hansen Odense's *Filosofiske Disputaats om Spøgelser* (*Philosophical Disputation About Ghosts*, 1673), Jens Nielsen Mundelstrup's *Prøve paa den endnu i vore Dage levende Hedendom* (*Examination of the Paganism that is Still Alive in our Days*, 1684), and Sixtus Aspach's *Om forskellig Overtro* (On Superstition of Various Kinds, 1687).

But the most important work was published by the Danish pietist, Bishop Erik Pontoppidan (1698–1764), to mark the 200th anniversary of the Reformation in Denmark-Norway in 1736: *Fejekost til ad udfeje den gamle Surdejg eller de i de danske Lande tiloversblevne og her for Dagen bragte Levninger af saavel Hedenskab som Papisme* (*A Broom to Sweep Out the Old Leaven, or the Remnants Both of Paganism and of Papistry that have Survived in the Danish Territories and are Here Brought to Light*).[46] Many of the superstitious elements that Pontoppidan found to be flourishing among the Danish peasantry as a whole concerned children (see Figure 2.5), and these are largely the same that I have discussed here. To see omens of success or failure, life or death, merely betrays "blind paganism, not in the least an enlightened Christianity. Let us therefore be done with that dense and empty superstition that puffs up credulity's false hopes with its deceptive outward appearance and inspires in simple minds a foolish fear that not seldom leads to the consequence that even the most mendacious omens seem to have contained some truth."[47]

In Pontoppidan's opinion, those popular beliefs with regard to sacred things was a remnant from Catholic practices. He gives the following examples:

> The following superstitious beliefs are of the same yeast: that the dark-skinned children become white after baptism; that one who has been bitten by a mad dog recovers if he is burnt with a glowing nail from the church door; that one should cut off some threads from the christening robe and sew them into the infant's swaddling clothes, to prevent it from being taken away and exchanged by the underground people.[48]

And further:

> There is an exceptionally well-proven means of protecting unborn children who, it is thought, are exposed to the risk of being exchanged by spirits or by the underground people: namely, that one should wind steel – or, what is best of all, scissors of steel (perhaps because this resembles the shape of the Cross) – into their swaddling bands; we may add that the hags sometimes prefer to fix two crossed needles over them.[49]

Figure 2.5 The attempt was made by means of "creeping" to cure children who suffered from epilepsy, hernia, or rickets. The sick child was drawn three times through an opening made by nature itself (for example, in a tree) in complete silence. Photograph: Nordiska museet in Stockholm, 1918, after Carl Herman Tillhagen, *Folklig Läkekonst*, Stockholm 1962.

And one last example:

> In order that those women who die in childbed without having brought children into the world may not disturb the house by coming back as ghosts to demand the care and attention that is due to their children, clothes for the fetuses and, in any case, needle and thread, should be laid in the coffin beside the corpses.

The author concludes his book with the wish that, God willing, it may be a burning inspiration to eradicate the last remnants of pagan and "Catholic superstition":

May God who is all-good and almighty grant that my insignificant book may have a barb that it can leave in the readers' minds, so that by means of the trumpet blast of this serious warning, the courageous soldiers of the holy fight may in any case be spurred on and inflamed to wage war on the survivals of both paganism and papistry.[50]

The fight against superstition among the people was also a common concern for state and church, for rationalists and pietists alike, in Norway in the eighteenth and nineteenth centuries.

Generally, it was probably the "Enlightenment pastors" who most effectively worked against these practices, since they reached a majority of people through their preaching, while at the same time helping to demystify and kill off superstition through rational arguments. One of the most prominent was Peder Hansen (1746–1810), a Danish professor and bishop in Kristiansand diocese (in southernmost Norway) from 1798 to 1803. In his short period as bishop, "he drew especial notice through several measures undertaken to strengthen the school system and to eradicate popular beliefs and practices that he regarded as harmful and as opposed to the Enlightenment."[51] His commentaries on the *Levninger af Overtroe* (*Remnants of Superstition*) in the diocese, which Peter Ludvig Lund (1760–1826), pastor in Valle, sent him around the year 1800, show very clearly how all that was strange and "supernatural" is ascribed to natural causes, whether visions in dreams, goblins, wood nymphs, the *åsgårdsrei* (crowds of evil spirits on horseback who swept people away with them), or changelings:

> If one bears in mind how easily it can happen that a mother during pregnancy can make an unfortunate movement while she is working hard, or can move carelessly in her bed, or that other natural causes can occur, thanks to which the fetus takes on a deformed shape; one need not pursue hidden causes here, where everyone can see the natural causes. Similarly, there are good reasons in the defective state of the brain for the weak mental abilities of many children, and in the bad treatment of children with regard both to their mental and to their physical faculties, which often leads to madness. Given the force with which infants are crammed into the so-called swaddling clothes and bands, it is more to be wondered at that there are not more who are harmed in their external limbs and their inward parts. Likewise, it is to be wondered at that there are not more children whose brain is unsettled by the vigorous shaking in a wooden cradle that gives the child the most terrible joltings on uneven paths.[52]

Everything suggests that the fight against folk beliefs also met with its greatest success among the Haugians (adherents of the influential Lutheran lay preacher Hans Nielsen Hauge, 1771–1824) and in the Free Church movements; this was the experience of a number of Norwegian folklore collectors in the nineteenth century. For example, in his account of his travels in Nord-Østerdalen (eastern part of southern Norway) in the summer of 1851, the famous folklorist and zoologist, Peder Christen Asbjørnsen (1812–1885), notes that "Haugianism and 'letting one's head droop'" were not environments conducive to popular poetry of any kind,[53] and when the folklorist Moltke Moe (1859–1913) visited Heddal in Telemark (southern inland Norway) on his collector's travels in 1878, he noted with regret the existence of a general belief "that all supernatural beings of which the traditions speak are merely various forms in which Satan reveals himself."[54] And many knowledgeable farmers and teachers refused to let themselves be interviewed about such topics for fear of legitimating superstition and keeping it alive. The most important factor in devaluing superstition about children in people's judgment was, however, the new scientific knowledge about pregnancy, obstetric aid, childcare, and children's illnesses. This largely ousted the old caring functions and made life safer for both mother and child.

Folk beliefs did not, however, disappear completely in the encounter with modern Enlightenment society. Pastors and other officials had elaborated detailed geographical descriptions of Norwegian regions already in the eighteenth century, with information about the natural environment, buildings, and communications. These topographers were also interested in folk beliefs and other antiquarian ideas, and when the collection and publication of popular culture became one main contribution to the national Norwegian cultural heritage project after independence from Denmark was achieved in 1814, superstition too was accepted—but as cultural history. Several pastors and theologians played a prominent role here.[55] This positive involvement also contained an appreciation of the ethical norms and attitudes that were certainly not foreign to popular belief. In their own way, folk beliefs helped to defend and deepen the recognition of the unique status of a child as a human being deserving protection in a dangerous and insecure world.

Folk Beliefs and the Care of Children in Recent Times

Most of the elements of folk beliefs concerning children that we have discussed here are much older than the eighteenth century, but very few of them survived into the twentieth century. Scholars have surmised that they survived longest in remote valleys and mountain villages, but this is highly uncertain. It is more likely that the duration of these elements was connected with social rather than with geographical conditions. In other words, the degree of Enlightenment, the educational level, and economic circumstances were more decisive. For example, a number of living folk beliefs with regard to children were registered in poor areas in the East End of Oslo well into the twentieth century, especially in the area of popular medicine.

It is not possible to determine what kind of folk beliefs survived longest, but there are many indications that the belief in dangerous spirits and beings in woods and outfields put up the greatest resistance. Many informants in the mid-twentieth century told how they had met the children of wood nymphs when they themselves were small, and they told their own children about this later. "They got the impression from their father that he fully believed in these beings" (Herland in Østfold, south-eastern Norway, 1952). As late as in 1966, the folklorist Otto Blehr published a large collection of living popular belief from Sørkedalen near Oslo, where the following quotations are far from isolated: "Father had seen the wood nymph at Bjørdammen several times. There is a big hill there, you see, and she had gone strolling forwards and backwards. And his wife's grandfather had seen the wood nymph at a hill here, 'Hulerbærje'" (hollow hill).[56] And: "Mother and Father told us that there was a corner in Fyllingen where a knocking was heard at midnight. So, they agreed that they would get up and ask it what it wanted. It said that they should dig up what was buried at the right, or rather the left stone pillar of the barn and lay it in Christian soil, and it was the skeleton a child. After they did this, everything was silent ..."[57]

The traditional material shows that folk beliefs were important elements in the education of children over a long period, and helped in various ways to set boundaries for them and to communicate and inculcate attitudes and norms that were meant to protect them from bad things later in life (Figure 2.6). Without a basis in genuine beliefs, these threats would surely

Figure 2.6 Traditional material shows that elderly persons contributed by means of their sagas and adventure stories to keep alive in the youngest members of the household the belief in spirits and ghosts that laid down norms. *The Woman Who Told Adventure Stories*: a drawing by Adolph Tidemand (1814–1876). Photo: Dag A. Ivarsøy / The National Museum of Art, Architecture and Design, Oslo.

have had no effect on children. Examples are: "The water spirit lives in the wells where people fetch water. They said that he was very greedy for small children. He was employed to frighten the children so that they did not go to the well."[58] And: "When the households sat together in the living room in the evenings in olden days, the old people told tall tales about wood nymphs and trolls, so that the kids were absolutely terrified and did not dare go out alone when it was dark."[59] And: "They often frightened the children with the Christmas fancy dressed child and the Christmas goat, with trolls and goblins, so that they would be well-behaved and obedient. 'Oh yes, they said. Now the troll will come to take you. The Christmas goat is not far away now. Just listen now.' Then the children became well-behaved, and did not open their mouths."[60]

These last quotations can serve as examples of the contrast between total rejection and pragmatic acceptance that gradually came to influence ordinary people's attitude to superstition. When the primary matter was care for the child, many people found that this more than justified the frightening stories. Without this perspective of care, it is impossible to appreciate the positive significance of all the old rules of conduct, warnings, protective rituals, and terrifying ideas with which superstition surrounded the child. "The child was their most precious possession in olden days too. It had to be protected in every way, so that nothing bad could affect it," said the folklorist Edvard Grimstad (1886–1955) from Nord-Gudbrandsdalen (central southern Norway) in 1945.[61] This was what they tried to do with the means that were available, the means in which they believed. Most of this would be called "folk beliefs" today, but "folk beliefs" too had their values. The child was regarded as holy and inviolable, and as a central point in the battle between the good and evil powers in the human world. This drama was decisive for whether the child's destiny would be sad and bad, or bright and good.[62]

Notes

1 To these we should add Johannes Skar 1961 and Storaker's collections both published in the early twentieth century.
2 Wigström (ed. Stenklo) 1952; Kristensen 1871–1987 (13 volumes).
3 Examples of studies of this kind from Norway are Amundsen 1983; Bø 1987; Holck 1996; and Skjelbred 1972.
4 Norsk Folkeminnesamling (hereafter NFS) Eldrid Hoprekstad 2, 1954: 5.
5 Lunde 1969: 29.
6 Storaker 1935: 10–11.
7 Amtsfysikus (Medical Officer) in Østfold 1851. Holck 1996: 138.
8 Kristensen 1883: 252–3.
9 Wigström (ed. Stenklo) 1952: 63.
10 Weiser-Aall 1968: 59.
11 Borchgrevink 1956: 15.
12 Ibid.
13 Holck 1996: 137.
14 Borchgrevink 1956: 15.
15 Fjellstad 1945: 112.

16 Gjest Bårdsen (1791–1849) is Norway's best known large-scale robber; Christian II (1481–1559) was a Danish-Norwegian warrior king who reigned from 1513 to 1523.
17 Opedal 1934: 172.
18 Storaker 1935: 13.
19 Hagberg 1949: 18.
20 Røstad 1931: 43.
21 Hagberg 1949: 17.
22 NFS Jacob Andreas Samuelsen 14 (1935): 24.
23 Opedal 1934: 175.
24 Wigström (ed. Stenklo) 1952: 210.
25 Grimstad 1945: 13.
26 Røstad 1931: 112.
27 Hagberg 1949: 21.
28 Troels-Lund 1929–31: 42.
29 Wigström (ed. Stenklo) 1952: 42–3.
30 Skar 1961: 104–5.
31 Wille, *Beskrivelse over Sillejords*, 1786.
32 Storaker 1935: 37.
33 Grimstad 1945: 14.
34 Sundt 1971: 180–1.
35 On the system of godparents in Norwegian local history and popular tradition, see Hodne 1979.
36 NFS Ola Talleraashaugen 4, 1928–30: 30–1.
37 Hagberg 1949: 31.
38 Ibid.
39 Hodne 1999: 51.
40 Tang Kristensen 1883: 255–6.
41 NFS Sjur Bøyum 2, 1929–30: 21.
42 Ibid.
43 Tang Kristensen 1883: 120–1.
44 Bø 1960.
45 *En klokkeringing for de Underjordiske*, 1877: 553–5.
46 See also the chapters by Markussen, Rørvik, and Aavitsland in this volume.
47 Pontoppidan, *FEJEKOST til at udfeje den gamle*, 13. See also the chapter by Markussen in this volume.
48 Ibid.: 49.
49 Ibid.: 53.
50 Ibid.: 68.
51 Amundsen 1999: 9.
52 Amundsen 1999: 11.
53 *Tradisjonsinnsamling på 1800-tallet*, 31.
54 Ibid., 136.
55 Examples are: Simon Olaus Wolff (1796–1859), Andreas Faye (1802–1869), Magnus B. Landstad (1802–1880), Jørgen Moe (1813–1882), Eilert Sundt (1817–1875), and Anton Christian Bang (1840–1913).
56 Blehr 1966: 76.
57 Ibid.: 59.
58 Mørch 1932: 39.
59 NFS Svale Solheim 1, 1930–32: 12.
60 NFS Peder Martin Guddal 1, 1964–65: 189.
61 Grimstad 1945: 7.
62 The text in this chapter has been revised by Lars Fredrik Janby and translated from Norwegian by Brian McNeil. Quotations in dialects and in archaic language have been translated into modern Standard English.

3   The Household Code

Protestant Upbringing in Denmark–Norway from the Reformation to the Enlightenment

Ingrid Markussen

The Reformation that Martin Luther (1483–1546) launched in the 1520s, and that spread from North Germany to all the Scandinavian countries, brought with it changes not only in church life, but also in people's everyday lives. The changes were aimed first and foremost at the adults, but children too became a particular target for the Reformation's demands with regard to upbringing and education. Luther's language about "the priesthood of all believers" was taken seriously in the Protestant lands. This meant that the individual was to be held responsible vis-à-vis God, and could pray to God without a confessional or intermediary authorities such as the Virgin Mary or the Church's priests and prelates, as had been the case in Catholic times. The universal priesthood also entailed the requirement of literacy and knowledge, so that the individual could read and understand the Christian texts and psalms that were now to be accessible in one's native language. Both girls and boys in the Scandinavian countries were to learn the same basic religious material, and the general result in Scandinavia was that not only men, but women too, were literate long before the obligatory primary school was established.[1]

Baptism was the Church's first sacrament and the first action that involved children. The adults were to give expression, on behalf of the child, to the Lutheran understanding of the faith.[2] As early as possible after baptism, girls and boys were to learn the Christian children's instruction, that is to say, Luther's *Small Catechism* of 1529. In this way, they used their childhood to prepare themselves for the next step in becoming an adult member of the Christian Church, namely, the Lord's Supper, which was the Church's second sacrament. No one could receive this sacrament without reciting from the Catechism by heart, and without being able to answer simple questions about the Lutheran faith. The contents of Luther's Catechism thus came to leave their mark on children's upbringing in the following centuries. It was the father, the head of the household, who was responsible for their upbringing. As attendance at school increased in the following centuries, it also became the task of the teacher to inculcate the children's instruction.

Luther's *Small Catechism* had five sections: (1) the Ten Commandments; (2) the Lord's Prayer; (3) the creed—all with brief explanations of each line, and with the biblical texts of the institution of the two Lutheran sacraments; (4) baptism; and (5) the Lord's Supper—with explanations here too. Luther had simplified the Christian message in the Catechism so that unlearned persons could familiarize themselves in a simple manner with the basic texts that presented the Gospel. It was, however, not easy for children to understand the abstractions contained in the texts.

The five principal sections in the Catechism, which were to be learned by heart, were given an appendix, the so-called "household code," in the second half of the sixteenth century. Together, the five sections and The Household Code constituted what was called the Gospel and the Law. The Household Code put the contents and the abstractions of the Catechism into a societal system that was much more concrete to relate to, both for children and for adults. In what follows, I shall concentrate on the part of upbringing that was connected to the Catechism's education for life in society. This is a relatively unknown aspect of the Lutheran thinking about education.

The Household Code and the Reformers

The Household Code was elaborated by Luther and his fellow Reformers, especially Philipp Melanchthon (1497–1560); its golden age in Scandinavia was the seventeenth and eighteenth centuries. It divided society into three estates: the teaching estate (the clergy), the governing estate (the king and secular persons in authority), and the household. In all the estates, the five parts of the Catechism—the Gospel—was fundamental for leading a Christian life. But it was necessary to understand the message of the Gospel in its societal context. According to Luther, the individual human being was placed by God in an estate or (as was also said) an office or a vocation—this is often called the "Lutheran idea of vocation." One was in one's vocation in all three estates simultaneously, either as superior or as inferior. After the Reformation, a clergyman was *paterfamilias* in his house, and he was also the leader of his parish, but he was a subject in the country. The king was *paterfamilias* in his house, and he was the political leader of the country, but as a part of the clergyman's parish he was subject to the guidance of the teaching estate in questions of faith.[3]

In the household, a child lived as a subject under its parents, especially the father, but after its baptism, the child also belonged to the Christian parish and was a subject in the country. The father was *paterfamilias* and leader of the household, but he was subordinate to the clergyman in the parish and to the king as a subject. Women and children were subordinate to a "father" in all three estates.

The Reformation made the family important for those who practiced the Lutheran faith, as marriage became a fundamental element in the state. Marriage ought to be blessed with many children, since the carnal love between man and woman was legitimated, from the Church's perspective, by procreation. This applied also to the clergy, who from now on were to

Figure 3.1 Epitaph from Køge Church, showing the Dean Christen Lauritsen Glob (1581–1633) with his total of four wives and six living and two deceased children. This picture is a clear expression of the Lutheran understanding of the ministers' role as a family man.

take part in social life as the head of a household.[4] In church paintings from the sixteenth and seventeenth centuries, we can see portraits of huge clergy families, with the children standing in long rows (Figure 3.1). If the wife died, the husband ought to marry again, so that the rows of children could be extended.[5]

The Household Code, also known as the "doctrine of the three estates," was fundamental for the systematic order that characterized the Lutheran education of children and adults. In the first part of this chapter, therefore, I shall illustrate its ideology and its societal significance. I shall then present an example of how The Household Code was understood by the pastor and the parents in a local region in Sydfyn in Denmark in the 1780s and 1790s. This sheds light on the inevitable conflict that occurred at the close of the eighteenth century between the rationalistic reform-pedagogical thinking of the Enlightenment and the Church's Lutheran educational principles.

The Household Code and the Doctrine of Three Estates

The Household Code was not an independently formulated text. It was a collection of biblical quotations from the New Testament that the Reformers found appropriate to the obligations of the three estates. Most of these are quotations from Paul's Letters to the first Christian communities. The Danish name, *Hustavlen,* is probably derived from a tablet (*tavle*) that could be hung on the wall in the home. It made up roughly seven of the circa seventy pages of the Catechism and laid down disciplinary regulations for each estate.

The Household Code was meant to help people to keep to the right path in life, so that they could obtain salvation and eternal life after death. This is why it was immeasurably important to learn and understand the five fundamental parts of the Catechism. The task of the teaching estate was thus to educate the people in both the Gospel and the Law. Since the *paterfamilias* was a kind of priest in his home, he was responsible for the children's upbringing.

The obligations prescribed by The Household Code were reciprocal. Parents were told: "And, ye fathers, provoke not your children to wrath: but bring them up in the nurture and admonition of the Lord." (Eph. 6) This text demands that the parents bring up their children in keeping with Christian maxims, so that they will keep to the right path and not direct their aggression to others or to their parents.

The Household Code told the children: "Children, obey your parents in the Lord: for this is right. Honor thy father and mother; (which is the first commandment with promise). That it may be well with thee, and thou mayest live long on the earth." (Eph. 6.1) This precept declares love and obedience vis-à-vis one's parents to be a cornerstone in the Christian faith.

Although obedience is a primary principle for children, both texts speak of reciprocity. If the parents brought up their children in a correct Christian manner, they would reap the reward of obedient and grateful children— and, one may suppose, children who would later, as adults, take care of their elderly parents.

The doctrine of the three estates, which Luther first set out circa 1520, grew out of the mediaeval focus on *the concept of father*, a hierarchy that passed from God, the father of all human beings, to the pastor, the king, and the *paterfamilias*, who were the superiors in the three estates and therefore a kind of father for their subordinates.[6] This doctrine thus cemented a patriarchal view of society in which the focus was always on the man. The Household Code demanded care and love in the exercise of the paternal function, just as a father showed love for his children. The superiors in every estate could expect respect and obedience from the inferiors. After the Reformation, the school and its teachers became the humblest members of the teaching estate. They were to support the house and home in the Christian instruction of children.

The doctrine of the three estates was not about the social distinctions that existed in the country, but about relationships within and between the individual estates. At the same time, it contained an interesting idea about equality. In the exercise of his "office," the father in each of the three estates had the same relationship to God. In other words, the peasant was the equal of the clergyman and the official in the responsibility he bore for religious upbringing.

No other disciplining ideology in Scandinavian history was ever more comprehensive and strictly elaborated than the Lutheran household. Despite this, relatively little attention has been paid to this phenomenon in Danish–Norwegian historiography, although it has been the subject of lively discussion by Swedish scholars.[7]

The biblical quotations in the Lutheran household code are largely identical in all the Scandinavian countries. In Finland and Sweden, it is found not only in Luther's *Small Catechism*, but also in the hymnal.[8] In Denmark–Norway, it is found in the Catechism and in the explanation of the Catechism. Since it contains obligations and rules that were to be carried out and obeyed in the three estates, it could be used in all the Scandinavian countries as one element in the disciplining education of the people not only in an ecclesiastical, but also in a secular context.

The thinking in The Household Code has left its traces long into the modern period. Many individual elements in the disciplining ideology, such as the basic patriarchal element, can be found today in most other countries and cultures. But the combination of the obligations to obey in an elaborate doctrine of three estates, encompassing the home, the parish, and the state, is specific to the Protestant countries in northern Europe. It must have left its mark on the upbringing of children in the centuries that followed the Reformation.

The Norwegian "Trumpet" Petter Dass and The Household Code

There are no sources that provide concrete information on how The Household Code was used in practice in the education of children. But we can see how the biblical quotations were understood by one clergyman at the beginning of the eighteenth century, Petter Dass (1647–1707), pastor of Alstahaug in Nordland, a coastal region in northern Norway.[9] He was a great poet, with an ability to express the Lutheran doctrine simply and powerfully in verse. His twelve household code hymns are included in his *Catechism Hymns*, published in 1715.[10] The fact that The Household Code verses were sung by the parish is completely in accord with the collective thinking of the code itself.

When one reads the many verses in Petter Dass' household code hymns, one understands the powerful impact they must have had on the Norwegian population. When the parish sang about the teaching estate, they affirmed that the bishops must refrain from adultery and drunkenness, so that they could defend the pure Protestant doctrine with seriousness and with "steel gloves." They would be rewarded by the parish, which was "an ordinance appointed by God." The hymn about the governing estate stated that as "God's under-lords on earth," it must be obeyed by the people and receive taxes and tolls in return for its work in "using God's weaponry" to punish those who went astray and ruined their own lives.[11]

With regard to the household, they sang that the woman must obey her husband, because "when the man is honored, God is honored," but also that the man should govern his house with care and "be aware of the woman's weakness."[12] The patriarchal thinking was thus laid down with a reference to God. Children and other members of the household must likewise obey the *paterfamilias* and overlook instances where he did not follow The Household Code's principles for correct governance.

Petter Dass was a mild-mannered moralist who put a humorous edge on the biblical rules about obedience, but his household code hymns laid down with unshakable orthodoxy, the rules that the Church preached. Disciplining is the primary message—disciplining in agreement with Protestant ethics. Women, children, and servants were the subordinates in all the categories. Petter Dass concluded with advice about how the entire parish should relate to each other in love, on the basis of the commandment that one should love one's neighbor as oneself.

Pontoppidan's Pietistic Explanation of the Catechism

In the first half of the eighteenth century, the country was influenced by a religious current known as "pietism," which demanded a personal conversion and a strong spirituality to be sure of eternal salvation. In 1737, the Danish–Norwegian government made the use of one particular explanation of the Catechism obligatory in religious instruction. Before this, there had been innumerable explanations of the Catechism that were used to help pupils learn Luther's *Small Catechism*; now, the pietistic court chaplain Erik Pontoppidan (1698–1764) was commissioned by the King to write an explanation entitled *Sandhet til Gudfrygtighed*, which, together with Luther's *Small Catechism*, was obligatory material in the preparation for *confirmation*, which was introduced by law in 1736. Confirmation and the explanation of the Catechism were central elements in the school law that took effect in Denmark–Norway in the years around 1740.

From that time, it was necessary to be confirmed before one received the Lord's Supper. Confirmation became an examination of the religious instruction in both the home and the school, a needle's eye that all children, boys and girls, had to go through to become full adult members of the parish. Confirmation, with a prescribed curriculum that was identical for all children, thereafter, ensured a uniform religious upbringing, since all the children were taught from the same basic books.

Pontoppidan's explanation of the Catechism has the structure of a series of questions and answers that follow the five parts of the Catechism. It is worth noting that The Household Code's biblical quotations are not collected under the term "household code," but are split up and placed under the fourth commandment of the Catechism ("Honor thy father and thy mother; that thy days may be prolonged, and that it may go well with thee, in the land") and the sixth commandment ("Thou shalt not commit adultery").[13] This meant that the biblical quotations for the governing estate and the teaching estate came under the fourth commandment, and the biblical quotations for the household under the sixth; but the contents are the same. Under the fourth commandment, Pontoppidan writes:

> *To whom do the names of father and mother refer?*
> First, to our natural parents, and after them, to all those who in any way are charged to command us, such as persons in authority, guardians, heads of households, clergymen, schoolmasters and the like, all of whom are parents, each in his own estate.

> *How many principal estates exist?*
> Three: (1) The governing estate, in which kings, princes, and other persons in authority are parents, whereas the subordinates are their children. (2) The teaching estate, in which clergymen and schoolmasters are parents, but their pupils and listeners are children. (3) The household, in which father and mother, husbands, wives, guardians, benefactors, and honest elderly persons should be respected like parents by children, grandchildren, stepchildren, servants, wards, and other young persons.

The placing of the three estates under the fourth commandment highlights the patriarchal principle where God, as father, is superior to the other "fathers" (the king, the clergyman, and the *paterfamilias*). The inferiors in every estate are to be regarded as children, the superiors as parents. The relationships between the estates are not mentioned, and this conceals the fact that the king too, as a member of the parish, is subordinate to the guidance of the clergy on questions of faith.

With regard to the third commandment, "Remember the day of rest, to keep it holy," children encountered in Pontoppidan's explanation rules that also applied to Sunday as the day of rest on which one attended church.[14] The question ran: "How does one profane the day of rest?" The answer was: "By not refraining from physical work, as well as through sinful pleasures such as dancing, playing at cards, comedies, going to public houses, and such things that are always sin *per se*, but are doubly sinful on holy days." A new question followed: "Are then no external works allowed on Sunday?" And the answer was: "Yes, truly necessary works that cannot be postponed, and the works of love that are always carried out."

Since the children were required to attend church together with their parents, it was not by chance that they too learned these rules. The works of love that often prevented the older children from taking part in worship included looking after smaller siblings while the family was in church.

From 1736, children were not only to learn Luther's *Small Catechism* by heart. They were now also to learn Pontoppidan's explanation by heart. This was a comprehensive work—the book had more than 200 pages and was divided into a total of 759 questions and answers. Pontoppidan realized that it was not possible for everyone to learn so much material by heart, and he specified in his preface that the clergy could dispense from this requirement in the case of children with a bad memory and little schooling. Pontoppidan himself elaborated several pedagogical instructions for schoolmasters and clergymen, with the aim of making their teaching task easier.[15] Here he states that the teacher should use practical examples and illustrative stories based on things that the children could see and that they knew.[16] Later in the century, Pontoppidan's explanation was published in abbreviated editions, to make the path to confirmation easier.

It was certainly not easy for all clergymen to fulfill the obligation to supply explanatory examples, and learning by heart was consistently a torment for the children. In a guide for newly trained clergy, *Collegium Pastorale Practicum*, which Pontoppidan wrote in 1757 to aid young pastors in their parish work, he writes about a meeting he had with a clergyman who taught young people in preparation for confirmation.[17] One of these had been a girl who was unable to learn by heart. She had wept copiously because she could not reach the required level of knowledge. Without confirmation, she would not be able to receive the Lord's Supper, and she would thus be unable to get betrothed or to marry; this was how things had been since the Reformation. The clergyman himself was deeply despondent about her situation, but he found a solution: he began to tell stories from the Bible. It may be that he had discovered the Bible history published in 1714 by the German schoolmaster Johann Hübner, which had appeared in Danish in 1728: *To gange To og Halvtredsindstyve udvalgte Bibliske Historier af det Gamle og Nye Testamente, Ungdommen til Beste*. The girl wakened up; her interest was kindled. Her keenness increased, and she finally attained the level that was required for confirmation.

Pontoppidan concludes the story with a striking pedagogical directive that has lost nothing of its relevance even today: "Pleasure strengthens the will, and the will opens the door to understanding, because the powers of the soul stretch out their hands to each other."[18] With his use of concepts such as pleasure (i.e. motivation), will, and understanding, Pontoppidan points ahead to the Enlightenment pedagogy. Bible history became solidly established in the second half of the eighteenth century, and was an essential element in the religious instruction of the Enlightenment period.

Tradition and New Beginnings in Christian Education after 1750

It is easy to give a description of the public children's school that functioned in Denmark in the second half of the eighteenth century because all the sources agree in the picture they give of teaching.[19] Children of all ages came to school at the same time, when school could be integrated into the pattern of their other tasks at home or as the servants of other families. They found a seat and took out their reading primer or ABC book, and the

Catechism—or, if they had finished with it, Pontoppidan's explanation or a Gospel book—and began to read aloud the lesson about which the teacher would ask questions in the course of the day.[20] All the children read aloud, and the noise could be deafening. It was, of course, the intention of the law that the pupils should understand what they read, but mostly, they learned to rattle off the reading lesson without really thinking about what they were reading. It was held that understanding would come as they got older.

The reaction came with the breakthrough of the Enlightenment in the 1780s and 1790s. A development at a Danish country estate that was influenced by the reform at the close of the eighteenth century can give us an impression of the conflicts that arose when new pedagogical ideas weakened the traditional power of the Lutheran Church, while at the same time also clashing with fathers' understanding of their responsibility for the religious upbringing of their children.[21]

The philanthropic Count Johan Ludvig Reventlow (1752–1801) introduced comprehensive land reforms and school reforms on the estate of Brahetrolleborg, on the south of the island of Fyn, in the 1780s and 1790s, which became exemplary for the entire country. Reventlow employed the school as an educational institution and intervened in the upbringing that was given both in the home and in the church. With good support from the Danish state, Reventlow had a completely different agenda from the traditional Church, namely, an education aiming at the use of reason and activity, with an emphasis on usefulness that could make the farmers agricultural entrepreneurs and good Christian citizens.

In a new school ordinance in 1783, Reventlow forbade the learning by heart of religious texts the contents of which the little children did not understand. He consequently removed the Catechism from the initial instruction in reading, and had the children learn to read through a secular moral reading book that came from the pen of the German estate owner, pedagogue, and philanthropist Friedrich Eberhard von Rochow (1734–1805), who himself had founded three schools for farmers' children on his estate of Reckahn in Brandenburg. This reading book, *Børnevennen* (*The Children's Friend*), described daily life in the countryside and built on observations that were familiar to the children. It was unquestionably the first secular reading book in Denmark—Norway, and it aimed to promote rational reasoning in the children.[22] The table of contents lists good and bad character traits, which the texts then illustrate by means of various children and adults: "The honest child"; "The little lying girl"; "The little thief"; "The foolish child"; "The wise mother"; "The good servant girl"; "The good male servant"; "The child who does good"; "The grateful son"; "The timid one"; "The superstitious one"; "The bad male servant"; "The impatient one"; and "The meek one." But we also encounter character traits that were more useful to society in texts about: "The prudent householder in a time of high prices"; "About the happiness of the virtuous person already here on earth"; "On the usefulness of those in authority"; "On the advantages of life in the countryside"; and "On the woman whose uncleanliness made her a bad housewife." Natural scientific knowledge was communicated in texts about the growth of plants and the artificial globe.

The reading book also addressed the pupils with texts that displayed reflective children: "A schoolchild's questions to its teacher"; "The two schoolchildren"; "Child and father—a conversation." Intellectual abstractions were also explained in texts about great and small, about truth, about the essential and the contingent, and in proverbs such as the following: "A thin settlement is better than a fat court case." The texts in the final section of *Børnevennen* take up religious questions, with titles like: "The master and the gardener—or how to use the Bible"; "Springtime—an image of the resurrection"; "On blessedness"; "On the explanation of perfect prayer"; "On God's blessing." The book concludes with tests of the children's knowledge of general religious truths and of the meaning of strange words.

This was a completely new way to prepare for the reading involved in confirmation. But the explanation of the Catechism that was used on this estate to supplement Luther's *Small Catechism* also lay outside the general norms in Denmark–Norway, since it was not Pontoppidan's explanation. Reventlow had received permission from the Danish chancellery to use the *Brief Instruction in Christianity* by the German theologian Johan Andreas Cramer (1723–1788) in the three schools for farmers' children on his estate.[23] It was translated into Danish in 1785 and was introduced immediately into the Brahetrolleborg school system. In his book, J. A. Cramer focused almost exclusively on life here and now.[24] His rationalist attitude can perhaps be best seen in his introductory questions to the children: "Do we not all want to be content and happy?" In Pontoppidan's explanation of the Catechism, the question was: "Dear child, do you not want to be happy on earth and blessed in heaven?" Cramer removed the dimension of life after death and concentrated on life on earth; his question had a general reference, and was not addressed to an individual child. His explanation also contained a number of explanations of terms in a natural language, so that the children could grasp what abstract expressions such as "almighty," "justification," and "truth" meant. The Enlightenment demand for rationality and the idea of usefulness left their mark on the book.

This book also shows that the rules about obedience in The Household Code had developed in Cramer into a general teaching about obligation and social ethics. We do not find The Household Code, the doctrine of the three estates, or the traditional exposition of the Ten Commandments in Cramer. Instead, we find an exposition of the human being's *obligations to God, to oneself, and to others*. However, The Household Code is not forgotten. Its biblical quotations about obligations between the individual and his or her superior are replaced here by "*true Christians' special and social obligations.*" This means, *inter alia*, that the relationship between the teaching estate (the clergy) and the other two estates more or less disappears from sight.

Cramer's book caused Reventlow problems with the ecclesiastical authorities, the provost and the bishop in the 1790s, since they disliked its rationalism. Throughout the whole period, however, the Chancellery supported his use of the book, although it was authorized for use only in the duchies of Schleswig and Holstein. In other regions of the kingdom, the traditional teaching of the Catechism was retained.

C. C. Birch and His Attitude to The Household Code

Carl Christian Birch (1753–1808), the parish minister in Brahetrolleborg, was a warm supporter of Reventlow's new school order. At the same time, he had a solid foundation in the Church's traditional thinking with regard to education, as we see in a collection of regulations that he drew up in 1784 for use in teaching writing in schools and in evening classes for young persons who had already been confirmed.[25]

The Lutheran idea of the three estates emerges most clearly in a text for the oldest schoolchildren of both sexes, who were to work as servants of other farmers after finishing school. In 1784, the peasants on the estate had not yet been freed from the obligation to remain on the estate where they had been born. This meant that until 1788, their relationship to the landowner resembled that of servants. In his collection of regulations, Birch taught the children to write:

> *Obligations of servants of both sexes to their master and mistress*
> God himself, the wisest and best Father, places each person here in the world in that estate that serves him or her greatly.
> A peasant is bound with zeal to the place of his birth, and is thus born to be a servant; here, the vocation from God comes already at birth.
> A vocation that is just as holy as if God had uttered it from heaven; rejoice at this and think that God, who knows all things in advance, knew that this was the most serviceable thing for you.
> For if he had thought that it was better for you, he could have let you be the child of other parents.
> Think, therefore, of these words of Paul in First Corinthians 7:21: "Art thou called being a servant? Care not for it." V. 20: "Let every man abide in the same calling wherein he was called."[26]

This prescription is completely in accord with Luther's thinking about vocations and estates, which exhorted each one to be content with his or her state in life, since that was an expression of God's will. Birch does not mention The Household Code or the doctrine of the three estates here, or anywhere else in the collection of regulations. But like The Household Code, he sets out the simple obligations of the household.

The aspect of obedience is strongly emphasized in his regulations about children's upbringing. The following regulation is addressed to young people in their twenties, as future parents:

Accustom your children to obedience
Prudent parents establish such respect for themselves in their children that they respect their parents as those who have the authority to tell them what to do.

And if you want your children to respect you in this way, enjoin upon them that they should do exactly all that you command them. Reflect therefore exactly on what you say; and nothing—neither kindness nor tears—should move you to change what you have once commanded.

Never be such poor parents that the child can come to one of you and get permission for something that the other parent forbids.

If you behave in such a way, from the time that the child can understand, that the child must always obey you, you will spare yourselves from punishing your children with corporal punishment.[27]

This regulation is his own personal guidance for the upbringing of children, since none of the apostles dealt so deeply with parenthood as Birch does here. He was also a man who spoke from experience, since he was at that date the father of five or six children.[28]

Birch's adherence to the traditional Lutheran thinking can also be seen in the speech he delivered in December 1783 before the assembled parents at the inauguration of the new school order.[29] When he wanted to explain why the parents should now send their children to school every day and not (as in the past) when it fitted into the work they had to do at home, his starting point was Paul's Letter to the Ephesians (6:4): "And, ye fathers, provoke not your children to wrath: but bring them up in the nurture and admonition of the Lord." Birch added his own comment, which he regarded as a consequence of Paul's Letter to the Ephesians: "Enjoin on your children that they come industriously to school." If parents were to bring up their children in the nurture and admonition of the Lord, this meant after 1783 that they also must send them to school every day, as the regulations on the estate prescribed.

The last consideration that Birch believed the parents ought to display was toward himself as their spiritual guide and teacher. In this area, the obligations of the parents, and especially of the *paterfamilias*, concerned both their own children in the household, the clergy, and the rulers who represented the king and his government—in this case, Count Reventlow.

When he spoke the following day to the schoolchildren during the opening of the first school, he said that the school was for the children what the church was for those who were older. The school was a house of God in which the children were to get to know Jesus and to understand how much Jesus loved them. If they showed that they were good children, Jesus would take them into heaven, where they would see him. "Is it not good to come to heaven?" asked Birch, and answered his own question: "Oh yes, indeed it is good. No matter how good your life may be here in the world, you will have a much better life there."[30] These words show that even in the ongoing period of reform, the school continued to build on the same foundations as during the Reformation. The highest aim of the school and of the church was identical—the salvation of human beings and an eternal life in heaven. It may seem paradoxical that life after death should have such a prominent place in Birch's speech in connection with a school reform that was meant to prepare the children for an active and useful adult life, but here he was following the Lutheran thinking that we have seen expressed in Pontoppidan's explanation, where the introductory question to the child was: "Dear child, do you not want to be happy on earth and blessed in heaven?"

The Parent's Protest and the Schoolmaster Pade's Defense

How did the parents react to the modern teaching methods and textbooks that were now introduced into the school? The answer is found in a comprehensive legal case that was brought in 1795/1796, when seventeen heads of households addressed the ecclesiastical authorities.[31] They held that their children were not receiving the correct Protestant doctrine and teaching that they themselves had received in their childhood, and that they believed the ecclesiastical authorities (provost and bishop) desired. The parents were disappointed that their children sat in the classroom with *Børnevennen,* instead of learning *Luther's Catechism* by heart after several months in school. The clash was between the modern Enlightenment principles regarding the teaching of reading and the Church's traditional Lutheran view that the children's parents put forward.

Johannes Pade (1750–1836) was the teacher about whom the parents complained. He defended himself in a long text in which we find a deepened understanding of the new principles, which offered a different approach to religious education than the traditional approach. Like the other schoolmasters in Brahetrolleborg, Johannes Pade had been trained at the Seminary in Kiel under Johan Andreas Cramer. He was highly respected by Reventlow, and he consistently followed the guidelines for teaching that Reventlow had laid down in the 1783 school regulations for Brahetrolleborg.[32] In his defense text, he states that while the children learned religion, they were at the same time to learn to think for themselves and become able to express their thoughts both orally and in writing. Pade writes:

> Although the educational principles of those who accuse me disagree profoundly with my own principles, I know that they would agree with me that Jesus was the most excellent teacher and that his way of doing things was also the most excellent.

Pade goes on to affirm how Jesus (in his view) communicated his message in an exceptional pedagogy to his simple listeners. Jesus did not ask anyone to learn abstract concepts by heart. On the contrary, he spoke to his "simple" listeners about situations that were well-known and relevant to them. He employed parables and narratives, for example, about work and daily wages, about a despairing father, about flour and yeast, about a sower, about wheat and chaff, about fishermen and their nets, about a wedding and the guests, and about various kinds of soil. Pade writes that Jesus wanted to catch his listeners' attention in a pleasant way and to get them to reflect, so that he could then take them further. When Jesus' disciples were surprised that he spoke in parables, he replied:

> Because it is given unto you to know the mysteries of the kingdom of heaven, but to them it is not given. Therefore speak I to them in parables: because they seeing see not; and hearing they hear not, neither do they understand.
>
> (Matthew 13:11, 13)

Pade concluded his argumentation by noting that when Jesus had spoken in this way to his disciples, he finished by asking them: "Have ye understood all these things?" (Matthew 13:51).[33]

There can be no doubt that Pade and Reventlow looked at the farmers in the same way that they assumed Jesus looked at his listeners: as simple persons, that is to say, persons who did not reflect on what they saw and heard, but took everything at face value, without going more deeply into things—or simply did not understand what was involved. *Seeing they did not see, and hearing they did not hear.* This was a simplicity that the school now had to tackle. Pade's argument went on to warn against the problems that would follow from learning by heart without understanding. Once again, he quoted Jesus: "Take heed therefore how ye hear: for whosoever hath, to him shall be given; and whosoever hath not, from him shall be taken even that which he seemeth to have" (Luke 8:18). "Take heed therefore that the light which is in thee be not darkness" (Luke 11:35).

Pade applies to his own pedagogy Jesus' admonition that the light that is in the individual can be changed into darkness. He warns that if one does not take prudent care of the light or the ability that the individual child has received (from God or from providence), but allows the child to grow up without learning to think and to reflect, the light or the ability will be extinguished over the course of time, especially in a child who has not received much light from the outset. The adult will then land in a permanent darkness (and simplicity). On the other hand, the child who has received a great light or ability from the outset will be able to develop the light into a brilliant light, if he or she receives prudent teaching. This is a very interesting and logical exposition of Jesus' words that "whosoever hath, to him shall be given; and whosoever hath not, from him shall be taken even that which he seemeth to have."

After this powerful introduction, Pade explains the teaching method that was followed in the schools. The teachers began their instruction by talking with the children about concepts that were well-known to them from their daily lives. They made use of narratives and illustrative stories that the child could find *inter alia* in the reading book *Børnevennen*. In this way, the children acquired concepts to think with, and they learned how to express their own thoughts in conversations with the teacher. As time went on, therefore, they would grasp more abstract concepts. It was important to the teachers that the children did not learn something by heart without understanding what they were learning. Pade's defense statement is in reality a defense of Enlightenment pedagogy as a whole.

Conclusion

Children in Scandinavia encountered Luther's thinking about society through the most widely used textbook that has ever been published in Scandinavia, Luther's *Small Catechism* and its appendix, The Household Code. This taught them about the hierarchical system of which they and their parents were a part. According to God's plan for human beings, they were all born into one particular estate, and all had received the vocation from God, which located them in a superior or an inferior position where they were to carry out the duties inherent in their vocation.

Luther's *Small Catechism* and the many explanations of the Catechism that were elaborated over the next two centuries incorporated The Household Code's biblical quotations into the text to make concrete the doctrine of the three estates. The quotations laid down rules concerning obedience, determining how children should relate, not only to the adults in the house (and especially to the *paterfamilias*), but also to ecclesiastical and secular authorities. At the same time, The Household Code made paternal love a focal point for the relationship between inferiors and superiors, and maintained the Reformation's patriarchal view of the relationships in society. This, however, did not prevent girls and women from having the same chance as boys and men to learn to read, after the Reformation. They were equal with regard to understanding the Christian message.

It is hard to document the significance that The Household Code had for children's and adults' view of societal conditions and, not least, of women's position in the home and in society. At any rate, the local example from Brahetrolleborg country estate shows that in the heart of the Enlightenment reform years in the 1790s, The Household Code still appears to express a world of ideas that held good for both the clergyman and the children's parents. This material shows that the parents wanted to keep control over the children's religious instruction, thereby living up to the responsibility that Luther had enjoined upon parents during the Reformation. Throughout the entire court case, no one asked about the mothers' views; it was the fathers who expressed themselves, and in the few instances where some of them involved their wives in the discussions, this concerned teaching the children to read at home. On this point, therefore, the women were just as qualified as their husbands. The Household Code was never mentioned explicitly during the legal proceedings, but the world of its ideas was a living reality for the seventeen farmers who brought the case.

Time was running out for The Household Code's hefty rules about obedience and for the Lutheran Church's traditional religious instruction by means of learning by heart and rules about obedience. In Brahetrolleborg, the children were faced with new demands that they understand the concepts they encountered in their instruction, so that they could develop a rational thinking that would make them active citizens.

In 1814, Denmark was given a new school law, but this did not apply to Norway, since it was separated from Denmark that year as a result of the peace negotiations in Vienna after the Napoleonic wars.[34] Many of Reventlow's ideas about schooling were incorporated into the law, which applied to the entire kingdom of Denmark, both town and country. Nevertheless, the Church succeeded in retaining its power over the school through inspection by the clergy. This meant that the Lutheran education, with the Catechism and an explanation as the basic textbooks, remained in place throughout the nineteenth century. At the same time, the teaching of the Danish language was given a higher priority as the second subject in the schools—and here, as in Brahetrolleborg, a secular reading book was now to be used as the basis for understanding concepts and for rational thinking.

After 1814, confirmation was always linked to the conclusion of schooling as a kind of ecclesiastical examination of the religious instruction that had been received in the school. This was very significant far into the nineteenth century for the young person's chances of finding an apprenticeship and getting married. One who was not confirmed was always regarded as not fully a member of society. This meant that confirmation was the goal for teaching even in institutions for disabled children in the second half of the nineteenth century.[35] After 1814, the goal of the school was widened to include the young person's development into an active citizen in the state. The Household Code's rules were replaced in the 1814 law by socio-ethical teaching about obligations to God, to oneself, and to others. This natural law shift of focus from the estate and the family to the individual points ahead to the individualization in later periods, where it was no longer possible to justify the child's obedience on the basis of a collective religious thinking in terms of estates.[36]

Notes

1 Johansson 1981: 193–224; Guttormsen 1981: 123–65; Markussen 1995; Appel 2001.
2 Troels-Lund, *Dagligt Liv i Norden*, vol. 4, Book 12. *Dagligt Liv i Norden i det 17. og 18. århundrede* is the major Scandinavian work on cultural and religious praxis before and after the Reformation.

3 Johansson 1981: 200; Stenbæk 1990: 72.
4 Troels Lund, vol. 4, Book 12: 82. See also the chapters by Aavitsland, Jacobsen, and Rørvik in this volume.
5 Troels Lund, vol. 2, Book 8: 83–95; vol. 4, Book 12: 82.
6 Maurer 1970: 18.
7 See Markussen 1995, and Bregnsbo 1997. For an orientation on Scandinavian research, see Markussen 2013. See also German literature on the Haustafel and the three estates in Schorn-Schütte 1998; Behrendt 2009.
8 Appel 2001: 177–8.
9 Petter Dass is one of the best known Scandinavian clergymen. His many poems and hymns that are still read and sung today include "Nordlands Trompet," which was first published at the beginning of the eighteenth century. Its title has often been used to characterize Dass himself.
10 Haarberg 2013: 517–43; Markussen 2013: 37–51.
11 Haarberg 2013: 515–20.
12 Haarberg 2013: 528–32.
13 In the Old Testament/Hebrew Bible, the commandments are found in Ex 20:1–17 (and Deut 5:6–21). In the Catechism, Luther omitted the second commandment (the prohibition of images), and divided the tenth commandment into two. This meant that the number of commandments remained the same, while the enumeration is partly divergent.
14 In the Old Testament/Hebrew Bible, the commandment applied to the Sabbath (Saturday), not to Sunday.
15 Pontoppidan, *Oppvækkelige Hydre-Breve*; Pontoppidan, *Kort og eenfoldig Underviisning for Skoleholderne*. See also Johnsen 1998.
16 Johnsen 1998: 55–62.
17 Pontoppidan, *Collegium Pastorale Practicum*, 1757: 416.
18 *Ibid.*, 416.
19 Markussen 1988, ch. 2; Appel and Fink-Jensen 2013, chs. 13 and 20.
20 The reading primer was a page with the alphabet and monosyllabic words pasted onto a wooden board with a handle.
21 See also the chapters by Lahtinen and Rørvik in this volume.
22 Rochow, *Der Kinderfreund*, 1777 (Danish trans. by Weiss 1785).
23 Cramer, *Kort Underviisning i Christendommen*, 1785. The Danish Chancellery was the supreme central authority for the educational system and for the Church in Denmark. This book was an explanation of the Catechism. Cramer received royal authorization in his time as superintendent to introduce it in the schools in the duchies of Schleswig and Holstein.
24 After his appointment in 1754, Cramer was a popular pastor at the court in Copenhagen and the author of many hymns, but he was removed from office by J. F. Struensee (1737–1772) and his government in 1771. He then became superintendent in Lübeck. He was appointed to a professorship at the University of Kiel in 1774, where he later became pro-chancellor. He founded the Seminary in Kiel in 1781 and became its rector. He was a close friend of J. L. Reventlow.
25 Birch, *Forskrifter med Anviisning*, 1784. These regulations were not printed; they are in the archive of the Brahetrolleborg estate.
26 Birch, *ibid.*: LXXIV.
27 Birch, *ibid.*: 144.
28 At the census in 1787, Birch had eight children. *Folketæling 1787*. Rigsarkivet. Daisy. Online. Birch had a total of eleven children, thus realizing in his own person the Lutheran understanding of the obligation of marriage.
29 Rasmussen, *De Reventlowske Skoler*, 1883.

30 Birch, *Tvende Taler holdne i Anledning af Skolevæsenets forbedrede Indretning i Brahetrolleborg Sogn*, Tale 2. Ved Indvidelsen af Haagerup og Gierup Skoler holden paa begge Steder den 18.de December 1783, online: 73.
31 Markussen, forthcoming.
32 Johannes Hansen Pade's recollections, which are found in the Landsarkivet in Åbenrå, have been used in several historical investigations; see Henningsen 2000: 77–148; Appel and Fink-Jensen 2013.
33 Retssagen mod Skoleholder Pade ("The court case against schoolmaster Pade"). Rigsarkivet. Odense. Brahetrolleborg godsarkiv. Pades forsvarsskrift.
34 Norway entered a union with Sweden in 1814 but was given its own constitution.
35 Wingender 1992: 325–30.
36 The chapter is translated from Danish by Brian McNeil.

4 "Let the Little Children Come to Me"

Representations of Children in the Confessional Culture of Lutheran Scandinavia

Kristin B. Aavitsland

The Protestant Reformation was introduced into the Nordic kingdoms in the middle of the sixteenth century. Lutheranism became the state-bearing religion in these countries, and has remained so, although the tight connections between church and state have been loosened in Sweden and Norway now, at the turn of the third millennium.[1] The Lutheran faith brought about, *inter alia,* a significant break in the attitudes toward childbearing and family life. The new ideals, communicated in legislation, education, and preaching, came to have a massive normative impact on the Nordic societies for at least three centuries. During this long period, the Lutheran family ethos was embodied in the figure of the royally appointed parish clergyman and his family, whose task it was to be an authoritative role model for the laity.

An important means of promulgating the exemplary status of the clergyman and his family was pictorial representation. This is an underdeveloped issue in the study of early modern culture in the Nordic countries, although the source material is overwhelmingly rich. In numerous parochial churches, painted memorial tablets depict parsons, curates, and other civil servants in the midst of their families, clearly promoting the family unit of father, mother, and children as an ideal state of social life. A prominent feature of eighteenth- and early nineteenth-century church interiors, this genre had its roots in the sixteenth century and its heyday in the seventeenth. These commemorative family portraits should therefore be studied throughout the whole period in which they were in use as a means of visual propaganda in the public sphere. To grasp the nature of their religious context as well as their visual rhetoric, it is crucial to look beyond the eighteenth century.

Although the commemorative portraits from the seventeenth and eighteenth centuries form a rich quarry for the understanding of Early Modern attitudes toward children and family life in the Nordic countries, they have barely been studied in this perspective.[2] This chapter offers close readings of selected examples from the joint kingdom of Denmark–Norway and the kingdom of Sweden during the seventeenth and eighteenth centuries. The readings aim to shed light on the normative patterns in which children's lives were understood in this period.

The objective of my chapter is twofold. First, I want to introduce the commemorative family portraits as a valuable source material for the field of historical childhood studies. Second, I want to emphasize the pre-Pietism and pre-Enlightenment Lutheran ethos as one of the sustaining foundation stones of what we think of, even today, as Nordic childhood. As an introduction to these issues, I will present Lucas Cranach's emblematic painting of Jesus and the children in Larvik Church in south-eastern Norway. Furthermore, I will briefly comment on orthodox Lutheran views on children and their role in the family. In addition to the group of selected seventeenth- and eighteenth-century commemorative portraits, I shall examine instructional texts from the same period, intended for didactic and pastoral use. Most of my sources are from Denmark–Norway, while a few are from Sweden. However, the ethos expressed in these normative sources was propagated by political and religious authorities in all the Nordic countries during the Reformation and in the ensuing centuries.

The Early Modern commemorative family portraits bear witness to the new interest in childhood which emerged in early modern Protestantism.[3] By tracking this new interest, the chapter highlights a validation of children and parents that lay at the core of a Lutheran understanding of society. These values came to shape thinking about family and childhood, and prevailed in the nineteenth century and through much of the twentieth, long after Lutheran orthodoxy had ceased to dominate the Nordic societies.

Jesus and the Children: A Lutheran View of Children and Family

To illustrate the changes in the conception of childhood, which the Protestant Reformation brought about, one could conveniently start in Larvik, a small merchant town on the Norwegian south-eastern coast, situated in the core area of the Danish–Norwegian aristocracy, where the citizens had a new church erected in 1677. The Danish governor in Norway, Ulrik Frederik Gyldenløwe (1638–1704), instituted a fund for the maintenance of the building, and donated a painting to embellish the new place of worship (Figure 4.1).[4]

This painting was probably purchased in Germany, but it is uncertain how long it had been in Gyldenløwe's ownership. When donated to the new church, the painting was about 140 years old, and was probably regarded as a very precious piece, as it still is. It was painted in the 1540s by the prominent German artist, Lucas Cranach the Elder (1472–1553), a close friend of Martin Luther and the most recognized visual interpreter of Protestant faith.[5] The painting represents a scene from the life of Jesus, mentioned in three of the four Gospels: Jesus welcomes the mothers who have brought their infants to him for blessing, and, to the surprise of the disciples who had wanted to expel them, Jesus proclaims: "Let the little children come to me and do not try to stop them, for the kingdom of heaven belongs to such as these" (Mark 10:14; Luke 18:16; Matthew 19:14).

Figure 4.1 Lucas Cranach the elder: *Let the Little Children Come to Me*, ca. 1550. Larvik Church, southern Norway.

Photo: NIKU (Norwegian Institute for Cultural Heritage Research), Oslo.

This biblical scene is virtually absent from art history before Lucas Cranach, whereas he and his workshop treated it at least twenty-three times.[6] This sudden "outburst" of paintings of Christ and the children in Saxony in the 1530s and 1540s doubtlessly had theological motivations. Martin Luther included the Gospel passage about Christ and the children in the baptismal liturgy, interpreting it as a divine authorization of infant baptism. He ardently favored the practice of baptizing children, unlike other Protestant persuasions such as the Anabaptists, the radical Reformation movement that practiced baptism of adults.[7] The issue of baptism was one of the big controversies among sixteenth-century Protestants, and Cranach's paintings of Christ and the children could well be understood in light of these theological debates.[8] Luther's views about infant baptism inevitably had a bearing on the status of children in Lutheran Protestantism, together with a changed valuation of family life. In my opinion, Cranach's painting in Larvik Church bears witness to both these aspects of childhood in early modern Lutheran culture.

Against the medieval ideals, which regarded a life in chastity and contemplation as the most secure way to sanctity, Luther propagated family life and procreation as the ideal Christian life path. He interpreted God's command to the first human couple, "Be fruitful, and multiply" (Gen 1:28), as *more* than a command; this was a description of the divine order of human life, impossible to ignore. To procreate was, in Luther's view, as necessary and inevitable as sleeping, eating, drinking, and emptying the bladder. In short, the breeding of children was simply a matter of nature, not of choice.[9] Family life was the God-willed vocation for man and woman alike, authorized by the model of the first human family. In a frequently quoted passage from a text on married life, Luther takes a surprisingly modern stance on the role of the father: "When a father goes ahead and washes diapers or performs some other menial task for his child, and someone ridicules him as an effeminate fool ... God with all his angels and creatures is smiling."[10] To breed and raise children and toil for their well-being was the primary Christian vocation: children were "fruits of life", *Lebens-Früchte*, they were tender plants in "the vineyard of the Lord," for the parents to look after and cultivate. Parents were like gardeners with the holy task of growing plants for God's paradise. A biblical legitimation of the idea was found in Psalm 128:

> Blessed is everyone who fears the LORD; who walks in his ways. You shall eat the fruit of the labour of your hands: you shall be happy, and it shall be well with you. Your wife shall be like a fruitful vine within your house: your children like olive shoots around your table.[11]

The high regard for marriage and family life was one of the main components of the positive view of children in Lutheran Protestantism.

Another element was inspired by Jesus' recognition of children as prominent citizens in the kingdom of God, which gave childhood a privileged status in Lutheran anthropology. Although small children also had their share of original sin, they had not yet grown aware of it, and were thus in a state of innocence that was pleasing to God. In accordance with medieval sacramental theology, Luther also declared every human child and infant capable of faith, because faith was a gift, received in the sacrament of baptism—rather than a rational and moral consent.[12]

Cranach's painting of Jesus blessing the children may thus be seen as an expression of Lutheran anthropology. In the seventeenth century, a period of consolidation of Lutheran faith in the Nordic countries that is often called "the age of Lutheran orthodoxy," the painting's message was undoubtedly understood by those who saw it in Larvik Church. One and a half centuries after its introduction, the Lutheran Reformation in Denmark–Norway seemed to be a success. This was due to the tight bonds between the Wittenberg Reformers and the theologians of Copenhagen University in the sixteenth century, the subsequent maintenance of a strict uniformity in religious discipline and observance, the suppression of heterodoxy, and the efficiency of a growing, centralized bureaucracy. These factors made the kingdom of Denmark–Norway look like an ideal Lutheran state.[13] Its homogenous confessional culture proved to be fertile ground for the cultivation of the Lutheran family ideals.

According to Luther (as we see in his widely distributed *Small Catechism*), society is composed of three divinely sanctioned estates, understood as orders of authority and obedience, of dominance and subordination. Among these, the household (*ordo oeconomicus*) is primary in relation to the two others, the government (*ordo politicus*) and the church (*ordo ecclesiasticus*).[14] As in medieval times, the household was conceived of as the extended family, including relatives, servants, and dependents, sharing a common dwelling. For the implementation of Lutheranism in Denmark–Norway, this unit became a privileged locus for the cultivation of the new Evangelical spirit. The head of the household, the *pater familias*, was legally obliged to ensure the piety of his house.

This duty was clearly communicated in Luther's *Haustafel* from 1529, a compilation of norms and obligations for the three estates in society, based on verses from the New Testament epistles. The role of the *pater familias* as the household's religious authority was reflected in the many literary and pedagogic adaptions of the *Haustafel* to the Danish language, as well as in the royally sanctioned legislation during the seventeenth century, the period of Lutheran orthodoxy.[15] Simultaneously, however, the privileged position of the household as the primary locus of religious education seems to be challenged, or at least supplemented, in this period by the concept of the biological family. As the nucleus of any household, the nexus of love between parents and children of course reflected the divine love between God the Father and his only begotten Son. But in the Lutheran confessional culture of the seventeenth century, the nexus between parents and children was also, and perhaps even more strongly, regarded as proof of the parents' realization of their sacred vocation to procreate. Luther's re-evaluation of human sexuality and the role he assigns to human reproduction in the scheme of salvation seemed to pave the way for a new idealization of childhood and parenthood in the Nordic countries in the seventeenth century. The relation of parents and children goes right to the core of the Protestant ethos, according to which they are mutually dependent on each other to fulfil their obligations as Christians.

This message is clearly communicated in the seventeenth- and eighteenth-century memorial family portraits. Such panels, often still *in situ*, flourished in the public space of Nordic parish churches from the seventeenth to the early nineteenth centuries. It is striking to see that they represent nuclear families of mothers, fathers, and children rather than the *pater familias* and his household. In what follows, I shall offer a close reading of a few of them.

"Some Children are Like Apes" Learning by Imitation

My first case is a commemorative portrait in the church of Søndeled, a small village on the south-eastern coast of Norway. It was commissioned in 1664 and is the work of an unknown painter (Figure 4.2). The commissioner, Christen Svenningsen (?–1684), was Danish-born, educated in Copenhagen and serving as a curate in Søndeled church. He had himself, his wife Johanne Nielsdatter Lem, and their four children portrayed in this ambitiously large commemorative portrait, which abounds with pictorial symbols and written messages.

Figure 4.2 Unknown artist: Christen Svenningsen and his family. Commemorative portrait, 1664, Søndeled Church, southern Norway.

Photo: NIKU (Norwegian Institute for Cultural Heritage Research), Oslo.

The family portrait follows well-established conventions for the representation of a devout, Lutheran family: sincere and serious, the curate and his stately wife present their *Lebens-Früchte* to the beholder. The children are testimonies to the fulfilment of the parents' duties as spouses, and are records of their God-fearing and productive lives. The sons are arranged by height and age in front of the father, and the one daughter in front of the mother. All the family members were still alive when the commemorative portrait was painted, their ages given in golden letters by their individual portraits: The curate himself was fifty years old, Johanne was forty-six, their daughter Marie Magdalene Christensdatter seventeen (the inscription has faded), and the oldest son fourteen. For the two younger sons, the numbers that indicate their age are so worn that they cannot be deciphered. By indicating the age, this painting follows a convention that was established in the sixteenth century. The group portrait thus captures the moment—or at least the year—in which the panel was painted. It arrests time in the life of this particular family, and thereby gives it a history.[16] As the portrait shows, the family is conceived of as a unit of adults and children, in which both categories are equally necessary and mutually dependent on each other in order to perform their God-given tasks—for the parents, to cultivate Christian virtues in their offspring, and for the children, to obey and honor their mother and father according to God's commandment.

The painter who portrayed Svenningsen and his family certainly reveals a quite provincial style. He was nevertheless skilled enough to catch the childishness of the three young sons and render them true to nature *as children*, with round cheeks, soft red mouths, and innocent expressions on their faces. But at the same time, the four children are clearly represented as mirror images of their parents—in clothing and posture, they take the parents as their gender-specific role models, carrying, as they do, flowers symbolizing Christian virtues.[17]

The family is depicted in an undetermined space between two tables, each with an open New Testament on top. An array of other books is set up at the far end of the table to the left, close to Svenningsen himself, indicating that he is a man of letters. He is represented as letting his children grow up between books, and as a curate, he probably taught them to read himself. The instruction of children is a crucial aspect of parents' care as Protestant Christians and gardeners "in the vineyard of the Lord."[18] The advocates of the Evangelical faith in the sixteenth century had heavily emphasized the tutoring of children.[19] Judging by their portrait, the Svenningsen family seemed to have followed what the Reformers of the previous century had eagerly espoused. The Reformers' pedagogy was based on a balance between the firm execution of discipline and the acceptance of children's nature as distinct from that of adults. This view is reflected in the Svenningsen portrait: the children are copies of their parents in dress and posture, but at the same time, they are rendered with childish features, clearly distinct from the parents. This represents a conception of childhood that laid the groundwork for educational ideals and pedagogic practice in the Nordic countries for several generations.[20] Thus, it may be worthwhile to take a closer look at the Reformers' stance on the instruction of children.

The major Protestant Reformer in the kingdoms, Superintendent Peder Palladius (1503–1560), addresses the issue in his influential *Visitasbog*, a handbook for the instruction in the new faith (1543). To his great satisfaction, Palladius has observed that in some Danish towns, the young pastors educated in Wittenberg gather boys and girls from four to six years old in the church two times a week. As they sit on the stairs leading up to the chancel, the curate would go to and fro with a little rod in his hand, teaching them prayers and commandments by heart.[21] Palladius is clearly aware that children learn not only by means of the curate's rod, but also, and perhaps even more so, because, as children, they love to play and make-believe. They should certainly be allowed to do so, Palladius claims, in accordance with Martin Luther himself, who in his 1524 essay on schools and pedagogy had noticed children's natural inclination to play.[22] Luther and Palladius agree that the suppression of children's nature is futile, and that the desire to play should be utilized prudently for didactic ends. If they are exposed to sound ideals, the children will learn through their play how to behave as good Christians. Palladius reports:

> Some children are like apes. This is clearly seen during summer, when the weather is nice, and they gather in the streets outside their parents' homes, sit down below the windows, and a little boy may act as a curate. He holds a rod and reads aloud for the others, and they say after him, then he distributes small pieces of bread of stones between them, calling them gingerbread, just as they have seen the curate act in church ... instead of running about, breaking windows and doing other

damage, they play what they have learned, absorbing it with delight, playfully and cheerfully.[23]

Palladius' description of children imitating adults has a certain idyllic air. His text should not, however, be interpreted anachronistically as an Early Modern instance of child-centered pedagogy, as this was developed in the following centuries, for example, by Jean-Jacques Rousseau (1712–1778), who emphasized the pedagogical outcome of play during a child's early years (*Émile*, 1762), and Friedrich Froebel (1782–1852), who, inspired by Rousseau, developed a theory of play-based childhood education and coined the concept of *Kindergarten* in the 1830s.[24] It is worth noting that the little boy acting as curate in Palladius' description carries the teacher's one distinct attribute—the rod. Punishment was regarded as an indispensable pedagogic means, necessitated by the stains which original sin had imprinted on human nature. The relation of a punishing, yet loving God to his fallen, sinful creature became a model for the relation between parents and children, teachers, and pupils.[25] A strict discipline was simply required to reach the indisputable ends of education: piety, obedience, and fear of God.

The Svenningsen children in Søndeled Church are clearly portrayed as living up to these ideals. Whether they had learned to copy their parents by way of play or by way of strict discipline, we will never know; but what is certain is that the parents, who had paid for the family portrait to be hung in Søndeled Church as an example of virtue for the congregation, wanted to represent them as mirrors of the virtuous adults their children were intended to become.

In accordance with these ideals, all four children carry small prayer books in their hands. The fact that both sexes hold books may be worthy of note. The presence of books for boys and girls alike may be explained in light of the literacy campaigns for all children, regardless of class and gender, which were carried out by the church authorities in Denmark–Norway during the seventeenth century.[26] These campaigns were naturally motivated to ensure upbringing in the Evangelical faith through compulsory reading of Luther's *Small Catechism*. The path of learning on which the children were destined to walk, led by their virtuous parents and assisted by education and literacy, is allegorically visualized in the family portrait: between the spouses, heaven stands open, depicted by a border of white clouds surrounding an area of shining golden light. From the ground, a ladder leads up to a wide-open door in the middle of the chain of clouds. Inside the door, the name "Jesus Christ" is written in red letters. This is the ladder of faith, leading to God.

The steps of the ladder depict the course of life as a gradual educative and spiritual development. The first step is the sacrament of baptism (*Daaben*), followed by hearing the word of God (*Guds ord*), leading to knowledge (*Guds Kundskab*), which prompts prayer (*Boenen*). This enables the growth of faith (*Troen*) and subsequently the other Christian virtues—patience (*Tolmodighed*), hope (*Haabet*), and constancy (*Bestandighed*). At the top of the ladder, a door stands open, inscribed with the name of Jesus Christ, who is "the door of the sheep" (John 10:7). To enter successfully through this door to eternal life was the ultimate goal for the Svenningsen family, as it was for all good and law-abiding subjects in the kingdom of Denmark–Norway. The portrait in Søndeled Church displays both the attitude required and the means available for the children, who are tender plants in God's vineyard.

Dead Children and the Hope of Resurrection

Chaplain Svenningen at Søndeled had the grace to see all his four children grow up. This was rather an exception to the rule, and most commemorative family portraits reflect—in one way or the other—the high level of infant mortality.[27] The monumental portrait of Curate Peder Gabelsen Krag (1590–1646) and his family, originally hung in Innvik Church in western Norway, is one of many examples (Figure 4.3).

This panel was painted by the Bergen-based artist, Elias Fiigenschoug (ca. 1600–1661), in the 1640s, and is one of the great pieces in the otherwise rather meagre Norwegian Baroque. The large panel represents Gabelsen Krag and his wife, together with their grown daughter Agnete between her two husbands, Bendix Friis and Absalon Jørgensen Beyer. The portrait of the latter was cleverly added to the painting after the death of the first, obviously by a painter other than Fiigenschoug. In front of the five adults are Agnete's four children. All of them came from her first marriage, but only two daughters, represented in front of their mother as miniatures of her, lived to grow up. One infant, probably a stillborn baby, is depicted beside the two girls, dead in its coffin with a white little face, closed eyes, and a wreath on its head. Their little brother, however, who likewise died as a child, is not depicted as dead. He seems to be three or four years old, which must have been his age when he passed away. Standing to the right of his sisters, he has turned his back to them. He has a skull in his hand, to which he significantly points. The pictorial language thus clearly signals that he was not among the living when the panel was painted. Similar pictorial strategies are found in numerous other commemorative portraits, like that of the nobleman and lieutenant Enevold Skaktavl (1627–1702) and his family, painted for Stange Church in eastern Norway in 1700 (Figure 4.4). Here, three babies with floral wreaths on their heads lie dead in a shared cradle. Their older sister stands beside them, catching the spectator's eye with her insistent gaze and serious little face, but the skull in her hands signals that she too was dead when the portrait was made.

These pictorial strategies are among a range of rhetorical means that were employed in seventeenth- and eighteenth-century Nordic commemorative portraits to include dead children in the family portrait. The visual language communicates the fact that they have passed away but are still regarded as an integral part of the family. One particularly striking example is a Swedish eighteenth-century panel from Släps Church near Gothenburg, commissioned to memorialize the curate and scholar, Gustaf Fredrik Hjortberg (1724–1776), and his large family (Figure 4.5).

Figure 4.3 Elias Fiigenschoug: Peder Gabelsen Krag and his family. Commemorative portrait, Innvik Church, western Norway.

Photo: Bergen University Museum.

In this panel, painted in the 1760s, the family is lined up, conventionally divided by gender: Hjortberg himself sits to the left, surrounded by seven sons and a rich display of items related to his intellectual, musical, and scientific interests.[28] His wife Anna Helena Löfman, portrayed at a distance from her husband's intellectual milieu, sits to the right together with the seven daughters and one stillborn son, lying in his white coffin at her feet. Another infant with closed eyes lies in a cradle.[29] The older girls surround their mother, wearing elaborate necklaces and richly decorated dresses,

Figure 4.4 Unknown artist: The deceased children of Enevold Skaktavl. Detail of commemorative portrait, 1700, from Stange Church, eastern Norway, now at Norsk Folkemuseum, Oslo.

Photo: Norsk Folkemuseum.

Figure 4.5 Jonas Dürch: Commemorative portrait of the Hjortberg family. Släps Church, southwestern Sweden.

Photo and copyright Vallda och Släps kyrkliga samfällighet.

similar to hers. Only half of this large crowd of children—eight sons and seven daughters—had the luck to grow up. Three sons and four daughters were alive when the painter Jonas Dürchs completed the family portrait. He differentiated the painted presence of the dead siblings: the stillborn brother is clearly dead in his coffin, and the baby sister in the cradle looks as if she is sleeping, whereas the other dead children are represented behind their living siblings, exposing only the forehead and one or both the eyes. The oldest brother turns insistently away from his father, showing only the back of his head. The pictorial language thus makes the dead children present and absent at the same time. Both parents display a list of the children's names and dates of birth—and for eight of them, their dates of death.[30]

What were the motivations for including dead infants and children in family portraits? Why are some of them represented as living, whereas others are depicted as dead? I have not seen these questions studied in depth, and would like to suggest two answers, which could indicate possible directions for further research.

First, the inclusion of dead family members probably mirrors the conviction that the family would be united again in Paradise. Thus, the commemorative family portraits anticipate this heavenly reunion—a theme most fitting for this genre, whose most important rhetorical function was to convince the one who saw the painting of the pious disposition of the portrayed—and thereby justify their confidence in salvation after death. This does not, however, explain the differentiation between the dead infants lying in their cradles or coffins and the toddlers and older siblings who are portrayed as living, yet are clearly represented as dead through gestures and symbols. Could it be that this differentiation addresses the highly problematic issue of the salvation of unbaptized children? Should the dead infants be understood as stillborn babies who never were included in Christianity, whereas their older deceased siblings lived long enough to receive baptism and some instruction in the Christian faith?

Another of Elias Fiigenschoug's commemorative portraits may elucidate, or perhaps rather complicate, this discussion. In the portrait of Pastor Thomas Uro (1606–1687) and his family in Ulvik Church in Hardanger on the western coast of Norway, the dead infant is given special attention, brightly lit and placed in the middle of the composition (Figure 4.6). Two

Figure 4.6 Elias Fiigenschoug: Commemorative Portrait of Thomas Uro and his Family. Ulvik Church, western Norway.

Photo: NIKU (Norwegian Institute for Cultural Heritage Research), Oslo.

siblings are depicted even more ambiguously—they stand in the same bright light, playing with a skull. Are they dead or alive? The visual language and the use of light suggest their salvation. If this was meant to be the message, it is in accord with several theological treatises from the Reformation period in Denmark–Norway.

The fate of children who died before baptism was an issue that engaged theologians and created anxiety for parents. The medieval, Catholic doctrine on this subject was that the unbaptized infants were destined for *Limbus infantium*, a place without pain, but also without the presence of God. They were clearly not damned, but they could never rejoice in the countenance of the Lord.[31] Protestant theologians addressed this issue, and some came, at least partly, to reject it. In accordance with the Protestant emphasis on family life and parenthood, the Reformers developed a special pastoral care for parents who expected children or who had lost them. In Denmark–Norway, a key figure in this development was the German theologian, Johann Bugenhagen (1485–1558), one of the central Reformers in the circle around Martin Luther. Bugenhagen lived in Copenhagen for a period and had a decisive influence on the introduction of the Reformation in the 1530s. In a consolatory treatise to parents of unbaptized infants, he argues that the stillborn receive the grace of God thanks to the faith and prayers of their still living family members.[32] He was instrumental in the shaping of the "Church Order" for Denmark–Norway (1537), a legal document that regulated the organization of the new Lutheran church. Here, the same position with regard to unbaptized children is expressed. In the paragraph on instruction to midwives and their handling of stillborn babies, Jesus' blessing of the children is explicitly referred to:

> Furthermore, the midwives shall entrust the fetus that is dead in the womb to the care of God … with the following words or their like: O Lord Jesus Christ, you have a special delight in the children who are brought to you, and you willingly receive them to eternal life, you who said "let the Children come to me etc". According to this word we bring this child before you, not on our arms but in our prayers: O Jesus, our dear Lord and Savior, receive it and let it enjoy your eternal deliverance, which you earned us on the cross. Amen.[33]

The Church Order emphasizes that the same prayer is valid for infants who die unbaptized shortly after birth. Grieving parents should thus trust God and pray that he will receive their dead child, taking as their role models the confident mothers who brought their children to Jesus for blessing (Figure 4.1). They should carry their dead babies to Jesus, not on their arms, but in their prayers. Salvation by faith was accessible to the unbaptized children too, because they would be saved through their parents' faith. I believe that these instructions for pastoral care form a relevant backdrop to the interpretation of the commemorative portraits and their careful rendering of deceased infants.

Out of the Church: The Absence of Parents

In the Nordic countries, commemorative family portraits on display in the parochial churches such as those discussed seem to belong chiefly to the confessional culture of Lutheran orthodoxy. This genre's popularity reached its peak in the second half of the seventeenth century. Although it lived on in the eighteenth, its popularity declined, before it faded away at the beginning of the nineteenth century. By the mid-1800s, commemorative family portraits had disappeared completely from the parish churches. By then, the ecclesiastical domain was obviously regarded as less relevant for the display of families and children, and portrait painting had developed as a genre primarily reserved for the salons and entertainment rooms of the bourgeoisie. In this setting, the transcendental dimension implicit in the space of the church was wanting. The allusions to piety, proper religious conduct, and hope for salvation beyond the threshold of death largely disappeared from the paintings.

An interesting shift in the representation of children from the public sphere of the church to the semi-private sphere of the bourgeois salon and cabinet is the absence of parents. Outside the public space of the state-controlled church, children are more often portrayed in art as figures in their own right rather than as members of the social unit of the family (Figure 4.7). In

Figure 4.7 C. W. Eckersberg: Portrait of C. F. Holm's children, 1832. The Hirschsprung Collection, Copenhagen.

Photo: Wikimedia Commons.

bourgeois portraiture, children are isolated in the realm of childhood.[34] They are represented as agents of their own, although they are becomingly shaped in the image of their parents. This tendency is exemplified by the 1832 portrait of the children of Minister C. F. Holm, painted by the Danish artist and professor at the Royal Academy of Art in Copenhagen, Christoffer Wilhelm Eckersberg (1783–1853).

Three siblings, two girls and a boy, gather around an illustrated book on a wooden table. Their pose is informal. The boy and one sister concentrate on the open book, whereas the second sister has raised her head and looks confidently out of the image. Their childish air and chubby faces are adorable. Eckersberg may have rendered them in this way to appeal to his commissioners' fancy for the charms of childhood. Probably, both painter and commissioner were guided not so much by the old Lutheran family ethos as by a modern concept of childhood as something distinct from adulthood, as the age of innocence. Developing in the wake of the Enlightenment in the eighteenth century, this "adultist" concept of childhood found visual expression not only in portraits, but also in genre painting, especially in French and British art.[35] In addition, the Eckersberg panel communicates a bourgeois appreciation of education and good manners.

Notwithstanding the great influence the Enlightenment thinkers had on the modern conception of childhood, this type of children portraiture originated in the seventeenth century. In parallel with the commemorative family portraits hung on church walls in the Nordic countries, a secular genre of children portraiture emerged.[36] An early instance, at least in a Nordic context, is a large panel from 1690, probably commissioned by some magnate in the Trondheim region in the middle of Norway (Figure 4.8).

Nine children, probably siblings, are lined up in a landscape, holding conventional symbolic attributes like fruits, flowers, flutes, and a little dog—in addition to the catechism or prayer book in the hands of the oldest boy. The rather crude provincial style of the painter has not quite managed to grasp the age of the individuals in this group of children, but inscriptions in gilt lettering above the heads of each of them helpfully give the figures. The oldest is seven years old, whereas the youngest is no more than six months. Further information about the identity of these children is lacking, as well as about the provenience of the painting. Hence, we will never know why they were portrayed and where the painting originally hung. It was probably not meant for a church. With the parents absent, the whole theological superstructure of Lutheran family ideals is gone, as is any reference to afterlife and salvation. The visual language of this panel testifies to a specific interest in the children as such—notwithstanding the "adult" style of children's dress at the end of the seventeenth century. The emphasis on the children's age is, as I have mentioned, a feature also found in the commemorative family portraits in the churches (Figure 4.2), and testifies to the wish of the commissioner to have these children portrayed while they were still children. Dressed up and neatly arranged in a row, the children are

Figure 4.8 Unknown artist: Children portrait of unknown provenience, 1690.

Photo: Nordenfjeldske kunstindustrimuseum (National Museum of Decorative Arts and Design), Trondheim, Norway.

clearly projections of the aspirations of the adults. They are bearers of their pride, objects of their investments, and carriers of their hopes. The portrait thus becomes a mirror reflecting the parents, despite their absence from the canvas. They are still there, thanks to the display of the children's discipline, grace, and good manners.

Conclusion

To sum up the argument of my chapter: the introduction of Lutheran Protestantism in the Nordic countries brought about a theologically moti-vated reevaluation of family life. The family was regarded as the primary social order, and child-bearing and child-rearing were considered a fulfill-ment of God's vocation for man and woman. The new ideals were effec-tively communicated in pictorial representation in the public sphere of the churches. During the seventeenth and eighteenth centuries, clergymen and other civil servants commissioned commemorative family portraits in which they, their wives and their children were represented as examples to be fol-lowed. In parallel, the semi-private, bourgeois genre of children's portraits developed from the late seventeenth century, depicting children alone, with-out their parents. This genre eventually replaced the commemorative por-traits in the sacred space of the church. The painted portraits of bourgeois children from the eighteenth and nineteenth centuries found a continuation in formal photographs of well-dressed and well-bred children from the nineteenth, twentieth, and even twenty-first centuries.

The children represented in the confessional Lutheran commemorative portraits were always included in the socially fundamental unit of the family and were put on display in churches. By contrast, the children in the bourgeois portraits outside the ecclesiastical space are left to themselves and the objectifying gaze of adults. The persuasive rhetoric about cultivation of plants for God's paradise gradually receded in the representation of children, to be replaced by projections of adults' mundane ambitions.

Notes

1 Sweden formally dissolved its state church in 2000 and Norway followed suit in 2012. In these countries, the former state churches are now autonomous juridical bodies, although they still enjoy special privileges. In Denmark, however, the monarch is still the supreme authority of the Evangelical Lutheran Church (Den danske folkekirke), and the Minister for Ecclesiastical Affairs is its highest administrative leader. In Finland, bishops of the Evangelical Lutheran Church are appointed by the President, and members of the Government and Supreme Court are represented on the Church's board.
2 Research into early modern Scandinavian commemorative painting is scarce. For sixteenth- and seventeenth-century commemorative portraits in Sweden, see Gilgren 1995. For the corresponding Danish material, see Honnens de Lichtenberg 1989 and Bøggild Johannsen and Johannsen 2011. For Finnish commemorative portraits, see Tuhkanen 2005. Apart from two Master theses from Bergen University by Eide 2006 and Holstad 2008, the body of Norwegian commemorative portraits has barely been studied as such. Selected samples are discussed in Aavitsland 2015.
3 Ariès 1973: 341.
4 Fonk 2011: 24.
5 Ozment 2011. For this topic, see also Chapter 3 by Markussen in this volume.
6 Andersson 1981: 53–5; Heal 2007: 301; Kibish 1955: 196–203.
7 Luther, *Das Taufbüchlein* (Wittenberg, 1523); Lohse 1995: 317–23.
8 Kibish 1955: 199–200.
9 Luther, "Vom ehelichen Leben, 1522", 275–6.
10 Luther, "Vom ehelichen Leben", 296.
11 This and subsequent biblical quotations are taken from the *New Revised Standard Version*.
12 See, for instance, passages in the chapter on baptism in Luther's *Large Catechism* in Martin Luther, "Der Grosse Katechismus, 1529", 218. See also Martikainen 2010: 100–2.
13 Grell, Lyby and Schwarz Lausten 1995: 135.
14 Bayer 1998: 127. See also Chapter 3 by Markussen in this volume.
15 A famous adaptation of Luther's *Haustafel* is the cycle of canticles by the Norwegian poet and clergyman, Petter Dass, published in 1715, *Hustavlesange*. For a discussion of Luther's *Small Catechism* and Danish–Norwegian commentaries, see Markussen, Chapter 3, in this volume, and Appel 2001. For legislation on household piety, see Aavitsland 2015.
16 Ariès 1973: 40.
17 Aavitsland 2015: 258.
18 The metaphor of the Lord's vineyard, repeatedly applied in the Bible as an image of the house of Israel, the chosen people, was reinterpreted by medieval exegetes

as the community of the Church, on earth as well as in heaven. For the Protestant Reformers, the vineyard of the Lord represented the new chosen people, justified by their Evangelical faith.

19 Appel and Fink-Jensen 2013: 37–51.
20 Appel and Fink-Jensen 2000: 25–30.
21 Palladius "Visitasbog", 94.
22 Martin Luther, "An die Ratsherren aller Städte deutschen Landes, daß sie christliche Schulen aufrichten und halten sollen (1524), 45–8.
23 Palladius, "Visitasbog", 95. Author's translation of the Danish original.
24 On Rousseau and Fröbel on play-based childhood education, see James, Jenks, and Prout 1998: 13–17.
25 Appel and Fink-Jensen 2013: 61.
26 Appel and Fink-Jensen 2013: 20.
27 The rates of infant mortality for Denmark–Norway in the seventeenth century were between 15 and 30%. See also Chapter 15 by Roos in this volume.
28 Hyltze 1995.
29 For the child in a cradle as a conventional iconographic sign of death in infancy, see Wilson 1990: 57.
30 For discrepancies between the dates in the lists and dates in the registers of the local church, see Hyltze 1995: 19–20.
31 Marshall 2002: 203–4.
32 Johannes Bugenhagen, *Der XXIX. Psalm ausgelegt*, 1542.
33 "Enn videre skal jordmødrene forholde seg slik med frukten og fosteret som finnes dødt i mors liv, at de overgir det til Guds varetekt [...] med diese eller sådanne ord: O, Herre Jesus Kristus, du som har et særlig behag i de barn som bæres til deg, og gjerne mottar dem til det evige liv; du som sa: La barna komme til meg etc. Etter dette ord bærer vi dette barn frem for deg, ikke i favn, men med våre bønner: O Jesus, vår kjære Herre og Frelser, ta imot det og la det til evig tid nyte din forløsning, som du har forvervet oss på korset. Amen. *Kirkeordinansen av 1537* (ed. Ellingsen: 73–4).
34 Higonnet 1993.
35 Higonnet 1993; Barker 2009. The concept of "adultism," analogous to sexism and racism, is coined by Kennedy 2006: 63.
36 Ariès 1973: 41.

5 Education of Children in Rural Finland

The Roles of Homes, Churches, and Manor Houses

Anu Lahtinen

In view of the welfare systems in the Nordic countries today, it is easy to forget that for many centuries illiteracy, child labor, and high infant mortality were typical characteristics of childhood there, just as in most other countries. Life was haphazard and unpredictable in many preindustrial Finnish families.[1] Until the nineteenth century, child mortality remained high, and despite a relatively high birth rate, communities were at best barely able, over a long period, to sustain a modest rise in population growth.[2] Universal access to education was only in its beginnings: for centuries, Finland, the region that now excels in the Programme for International Student Assessment (PISA) reports, had only some poorly financed schools and harsh, unpolished tutors.

It is true that as early as the seventeenth century, in the aftermath of the Reformation period, teaching literacy had become important for religious reasons; but this was limited to the ecclesiastic sphere and the tenets of the Lutheran Church. Despite some attempts at reforms in the eighteenth and nineteenth centuries, it was only on the eve of modernization, in the latter part of the nineteenth century, that active action was taken in order to offer more comprehensive schooling even for ordinary rural children. The Elementary School Law of 1866 started a change that slowly led to the building of a school network and a comprehensive school system over 100 years later. A look at the ordinary lives of rural children in preindustrial Finland reminds us that the Finnish children's path to becoming top pupils of the world was unforeseen.

This chapter examines the role of literacy in children's upbringing in southern Finland from the premodern era to modern times. My aim is to shed light on a previously neglected region and a frequently ignored period of the history of childhood in rural Finland before the modernization. My focus is on how rural Finnish children were brought up and how the function of literacy in their curriculum changed over time. I will use a variety of sources to follow the subtle shift from practical training and alphabet teaching motivated by religious views to a more formal schooling until the time of the Elementary School Law.

My source material is collected from rural southern Finland, especially in the villages of Kytäjärvi and Erkylä (both dominated by a large manor in the nineteenth century) as well as Hyvinkäänkylä and Ridasjärvi (which were inhabited by freeholders). These villages were situated on the border of the provinces of Uusimaa (Sw. *Nyland*) and Häme (Sw. *Tavastland*). The nearest parish villages, Nurmijärvi, Loppi, and Hausjärvi, were located some 20 to 30 kilometers away, so the sound of church bells never reached the small fields and huts clustered near the lakes of Kytäjärvi, Hyvinkäänjärvi, and Ridasjärvi. These villages have been chosen to represent ordinary Finnish rural communities that were not situated close to preparatory schools or institutions of higher education. For my analysis, I use local parish records of the inhabitants and their literacy, court cases, records of school children, early newspapers, and family records of local mansions.[3] The material is scanty, but a close reading of the sources and the analysis of the available information can place the local events in a larger context.

Although the villages that I study are rather ordinary, small, rural communities, there are some features that make them interesting. First, the events of the first significant novel in Finnish, *Seven Brothers* (*Seitsemän veljestä*), written by Aleksis Kivi in 1870, took place in the same church parish (Nurmijärvi) as the Kytäjärvi and Hyvinkäänkylä villages. Moreover, as one of the main themes of the novel is the problem of illiteracy and learning in an outlying village, the story offers an interesting point of comparison between nineteenth-century fiction and historical sources.

In addition, some educational arrangements in this area were actually groundbreaking. Some of the villages were among the first to adopt ambulatory schools and Sunday schools.[4] The village of Erkylä became a forerunner in public education, since the owner of the Erkylä Manor invested his money and energy in the founding of the first elementary school (Esko School) in Finland in 1856. In the nineteenth century, there was an emerging interest and a new sense of responsibility among the local population with regard to organizing theoretical education for all children.

New in my approach is the long-term analysis of an area in which outlying villages continued with little schooling even until the nineteenth century when they came into contact with some of the most progressive minds of the time. People in Finland tend to think today that literacy and education are a self-evident task allotted to institutions. It is important to put the present situation into perspective by presenting the very different conditions of the past. Accordingly, I shall discuss the influence of the family, the owners of the manors and individual tutors, and the very haphazard courses that children's upbringing could take. I shall examine the extent to which the living conditions of children reflect the ideological changes that took place in these rural communities as well as in the Nordic societies.

First, I will present what is known about schooling and literacy as a part of bringing up children from the early modern period to the turn of the eighteenth century. Second, I discuss the measures taken by the Church from the late eighteenth century to educate young people. And third, I shall deal with the changes that occurred in the nineteenth century, especially with the role of local manor owners as early pioneers of elementary school education in this area of Finland.

My study will end at the time when the villages were establishing their first permanent parish schools outside the control of the manors (Hyvinkäänkylä 1875; Ridasjärvi 1883). Until then, the popular education had mostly followed the idea of disciplining the subjects of the Crown and members of the congregation. Now, in the later part of the nineteenth century, the focus was directed at educating well-informed citizens who needed new knowledge to help build the new modern society.[5] I shall also describe this process and conclude with a discussion of the changes and continuities over time.

Children's living conditions in these rural communities will be set in the context of the history of childhood and education in the Nordic countries. After all, Finland was part of the Swedish realm until 1808, and although it then became a Grand Duchy under the Russian Empire (1809–1917), most Swedish statutes and practices related to education prevailed until the 1860s. Thus, an analysis of rural childhood in southern Finland offers an illustration and comparison of common characteristics and local peculiarities in the history of Nordic childhood.

Catechetical Teaching and the Role of Individual Households

One can hardly overemphasize the contrast between present-day Nordic childhood and childhood in the past.[6] If one looks at the modern Nordic societies, they appear to be highly regulated and indeed still are, despite some recent changes in welfare politics. The aim of the present welfare institutions is to monitor and offer support to every child to ensure equal possibilities in life. What happened to children in the past is uncertain, because our documentation is poor; what has survived is a matter of chance.

Generally speaking, the further we look in the past the more scattered the information available on Nordic rural childhood and schooling, and the more it seems to have been up to the households to decide how their children were brought up. This is very logical, given that local communities were small and mostly rural and that farms and families often depended also on children as a labor force.

Who, in the first place, was considered a child? An examination of the source material reveals that anyone under the age of ten was regarded as a child. The age limit between childhood and young adulthood, however, was blurred. Many statutes and norms suggest that childhood was thought to last until the age of fifteen; approximately at that age, a person was considered legally responsible for his or her actions and was expected to start paying poll-tax. Confirmation was usually held when a person was fifteen. According to the Law of the Realm in 1734, a girl could be wed at the age of seventeen, a boy at the age of twenty-one.[7] My focus will be on children from zero to fifteen years, but it is important to remember that even young adults aged eighteen could be referred to as children.

Ever since the Catholic Church became established in Finland in the twelfth and thirteenth centuries, it had been keen to promote knowledge of its basic teachings. From christening onwards, parents and godparents were responsible for guiding little children in the ways of Christian beliefs, and teaching them the common prayers and doctrines of the Church. For most, it was enough to memorize the important teachings, such as the Lord's Prayer.[8] During the Reformation period, literacy became more important, since all were expected to receive the Word of God with their own eyes. As there was a lack of schooling resources, parents were expected to ensure that their children learnt to read. Schools were established in the towns, but these institutions were not available for the vast majority of people who lived in the countryside. In addition, towns were few and far between in the eastern part of the Swedish realm. This meant that parents in general were expected to provide their children with a basic literacy.[9]

The significance of reading skills was consolidated by means of the Church Law of 1686, which prescribed that those who wanted to get married had to prove his or her ability to read. The local priest was to regularly organize parish catechetical meetings to investigate the skills of his parishioners in this. The aim was to provide people with a religious and literary foundation that would help keep them obedient to the Church and to the Crown. For a long time, much of the literacy was superficial, mainly a reciting of text by rote. Thus, a person who was declared literate in the church records was not necessarily good at reading at all. Many had merely learnt to memorize the elementary texts. This was enough for the authorities: secular aspects of education were secondary, and the demand of literacy was used to control the access to matrimony and reproduction.[10] Nevertheless, as has been argued, in the relatively early aims of promoting literacy for the sake of bringing the divine word to all, one can see parallels to the universal thinking of the later Nordic social security system.[11]

In the seventeenth century, then, popular education focused on the memorization of elementary texts such as the Lord's Prayer. In the eighteenth century, however, Martin Luther's *Small Catechism* became an important manual for learning the doctrines of the Church. The Catechism's Household Code (Germ. *Haustafel*, Sw. *hustavlan*, Fin. *huoneentaulu*) had an especially central role in pre-modern Sweden.[12] It taught an order of society where government was based on authority given by God. The teachings were often repeated in popular education. Short religious texts like the *Small Catechism* remained central educational textbooks for centuries. It was only at the turn of the eighteenth century that more entertaining educational books were written for children.[13]

Very often, sources provide information about what the Church and the Crown wanted the lives of children to be like, rather than about what the children's lives actually were like. Apart from the teaching of reading skills, regulations and institutions had control over only small parts of the lives of children and their families. And even the control of reading skills was initially weak. In Finland, it was common for people to live 20 to 40 kilometers away from the nearest church building. This could mean that people attended church only once a year, or even more rarely. A pastor might visit the outlying villages once a year—if he was not prevented by illness, drunkenness, war, or some other force majeure.[14] Besides this, rural people in southern Finland complained about the weather-beaten roads, saying that it was difficult to get to the church. Thus, many people could be born and even die with very little contact with the sacraments or the basic education of the Church.[15]

Even later, in the early eighteenth century, these outlying villages, which were far away from the church, were often neglected by pastors. When they were approached by uninvited external authorities, the village folk could express outright hostility toward any interference from outside.[16] This was especially the case during times of crisis, such as the Great Famine in the late seventeenth century, or the Great Northern War in the early eighteenth century, when any representative of the Crown or the Church was likely to present demands that were beyond the capacity of the local communities, heavily burdened as they were by wars and crop failures. The universality of popular education thus remained an ideal that was most likely to succeed in towns and densely populated parishes.

Under these conditions, children were most likely to focus on learning by doing. Literacy was not of primary importance for carrying out the tasks on little farms; the most important skills were acquired via socialization in everyday situations when children were working as helpers in their own family or in service outside their family of birth.[17] Since the administrative records often fail to recognize or refer to family relations of lesser members of a household, however, it is not always easy to draw distinctions between the children of the house, other relatives who lived there, and unrelated servants.[18]

Scholars generally agree that entering domestic service was typical in early modern northwestern Europe, where both young women and men of the lower social classes often did so before getting married. The practice was considered part of the training of young people who were later expected to manage households of their own. It was habitual for girls and boys of all social strata to be sent to other households, partly into service, partly to learn manners and household skills outside their home. In a period of low institutionalization, it was natural that the training was given in another household. Servant maids had low salaries, and many farms could only afford a female servant.[19] Male servants were less numerous, since many young men were taken to the battlefields or were given other tasks. It was not surprising, then, that in the beginning of the eighteenth century all but one servant in Kytäjärvi were female.[20] In the late eighteenth century, however, the situation was different and both female and male servants were more numerous.

One of the tasks that was often allotted to children was herding. Like many children in the other Nordic countries, young people in the rural areas of southern Finland were sent to herd the village's grazing cattle. In the seventeenth and eighteenth centuries, Swedish statutes forbade the use of boys in herding for fear of bestiality; girls and women were expected to take care of this task. In practice, labor shortages limited the choice of cowherds. Boys as young as eight years old are mentioned in the sources related to herding in Kytäjärvi, although girls and young women too were given this task.[21]

Cattle herding was a task that was often solitary and the weather conditions were harsh, especially in early spring and late autumn. It could also be scary and even perilous for young cowherds to try to keep wolves and other beasts away at bay. Especially in Kytäjä, but also elsewhere, there were steep hills that could be dangerous for both the herder and the cattle. The means to protect the cattle were often limited, the cowherd could, for example, blow a birch-bark horn or otherwise make enough noise to scare the predators. Although cattle herding was not highly appreciated, it was a task that taught children responsibility. It is an example of their complementary role in the division of family labor.[22]

Another task repeatedly allotted to children was that of helping in the stagecoach service. This was particularly important in Hyvinkäänkylä, as the village was situated by the side of the important road between the towns of Helsinki and Hämeenlinna. In cases where farms were obligated by the law to provide horses and service to travelers for a fixed fee, young boys and girls could be sent to accompany the horses and the carriage.[23] It could be frightening and even risky for a child to travel with strangers and return alone with the horse and carriage. However, as the size of the workforce on any farm was limited, there could be no alternative to having a child replace a grown-up driver.

Both cattle herding and stagecoach service are examples of how children were used as a reserve workforce for many auxiliary tasks. In the villages studied in this chapter, as well as elsewhere in the Nordic rural areas, children's tasks were flexible. Replenishing water and food supplies, assisting in the fields, and picking berries were jobs where children often worked on their own. One important task was looking after younger children in the household—sometimes a pleasant, sometimes a tedious task.[24] As has been observed both in rural Finland and Sweden, a division of labor according to gender was not as common in the case of children under the age of ten as it was for older children. In their teens, girls were more likely to take care of their siblings and have dairy work, while boys would deal with horses and other farm work.[25] In any case, the skills and training required for these tasks were mostly physical. In this context, literary skills were of minor importance; investing time in the survival of the farm was crucial.

The Clergy's Engagement with Literary Education

Generally speaking, some inspiration from the Enlightenment began to be felt in popular education during the eighteenth century, although it took almost one hundred years for these ideas to mature into practical decisions. In the rural context, the focus of any formal education was still on basic literacy skills and the teaching of the basic tenets of the Church. In Finland, there were around twenty grammar schools (*pedagogi*), fewer than ten schools that offered a more developed curriculum (*trivialskolor / gymnasier*), and one university, the Royal Academy of Turku (*Regia Academia Aboënsis*). These schools were for boys; schools for girls were established only in the first half of the nineteenth century. For people living in the small villages of northern Uusimaa, there were schools available some 60 kilometers away, in the towns of Hämeenlinna and Helsinki, and a little further away, in the town of Porvoo. However, it was only seldom that they attracted pupils from the outlying villages.[26] In the eighteenth century, there was public discussion about developing parish schools in the countryside, but the mission proved to be almost impossible, given the long distances and the acreage of parishes.[27]

In the latter part of the eighteenth century, however, one can see some changes in the attitudes of the upper social strata of the villages. In the parish village of Nurmijärvi, there was already a tendency to send wealthy farmers' boys to schools, mostly to Helsinki, for a couple of years. After the Great Northern War, in the 1730s and 1740s, many schoolboys from Helsinki had been lodged to Nurmijärvi for summer, and they may have served as an example for the next generations. Even from Hyvinkäänkylä, several boys—mostly sons on farms that were wealthy enough to equip a cavalryman—were sent to Helsinki. Boys of the "Hyvenius/Hyveen" family (the name was inspired by the name of the village) went to school in Helsinki before returning to their home farm.[28] There is one example of a boy going from Hyvinkäänkylä, Mutila estate, to Helsinki and taking his Bachelor's degree (*baccalaureus Mudelius* in Latin) at the Royal Academy.[29] One son from the Vatsia farm, situated on the outskirts of Kytäjärvi village, was known to have attended school in the town of Porvoo; accordingly, the word *scholaris* is used in the parish records.[30]

In some families, then, there were higher educational ambitions, and the change spread gradually from Helsinki and the south toward the north. In the Kytäjä (*Näs*) manor, situated by the lake in Kytäjärvi, there was also a library, and the manor owners may have organized some guidance not only for their own children but also for their employees and their families.[31] In the eighteenth century, however, the manor owners were not yet touched by philanthropic principles in the same way as later, in the mid-nineteenth century.

The question was sometimes raised whether separate schoolmasters could be hired by the parish to help the pastors. In practice, people in rural parishes like those studied here mostly felt that hiring teachers was too expensive, not to mention building actual parish schools.[32] In addition to being worried about the costs of a schoolmaster, parents were constantly worried that too much reading would destroy children's working capacity. In Nurmijärvi parish meetings farmers and clergymen discussed getting a schoolmaster, but it proved difficult to find teachers, even if the parish people had been willing (albeit reluctantly) to pay.[33] We do, however, hear in the early nineteenth century of some lay teachers who were self-taught individuals paid by parents to tutor the village children.[34] Unfortunately, as they were not officially working for the parish, very little is known about their work.

The conflicts related to teaching became apparent in Ridasjärvi village after 1765 when obligatory confirmation classes were imposed on the inhabitants. In principle, the idea was that young people should be prepared for confirmation by participating in a confirmation school regularly for two years. In practice, confirmation school often involved only a couple of days of teaching, and while children could have been tutored at home, the importance of reading skills seems to have dawned for many of them only when they reached the age of confirmation.[35] For instance, the parishioners complained that the assistant pastor, Master Fredrik Johan Zweygberg (ca. 1722–1775, assistant 1762–1769), took too many days to prepare the young people for confirmation. For many farmers, sending the young people away from the farm, and paying for their meals and accommodation, just for the sake of literacy and doctrine, felt like an unnecessary expense. Zweygberg himself felt that it was impossible for children to learn anything when many of them arrived at church only the night before confirmation. One can imagine the frustration of Zweygberg, who had studied at the University in Turku. The relationship between the assistant pastor and the parish was not good, and he was fired in 1769.[36]

In the nineteenth century, the confirmation school system was organized throughout Finland in such a way that the school now took several weeks in spring and autumn. Children were expected to read the Catechism and later also a Children's Bible.[37] On the local level, however, the schooling arrangements depended on the activity of the clergy and the goodwill of the parishioners. For Kytäjärvi and Hyvinkäänkylä, things changed in the 1830s when an active minister of the parish, Johan Fredrik Bergh (1795–1866), started the ambulatory parish school (*kiertokoulu*) and the Sunday school. This was pioneering work in Finland, and it was influenced by Pietism, which put even more emphasis on a person's ability to personally receive the word of God than the Lutheran Church traditionally had done.[38] In the ambulatory parish school, the teacher would visit every village for a couple of weeks and gather the children in one farmhouse to train their reading skills. The Sunday school was organized with the purpose of teaching children who came to the church for the Sunday sermon. Later, in the mid-nineteenth century, Bergh was also active in the preparations of the Elementary School Law of 1866.[39]

From then on, a hired ambulatory parish school teacher went from village to village, including Kytäjärvi and Hyvinkäänkylä, to observe the skills of children and young people before the time of confirmation. He would stay at one village for a couple of weeks, teach children, and make notes of their skills.[40] The pupils were boys and girls, rich and poor, mostly ten or eleven years old; but some were only six years old, while others had already passed the age of confirmation. The school books list farmers' sons and poor people's daughters alike; all were gathered under the same roof.[41] As the teacher still spent most of his time in the villages near the church, it is hardly surprising that children in the most distant villages were found to have the least skills and knowledge of letters.[42] On the other side of the provincial border, in Erkylä and Ridasjärvi villages in Häme, the local parish priest was not as ambitious as Bergh and his school teacher, and Sunday school activities started only in the 1850s.[43]

Teaching was far from the present-day ideals of equal communication between the teacher and the pupil. The methods included learning the alphabet by shouting together. Discipline was severe and treatment often harsh, and being disciplined by a pastor was humiliating for older pupils. The horrors of learning were famously presented by Aleksis Kivi (1834–1872) in his novel *Seven Brothers*, which tells the story of seven brothers who are already young adults but are lazy and illiterate, and would rather escape to the forests than suffer the humiliation of the parish clerk's hard-handed tutoring.

The horrors of learning to read were on display in catechetical meetings where even adults were expected to be present and to prove their skills in front of the clergy and their fellow parishioners. Everyone was required to attend these reading days and publicly prove his or her skills in reading. In this context, *Seven Brothers* reflects on the consequences of bad childhood experiences related to learning:

> I'll quote that fine boy Paavo Jaakola, who said: "Life would be all right with one less day of the year, that damned reading day." And he said too: "It's not the pain, but the shame." That was after his scalp had been badly stretched at one of those hair-pulling parties. – He was one of the cleverest and wittiest of young men, but his stepmother thrust the book upside down into his hands the very first time, and so reading-day became a day of terror for him. – Mikko Kukkoinen, a man as big and strong as a pine log – in a shed one reading-day he heard the chime of the preacher's sleigh-bells and it frightened him like a lamb. So awful it is – this hair-pulling, nerve-racking shinding.[44]

Seven Brothers seems to advocate milder teaching methods, and in the novel the parish clerk is brought to question the harsh methods that he has learnt from previous generations. Although the novel is fiction, the period at which Aleksis Kivi wrote coincides with new tendencies in education. Strict catechetical teachings were giving way to a wider understanding of education, the initiative moved from the clergy to the enlightened aristocracy, and this time Erkylä village was the forerunner.

An Age of Transition: Individual Initiatives for Rural Education

In 1854, Baron Johan Reinhold Munck (1795–1865), the owner of Erkylä Manor, published a newspaper article in which he expressed his commitment to popular education. Baron Munck thought that all children should receive the same basic education and the same religious and moral principles. He placed a strong emphasis on the teaching of religion and Christian principles for children, but he went beyond the traditional ideas of catechetical teaching. Munck ridiculed those who thought that literacy and numeracy would make the common people vain and arrogant. Moreover, he expressed his conviction that learning more about the world, its geography, nature, and history, would help to consolidate even ordinary young people's faith in God and his power. For Munck, popular education, prudence, and good workmanship were important tools for maintaining order in society.[45]

By the time Baron Munck wrote his article, it was clear that society was going through a period of transition. While agriculture remained the most important means of living for the majority of Finns, new industrial enterprises, means of transport, and communication changed the prospects of the common people. The communities presented in this chapter were rural and mostly inhabited by freeholders (*bönder*) and tenant farmers (*torpare*), but by the end of the period studied here, a new kind of community was being established, thanks to the construction of a railroad and a railway station in 1862 on the outskirts of Hyvinkäänkylä. Changes to the old order suggested a future where old traditions would no longer be sufficient for new generations. Instead of being regarded as subjects of the ruler, people were more often seen as active citizens who needed certain skills and knowledge in order to contribute to the modern society.[46] This trend can be seen also in the novel *Seven Brothers,* where this new citizenship was embraced by the youngest of the brothers, Eero, who not only learned to read but also started to subscribe to newspapers and to write local notices for these papers.[47]

The Nordic countries followed more or less the same process of development and modernization of the school system from the early nineteenth century to the 1870s.[48] This process was partly inspired by the Enlightenment, partly by new philanthropic thinking, and partly by nascent nationalist sentiments.[49] Some manor owners took the initiative and funded schools for local children, especially the children of their own tenants and workers. Local schools were first established by the elite, who felt it their duty to take care of and to educate and mentor their dependents.[50]

Baron Munck was an example of the nineteenth-century enlightened aristocracy with a keen interest in education. He had been head of the Cadet College in Finland and vice chancellor of the University of Helsinki. At a stay in St Petersburg, he had met local advocates of the Pestalozzi School and studied its principles.[51] As a senator, he would soon propose a motion for the organization of the school system in Finland. It was only natural that in 1856, the same year he proposed the organization of the school system on the national level, Munck opened an elementary school, Esko School, for children in Erkylä. He recruited a committed friend of the elementary schools, Olai Wallin (1832–1896), as the teacher. Wallin later became a pioneer in the Teacher Training Institution at

Jyväskylä. Wallin was dearly beloved by his pupils and much appreciated by the local inhabitants.[52]

At Esko School, as well as in the upcoming elementary school system, the parents were still expected to arrange the basic tutoring at home or else to entrust their children's education to the village teacher. Esko School offered classes for boys and girls aged between eleven and fifteen.[53] Along with the school came a village library, the first of its kind in Erkylä, which Munck equipped with over 170 books.[54] The school was primarily intended for the children of local tenants. Its catchment area was 25 kilometers at its widest. The school routes were onerous, and many pupils needed boarding for school weeks. This was one reason why the children attended school on alternate weeks. Older girls and boys were given classes separately—this was considered necessary for the sake of chastity. A coeducational school system was later heatedly debated on the national level before it became the prevailing arrangement.[55]

In the village of Kytäjärvi and the Manor of Kytäjä, Constantin Linder (1836–1908) and his wife, Countess Marie Linder (Musin-Pushkin, 1840–1870), took the same kind of initiative, some ten years later. They had bought the Manor of Kytäjä in 1860, and subsequently launched several projects to reform and develop the Manor and its surroundings.[56] That was how the Kukkumäki School was established in the Manor area. In 1864, Aleksanteri Rahkonen (1841–1877), a young student, poet, and translator, was hired to teach children mid-week and adults during weekends.[57] To begin with, the experiment was successful, and the long-lasting effects of this teaching were reported as late as in the early 1930s, when an old farmer living in Kytäjä thanked Rahkonen's school for his remarkably good writing skills.[58] As Munck had done in Erkylä, the Linder family organized a library in Kytäjä and provided school books for children.[59] The school experiment took an abrupt end, however, when Constantin Linder found the teacher drunk at a local farmer's place. In spite of their efforts, the Linder family could not find a substitute for Rahkonen.[60] It was only ten years later, in 1874, that the school activities were resumed. The school was funded by the owners of the Erkylä Estate until 1900. After that, it continued as an ordinary parish school.[61]

Baron Munck and the Linder family belonged to the exceptionally wealthy aristocracy. This made it possible for them to pay generously for the education of local children and to establish permanent schools. However, we also hear of some smaller manors in the neighboring parishes that offered informal small-scale teaching for farmers' children, even for a little beggar of whom the lord of the manor had become fond.[62] It is likely that there was more short-time schooling and peer-to-peer help among rural families than one might expect at first sight.

From the mid-nineteenth century, the need for education was not only a sentiment promoted by some of the most privileged. There were also local farmer families who felt that their lack of literary skills prevented them from aspiring to new positions and who, like Eero of the *Seven Brothers*, wanted to contribute to the building of the new society. The change was fully seen when they had a chance to arrange education for their own children at a later date. One of the most ardent advocates of formal education was Pelet Sykäri (1837–1922), owner of Sykärinsaari in Ridasjärvi, south of Finland. He himself had not learned much, and he keenly felt the lack of knowledge and literacy. His wife Ida, a farmer's daughter, had reportedly received elementary education in an informal manor school at a neighboring parish and mourned her lost chances to learn more. The couple put all their seven daughters to school, subscribed to the new children's magazines and encouraged their children to take university degrees.[63]

The difference in the prospects available for Ida and Pelet Sykäri and those available for their daughters illustrate the profound changes from the mid-nineteenth century. From the previous confirmation schools with their harsh methods, there were now broader prospects for children, who could receive much more education in their home villages.

At the same time, these prospects were limited. The schools of Esko and Kukkumäki were primarily meant to serve the children who lived near at hand and were subordinate to the manors. Many rural children still led the same kind of life as their parents and grandparents in the eighteenth and nineteenth centuries. Many still went out to service or to work as apprentices, struggled to find time (or motivation) to learn the alphabet and the four rules of arithmetic, and felt that the harvest or any other work on the farm was more important than their schoolwork. Little cowherds, childminders, and helping hands were still needed for many tasks in rural southern Finland as well as elsewhere in the Nordic countries.[64] Children in neighboring villages were also in a rather unequal position with regard to the availability of schooling.

In 1866, the Statute for Elementary Schools laid the basis for a unified school system, where in future the same kind of curriculum would be available for all children. This was a milestone in the development of equal education, although it would still take decades before every parish had a school. According to historian Marjatta Rahikainen, it was in the 1870s that changes in legislation, education, and economic trends created new possibilities in the lives and prospects of children in the Finnish countryside; and even then not everyone was able or willing to make use of the emerging opportunities.[65]

Conclusions

When we analyze childhood and children's upbringing within a specific geographical area from the premodern times to the eve of modernization, we note both local peculiarities and a pattern of development similar to many other places. In the outskirts of rural southern Finland, children were brought up in the same way as in many other rural villages: for centuries, they learnt the most important skills via the process of socialization and practical training. They were entrusted, at home or in service in another household, with tasks that would have taken up too much of the adults' limited time. This, however, provided children with possibilities of learning by doing; and this formed the core of their education for adult life. Despite some interest in sending boys to schools in the eighteenth century, physical training was of crucial importance, and learning to read and write was not thought worth much investment.

With regard to literary education, rural children depended mostly on what the nearest villages had to offer. Although they could sometimes travel by coach or walk in the forests along with the cattle, or visit the parish church, a distance of some 10 to 20 kilometers could nevertheless be too much when it came to going to school. Local differences in education remained huge in neighboring parishes, since this depended on the commitment and skills of the local clergy. While children in Kytäjä and Hyvinkäänkylä were among the first in Finland to be introduced to the nascent ambulatory school and Sunday school system, some decades later the families who were dependent on local manors of Kytäjä and Erkylä were the first to take part in the experiment of the Esko School, an embryo of the elementary school of the 1860s.

Our sources reveal that at the time when the elementary school was being formed, the first initiatives in the area studied in this chapter were taken by aristocrats who had the means and the motivation, and were inspired by the Enlightenment and philanthropy, to follow up on the current ideas about schooling for all citizens. In villages, where ordinary farmers had a stronger position, there was less wealth, with focus more on the practicalities of everyday life. Even in the 1870s, there was still a long way to go from the heterogeneous paths of schooling and upbringing to a standardized and regulated educational system. For many centuries, education for rural children mostly meant learning to read, and this teaching was motivated more by religious demands than by an enlightened interest in new information.

Notes

1 Rahikainen 2010: 341.
2 Tommila 1958/2003: 247–84; Lehto 1989: 55.
3 The article has been written as a part of my book project on the history of the area of the present-day City of Hyvinkää (2013–2016).
4 Tommila 1959: 312, 317.
5 Heikkinen and Leino-Kaukiainen 2011: 11.
6 For general presentations on the history of childhood and education in Sweden, see Sandin and Sundkvist 2014. See also Chapters 6 and 9 by Jacobsen and Rørvik in this volume.
7 Vilkuna 2003: 23–9; Hanska and Lahtinen 2010: 42–3.
8 Hanska and Lahtinen 2010: 18–20.
9 Sandin 1986: 364–9; Sandin and Sundkvist 2014: 19, 24.
10 Kallenautio 1976: 554–6; Sandin 1986: 363; Laine and Laine 2010: 258–64.
11 Lindmark 2011: 32.

12 See Chapter 3 by Markussen in this volume.
13 Laine and Laine 2010: 277; Lindmark 2011: 32–41.
14 Lehto 1989: 18–22; Junnila 1992: 16–17.
15 Leinberg 1892: 174–5.
16 Lehto 1989: 19–24, 187–90.
17 Tommila 1958/2003: 288–93; Lehto 1989: 55–7.
18 Lehto 1989: 50; Miettinen 2012: 67–80, 102–10, 308–10.
19 See the discussion in Lahtinen 2006; Lahtinen 2007.
20 Lehto 1989: 50.
21 Keskitalo 1964: 334–7; Lehto 1989: 57; Sjöberg 1997: 106–28; Rahikainen 2010: 321–5.
22 Sjöberg 1997: 106–28; Rahikainen 2010: 321–5.
23 Seppälä 1959: 200.
24 Sjöberg 1997: 121; Vilkuna 2003: 28; Rahikainen 2010: 333.
25 Rahikainen 2010: 332–4.
26 Puntila 1934.
27 Joutsivuo 2010: 148.
28 Ragnar 1936: 39, 62, 97.
29 Ragnar 1936: 36; Kotivuori 2005, online at http://www.helsinki.fi/ylioppilas-matrikkeli/henkilo.php?id=7515. Accessed 22.7.2016; Tommila 1959: 379
30 Carl Simonsson, scholaris, Loppi parish records on Vatsia farm, 1768–1773, Loppi parish records, the National Archives of Finland. I am grateful to Kaisa Kyläkoski for pointing out the source.
31 List of library books in Kytäjärvi manor, collected by Sirkka Lauerma, in the Hyvinkää City Museum Archives; personal observations by the author of this chapter at the private Kytäjärvi Manor Archives in Kytäjärvi Manor, September 2013. See also Chapter 3 by Markussen in this volume.
32 Joutsivuo 2010: 148.
33 Tommila 1959: 360–1; Joutsivuo 2010: 148; Laine and Laine 2010: 280–1.
34 Keskitalo 1964: 487–9.
35 Laine and Laine 2010: 280–1.
36 Dean's reports of inspection (rovastintarkastuspöytäkirjat), 1760–1770, Hausjärvi Parish records, Hausjärvi parish archives in the National Archives of Finland; Keskitalo 1964: 483–484; Kotivuori 2005, online catalogue at www.helsinki.fi/ylioppilasmatrikkeli/henkilo.php?id=6800. Reference 5 Nov 2015.
37 Keskitalo 1964: 48.
38 Tommila 1958/2003: 305–19.
39 Tommila 1959: 356–73; Tiensuu 2007.
40 School children register 1839–1857, Nurmijärvi Parish Archives, the National Archives of Finland.
41 School children register 1839–1857, Nurmijärvi Parish Archives, the National Archives of Finland; Tommila 1959: 368–9.
42 School children register 1839–1857, Nurmijärvi Parish Archives, the National Archives of Finland; Junnila 1992: 16.
43 Keskitalo 1964: 488.
44 Aleksis Kivi, *Seven Brothers*, ch. 11 (trans. Impola 2005).
45 'Tankar om Folk-underwisningen', 2 parts, *Helsingfors tidningar*, 4 March 1854 and 8 March 1854.
46 Heikkinen and Leino-Kaukiainen 2011: 11–12.
47 Kivi, *Seven Brothers*, ch. 14.
48 Thuen 2011:70–4; Sandin and Sundkvist 2014: 19–20, 43–8. See also Chapters 3 and 9 by Markussen and Rørvik in this volume.
49 Jalava 2011: 74–5.

90 *Anu Lahtinen*

50 Leino-Kaukiainen and Heikkinen 2011: 23.
51 Keskitalo 1964: 676–78. Johann Heinrich Pestallozi (1746–1827) was a Swiss pedagogue and educational reformer who founded several educational institutions across Switzerland.
52 Nurmi 2007; Ahonen 2011: 244, 246.
53 Keskitalo 1964: 678.
54 Keskitalo 1964: 726.
55 Keskitalo 1964: 678.
56 Lehto 2000, "Linder, Marie (1840–1870)."
57 Reports on Kukkulinna school activities in newspapers *Suometar* 5 Jan 1865; *Helsingfors dagblad* 10 Jan 1865; *Folkvännen* 18 Jan 1865; Lehto 2010.
58 *Hyvinkään Sanomat* 1932.
59 List of library books in Kytäjärvi Manor, collected by Sirkka Lauerma, in the Hyvinkää City Museum Archives; personal observations by the author of this chapter at the private Kytäjärvi Manor Archives in Kytäjärvi Manor, September 2013; Lehto 2010.
60 Constantin Linder to Marie Linder, 28 Feb 1865, Linder Family Archives, the National Archives of Finland; Lehto 2010.
61 Junnila1992: 428.
62 On informal education, available at smaller manors in southern Finland, see Hilma Sykäri's account of her parents, Ida and Pelet Sykäri, ('Agronoomi Yrjö Sipilälle joitakin elämäkerrallisia tietoja ...'), Private Archives of the Ascendants of Pelet and Ida Sykäri, Estate of Sykäri; Kuusanmäki 1954: 226–8.
63 Hilma Sykäri's account of her parents, Ida and Pelet Sykäri, ('Agronoomi Yrjö Sipilälle joitakin elämäkerrallisia tietoja ...'), Private Archives of the Ascendants of Pelet and Ida Sykäri, Estate of Sykäri.
64 Jalava 2011: 94.
65 Rahikainen 2010: 355.

6 Children's Rights and Duties

Snapshots into the History of Education and Child Protection in Denmark (ca. 1700–1900)

Anette Faye Jacobsen

The Nordic countries are considered strong advocates for children's rights, and children's rights are highly featured in both legislation and at policy level.[1] All five Nordic countries have set up official institutions to promote and protect children's rights. Established in 1981, the Norwegian Ombudsman for Children was, in fact, the first of its kind in the world.[2] Child rights and child protection feature prominently in the Nordic welfare state ideology, and there is a strong tradition of pedagogical thinking with a child-centered approach that takes into account the perspective of the individual child.[3]

Research into children's rights and welfare has also been widely conducted in the five countries,[4] focusing on the individual countries as well as on the region.[5] Surprisingly, however, very few studies have been undertaken on children's legal history.[6] This is also the case with historic studies on human rights more generally. It is possible that researchers may have been discouraged because the concept of rights is complex, and, indeed, subject to very different interpretations over time. Recently, however, studies have begun to appear.[7]

The aim of this chapter is to contribute to the legal history of children's rights. This is an interesting field because it shows that our current understanding of rights for children is a new phenomenon, as previous generations have had very different conceptions of both childhood and rights.[8] However, certain rights seem to have been protected across the centuries.

This chapter, more specifically, explores the major factors that have furthered the development of children's rights in Denmark between the period of approximately 1700 to 1905. The thesis is that children's rights were generated as a response to religious and social needs, in contrast to the "adults' human rights," which were developed for political reasons. Moreover, in its conclusion, the chapter identifies three important elements, which have been crucial to the development of the approach to children in the Nordic context—the roles of pietism and of the state *in combination* with the role of women.

The chapter covers a period of over 200 years and deals with a very complex evolution. To give an overview of this multifaceted history, the chapter is structured into three parts or "snapshots," each of which focusses on the key legal framework that shaped children's rights and duties during a specific epoch.

The first snapshot analyzes the rights and duties of children as they were conceived in a "traditional," household-based society divided into social estates and headed by a very small state structure. The second snapshot moves to the early modern era and presents the first major legislation, the compulsory schooling acts adopted in Denmark in 1814, which established the modern understanding of rights for children—addressing all children and with the state as the responsible implementing power. The third snapshot jumps into the era of industrialization and urbanization, and describes the next comprehensive state scheme aimed at children, the child protection system, enacted in Denmark in 1905. With this new institutional structure, the state undertook an obligation to monitor children's upbringing and education. The child care system was launched primarily to prevent youth crime, but, at the same time, it was seen as a protective measure that was "in the best interest of the child" (as this concept was understood at that time).

Through the three snapshots, the intention is to present three epochs with very different notions of children's rights and duties, as well as to analyze two of the crucial building blocks, which have served as foundations for the gradual expansion of state responsibilities in relation to children—compulsory schooling and child protection. Gradually and concurrently with these developments, the idea of children as individuals with their own rights was developing.

The chapter is based primarily on Danish source material and mainly follows developments in Denmark. However, in its conclusion, it outlines some features that are specific to the Nordic region. Even though the Nordic states have not followed parallel paths in relation to the history of children's rights, certain common features may be identified that have shaped the ideas of children's rights and duties in these countries.

Overall, the chapter prompts further research on the history of children's rights in the Nordic countries and beyond. Children's rights, from a historic perspective, developed very differently to "adults' human rights." Moreover, studying children's rights in different epochs shows how the concept of "the child's best interest" has had a range of interpretations over time, and, thus, indicates that our current understanding of children and their rights has a historical basis.

Snapshot #1: The Right to Life, Health, and Religious Education within the Household Regime (ca. 1700)

Denmark and Norway were dual kingdoms under the Danish king until 1814, and were regulated by a set of very comprehensive codebooks called *Danish Law* and *Norwegian Law* respectively.[9] The codes were issued by the absolutist king by the end of the seventeenth century and were the foundations for the two countries' legislation for several centuries.[10]

The codebooks aimed to cover all aspects of state regulation of the dual kingdoms, and they are an interesting source of information about state policies in relation to children and their families. The codes also represent a radically different and unfamiliar legal setting, when considered from a present-day perspective. A peculiar trait was that the state did not command a monopoly of law enforcement. The legal order was a pluralist system, within which the household was one of the cornerstones.[11] Most of the law under the household's legal order was customary and unwritten. The codes only provided a very general framework for the legal capacity of the household, while the practical administration of justice was in the hands of the household's head and his discretionary power.

The household law was hierarchical, with children and servants at the bottom of the hierarchy. Furthermore, under customary law, parents were required to care for children until the age of maturity, and in exchange, children had to show obedience in all matters within the household.[12] As this was customary law, it did not require written codification.[13] Only the limits of parental power were outlined in the codebooks:

> The house master may punish his children and servants with a stick or a switch but not with a weapon. But if he inflicts on them wounds, with edge or oak or damages their body or health, he shall be punished as if he had caused harm to a stranger ... The same right is for the house mistress to exercise over her children and servants.[14]

Interestingly, in a patriarchal society, the female head of the household was provided the same authority and punishing power within the family as the male, even though he was considered house master for her too.[15] Moreover, the notion of family was very differently from the modern notion, including in legal theory and legislation. Family membership was not a matter of biological bonds but of living together under the same roof, and the family consisted of the household heads, their cohabiting relatives (which were often their children), and servants.[16] Typically, in the household, male and female heads were in charge of the male and female servants respectively, while the children were under female care and tutelage during infancy and early childhood.

The codified state regulations, expressed in *Danish Law* and *Norwegian Law*, had the aim of protecting society's vital functions and institutions, and the household was such an institution, because most of rural and urban production was undertaken within the realm of the household. Consequently, the codebooks were preoccupied with guarding the parents' authority and executive power to ensure that control was maintained over the family functions. The codebooks devoted a whole chapter to this issue, entitled "About children's offenses against their parents, and equally against masters and mistresses."[17] In this chapter, we find the sections cited on the limits of punishment together with more detailed descriptions of parents' rights and children's duties. These include the parents' right to be obeyed, and children's duties to be honest, sober, peaceful, hard-working, and thrifty. If misconduct occurred in these regards and could be proven, then the children could be declared disinherited. Furthermore, if parents were sworn at or threatened by their offspring, then the latter would risk disinheritance, or could be punished with life imprisonment in the king's prison. If anyone beat their parents, they could be sentenced to death.[18] We do not know to what extent these provisions were invoked, but one study has documented that a number of children were imprisoned on the initiative of their parents or household masters in Denmark in the mid-1700s.[19]

The protection that the written law offered the child within the customary household—that punishment should not cause physical harm to children—can be described as relating to the right to health in the most basic way. This was supplemented by a number of provisions aimed at protecting the child's right to life. In particular, if the child was not born into a family, its life was at risk. Such a situation was dealt with in the codebooks in four consecutive sections.[20] Three of the provisions were aimed at punishing the woman who had given birth to the child out of wedlock and killed it or made it disappear. It was taken for granted that an infanticide was committed or organized by a single mother.[21]

It is questionable whether these clauses were meant for the protection of the child and as an endeavor to secure the child's right to life. In these sections, the codebooks are preoccupied with control and punishment of female sexual offenders rather than with saving children's lives. However, one clause does indicate an intention to protect the child's life. The punishment for leaving a child depended on the severity of the offence. The most severe penalty was given to an offender who had hidden a child in a remote place where nobody could be expected to find it, while the milder penalty was given to an offender who had placed the child in a busy place. Another provision punished parents who out of neglect had killed an infant by laying upon it in their asleep.[22] From such provisions, we may conclude that the state was anxious to protect the child's right to life, yet its power to enforce the right was limited to threatening perpetrators with severe penalties.[23]

The early modern provisions differentiated between rural and urban regions. It seems that in towns, the household heads were granted somewhat less autonomy than in rural areas. The codes stated that in towns, the local government should appoint two public trustees who were in charge of supervising "the youth, how it is raised as well as how the parents maintain their children." Moreover, the public trustees were required to monitor whether the parents sent their children to school or into someone's service. Parents who kept their children in idleness would be advised to find solutions within a given timeframe, otherwise the trustees were required to identify a position for the youngsters and the parents were asked to pay their maintenance. If they could not afford this, then the children, as with the foundlings and the fatherless, would be equipped from voluntary alms.[24]

Most importantly, the public trustees had to monitor the conduct of individuals who acted as legal guardians for the fatherless and others without legal capacity, and particularly their conduct in regard to the children's land or capital, if they had any. Through this role, the public trustees can be seen as part of the state's endeavor to guard the right to property for all, including for children. Other measures were a series of provisions in the codebooks protecting the right to inheritance.[25] This was not a right equally available to all. Sisters were only entitled to half the share given to their brothers, and children born out of wedlock were not entitled to inherit from their father unless he registered his paternity. The father could subsequently accord a share of his assets to such a child, although not exceeding half of what his or her siblings born in wedlock were entitled to.[26] The law, furthermore, distinguished between children born out of wedlock to unmarried parents and children born out of wedlock but with one or both parents married to others. In the latter cases, the child would not be entitled to inherit anything from the married parent, neither from the father nor the mother.[27]

Schooling as a universal right or duty for children was not a state goal during early modern times. The Danish and Norwegian codebooks contain a chapter that describes how schools may be organized in towns to train young people to serve God in churches, among other places, or to seek a secular occupation "according to the needs of ordinary people."[28] Nevertheless, education was not a goal in itself for the state, the nation, or the king. All major educational tasks were undertaken within the household unit by the parents, and for adolescents by the house master and mistress or other people within the household unit.

One provision in the codebooks had to be implemented universally for all children. This was the requirement of baptism for every child and parents who neglected this duty were to be heavily fined.[29] It is indeed questionable whether being christened should be seen as an entitlement for the child. It was first and foremost a duty, guaranteed and enforced by the state. But it was undoubtedly understood as a measure established for the benefit of the child to secure the child's opportunity of salvation. Even if the child was weak, the Christian parents were obligated to do their utmost to ensure that "no means of salvation were uncared for."[30]

As a follow up to the baptism, another duty and right for every child was that he or she should be taught the basic doctrines of Lutheranism. It was one of the responsibilities of the parish vicar and his clerk to teach and subsequently to test that the core evangelical curriculum was learned by heart as well as understood. This test was a prerequisite to celebrating the Eucharist, which was again obligatory for everyone to receive at certain intervals.[31] Even if the legislation to enforce the Eucharist may be understood as a state and church endeavor to control the official Lutheran disposition of their subjects, it was, at the same time, considered to be a means of grace essential for salvation.

To sum up this snapshot of children's rights in Denmark and Norway in the early modern era, the family and household were in charge of caring for and educating children according to customary law. The central government apparatus was very limited, and the state statutes only outlined the most basic universal entitlements for children. The overall social structure was divided into distinct estates, and rights were dependent on social position, gender, and age. There was no expectation or intention that individuals be granted equal rights, and the child was placed at the lowest position of the age hierarchy. Still, the right to life was protected, as well as a very basic right to health.

Taking a comparative perspective, Danish and Norwegian children were not entitled to more rights than children in other countries. What is peculiar to the dual kingdoms is the ambitious and comprehensive compilation of rules and regulations into written law, enacted by the young absolutist state to gain more control over society and the competing powers of the landlords.[32] The active state involvement increased dramatically over the next century. The second half of the 1700s saw state reforms initiating one of the most important agricultural reorganizations in Danish history, which also had a strong influence on children's rights. The next section will focus on Denmark because the dual kingdoms were divided in 1814 and Norway followed a different path.

Snapshot #2: Universal Schooling Secured by the State (ca. 1800)

In 1814, the Danish king enacted five statutes regarding elementary schooling. This initiative established a right and duty for every child in the Danish king's realm to receive obligatory primary education. The five documents were special acts covering different sectors and regions, and one religious minority. One act was aimed at schooling in the capital, Copenhagen, one covered the provincial towns, another targeted the rural districts, and one was directed specifically at the two duchies, Schleswig and Holstein, south of the Danish border. The fifth statute concerned the Jewish community in Denmark. It was not a schooling act as such, but it made religious education followed by an exam compulsory for all Jewish youth. The test in Judaism was, thus, analogous to the Lutheran confirmation, which concluded the compulsory schooling of the Christian children.[33]

The 1814 school statutes were prepared over several decades and were a landmark reform for the Danish state and society.[34] They can also be seen as the documents that established the right to education in the modern sense, namely as a universal right (and duty) guaranteed for every child by the state.[35] The purposes of the new school system were explained as follows:

> The teaching of the children will in general be aimed at educating them to become good and righteous humans, in accordance with

the Evangelical-Christian teaching; and should confer to them the knowledge and skills necessary to become useful citizens of the State.[36]

Compared to the situation a century earlier, this was a radically different approach to parents, children, and children's rights. The 1814 school legislation was a strong signal of expanding state influence and control over children at the expense of household autonomy. Making schooling obligatory meant that the authorities, in practice the teachers, would dispose of children's time and energy on a regular basis. For many parents, as well as masters and mistresses, this was not at all welcomed, as it took away an important workforce from household activities. The struggle over children's time, in fact, continued for almost a century after the adoption of compulsory schooling.[37]

What had also changed was the aim of education. It had developed from exclusively focusing on the Lutheran teaching to a broader objective. There was still a strong emphasis on Christian learning (which included the ability to read), but it was supplemented by other knowledge and skills that would contribute to the children becoming citizens of the state (as stated in the quotation above) and not merely subjects of the king. New learning objectives beyond the religious curriculum were introduced, primarily writing skills and arithmetic, together with a basic knowledge of the homeland. From a rights perspective, the notion of citizenship is important. The word has a long history in many European languages, yet the meaning had become loaded with political connotations during the Enlightenment era of the second half of the 1700s and even more in the aftermath of the French Revolution. It now signified an individualization of the former subjects and them becoming members of the common society.[38]

The 1814 statutes were an important step in the establishment of a universal right to education for children. The provisions differed, however, from the modern human right to education, since it was not meant to be an *equal* right. This is one of the reasons why there were several statutes instead of one. Society was deeply divided, along gender lines, between social classes, as well as between rural and urban communities, and the government had no intention to bring about equality. Instead, the school regulation tailored to societal differences. For instance, children in urban schools were to have more lessons per week than their rural peers. Furthermore, the public schools were intended primarily for poor children. The elite, as well as the urban middle class, merchants, civil servants, and independent craftsmen, would often choose to send their offspring to private schools, or, later in the nineteenth century, to public fee-paying schools with much more extended curricula and teaching hours.[39]

Still, the aspiration to introduce universal basic schooling was extraordinary for the time. First, it was remarkable logistically because the 1814 statutes required huge bureaucratic efforts including funding, which was a heavy burden on local taxpayers.[40] It was also remarkable ideologically because the principle of universal schooling was, in several ways, at odds with the tradition of segregating people based on class, denominations, and localities. Seen from this perspective, the 1814 statutes were a milestone in Danish and maybe even in European social-economic history, as well as in the history of human rights—at least in the symbolic sense. The classic idea of human rights evolution is described in the chronological stages of the development of civil rights, followed by political rights, and completed by social and economic rights.[41] But when it comes to children's rights, social and economic rights appeared even earlier than the political rights of adults.

What was the background for this important reform? There were a range of intertwined causal factors that contributed to it but two major movements were decisive: the religious, Pietistic influence from the first decades of the 1700s, and the economic-social restructuring that profoundly changed the agricultural sector during the last decades of the eighteenth century.

Pietism has been described as the single most influential force behind compulsory schooling in Central Europe.[42] A key objective of pietism was to revitalize each individual's inner devotion to the Christian message through the personal experience. It implied a renewed incitement for everyone to read the scripture. This, again, made literacy an important goal for the truly Christian individual as well as for the Christian state.

Pietism was a complex and broad movement, and had an impact on all the Nordic countries.[43] It was particularly influential during the first three decades of the eighteenth century.[44] In Sweden, it led to a decree that obliged parents to teach their children how to read. However, to strengthen implementation and to suppress potential unauthorized religious practices among lay people, a general system of annual investigations of all households was established and children were tested in literacy and knowledge of the Lutheran catechism.[45]

In Denmark–Norway, the new devout current gained influence in the first decades of the 1700s through the royal family and gave impetus to the building of schools and the inclusion of schooling in legislation. The motivation behind the education programs was multifaceted. In Denmark, the earliest plans to establish school programs were built into ordinances for poor relief.[46] Moreover, the establishment of compulsory military service, characteristic of early modern regimes, sparked a need to strengthen loyalty and devotion to duty in the future soldiers.[47] The Pietists' approach to education was instrumental to both these reform areas. The basic aim of the education was to inculcate in the individual a sense of personal responsibility for his or her salvation, combined with a strong self-discipline and commitment to attend to one's duties. Furthermore, Pietism was occupied with the personal development of the individual, and supportive of popular involvement in social and religious issues.[48]

By the mid-1700s, Pietism had given way to Rationalism within the state church. Yet, much of the Pietistic ideas and values had transplanted into the political thinking behind reform efforts, which were implemented in the rural sector during the second half of the century. Educating the peasants was seen as one of the core ways of strengthening the state's capacity, and the leading reformers saw compulsory schooling as an important means in this endeavor.[49] Compulsory schooling was thus motivated by very worldly aims, but religion still played a major role in the school statutes of 1814. All education and schooling at the primary level was deeply influenced by Christianity throughout the nineteenth century.

Essentially, the religious curriculum was the universal part of the state sponsored primary education, as the same religious syllabus was obligatory for all children regardless of their gender, social class, and urban or rural background. Only the Jewish children had a different curriculum but it was state sanctioned in the same way as the Lutheran one. The religious test, whether it took place in a church or a synagogue, was the conclusion of primary schooling and was also considered a kind of citizenship exam for both congregations. Completion of the test gave access to civil rights, including marriage as well as legal capacity in relation to employment and property.[50] According to the statutes, religious education was inextricably linked with the aim of conveying knowledge and skills necessary to becoming useful citizens of the state.

Historians have paid little attention to the religious aspects of compulsory schooling and it has often been seen as a conservative force undermining progressive developments. In the Danish and Norwegian context, however, Pietism (resurrected as popular "awakening" movements in the 1800s) revitalized pedagogical debates.[51] In Denmark, it brought about a "free-school movement," and generally gave inspiration to more child-centered teaching methods that found common ground with the pedagogic currents toward the end of the nineteenth century.[52]

Snapshot #3: Legal Systems of Child Protection and the Child Act (ca. 1900)

In 1905, a new act was adopted by the Danish Parliament, which established a nation-wide child protection system with the objective "to monitor the moral education of the young generation."[53] The Child Act was a remarkable new step of state interference in parents' rights.[54] Similar acts were adopted in the Nordic countries around the turn of the century.[55]

Comparable legislation was also initiated in many European states from the mid-1800s, most often as a reaction to the fact that crime rates among children and young people were steeply rising. Some believed that there was a need to systematize efforts to keep children away from prisons and to protect children at risk of sliding into crime. In France, the courts could decide that children should be taken away from their parents because of a criminal record, as well as if the parents' lifestyle was such that it was a threat to the child's safety, health or morals. In the United Kingdom, courts could send a child at risk to a reformatory or an industrial school. The Nordic model, however, was primarily inspired by Germany. The important difference was that the child protection system was not linked to the judicial machinery.[56]

This new legislation reflected a changed perception of children that had gained ground among broad segments of decision makers and opinion leaders in the second half of the nineteenth century. Delinquent children were increasingly seen as needing protection and education, rather than punishment. This was a recurrent issue on the agenda of international meetings and conferences organized by new networks of jurists and criminologists from the 1880s.[57] These fora were informed by the concurrent development of systematic statistics, which documented the sharp rise in crime rates among adolescents. This rise was probably partly a result of more prosecutions of children and an increase in the regulation of urban public spaces.[58] The jurists and criminologists were, moreover, influenced by new sentiments toward children advanced by philanthropic movements. These movements were made up of individuals and associations that had organized around social issues, as a reaction to destitution and overcrowding, which was becoming more and more visible in the swelling cities.

Young children were seen as potential victims of the migration and industrialization processes of the second half of the 1800s. A growing anxiety that social cohesion and security were jeopardized sparked the mobilization of religious and social activists, in particular from the urban middle class, to aid the poor and especially their children. Civil society organizations were a fast expanding trend of the social and political life of the nineteenth century. A large number of these activists had a background in religious groups and saw their involvement in philanthropy as a Christian deed and duty. They considered it to be their social commitment to "save the children," and they saw themselves as "child savers."

One of the most influential philanthropic associations behind the Child Act of 1905 was the Christian Association to Save Errant Children (the Christian Association).[59] There were many similar organizations in the other Nordic countries and beyond.[60] The Christian Association was set up in 1898 and attached to the Copenhagen Inner Mission, one of the descendant groups of the Pietistic awakening movements of the nineteenth century. The main goal of the Christian Association was to lobby for the enactment of the Child bill. Another aim was to find new homes for children in need, either with foster families or in children's homes.[61] The philanthropic activists did not apply a rights discourse but rather focused on the needs of the children. As the founder of the Christian Association, Siegfred H. Nissen explained, an errant child in the urban slum needs to be placed in a "good Christian home in the countryside, a home that would receive the child with joy and love, assist it and guide it with love and lead it to its Saviour."[62]

The aim of the child saving movement was to protect children against evil forces. That required for the child to be guided by a series of moral and social rules and norms through a caring and loving homely environment.[63] This view was, to a large extent, shared by opinion makers and lobbyists engaged in child policy. One of the very prominent political spokesmen for children was a Social Democratic Member of Parliament, Peter Sabroe. He had also been actively involved in the preparation of the Child Act. For Sabroe, the vision was that "the children's rights are the primary concern." In the labor movement, "rights" were a recurring theme in the political discourse, but the objectives for child protection did not differ much from the objectives of the philanthropic activists, even though the labor movement did not apply a religious rhetoric.

The ideals of a good childhood and a proper upbringing were primarily generated from the urban middle class and were also embraced by the social democrats active in the field. It was stressed that a child should not be exposed to a rough and careless upbringing. A slogan of the time was that a child had a "right to be a child."[64] This reflected a new attitude, inspired by romanticism, that the child was an innocent being, essentially unspoiled by the cynicism of the adult world.[65]

This protective approach to children also implied the prolongation of their immaturity. The Child Act was followed by an amendment to the penal code, which raised the age of legal competence from ten to fifteen years. A young child could no longer be held accountable for any criminal offence. In contrast to present-day child rights thinking with its emphasis on the child as a competent agent, the prevailing efforts of the child savers around the year 1900 were directed at easing the responsibilities placed on children from poor families. These children often had to manage on their own because their parents were busy from dawn till dusk sustaining a living.

The Child Act of 1905 described two main objectives for the new child protection system. The first was to monitor children's moral education and, thus, safeguard the young generation against moral corruptness; and the second was to prevent a future burden on society.[66] In the eyes of the drafters of the Child Act, there was no conflict between the two goals. The parents might have seen the intervention into their family life as unfair, but it was justified by the idea that "the best interest of the child must prevail."[67] Interestingly, these words are very similar to one of the core principles of the United Nations Convention on the Rights of the Child, adopted more than eighty years later. There is no doubt that the new legislation was introduced for the purpose of protecting vulnerable children. The ambition of the legislators, however, was very limited, from a modern perspective, as it was emphasized that "it was obviously not the intent that the new rules should be applied everywhere where children are needy or suffering hard treatment, but only if their health or normal bodily development are in serious danger."[68] The reason for the limited intentions was a very realistic understanding of the scarce state and local resources. However, the introduction of the Act also represents a belief in the state's capacity to regulate and implement systemic interventions into the family life of citizens.[69]

Only a few years after the enactment of the Child Act, scandal after scandal about child abuse and maltreatment within the system were revealed.

These did not lead to any structural changes and it took half a century of further democratization before the parents of the removed children were granted better legal protection.[70] Nevertheless, the ambitious child protection systems introduced at the beginning of the twentieth century marked an important step in the direction of modern day child rights thinking. This may not be obvious, as the intention to protect children was very limited with the emphasis of the regulation on the protection of society. Still, the child protection systems represented an important political shift toward what is characteristic of modern child rights—strong political support for the state monitoring and interfering in family life in order to protect the child's best interest.

Conclusion

The snapshots of these three points in time during the period of approximately 1700–1900, make it very clear that approaches to children's rights were radically different during the three eras. Nevertheless, parents and legislators in all the epochs believed that the educational efforts of their times were in the "best interest of the child."

It was believed that the best interests of the child were promoted in the Danish and Norwegian codebooks of the seventeenth century through securing christening and an education, which emphasized submission to the parents as well as to God. The codebooks, moreover, had the aim of protecting the child's right to life and safeguarding against serious physical harm. However, child protection was, to a great extent, in the hands of parents, who were monitored by the local church vicar. The state was not equipped to undertake the responsibility of protecting children as a group, let alone as individuals.

The role of the state markedly changed in the epoch of the enactment of the schooling statutes. With this ambitious reform, the first child right, in the modern sense of the term, was adopted: an entitlement for every individual child to attend school (whether the child was a boy or girl, rich or poor, or from urban or rural areas) and this entitlement was guaranteed by the state. A century later, the 1814 statutes implied a different idea of what was in the best interest of the child. It was considered necessary that each child was provided with expanded knowledge and skills, not only to learn to fear God but to prepare the pupils to become useful citizens. With these objectives, the children were not only seen as obedient subjects and believers but also as the future agents of the enhancement of welfare and happiness in the state and society.

The third snapshot described a new state task vis-à-vis children that was increasingly demanded during the last decades of the nineteenth century. Interventions in the moral upbringing of the child were to be much more proactive than before, to save the child from corruption and abuse, and, thus, eventually to protect society. With the Child Act of 1905, child rearing was no longer solely an obligation of the parents but, in principle, a responsibility of the state. The Child Act marked yet another change in the perception of what was in the best interest of the child. It was no longer sufficient for the state to offer basic schooling. Every child deserved a morally safe childhood and this called for a monitoring mechanism with a mandate to interfere in families failing to safeguard their children against moral downfall or crime.

Finally, the question was raised: To what extent has the development of children's rights and duties followed parallel paths in the Nordic countries? When looking at the detailed and specific history of each country, the differences are magnified and the similarities diminished. In the field of compulsory education, Denmark established obligatory education in 1814, while in Sweden a general schooling statute was enacted in 1842.[71] There are also overlaps between the development of children's rights in the Nordic countries and other northwest European states, and the uniqueness of a shared Nordic history in this field should not be overstated. However, it is this author's view that three major factors have contributed to shaping attitudes as well as rights and duties of children in a common direction, specifically in Denmark, Norway, and Sweden. They include the roles of religion, of the state, and the role of women.

Lutheran teachings always emphasized the importance of reading skills for all parishioners, male and female alike. Furthermore, the strong influence from Pietistic movements and their successors in the Nordic countries have had a range of impacts. During the nineteenth century, these religious movements inspired a more individualized pedagogy with a focus on the child's perspective. This paved the way for the reform pedagogy, which played a very important role in the Nordic countries from the last decades of the 1800s and well into the twentieth century.[72]

The Lutheran state churches have enjoyed a monopolistic status in the Nordic countries, and the strong local presence of state church representatives facilitated the bringing about of a high literacy rate—even if compulsory schooling was instituted at very different times between the countries.[73] The active reform agenda was another characteristic of the Nordic states. Even though the role of women was not discussed in the analysis above, it is the view of this author that the *combination* of state initiatives and the early involvement of women in education and child protection have been important in shaping the Nordic tradition in relation to children's rights.

There is a widespread tradition of collaboration between state and private actors, and women were granted new opportunities through such partnerships. In Denmark, for example, an important element of the education system was a system of state accreditation, which supported women in establishing private schools and offered them teacher training. The child protection systems, too, involved women.

It is certainly not an exclusive trait of the Nordic countries that women were active in philanthropy during the nineteenth century. Rather, what was characteristic of the education and child protection systems in the Nordic countries was the professionalization of women. This process was generated through networking and dialogue between state and private actors.[74] To give a few examples: the private female school principals and teachers organized themselves and engaged in lobbying when new reforms were being negotiated in Parliament.[75] In the child protection system, women were appointed as representatives in the municipal protection committees.[76]

Altogether, the relatively stable and ambitious states and the monopolistic Lutheran churches of the Nordic countries facilitated the implementation of children's rights to literacy and schooling. At the same time Nordic states were influenced by religious movements (often inspired by Pietism) and, during the second half of the nineteenth century, by women's groups, tirelessly working to influence government policies in relation to children. These activists and opinion leaders had a large range of ideas and political goals, but they shared the idea that the child was an individual in his or her own right, and that adults should strive to involve the child and the child's perspective, at least to some extent.

This chapter contends that the commitment from a wide spectrum of civil society activists, including women, to the promotion of what they saw as the best interest of children *combined* with a confidence in and collaboration with the state and its endeavors to professionalize child-related work are typical for the Nordic countries.

Notes

1 See, for instance, Therborn 1993: 256, and Kristjansson 2006: 19–20.
2 Flekkøy 1991: 162.
3 Carlgren et al. 2006: 301–2. As for the best interest of the child, cf. also Chapter 2 by Hodne in this volume.
4 The sociology of childhood has been particularly strongly endorsed in Norway. The Norwegian Centre for Child Research was established in 1982 with an academic journal, *Barn (Children)*, started in 1983. In 1992, the Centre was instrumental in establishing one of the leading journals within interdisciplinary child research, *Childhood*, established in 1993. In 1989 in Sweden, the University of Linköping established an interdisciplinary centre, Child Studies (*Tema Barn* in Swedish) with academic programmes in child studies, often with an emphasis on historic perspectives.
5 The Nordic Council of Ministers has a strong tradition of funding research with a Nordic perspective. Welfare studies, including on children's issues, have been one of the organization's priorities. Most of this research has been published in the Nordic languages, although publications in English are increasing. A few examples of child research are De Coninck-Smith, Schrumpf, and Sandin 1997; and Einarsdottir and Wagner 2006.
6 In a broader international context, an outline on children's rights through history can be found in Fass 2004: 539–41; Hawes 1991: 1–11; and Cunningham 1994: 2–4. For more details on the US, see Mason 1994: 1–49.
7 Research in the history of human rights is still fairly young. Hence, current debates struggle with definitions of human rights over time, while the conventional, somewhat naive narrative of a straight evolutionary progress of rights is

criticized. An overview of recent debates can be found in, for instance, Hoffmann 2011: 1–26; Alston 2013. The view implicit in this chapter is that certain paths of continuity may be traced back in time, but that multi-dimensional concepts such as "rights" are always defined historically in a specific context. On the history of children's rights in Denmark, see Faye Jacobsen 2015.

8 Following Ariès 1962, the concept of childhood, and perceptions of the "nature" of the child as such, have been discussed extensively by historians. Research questions have included: Has childhood always been considered a distinct age, and how did parents comprehend their children? A good overview of the theoretical positions among historians and sociologists since Ariès, with a link to the concurrent development of the idea of children's rights, is provided in Shanahan 2007.

9 The two titles *Danish Law* (issued in 1683) and *Norwegian Law* (issued in 1687) are literal translations from the descriptive names of the books in Danish and Norwegian. They are found in the Bibliography under their popular book titles *Danske Lov* and *Norske Lov*, respectively. As many provisions in the two books are identical, references are made to both codes together, and using the conventional format: Book part number, chapter number and section number, for instance, 3-17-34. Only if references differ from one another, then the two books are referenced separately. For this snapshot, see also Chapter 3 by Markussen in this volume.

10 Tamm 1983: xxxiii–xxxvi. Also, Iceland, as part of the Danish Kingdom until 1918, adopted sections of both the Danish and Norwegian Code Books during the eighteenth and nineteenth centuries, Sigurðsson 1983: 66–347.

11 Faye Jacobsen 2008: 187–8; Brunner 1968: 107–11; Miller 1998: 13–17.

12 Legal majority was eighteen years, except in relation to property and guardianship, which was twenty-five years: Danish Law 1683/1929 (hereafter cited as DL), 3-17-34; 3-17-35 and 3-17-2 and Norwegian Law 1687 (hereafter cited as NL), 3-19-34, 3-19-35, and 3-19-2.

13 There is very little research on customary law in the Nordic context, cf. Faye Jacobsen 2008: 43–7, 85–7.

14 DL/NL, 6-5-5 and 6-5-6.

15 Appel 1999: 159.

16 Nørregaard 1784: 299; Hurtigkarl 1813: 281. See a description of rather similar socio-legal patterns in the US during colonial times and based on the common law tradition in Mason 1994: 4–8.

17 DL/NL, 6-5.

18 DL/NL, 6-5-1 to 3.

19 Markussen 1988: 41–2.

20 DL/NL, 6-6-7 to 10.

21 Nielsen 1980: 3–8.

22 DL/NL, 6-11-14. Nielsen 1980: 3–12

23 The number of actual convictions was relatively small, Nielsen 1980, Hæfte I, 3-72-76.

24 DL, 3-19-2, 7; NL, 3-21-2, 7.

25 DL/NL, 5-2: "*Om Arv og Skifte*" (English translation: "On inheritance and estate administration")

26 DL, 5-2-29, 70, 72; NL, 5-2-29, 71, 73.

27 DL, 5-2-71; NL, 5-2-72. A reform of the discriminatory provisions was debated by parliament in the end of the 1880s but nothing was decided (Bentzon 1906: 203–7). In 1937, children born out of wedlock, as from 1938, were given equal inheritance rights to children born in wedlock. (Højberg Christensen, Grue-Sørensen, and Skalts 1953: 100–1).

28 DL/NL, 2-18-1.

29 DL/NL, 2-5-6, 7.
30 DL/NL, 2-5-6.
31 DL.2-5-11, 27, NL 2-5-11, 26.
32 In 1665, the early Danish–Norwegian monarchy was the only regime in Europe that enacted a written absolutist constitution. This was followed by the two codebooks, which served as models and inspiration in codification efforts in southern Europe, as well as in France, Prussia, Russia, and Sweden during the eighteenth century (Wagner 1983: 223–34). Faye Jacobsen 2008: 187–90.
33 Larsen, Nørr, and Sonne 2013: 138–41.
34 Larsen, Nørr, and Sonne 2013: 69–89.
35 The right was not granted in the entire jurisdiction of the Danish king, since Iceland, the Faroe Islands, Greenland, and a couple of tiny tropical colonies were not included in the reform. This would have been far beyond a realistic scope of the project. Larsen, Nørr, and Sonne 2013: 275–89.
36 *Anordning for Almueskolevæsenet paa Landet i Danmark af 29. Juli 1814* (ed. Larsen 1914, § 22).
37 De Coninck-Smith 1997.
38 Riedel 1972 (vol. I): 702–4; and Bregnsbo and Ihalainen 2011: 111–16. See also Chapter 9 by Rørvik in this volume.
39 Larsen, Nørr, and Sonne 2013; and Gjerløff and Faye Jacobsen: 2014.
40 Larsen, Nørr, and Sonne 2013: 149–53.
41 T. H. Marshall launched this theory of historical stages in his influential essay "Citizenship and Social Class" already in 1950; Marshall and Bottomore 1992: 17.
42 Melton 1988: XIII.
43 The term is used here as a collective name for a variety of trends including the Hernnhuts, radical forms and different state sponsored trends in the Nordic countries, Brecht et al. 1995: 446–541.
44 Brecht et al.1995: 449–54.
45 Hope 1995: 153–; and Barton 1977: 524–5.
46 Appel and Fink-Jensen 2013: 22.
47 Reeh 2006: 32–43.
48 Melton 1988: 23–30.
49 Markussen 1988: 112–81.
50 Schwartz Lausten 2002: 323.
51 Hope 1995: 369–72; Myhre 1992: 38–41; and Gjerløff and Faye Jacobsen 2014: 105–10.
52 Faye Jacobsen 2013.
53 Kommissionen angaaende Statstilsyn med Børneopdragelsen (*Betænkning* 1895: 8).
54 "Lov om Behandling af forbryderske og forsømte Børn og unge Personer" Nr. 72 af 14 April 1905. The popular title of the act was the Child Act, in Danish: *Børneloven.*
55 More precisely in Norway, Sweden, and Denmark. Similar Acts were prepared and adopted by the Finnish Parliament in 1908 and 1914, but were turned down by the Russian Tsar who had the supremacy over the country, and legislation on child protection systems both in Finland and Iceland had to wait until the 1930s (Andresen et al. 2011: 148–9, 153). See also Chapters 8 and 10 by Sandin and Markkola in this volume.
56 Kommissionen, *Betænkning*, 43–4.
57 Kommissionen, *Betænkning*, 24–6; and Løkke 1990: 29.
58 Løkke, *Vildfarende Børn*, 30–31.
59 In Danish: *Kristelig Forening til Vildfarne Børns Redning* (as from the year 1900). The association has changed its name a number of times. The names can be seen by searching the online database in the Danish National Archives on https://www.sa.dk/en (accessed 24.07.2015).

60 Stang Dahl 1978; and Grinde 1989: 25–31.
61 Løkke 1990: 49–54.
62 Quoted from Løkke 1990: 50.
63 *Kristelig Forening til Børns Redning*, 1923.
64 Peter Sabroe, quoted in Løkke 1990: 39.
65 The romantic image of the child is primarily ascribed to J.J. Rousseau, cf. Fass 2004 (vol.2): 718.
66 Kommissionen, *Betænkning*, 8.
67 Kommissionen, *Betænkning*, 42.
68 Kommissionen, *Betænkning*, 72.
69 Kommissionen, *Betænkning*, 52–9.
70 Faye Jacobsen 1989: 276–7.
71 Richardson 1992: 8.
72 Hatje 1994: 93–8.
73 Ihalainen et al. 2011: 7–8. On literacy, see Green 2008 with a focus on Sweden; and Appel 2005: 325–6, on Denmark.
74 Taussi-Sjöberg and Vammen 1995: 7–8.
75 Gjerløff and Faye Jacobsen 2014:155–71. A similar pattern is seen in the kindergarten movement. Cf. Vammen 1999: 79–132. In Sweden, women's organizations were actively engaged in lobbying for a child welfare officer system cf. Bergman 2003: 65–93.
76 Jørgensen 1921: 160; and Stang Dahl 1978: 163–4.

Part II
Children's Development
Formation, Education, and Work

7 "A Plain and Cheerful, Active Life on Earth"

Children, Education, and Faith in the Works of N. F. S. Grundtvig (1783–1872, Denmark)

Marcia J. Bunge

Since the mid-sixteenth century, all Nordic countries have been and continue to be predominantly Lutheran, and over the centuries many Lutheran theologians and religious leaders in northern Europe have significantly shaped ideas and policies regarding children, education, and child well-being. At the beginning of the Reformation, for example, when formal education was limited primarily to the nobility or to boys, Martin Luther recommended that all children, including girls and the poor, be given a basic education. Luther and the early reformers also established a "common chest" to provide for those in need, including orphans and children in poverty. Later, Lutheran Pietists, such as A. H. Francke (1663–1727) in Halle, established many orphanages, hospitals, and schools. Lutheran theologians, such as J. G. Herder (1741–1803) in Weimar, contributed significantly to theories of education. In the Nordic countries, several Lutheran pastors and lay leaders also introduced educational reforms and significantly influenced ideas and policies regarding children. They expressed ideas about children not only in formal essays or tracts but in poems, hymns, songs, sermons, stories, or catechisms. Thus, many Lutheran religious figures are cited in Nordic histories of childhood and education as well as music and literature, such as the Icelandic pastor and hymn writer, Hallgrímur Pétursson (1614–1674), the Norwegian poet and pastor, Petter Dass (1647–1707), the Danish bishop and historian, Erik Pontoppidan (1698–1764), the Swedish Pietist, Carl Olof Rosenius (1816–1868), or the Swedish hymn-writer Karolina W. Sandell (1832–1903).

Although Nordic views of children have been greatly informed by Lutheranism, expressions of Lutheranism vary across Nordic countries and centuries. This chapter focuses on the conceptions of children expressed in selected works of one leading nineteenth-century Lutheran pastor in Denmark: Nikolaj Frederik Severin Grundtvig (1783–1872). Grundtvig is a key figure in Danish histories of religion, education, literature, music, and the founding of modern Denmark. He was a pastor, poet, and politician who promoted the education of young adults and life-long learning in Denmark. He is also known as the founder of the "people's high school" movement, which aimed to provide education for all citizens, including the rural poor. He is cited in histories of literature for his translations of the ancient epic, *Beowulf,* and for his groundbreaking studies of Anglo-Saxon literature and Nordic mythology. Grundtvig is characterized by some as a model of the "happy Dane" and a radical Renaissance man who criticized both pietism and rationalism as well as his Lutheran contemporary, the philosopher Søren Kierkegaard (1813–1855), the "father" of existentialism. Grundtvig's religious ideas and the many songs and hymns he composed (almost 1,500) helped to revitalize the church and attracted a number of followers, called "Grundtvigians." Today he is known around the world for his innovative approaches to education, emphasis on life-long learning, ideas about nation-building and splendid hymns.[1]

Although Grundtvig played an important role in shaping ideas and reforms that benefited not only adults but also children, little scholarly attention has been paid to his precise conceptions of or commitments to children. Given his role in creating the "people's high schools," many studies focus on his view of the education of youth or adults. Some historians even claim that he focused on youth as opposed to childhood as the real period of education.[2] Those studies that do mention his view of children often attribute his focus on freedom, equality, and education to ideals of the Enlightenment and his emphasis on child development, creativity, and play to Romanticism or to the Genevan philosopher Jean-Jacques Rousseau (1712–1778). Although certainly a man of his time, Grundtvig was an expansive and complex thinker who was intimately involved with children and thought much more about childhood than current research indicates. For example, he was home schooled until age nine and writes about his own "happy childhood years."[3] His essays on education are not simply about adult education but include attention to infants, children, child development, and schools. His hymns, songs, and sermons are filled with references to children, joyful days of childhood, "childlikeness," and the birth and childhood of Jesus. He wrote rhymed histories of the world, songs, and other texts for children. He was a tutor, director of a "people's high school," and the board director of a charity school for children (ages seven to fourteen).[4] As a pastor, he was also surrounded by children. Grundtvig lived to be nearly eighty-nine years old, was happily married three times (outliving his first two wives), and had five children.[5] He home schooled his own children, enjoyed them, and refers lovingly to them and his wives in many poems and songs. One of his most famous poems that is still sung today, "A plain and cheerful, active life on earth," was adapted from a longer poem that was addressed to his first two sons and entitled "Open Letter to my Children" (1839).

The aim of this chapter is to contribute to Grundtvig studies and the history of childhood by exploring elements of Grundtvig's conceptions of children found in some of his most significant songs, hymns, and essays on education, Nordic mythology, and Christianity. Grundtvig was a prolific preacher, speaker, and writer throughout his lifetime, and his life spanned almost a century! Many of his works have not yet been edited or published, even in Danish. According to one scholar, if published, his collected works would comprise 120 to 130 large volumes.[6] Nevertheless, by paying close attention to child-related ideas expressed in just a few selected seminal songs, hymns, and texts that have already been published and translated into English, we learn much about Grundtvig's ideas of and commitments to children.[7]

Based on these seminal sources, the chapter explores aspects of his ideas on children related to his views of humanity and education, and it outlines some of the ways in which Grundtvig combines his commitments to the common good and to children—indeed to all human beings regardless of faith or no faith—with his belief in the ultimate truths of Christianity. The chapter finds that Grundtvig articulates a multi-faceted and holistic view of children as made in the image of God; a mixture of nature and spirit; vulnerable yet also full of vitality; future citizens; creative and free individuals; and "glorious mysteries." Furthermore, his ideas on children interweave Lutheran beliefs and practices with elements of his notion of the "Nordic" and provides powerful grounds for his attention to the well-being of all children.

By exploring Grundtvig's conception of children, the chapter highlights the significance of child-related themes in his work and invites further study about childhood in the works of Grundtvig. Furthermore, given his significance beyond Denmark, the chapter provides some insights into the complex history of childhood in Nordic countries and the numerous sources that have informed contemporary Nordic commitments to universal education, child protection, and children's rights. In addition, the chapter illustrates the significance of exploring multiple sources that shape past and present notions of childhood in other parts of the world, and it invites all readers to reflect seriously on their own conceptions of and commitments to children in their own communities and around the world.

Foundational Conceptions of Children and Humanity: Made in the Image of God and Embodied Spirits

One of Grundtvig's most foundational ideas on children is that they are genuine human beings made in the image of God and possess, like all human beings, a fundamental God-given equality. He bases this conception on Genesis 1:27, which states that God made human beings "male and female" in "the image of God." Throughout his writings, he emphasizes that all people are made in the image of God—poor, rich, Christian, non-Christian, male, female, young, old. Few Lutherans, as one scholar states, "Have spoken so directly to the question of [humankind] created in the image of God, as N. F. S. Grundtvig ... Creation and the created order of things are basic to his whole understanding of [humankind]."[8] Furthermore, whether reflecting on individuals, nations, or the whole of humanity, he includes children. When he criticizes Søren Kierkegaard for claiming there are no "true Christians" because no Christian has reached "Christian perfection," Grundtvig states: "This is as if we would deny that our children were genuine human beings because they are as yet far from knowing, or in word and deed unable to express, their humanity as vigorously or as clearly as we are."[9] He also specifically affirms the full humanity of both boys and girls, sons and daughters, and underscores in several songs and poems his respect for children and women.[10]

He also emphasizes that what makes humans distinctive from other animals is their capacity for language. In his *Den kristelige Børnelaerdom* [*Basic Christian Teachings*], for example, he states that human speech must be seen as "a marvelous something, a matchless gift which no bird or animal can be taught to imitate."[11] Speech gives human beings their capacity for power, truth, and love, and is essential to their relationship to one another and to God. As he says in his poem, "What a Great Wonder is Human Life":

> Humans are all in God's image made,
> with living words making for union,
> and wand' ring mid forests and animals they
> with gods can enjoy sweet communion.[12]

Furthermore, he believes the image of God cannot be corrupted or erased, as some theologians might claim. Even though human beings err and make mistakes, the image of God in all people and through all ages has never been distorted or destroyed. "Human life in its most obscure, most poverty-stricken and uncleanest form is nevertheless of the same kind of human life in its richest, purest, and most clarified shape."[13] The same image of God is in Adam, Abraham, and Moses. The same image is in Christian, Jew, or Muslim. For Grundtvig, human beings err, and in this sense have all "fallen," but "humanity is similar and the same before and after the Fall as well as before and after the rebirth."[14]

A second foundational conception of children expressed in his view of humanity generally is that children, like other human beings, are embodied spirits that are both vulnerable and full of vitality. In his *Nordic Mythology*, Grundtvig speaks about human beings, including children, as an intricate union of nature and spirit, body and soul, and "glorious, incomparable" creatures.[15] As a glorious mixture of nature and spirit, human beings are also vulnerable yet full of vitality. Grundtvig pays particular attention to the vulnerability and vitality of children when he discusses how children suffer because of false ideas about the opposition of body and soul. In his work, *The School for Life and the Academy in Soro*, for example, he says that children's brains and bodies are still developing, and he strongly believes that their development can be harmed by an education focused solely on book learning or learning by rote. Schooling devoted to "exhausting brainwork" or to implanting in children "the order, quietness, reflection and wisdom of

old age" can "completely destroy the vitality of most of the children."[16] He
believes many problems in education can be traced to "the conflict that is
imagined between the body and the soul, so that what the body loses, the
soul must win."[17] Grundtvig states that although the opposition of body and
soul has little to do with the genuine spirit of Christianity, Christians who
buy into this opposition by neglecting the body or focusing solely on heaven,
damage not only children's bodies but also their souls.[18]

Grundtvig greatly delights in and celebrates the vulnerability and vitality
of children. Throughout his writings he emphasizes life, growth, and vitality, referring to countless and detailed elements of the natural world, such as
groves, forests, beeches, woodlands, fields, and particular flowers and birds.
In songs and hymns, he depicts the vulnerability of children and their need for
protection. They are small, sweet, fair, tender, little, and gently sleeping. They
are held, nourished, suckled, cradled, bathed, embraced, kissed, welcomed,
protected, and loved by others, including God. Children are also vibrant and
alive – their "childhood cheeks a-glowing."[19] Infants suckle with zest, cry,
crow, smile, and laugh. Little children wonder, speak, contemplate, sing,
leap, play, peek, and hide and seek. Children, for Grundtvig, are not empty
vessels, blank slates, or clay to be molded, as we see in some conceptions of
children in Western thought, but rather active, alert, and full of vitality.

Grundtvig sometimes uses the image of "tender flowers" or "little birds"
to describe the delicate yet vibrant nature of children, and he describes their
development in dynamic terms, such as flourishing, blooming, thriving, and
growing. For example, he calls his own baby daughter "my pretty child ...
who with other tender flowers peeps out now above the clay."[20] In this verse
of a Christmas hymn, he states:

> In humble homes as in mansions rare
> With light in the windows glowing,
> We harbor the babes as sweet and fair
> As flowers in meadows growing.
> Oh, deign with these little ones to sharet
> The joy from your message flowing.[21]

Christian and Nordic Elements in Grundtvig's Conceptions of Children and Humanity

In these two foundational conceptions of children and humanity, Grundtvig
interweaves Christian understandings of the image of God, goodness of creation, and the care of children with elements of his own notion of "Nordic."
Grundtvig was a Lutheran pastor, and his notion of the image of God is
biblically based and grounded in the belief that God has created all human
beings and indeed all of creation. Even Grundtvig's view of the power of
human speech is connected to his view of a God who creates all things and
continues to communicate with human beings through the power of the

Word. Related to his Christian understanding of the goodness of creation is his emphasis on the goodness of the body and the beauty of creation. The Christian tradition also emphasizes the care of the weak and vulnerable, including women and orphans. Many biblical passages express the command to "love your neighbor as yourself" and "to care for the widow and orphan." Jesus also fed the hungry, reached out to the marginalized, and blessed and healed the sick, including children, and he called his followers to love even their enemies.

Although Christianity certainly affirms the image of God, honors the goodness of creation, and emphasizes the need to care for the most vulnerable, Grundtvig adds certain "Nordic elements" to these ideas and his conception of children that greatly affirm their embodiment as well as their vitality and their vulnerability. Grundtvig was immersed in and preoccupied by Nordic myths and wrote extensively about them. He also interweaves Christian and Nordic ideas and figures in an almost seamless way, writing, for example, about the Nordic god, Odin, and Jesus Christ all in one brief, breathtaking poem, "High Odin, White Christ."[22] Thus, it is difficult to pin down precisely all the elements of his notion of the "Nordic" or "the North" (which for Grundtvig included the Nordic countries and England). However, there are at least four common and related Nordic elements in his writings that can be seen in his view of children: (1) growth and vitality; (2) a joyful presence in the world; (3) "spirit in action"; and (4) a certain combination of strength and mildness. As scholar, Uffe Jonas, notes, Grundtvig adds "a certain extra element of earthiness, a joyful, lively and compassionate presence in the world, to the more detached and otherworldly tendencies of monastic Christianity."[23] Grundtvig also perceives the poetic and philosophical spirit of the North as one of "spirit-deeds" or "spirit in action."[24] In other words, a certain vitality and creative energy that is able to manifest itself in words and deeds in the world. In his references to Vikings or Nordic myths, Grundtvig also highlights the dynamic Nordic combination of strength and mildness, courage and ease, valiance and love. All of these elements and more are interwoven into his view of children.

Children as Future Citizens, Creative and Free Individuals, and "Glorious Mysteries"

Three additional ideas on children are visible in Grundtvig's promotion of universal education, life-long learning, and innovative approaches to education. He writes extensively about his vision of education for the sake of individuals, nations, and humanity in several texts, including *Nordic Mythology* (1832), *The Danish Four-leaf Clover* (1836), and *The School for Life and the Academy in Sorø* (1838). Although they broadly address education and are not focused directly on children, reading these texts with close attention to children reveals much about his conceptions of children and their development.

First, like Luther and in line with Lutheran understandings of vocation and calling, Grundtvig believes that children are future citizens and participants in society, and parents and the community have a duty to educate all children (whether poor or rich, girls or boys) so that they can cultivate their gifts and talents and contribute to the common good. Their particular callings or vocations in life are ways in which they love and serve others in the world and become productive citizens. By providing children with a basic education in the humanities and natural sciences, children become equipped to use their gifts in service to others, thereby strengthening the community and building for the future. Thus, like Luther, Grundtvig supports universal education and assumes that it not only helps all children read the Bible and participate actively in the Church, but also prepares them for carrying out particular roles in society and becoming productive citizens.

Second, unlike Luther and writing 300 years after the Reformation, Grundtvig emphasizes that children and adults are creative and free individuals who are continually developing, and thus the purpose of education is not simply to gain knowledge or to prepare oneself for certain roles and professions that serve both church and society, but also to foster an individual's continuing development, self-understanding, and zest for life.[25] Given his view of human beings as continually developing, he pays attention to education across the life span, becoming a pioneer in adult education and a champion of "life-long learning." He also believes education should engage children and be pleasurable. In his song, "As sunshine is to the dark brown earth," for example, he says, "true education will serve all earth's friends," involves "knowing God and the way your life tends," and is "mild and soft, and to our heart it must bring much pleasure."[26]

Third, in his *Nordic Mythology*, Grundtvig emphasizes that children and human beings are a "glorious mystery" with a spiritual nature, and genuine or true education must also honor this spiritual nature. For Grundtvig, human beings are, as we have seen, "glorious, incomparable" creatures, and they are ultimately a mystery or an enigma to themselves. Furthermore, their desire to understand their own mystery leads them to seek knowledge of the world and God's mystery as well. According to Grundtvig, the spiritual nature of human beings is part of the "Jewish-Christian" worldview, but it is also a truth that can be grasped by people of all faiths or no faith at all. He states, for example:

Be he Christian or heathen, Turk, or Jew, every man who is aware of his spiritual nature in himself is such a glorious mystery that he casts absolutely nothing aside merely because it is strange and seems as inexplicable as himself. On the contrary, he is almost irresistibly drawn to what is strange, because at heart it resembles him, and because in it he expects to find the answer to his own mystery ... Such a person, whether in fact he is of this, or that, or no faith in the Godhead, never finds himself attracted to transparently enlightened people whose whole wisdom can be learned by heart in an hour ... Rather he is attracted precisely by the mysterious, deep natures that sense more than they see, feel more deeply than they can fathom, and speak with far greater spirit than they themselves are aware of.[27]

The School for Life and the School for Death

Given these three notions of children, what kind of schooling prepares them to be future citizens, honors their creative capacities and freedom, and opens them to their own "glorious mystery"? What kind of schools did Grundtvig envision? His ideas on education are expansive and address all levels of learning across a lifetime. However, by highlighting just a few of his ideas, we learn much about his views of both education and children.

In several writings, he contrasts the current school system, what he calls the "School for Death," with his own vision of a "School for Life." He criticizes the school system of his time because he claims it destroys a child's vitality and desire to learn by emphasizing memorization, book learning, Latin, strict order, and lectures. Grundtvig himself was initially home schooled by his parents and grew up with the stories told him by Malene Jensdatter, the live-in maid at his childhood home. When he was nine years old, he was sent away to a private tutor to prepare him for high school, which he entered at the age of sixteen. His own experience of the school system was deadening, and his view of the School for Death is well summarized in the following stanza:

> With sadness then I view all boys' ambition,
> whose eyes light up, as daily they grow tall;
> they too must go to school and learn addition,
> and even as they grow are growing small!
> Before her sweet perfume is liberated
> the rose must wither in sepulchral air;
> the eye must break before it is translated,
> the light is gone before we are aware![28]

Grundtvig's own view of education, the School for Life, emphasizes engaging children's questions, attending to their need for physical activity and play, and incorporating singing and storytelling. Even though unmusical by his own admission, he writes extensively about the many benefits of music, including for education. Thus, song, play, and children's own voices and ideas are part of his vision of a School for Life. His "Free School Song," for example, opens with the lines: "Where Spirit has a mouth and voice/through clouds a sun is winging;/ like little birds when woods are green,/ the child-like souls are singing."[29] In his poem, "In the Queen's Charity School," he says that in this school:

There is room to play indoors
just as on the terrace!
Songs sung in these lofty rooms
make a splendid chorus![30]

And in "The Chirping of the Birds" (*Fugle-kvidde*, 1840) he even coins the phrase, "Sing yourself happy!"

Furthermore, like J. G. Herder, Grundtvig believes human beings are shaped by their cultures, communities, and language, yet also part of the whole of humanity. Thus, he says that Danish children should be taught in their own language (instead of Latin) and learn about Denmark. His list of qualifications for teachers, therefore, includes knowledge of Danish history, literature, folklore, geography, and law, as well as the capacity to tell stories, sing, and bring to life Danish stories and folksongs.[31] Yet, even as Grundtvig's view of education honors one's natural vitality, native language, and culture, it also seeks to awaken the spirit and to appreciate what is true and noble in all times and places. Thus, he suggests studying the great myths, poems, stories, and histories of other cultures, which also fosters a love for truth and humanity.

Another key element of his approach is what he calls "living interaction" or the "living interplay" of ideas. When information is presented in lecture form, "No living interaction is reached between your thoughts and mine."[32] Furthermore, true living interaction awakens the spirit. In describing his vision for a joint Scandinavian high school, for example, Grundtvig states: "Everything that strongly attracts or awakes the spirit was in the form of a constant brisk interaction in the well-regulated conversation."[33] Even the relationship between human beings and God involves, for Grundtvig, a "hearty, spiritual mutuality, inclination, and interaction."[34]

In these and other ways, a "School for Life" instead of a "School for Death" fosters self-understanding and creativity, full participation in the community and civic society, love for humanity, and openness to mystery.[35] For Grundtvig, such an education is crucial not only for one's own individual development but also for the development of a *people*. As he states in *Nordic Mythology*: "To try to make everybody equally wise at once is folly ... But to offer basically the same education to all classes and to open up to everyone the path to continuous progress is, like everything that leads to a free yet methodical development of one's powers, not only wise but absolutely necessary, if nations and states are to prosper."[36] He certainly believes that nations need excellent academic universities to educate lawyers, professors, pastors, and other professionals, yet he advocates helping everyone in society to be educated so that all can develop their capacities as well as contribute to the common good and fully participate as citizens. "Finally we have too *many* institutions rather than too few, too large rather than too small, in which to educate our clergy and our professors, whereas we have none at all in which to educate Danish citizens."[37]

Christian and Nordic Elements of Education, Equality, and Freedom

Just as in his view of humanity, Grundtvig combines Christian and "Nordic" elements in his view of education and notions of freedom and equality. For example, one of his most cited verses that captures his concern for equality and community comes from his poem, "Far higher are mountains elsewhere on the earth":

> Far more of the ore, both the white and the red,
> have others from digging or selling,
> but Danes never lack for their own daily bread,
> no less in the poor peasant's dwelling.
> In this lies our wealth, on this tenet we draw:
> that few are too rich, and still fewer too poor.[38]

This verse and the poem overall lift up Denmark and the Danes, yet build on biblical notions of justice and care for the vulnerable. The last two lines, as Jonas notes, are "an almost exact quote from Exodus 16:18, where Moses instructs his followers in the rules of just distribution."[39] Grundtvig accepts that some will be rich and others poor—the key word is "too." To this day Grundtvig's line informs part of the national debate on the role of government in a welfare state.

The most cited verse about human freedom comes from Grundtvig's poem, "Rhymed Letter to Our Nordic Next-of-kin" is:

> Freedom our watchword must be in the North!
> Freedom for Loki as well as for Thor.[40]

Directly following these famous lines and throughout his work, Grundtvig also refers to the power of the Word that creates, enlivens, and is itself free.

> Free is the Word in the spirit's new world,
> which the Word has created on this early shore,
> this country of learning, of thought, and of faith.[41]

Grundtvig is himself aware that his vision of education and his worldview spring from Christian and what he terms "Nordic" values and beliefs. For him, part of the spirit of Christianity itself is that it is lived out and enlightens peoples in their own cultural contexts. In one striking passage about the People's High School, he states:

> On the one hand, a living Danishness is always aware of the omnipotence of Christianity and its own impotence; on the other hand, the spirit of Christianity always borrows its mother-tongue from the people

among whom it dwells and whom it enlightens and enlivens, just as Christ Himself borrowed the womb he would dwell in from the people in whose midst he wished to live and work as a human being.[42]

"Human Comes First, and Christian Next": The Role of Faith and Community in Grundtvig's View of Children's Well-Being and Happiness

In line with Grundtvig's views of human freedom and equality, Grundtvig is a strong advocate of freedom of religion. As he states in the poem, "Constitution Day 5 June 1854," "Freedom to believe and think and speak are people's ancient rights!"[43] One of the phrases that captures his high regard for humanity and freedom of religion comes from the title of his poem, "Human Comes First, and Christian Next!"[44] In the poem, he speaks of evils committed in the name of Jesus and reminds readers of so called "heathens" who stood in God's grace, such as Adam, Noah, Abraham, David, and John the Baptist. The poem emphasizes that Christianity can never be compelled or forced, claiming:

Human comes first and Christian next,
this is a major precept;
our Christianity comes free,
a gladness pure and perfect.[45]

Although he is a strong advocate for freedom of religion, Grundtvig is also a pastor, bishop, confessing Christian, and self-identified Lutheran who believes firmly in the truths and renewing power of Christianity. He rejects coercion, yet also believes and professes that Christianity is a compelling and truth-filled worldview that addresses deep human needs for forgiveness and renewal. Throughout his writings, he speaks in down-to-earth terms about the tendencies of human beings to be so self-centered that they neglect the needs of their neighbor. For Grundtvig, this truth should be obvious to people of any faith or tradition as well as to humanists and atheists. Whether one uses the term "sin," as Christians and Jews do, the great myths, worldviews, and religions of peoples around the world recognize and seek to address the problem of human error, selfishness, or wrongdoing. For Grundtvig, since all human beings err, all are in need of healing, forgiveness, and renewal, which Christianity abundantly offers. In his text, *What Constitutes Authentic Christianity?*, for example, he assumes that many people are "convinced" by their conscience about their own sinfulness and "conscious" of their need for forgiveness and rebirth. He warns Christians, however, "We should never seek to convince those of the truth of Christianity who manifestly have no feeling of any need for a Savior, for a divine word of grace, and for the gospel of peace."[46] Such efforts, for Grundtvig, are ineffective or futile. In the meantime, everyone in the nation (religious or non-religious, Christian or non-Christian) can and should work together for the common good.

Nevertheless, since Grundtvig believes that Christianity is a compelling and true vision of life, offers forgiveness and renewal, and sparks hope and joy, he has much to say to Christian parents and church leaders not only about educating children but also raising them in the Christian faith. Grundtvig understands faith to be a matter of the heart that is shaped primarily in the home and in the worshipping community. In his essay *Is Faith Truly a School Matter?* (1836), he explains that faith is something "sacred," the "heart's treasure," and a child's "best inheritance."[47] Faith cannot be handed down to children through book learning or memorization. This is the approach taken in his contemporary schools, and for this reason, Grundtvig believes that faith cannot be taught in schools as they exist. Furthermore, many teachers do not teach it as a living faith, and no child should be force fed religion. Thus, for him, "Christian schools" have never existed and never can exist except in "individual households."[48]

Grundtvig expresses many ideas for nurturing children's faith in the home and the congregation, and many of his theological ideas and practical approaches are similar to those of Luther. For example, for both, faith is enlivened by the Holy Spirit and comes through hearing the Word and participating in the sacraments of Baptism and Holy Communion (which are understood as visible forms of the Word). Thus, both believe that parents should worship with their children. They should also baptize them and prepare them to participate in Holy Communion because the sacraments are commands of Christ that offer forgiveness of sins.[49] Luther and Grundtvig also emphasize that the sacraments offer comfort and renewal for daily life and throughout one's lifetime.

Furthermore, for both Luther and Grundtvig, parents should also read the Bible with children, pray with them, and teach them fundamentals of the faith. Although Grundtvig was critical of trying to nurture faith through book learning, he did not dismiss the importance of teaching children basic elements of the Christian faith, such as the Apostle's creed, the Lord's Prayer, and the meaning of the sacraments. Grundtvig wrote texts that outlined central elements of the faith for lay people, such as his *Den kristelige Børnelaerdom* [*Basic Christian Teachings*] (1855–1861) and *What Constitutes Authentic Christianity?* (1826).[50] He places particular importance on the Apostles' Creed, since he believes that this creed was passed down orally by early Christians even before the writings of the New Testament and has been held in common by all Christians for centuries. He also praises Luther for recognizing the importance of this Creed for all Christians, including children, since he places it in his *Small Catechism*.

> It is finally certain that no one elevated the simple childhood faith above all education more than Martin Luther. He could not show his reliance upon the foundation of the church more clearly than by tying

the apostolic confession inseparably to baptism and by placing it in the Small Catechism as the basis for childhood faith and childhood teaching.[51]

Like Luther himself, Grundtvig also recognizes that singing is a powerful and central vehicle for enlivening faith both at home and in the congregation. Luther and Grundtvig are both famous hymn writers who write eloquently about the power of music in the Christian life. In his preface to the *Large Catechism*, for example, Luther reminds readers that children do not retain Christian teachings from sermons alone; teaching must be supplemented with singing. He also claims in his preface to *Wittenberg Songbook* (1524) that good and pleasing music is good for the youth. He praises music by saying, "Next to the Word of God, music deserves the highest praise."[52] Grundtvig also speaks eloquently about the power of hymn singing and wrote over 1,500 hymns and songs, including biblical songs for children.[53] He believes the Word of God is made alive through hymns "... since sound is the life of the Word and tone is the power of the sound which reveals the Spirit."[54] As Thodberg notes, for Grundtvig, "It is above all else the hymn which testifies to the life of Christianity."[55] And as Broadbridge explains, "[Grundtvig] is still by far the best represented poet in the *Danish Hymnbook* (2002) with 253 out of 791 hymns, and in the *People's High School Songbook* (2006) with 86 hymns and songs out of 572."[56]

Even though his approach to the formation of children's faith is similar to Luther's in these and other ways, Grundtvig adds his "Nordic" elements of growth and vitality, spirit in action, and joyful presence in the world by greatly emphasizing spiritual growth, the importance of the living witness of the community, and the joy of faith in this life (not just the next). For him, a living faith, like a "true education," develops, grows, and thrives. Growth is a sign of God's grace. For Grundtvig, without spiritual growth and generation, there is only spiritual death. He underscores the growth and vitality of a living faith in many sermons, poems, and hymns, describing faith as regenerating, flourishing, nourishing, and growing.

For Grundtvig, faith grows and is nourished in the spiritual practices and living witness of the faith community. For him, the Word and Jesus himself are present in the living witness of the Church, with its spiritual practices of hearing the word, singing, baptism, and communion. All these practices and manifestations of the spirit are life giving, nourishing, and refreshing. As he says in one hymn, the Word of God has created all things, "consecrates" baptism, and "blesses" the bread and wine, and thereby "all souls refreshes." "This word imparts a happy lot,/ for child-giants [*barnekaemper*] in Your keeping,/ so they can laugh at mortal wounds,/ and over graves go leaping." The Word "turns water into wine /and deserts into gardens." The glory of *God's* kingdom on earth "glows like ears of corn, /like beechwoods all in motion, /its splendor like a choir of birds, /or sunrise from the ocean."[57] In another hymn, "Homely Your dwelling," he says in the church, the "Gracious Creator" welcomes all; gently nourishes "children small" so "they may flourish"; and He refreshes us "as we sing."[58]

Given his emphasis on the life-giving Word, religious practices, and the witness of the church, he criticized the common approach of focusing children's faith formation on the reading of Luther's *Small Catechism*. Although Grundtvig appreciates the text, he warns his contemporaries not to place Luther's (or any other individual Christian's) interpretation of Christianity above the Church's own living witness. "Luther's catechism, no more than any other book by an individual Christian teacher, even if it were by an apostle, can be compared to the witness and instruction that comes to us through the living voice of the Church."[59]

In the church community and through the sacraments, Grundtvig believes one also encounters the tangible and nourishing presence of Jesus. For example, one way he often speaks about the renewing power of baptism throughout life is in terms of returning to the arms of Jesus. Grundtvig wrote much about baptism, claiming "Jesus spoke of the water in baptism as an inseparable part of the spiritual regeneration without which one cannot anew become a child of God."[60] In several passages, Grundtvig speaks about the refreshing and renewing power of baptism as the ability to continually return to the loving embrace and arms of Jesus. In this hymn, for example, he states:

> See, His [Jesus'] arms are open wide,
> little ones find blessing!
> Children come to Jesus' side
> in His love progressing.
> Lord, baptize them now, we pray,
> let them grow to ponder
> their new birth, so from Your way
> they may never wander![61]

Grundtvig also believes that baptism (in which a child's forehead is "marked by the cross of Christ") offers a sense of ease, rest, and refuge in the face of life's troubles, fears, and sorrows, as can been seen in the popular baptismal hymn, "Dear child, sleep sweetly" [*Sov sødt, barnlille*]:

> Dear child, sleep sweetly,
> and rest now completely
> as birds in the trees
> as flowers at ease,
> asleep in their Father's safekeeping!
> "Come, angels," He said,
> "stand guard round the bed
> wherever my children lie sleeping!"

God's fingers have signed you,
His cross has defined you
On brow and on breast
a child by Him blessed.
No devil shall harm His creation!
In baptism's bowl
your heart and your soul
may rest in the hope of salvation...

The child who is sleeping
in angels' safekeeping
can rest safe and sound
as manna drips down;
no doubt you will find it tomorrow.
So clear-eyed and bright,
bid now your goodnight
to doubt and to fear and to sorrow.

Dear child, sleep sweetly,
and rest now completely,
and murmur that name
whose grace you can claim,
salvation to earth guaranteeing.
Sing, "Jesus is mine,
so fair and so fine,
the light and the life of my being!"[62]

Although it is often sung at baptismal services for infants, this hymn and many others refer to both children and adults as "children of God." As God's children, young and old find light, life, and comfort in relation to Jesus and are embraced in his loving arms. "Dear child, sleep sweetly" was written during a time of depression in Grundtvig's own life.[63] In another hymn "To bid this world farewell aright," he calls Jesus "brother sweet and Lord," imagines talking to Jesus "as friend to friend," and closes with these lines:

Before death with his icy gust
divides my spirit from my dust,
and leaves my heart-warmth dying,
I happily shall come to rest,
and like a child at mother's breast,
saved in Your arms be lying.[64]

Deeply connected to his view of Jesus, spiritual growth, and the living witness of the community, Grundtvig claims Christianity offers genuine gladness in this life (not just the next). He devotes much attention to the role of joy, gladness, and happiness in childhood and Christian life on earth. Grundtvig's vision of the joyous Christian life and spiritual growth is

expressed eloquently in his "Open Letter to My Children" (1839), probably written to his sons, Johan and Svend, in honor of their confirmation.[65]
He reflects on their childhood, his desires for their well-being, and how he
sought to nourish their growth in the School for Life, and he weeps and
laments for other boys who "grow tall," yet, because they were submitted
to the School for Death, have lost their youthful "vigor" so that "even as
they grow are growing small!" He hopes his children will strive beyond the
common but narrow goal of an "assured livelihood" and, instead, "show
ancient Nordic taste for great and glorious, for feats of giants followed by
heart's ease" and grow and flower in God's grace. The letter includes these
two famous verses, which are later included in perhaps his most famous
song, "A plain and cheerful, active life on earth":

> A plain and cheerful, active life on earth
> as such I would not for a king's life barter,
> the path enlightened by our fathers' worth,
> where high and low-born shared an equal charter;
> our eye, as it was made, to heaven turned,
> alert to beauty and by greatness greeted,
> yet knowing where the deepest longings burned
> alone by God's great light shall be completed.

> A path like this for all my kin I sought;
> on how to pave it for them I reflected,
> and when my searching soul grew overwrought,
> the Lord's Prayer to my heart its peace directed.
> The comfort of His truth I understand:
> our garden round with happiness is bordered,
> when mortal clay is laid in His good hand,
> and all things are in Nature's fashion ordered.[66]

Grundtvig's view of a "cheerful, active life on earth" is also in line with
his view of Jesus. He acknowledges that Jesus suffered and that life for all
human beings on earth involves hardships, and yet he sees in Jesus, and for
those who follow him, a life of joy and deeply rooted happiness. Although
he is indebted to Luther, he reproaches him, as one Grundtvig scholar states,
"for having placed too much emphasis on Jesus' suffering and too little
on the spiritual rebirth" in human beings and "the consequent growth in
God."[67] Grundtvig also criticizes his contemporary, Søren Kierkegaard, for
failing to appreciate the fellowship and joy of the Christian life on earth. As
Grundtvig states in a sermon from 1855:

> But this Christian life, this life in the Lord, is by no means what the
> false prophets proclaim, a life of constant sorrow and anguish, pain and
> plague, for such was not the life which our Lord Jesus Christ himself

lived on earth; and we shall become as he was in this world. Who can doubt that the life of our Lord Jesus Christ, despite his worldly lowliness, poverty, adversity, and temptation and, when his hour of suffering came, even pain and death, still was in its totality the most joyful, the most blissful human life that has been and even can be lived in this world.[68]

In his hymn, "O life lived in Christ!" Grundtvig speaks about this life as a life "redeemed from despair" and empowered by "radiant love." It is a life in which cold hearts are melted, and "Then filled with such gladness of heart we shall thrive /in being alive!"[69]

Conclusion

Although this chapter explores only a few of the seminal texts and hymns by Grundtvig translated into English, even this small sampling provides some indication of the breadth and depth of his thinking about children. By combining elements of Lutheranism with his understanding of "the Nordic," Grundtvig articulates a comprehensive and holistic view of children as made in the image of God; embodied spirits; vulnerable yet full of vitality; future citizens; creative and free individuals; and "glorious mysteries." Such ideas provide strong foundations for regarding children as fully human and valued members of families, communities, and the whole of humanity; treating them with kindness and respect; caring for their physical, intellectual, and spiritual needs; appreciating the importance of their cultural and religious identities; and honoring their own freedom, creativity, questions, and capacities to grow and flourish.

Furthermore, Grundtvig's ideas about children have many and varied sources. Certainly, he lived in a dynamic time in his own nation and in Europe, when Romantic and Enlightenment ideas were shaping perceptions of childhood and education. Yet his conception of childhood has many other direct sources of inspiration: biblical understandings of God and human beings; Lutheran beliefs, spiritual practices, and educational and musical traditions; and his notion of "Nordic" qualities of growth and vitality, spirit in action, and joyful presence in the world. This interweaving of Christian and Nordic sources is also fed by many other experiences, such as his happy childhood memories; his warm relationships to his children and wives; his love of creation and the Danish landscape; his work as a pastor; his sweeping view of Church and world history; his experience of human error and God's grace; and his own intimate relationship with Jesus.

By exploring Grundtvig's ideas on children, the chapter highlights the significance of child-related themes in his work and invites further study about childhood in the works of Grundtvig, and his influence in the Nordic countries. This chapter has tapped into only some of the best-known sources, and there is much to uncover about children in his published and unpublished works. Furthermore, although it is outside the scope of this chapter to chart the precise influences of Grundtvig's ideas about children, his hymns and songs have certainly enjoyed broad appeal in the Nordic countries and in other Lutheran communities around the world. Thus, in studying the history of childhood, more attention could be paid to his conceptions of children not only in his essays on education but also in his hymns and songs. Given his affirmation of children's full humanity and equality, more work could be done to understand his actual treatment of children, including his own, and his precise role in shaping commitments in Denmark and other Nordic countries to universal education, child protection, and children's rights.

Given the varied sources and multi-faceted dimensions of Grundtvig's views, the chapter illustrates the significance of exploring the multiple sources that shape conceptions of and commitments to children in other times and places, including today. Understanding conceptions of children, whether today or in the past, requires appreciating their varied dimensions and sources of inspiration. Yet, too often in the history of childhood or in public debates today, we are tempted to define views of children too narrowly or to attribute them to one or two sources alone. As the study of Grundtvig illustrates, European views of children as playful cannot be attributed solely to Romanticism, or children's rights and education primarily to the Enlightenment. Such notions had many and varied sources, including Christian beliefs and practices. The religious sources of Grundtvig's own thinking also underscore the importance of taking into account diverse religious perspectives (both within and across religious traditions), especially since religion was and is a force and factor in the lives of children in many parts of the world. Finally, Grundtvig's comprehensive view of children, which undergirded his strong commitment to them and their ability to thrive, invites all readers to reflect seriously on their own conceptions of and commitments to children in their own and other communities around the world.

Notes

1 For general introductions to Grundtvig in English see, for example, Allchin 1997 (2nd ed. 2016); Koch 1952; and Korsgaard 2014. See also Chapter 14 by Olsen in this volume.
2 See, for example, Bugge 1983: 216–17.
3 He speaks about "those happy childhood years," for example, in his poem, "Udby Have." Translated as "Our Garden at Udby" in *Living Wellsprings* (ed. Broadbridge 2015) (#105): 211–14.
4 The school was opened November 3, 1856 for adults and called "Marielyst" (literally, Marie's Pleasure), in honor of his late second wife, Marie Toft.
5 The names of his wives: Lise Blicher (d. 1851); Marie Toft (d. 1854); and Asta Reedtz (d. 1890). Names of his children: Johan (b. 1822); Svend (b. 1824); Meta (b. 1827); Frederik (b. 1854); and Asta (b. 1860).
6 Nielsen 1968: 160.
7 Several of these seminal texts have been recently edited by a team of scholars at the Grundtvig Study Center (Copenhagen), newly translated into English by Edward Broadbridge, and published in a series of Grundtvig's works in English. The first two published volumes in the five-volume series are: *The School for Life: N. F. S. Grundtivg on Education for the People* [hereafter abbreviated as

TSFL], (ed. Broadbridge, Warren and Jonas 2011); and *Living Wellsprings* [cited above and hereafter abbreviated as LWS].

8   Nielsen 1968: 169.
9   Grundtvig, *Selected Writings* (ed. Knudsen 1976: 106).
10 See, for example, LWS 170, 179 ("Whether low or high connected, children, women are respected"), 182.
11 Grundtvig, *Den kristelige Børnelaerdom* (sometimes translated into English as "Christian Childhood Teachings" but aimed at adults and also translated by Knudsen and others as "Basic Christian Teachings" in *Selected Writings*, 74).
12 LWS (#85), 183.
13 Grundtvig, *Selected Writings*, 75.
14 Grundtvig, *Selected Writings*, 77.
15 Grundtvig, *Nordic Mythology* in TSFL, 66.
16 Grundtvig, *The School for Life and the Academy in Soro* in TSFL, 195.
17 Grundtvig, *The School for Life and the Academy in Soro* in TSFL, 195.
18 Grundtvig, *The School for Life and the Academy in Soro* in TSFL, 196.
19 "Cheeks a-glowing" is a common image when Grundtvig describes children. See for example, "Open Letter to my Children," in TSFL, 259.
20 "To My Wife, Asta," in LWS (#161), 329.
21 "Be Welcome Again, God's Angels Bright" (1825), [*Velkommen igen, Guds engle små*], translated by J. C. Aaberg.
22 LWS (#111), 225.
23 Uffe Jonas, "Earth and Heaven, Be United: Grundtvig as poet and hymn-writer," in LWS, 61.
24 Jonas, "Earth and Heaven," 34.
25 Arden states that Grundtvig saw "the essential purpose of education is not to impart knowledge, but to awaken an understanding of and a zest for life, for all of life, for life whole and complete." Arden 1964: 97
26 LWS (#83), 179.
27 Grundtvig, *Nordic Mythology* in TSFL, 60.
28 "Open Letter to My Children" in TSFL, 260.
29 "Free School Song" in TSFL, 290–1.
30 LWS (#137), 282.
31 See the introduction to "On the Establishment of Sorø Academy as People's High School" in TSFL, 293.
32 From Grundtvig's *Within Living Memory* (1838); cited in Bugge 1983: 218.
33 From Grundtvig's *Within Living Memory* (1838); cited in Bugge 1983: 218.
34 Grundtvig, *Selected Writings*, 75.
35 For more on Grundtvig's view of education, see, for example, Bugge 1983: 211–25.
36 Grundtvig, *Nordic Mythology* in TSFL, 66–7.
37 *The School for Life and the Academy in Soro* in TSFL, 199–200.
38 LWS (#91), 191.
39 Jonas, "Heaven and Earth," in LWS 36.
40 "Rhymed Letter to Our Nordic Next-of-kin," in LWS (#116), 236.
41 "Rhymed Letter to Our Nordic Next-of-kin," in LWS (#116), 236.
42 Cited in TSFL, 347.
43 LWS (#139), 285.
44 LWS (#123), 249–51.
45 LWS (#123), 251.
46 Grundtvig, *What Constitutes Authentic Christianity?* (trans. and ed. Nielsen 1985: 96).
47 "Is Faith Truly a School Matter?" in TSFL, 124.
48 "Is Faith Truly a School Matter?" in TSFL, 125.
49 For more on Grundtvig's view of baptism, see Thodberg 1994.

50 N. F. S. Grundtvig, *What Constitutes Authentic Christianity?* In the "Translator's Preface," Nielsen states the text originally appeared in the monthly journal of theology called *Theologisk Maanedsskrift* in 1826 (Jan, Feb, March, June) and can be found in Grundtvig's *Udvalgte Skrifter* [Selected Works], vol IV. See "Translator's Preface," 12.

51 Grundtvig, *Selected Writings*, 18–19.

52 See Luther's foreword to "Georg Rhau's *Symphoniae iucundae*" (1538) in *Luther's Works* (ed. Pelikan and Lehmann 1955–1986, 53: 323).

53 See, for example, LWS (#101, 102, 103), 205–9. For a full discussion of Grundtvig's hymns, see Jonas, "Heaven and Earth," in LWS; and Thodberg 1953: 160–96.

54 "Sermon on Christmas Day" (1822). Cited by Thodberg 1953: 166.

55 Thodberg 1953: 167.

56 Broadbridge, "Preface" in LWS, 19. See also Chapter 14 by Olsen in this volume.

57 "The Kingdom of our Lord on Earth," LWS (#39), 119–20.

58 "Homely Your Dwelling," LWS (#56), 140–2.

59 N. F. S. Grundtvig, *Den kristelige Børnelaerdom* (3rd ed. 1883: 4). Quoted from the English trans. in Nielsen 1968: 168.

60 Grundtvig, *What Constitutes Authentic Christianity?* 51.

61 "See, His arms are open wide" [Herren straekker ud sin arm] in LWS, (#59), 144. The hymn in another translation is found in *Selected Writings*, 139; and in the hymnbook, *Evangelical Lutheran Worship*, Hymn #444.

62 LWS (#68), 155–6 (verses 1, 2, 6, and 7).

63 LWS, 350.

64 LWS (#64), 148–9.

65 "Open Letter to my Children," in TSFL, 259–63.

66 "Open Letter to my Children," in TSFL, 260. The popular song, "A plain and cheerful, active life on earth," can be found in TSFL, 263–4; and in LWS (#86), 184.

67 Lundgreen-Nielsen 2003: 244. Here Lundgreen-Nielsen refers to Grundtvig's *Christenhedens Syvstjerne* [The Pleiades of Christendom] (Copenhagen, 1860) and *Den nordiske Menighed* (stanzas 62–86).

68 Grundtvig, *Selected Writings*, 110 (the sermon was from the 8th Sunday after Trinity, 1855).

69 "O life lived in Christ!" [*O kristelighed*], LWS, 122–3.

8 "Educating Poor, Rich, and Dangerous Children"

The Birth of a Segregated School System in Nineteenth-Century Sweden

Bengt Sandin

Sweden today is known around the world for its commitment to child well-being and education for all children through its comprehensive social welfare system and its egalitarian school system. Sweden's school system aims to create equal educational opportunities for all children, regardless of their gender or socio-economic class. Sweden is internationally recognized for its long historical legacy of commitment to the welfare of the population based on social trust, consensus, and egalitarian values.

Less well known globally is that Sweden's current egalitarian educational system was created rather recently; it was introduced in the 1950s and accompanied by strong criticism of the former Swedish education system, commonly called the "parallel school system." This former system was characterized by the class and gender segregation of children, who were placed in different schools. This history is perhaps less well known because it runs contrary to common perceptions of the significance of egalitarian values in Scandinavia.

This chapter closely analyzes the story and the historic roots of the parallel school system in Sweden in the early nineteenth century. Although the parallel system was discontinued in the 1950s, by examining its history, the chapter reveals that education systems in Sweden were not founded on choices about schools or education alone, but on a variety of other institutional, social economic, and political factors. Many of these factors are left out of the history of education in Sweden or public debate today, although they were an important factor for the way in which the alternative policies shaped an egalitarian educational policy during the twentieth century.[1] Furthermore, the chapter illustrates how educational changes and the conflicts over the organization of schools also shaped the changing understanding of the meaning of childhood.[2]

This history is of particular relevance not only for Sweden but also for parts of the world where education systems struggle with issues such as child labor, poverty, and class and gender segregation in educational institutions. This specific history in Sweden prompts readers to explore the complex relationships that influence policy and public discourse about education and childhood and the role of education in children's lives both in the contemporary world and in the past.

Larger Historical Context

The historical context in which the parallel school system emerged is complex. During the early nineteenth century, education was in a process of major transformation. The Napoleonic War, economic blockades, and a major constitutional crisis in the wake of a coup d'état in Sweden, exemplify how urban authorities trying to come to grips with an increasing level of poverty reshaped the political landscape. The actors in this process were many, and from varying political levels: religious leaders, bishops, and local clergy; urban magistrates and central government elites; poor-relief authorities; and a few intellectual elites. Much of the interaction took place in a series of government inquiries about the organization of poor relief and education, and in public debates about the role of education among various political bodies, such as the magistracy and the church governance board, known as the "Consistory." At the core of these inquiries and the consequential political and administrative policies was the issue of the role and character of education in childhood.

A common religious educational base for the entire population had been a cornerstone of the Lutheran State Church since the seventeenth century but ran into difficulties in urban centers due to the large number of poor families.[3] The urban church schools could traditionally recruit students from a broad social stratum, because the schools encouraged children to beg or to solicit donations for their support in public places and in the church. Philanthropic educational institutions developed to care for the growing number of poor urban children, particularly illegitimate children and girls. The poor-relief authorities in Stockholm, as well as in Copenhagen and other European cities, struggled with questions of the deserving and undeserving poor, of who had legitimate claims to be supported, and an apparently growing number of street children.[4] Some of these children and their parents clearly understood schooling as a means of accessing the right to beg in the streets, or, for some parents, simply to keep children off the streets. For other children, schooling involved access to arithmetic, reading, and writing skills. These different childhood experiences gave rise to conflicts over the role of schools and the role of poor-relief authorities with regard to schools for the poor. For example, the middle class claimed that it was difficult to send children to the public schools in the cities, which tended to be filled with poor children. Still others held that education in public schools was too narrowly geared to ecclesiastical interests and too little to the needs of the middle classes.[5]

The debates in Sweden also addressed a general need to develop urban governance, community policing, and nation building. Swedish elites looked for models in the rest of Europe and the United States: the French secret police, the English police street patrols, the German poor relief and education, as well as the penitentiaries in Pennsylvania were presented as models.[6] The education reform movement in Europe also merged with the principle of nation building during the early nineteenth century, as Europe reorganized after the Congress of Vienna (1814–1815).[7]

What was the role of schools in all this turmoil? Why should children go to school, and could children from different socio-economic backgrounds go to the same schools? Were schools also appropriate for the education of working-class girls? Both the reorganization of the system of poor relief and changes in the urban and public schools had reason to address the plight of children, and both poor-relief authorities and public schools made claims to organize the life of children.

Poor Relief and School Reforms: Setting the Stage

Given this broader context, the chapter begins with how the poor-relief authorities claimed access to the schools to solve their problems with the poor at the same time as educational reforms aimed to improve education for the middle classes. In the first decades of the nineteenth century, poor relief in Stockholm, Gothenburg, and Malmö underwent a major reorganization, which included the establishment of schools.[8] Poor relief had been a constantly growing problem for decades. The main clientele of poor relief consisted of the sick, the elderly, and children. The authorities tried to limit the movement of poor families into towns by issuing city decrees.[9] These decrees shed some light on the living standards of the underclass and also on the repeated prohibitions and complaints about begging women and children that were heard in all the towns of Sweden in this period.[10]

The struggle of the urban authorities against the begging of families and children was part of the program of urban reorganization. The focus was on the policing of the communities in a broad sense, including street cleaning, the creation of parks and road networks, and so.[11] The education of paupers' children was regarded as a significant aspect of these reforms.[12] In major cities schools were founded both at the poorhouses and workhouses, as well as in the form of independent schools. Instruction in these schools was not limited to children who were inmates of institutions or whose parents received poor relief; it was also aimed at children whose parents could afford to provide for them but who were unable to manage their education.[13] This meant, among other things, that the ambitions of the poor-relief authority in Stockholm collided with other interests, because it aimed at sending poor children to the schools already operating in the capital. The existing schools were in a process of modernization in 1807, with the addition of learning languages and subjects such as geography, geometry, and the natural sciences.[14] The old 1724 school law had required pupils (boys) to be able to read on admission, but in 1807 these requirements became considerably more stringent.[15] These schools were no longer intended for boys with only a bare minimum knowledge of the catechism.

But these changes kindled the conflict over the role of education in the class society. Different schools were required for public officials, for the peasantry, and for the bourgeoisie. Some claimed that primary education must be the same for all children. Others argued that the public should fund only the education and training of public state officials, that is to say, implicitly only of middle- and upper-class boys. For this purpose, the secondary education system needed improvement, but other kinds of education were left to private interests.[16]

Thus, there were two social developments: one that addressed the issue of popular elementary education and also mobilized the poor-relief authorities; and another that addressed the issues brought to the fore by the development of secondary education and the demands of the middle classes. The link between these developments became a central problem. In 1812, a motion to establish comprehensive schools was rejected, but a national committee was set up to consider the design of the school system.[17] The Education Committee was established in 1816 and given the additional task of suggesting a reorganization of the Stockholm school system in light of the proposed national school ordinance. The challenges were not minor, since the education of paupers' boys and girls was a political issue of paramount importance that was addressed by poor-relief authorities and the school administration.[18] Let us take a closer look at the alternatives.

The Poor-Relief Ordinance of 1807: Keeping Children off the Streets and Away from the Family

In 1805, the governor established a "Committee of Inquiry" into poor relief in Stockholm.[19] The first initiative of the Committee was to suggest a prohibition on migration into the town. The Committee's main proposal for the organization of poor relief was approved in 1807, and it was applied for a trial period of three years.[20] A central directorate for poor relief was established and divided into four departments: provision, institutions for work and correction, education and tuition, and care of the sick.[21] Education was considered such a central element of poor relief that a special department was necessary; this would function under the directorate of the poor-relief administration to supervise the schools and pupils and, to some extent, the teachers as well. It was also intended to supervise "everything to do with the education and teaching of the poor children."[22] The various school institutions and their headmasters were also subordinate to the department. It was their duty to ensure that children attended schools and that teachers carried out their duties.[23]

The frightening conditions exposed by the inquiry into education justified such ambitions. As few as 800 pupils had places in the schools, and very few of these were reserved for girls, who were refused admission to church schools and schools at the garrisons. The number of educational institutions was generally insufficient in relation to "the amount of children whose parents can support them but cannot afford to pay for their education."[24] The expected influx of pupils would be dealt with by expanding the existing schools and, depending on needs, through the foundation of new poor schools. It was suggested that some schools should be reserved for girls. The poor schools would be under the supervision of the poor-relief authorities, while the schools already subordinate to the church government would remain so.[25] The proposed school ordinance recommended in a roundabout way that "all the children of both the male and the female sex whose education their parents, whether enrolled paupers or not, cannot afford to finance" should be educated.[26] This was a radical expansion of the school system for children of the lower classes and girls that was adopted with the Poor-Relief Ordinance of 1807.

The Committee believed that a key reason for poverty and misery was the negligent upbringing in poor families. The children grew up in inadequate environments, no matter where they spent their time: in the home, on the street, or in the factory. The way in which proletarian families reared their children failed to satisfy the members of the Committee, who criticized the parents on a number of points. One passage is worth quoting:

> As child rearing is today, it cannot but spoil the children of the poor ... wretchedness is grounded in childhood, the children grow up amidst their parents' quarrels, fights, and oaths, see their immoral way of life, and are not infrequently beaten, perhaps cursed as being a burden on their parents ... they are brought along to beg in the streets and are introduced to all the deceits and excesses associated with that. If they cannot be brought along they are either locked in or they are allowed to roam the streets without supervision and freely perform all the misdeeds they can think of. If they are finally sent to some school, this happens highly negligently and often rather late.[27]

The Committee concluded that the consequences were grave: "uneducated and immoral girls cannot become anything but unskilled, ever to fulfill the duties of a servant, much less those of a wife and mother."[28] The education of girls was evidently of special importance, precisely because the schools could not replace the parental care in the first years, specifically maternal care. For this reason, it was necessary for society to extend its care in equal measure to both genders.[29] The proletarian family was simply not considered competent for the task of bringing up children.

Children were to learn to read, write, and count, and they were to be taught religion, morals, general knowledge about nature, the laws of the fatherland, civic institutions, duties, and more. The skills were to include handwork of different kinds.[30] For example, the craft curriculum was justified in the report by pointing out the need to train children for their future lives so that, in the absence of other work, they could later support themselves using these skills. However, the work children did was not to be so hard that it suffocated "the cheerfulness of childhood years"; body and mind were to be developed alternately.[31] The argumentation also shows that the Committee did not consider the lower-class parents capable of giving their children the necessary practical or theoretical education. It also demonstrates an understanding of childhood as a separate, special, and valuable stage of life.

The education system outlined in the poor-relief plan for Stockholm meant not just economic sacrifices for the prosperous classes who financed it; it was also an attempt to limit the voluntary nature of the school and to create a compulsory institution. According to the statute, children were expected to continue their education without interruption, and both parents and children were required to obey the terms stipulated in the school regulations. Exceptions from school attendance could be granted only in extraordinary cases.[32] In the Committee's opinion, it was not possible to give the parents the freedom "to send their children there as they see fit ... and strictly compelled to send their children properly to school and only keep them from it in cases of extreme need, but never without due permission."[33] According to the curriculum, children were expected to go to school between their sixth and twelfth or thirteenth years. No pedagogical reasons were given for the duration of the schooling, but a very concrete explanation was offered. Children were to go to school until "they can generally be considered competent to enter into apprenticeship or service, but if there is no opportunity for this, they shall be occupied at the poor-relief workhouses ... as it could be hazardous to leave them on their own all at once."[34]

The ambitions of poor relief were twofold: to keep the children occupied until they could find a job, preferably in a way that simultaneously contributed to the family's economy and limited the costs of education; and to channel the children into working life without problems. The poor-relief authorities were thus supposed to keep a vigilant eye on children after they finished school. A further step in this direction was the Sunday school, where children would maintain their knowledge, and preferably expand it.[35] Education in the Sunday school was to take the form of public lectures after the church services, "chiefly on religion and morality, but also on civic duties."[36] The Committee envisaged a development toward an increased knowledge of Christianity thanks to the establishment of schools, which would be the basis of a more general education.[37] The new school would replace earlier attempts to compensate for inadequate parental instruction. Moreover, poor relief was to take over some of the traditional responsibility of parents and masters to ensure that children found work and that they were brought up to embrace the accepted norms of society. This was also stressed by the high frequency of examinations: children were to be examined publicly twice a year.[38]

Education and Leisure Time, Families, and Policing the Streets

The school system and the poor-relief institutions were to be supported by rules about the policing of the poor relief. These rules indicate that schools had been established chiefly to curb begging. To enforce the ban on begging, poor-relief bailiffs were employed and given an authority comparable to that of the police. In addition, strict instructions were issued to deal with people who were reported for or caught begging. For instance, individual citizens were forbidden to give alms, and the authorities imposed a ban on protecting beggars from the bailiff's raids.[39] Naturally, these rules were also aimed at parents or foster parents who "ordered or permitted or did not prevent their children from begging when it was in their power to do so." Parents would be punished as if they themselves had been begging.[40]

Other rules imposed stricter requirements for an orderly family life and regular school attendance, and parents were enjoined to put their children into apprenticeships when they were old enough. The Committee deemed it important to stress the necessity that parents fulfilled their duties. In the Committee's view, begging reflected the inability of families to socialize their children.[41]

The Committee submitted its report and a plan for the organization of poor relief on April 4, 1807, which was ratified and passed by the King in Council on August 12 that same year. By means of this statute, Stockholm acquired a poor-relief organization that included the whole city. It meant that the school system would be managed according to the principles suggested by the inquiry. The character of the church schools as a place for the poorest classes and girls was confirmed. The organization established for poor relief was to be tested over three years.[42]

Unfortunately, it is difficult to know how the school system worked during this trial period, because the documents of the Stockholm education department have not been preserved.[43] The minutes of the church's governing board, or Consistory, from 1808 show that serious attempts were made to put the school plan into practice. The church listed the schools that would be opened in the future to teach girls. One point in the school plan that generated some discontent among teachers was the decision that pupils should also be taught during vacations. Apart from the limited vacations around church holidays, children were only to be "free for 8 days after Midsummer," and this required a great deal of extra hours from the teachers. The Consistory flattered the teachers as much as possible when presenting the new regulation by admitting that: "it would be superfluous to show such enlightened and experienced men as the schoolteachers of Stockholm the dangers of the long vacations now customary in schools."[44]

Vacations had previously been restricted at some schools, but now such restrictions were to be more generally applied. It seems that the majority of teachers agreed to teach children during the vacations.[45] The church schools likewise reduced the length of vacations. This idea was not new. In 1792, the teachers at the public poor-relief institutions and the church schools were paid for teaching during the summer and winter vacations.[46] In other words, the model for study during vacations had been practiced even before the poor-relief committee's school plan was implemented.

The poor-relief authorities also drew up rules for the relationship between parents, children, and the school. Great importance was attached to regular attendance, cleanliness, and order. Parents were expected to help send their children to school and to be at the disposal of the teachers, when needed. At the same time, these rules clearly show that the parents were not viewed as positive examples for the children. The parental declaration about parents demonstrates that public education had definitively given up the exclusive pedagogical foundation on home instruction.[47] Other measures were taken to increase the system of control of catechetical knowledge; this may indicate that the more ambitious plans had not been fully successful. [48]

With regard to other parts of the poor-relief plan for children's education and the efforts to make them function, it is safe to assume that they could not be implemented during the short period in which the plan was enforced. This will be discussed in the following section.[49]

A School for all Classes, the Selected Few, or Both?

When the three-year trial period was over, the poor-relief organization was heavily criticized both with regard to finances and administration, and because no adequate solution had been found for problems of poor relief.[50] The economic crisis that struck the factories of Stockholm in 1809 had repercussions on the whole city. The inherent weakness of the poor-relief plan that had been launched was its failure to cover the most vulnerable and poverty-stricken groups in Stockholm.[51] The factories were expected to solve their own poor relief problems.[52] Since in reality they assumed no responsibility for all the workers they employed, the after effects of the crisis from 1809 onward revealed the defects in the organization of poor relief.

The information from the parishes about the organization of poor relief served as the basis for a report presented on February 19, 1812. The idea of a central organization was abandoned, but not the ambition to teach the poor. This document suggested that poor relief should be organized by the parish, and that the paupers of the garrisons should be looked after in their respective parishes. It claimed that this new type of organization of poor relief would have great advantages, such as a better control over the expenses, and a clearer estimation over the actual needs. However, it was considered desirable to level out the costs among the different parishes. This was the only sense in which poor relief was to be a shared concern.[53]

In another respect, however, the ideas in the earlier poor-relief plan were abandoned. On the basis of the report about poor relief from two parishes in Stockholm, which had won the approval of the Committee, the first constituent of a good poor relief was "the education of poor children." The only long-term way to curb the increase in poor-relief expenses was to attack these costs at the root by education. It was essential, according to the report, to counteract the immorality and the careless manner of child rearing in the lower classes.[54]

All those children who could not be cared for in the public children's homes were to be given the opportunity for instruction in "Christianity and good customs, and other knowledge of benefit to them."[55] Boys were to be taught in the church schools, which were designed as pedagogies and thus suited to the teaching of poor children. This meant that other children were referred to the "trivial schools." The proposal entailed that church schools would be wholly devoted to teaching the poorest children. The committee believed that, since the teachers at the church schools could count two years of merit for each year of service and were also well paid, they should continue to teach children during vacations, or else children "would mostly forget what they had learned during term and be left without supervision of their behavior." The teachers were to receive an additional salary from the poor-relief authorities.

Another point that the new proposal and the earlier education plan shared was that girls were to be trained for domestic tasks. In the future, it would remain an important "part of the supervision at these schools that children, according to their age, are accustomed and urged to attend public services and not go idle or hang around in the streets and other places where bad habits are learned."[56]

The statute issued on March 18, 1812 followed some of the recommendations of the report. The new statute ruled that only boys should be taught in the church schools, the garrison schools, and some other local schools. These schools would also be open to poor boys "insofar as space and other circumstances permitted."[57] It was obvious that the church schools would not function solely as an institution for the poorest children. The statute stated that these schools should "not only serve as places of education for those whose indigence or inclination seems to destine them for the lowest occupations among the working class but also, as hitherto, serve as elementary schools for those who wish to acquire more knowledge than the most indispensable."[58] The ordinance thus underlined the link between the church schools and the higher education system and recognized the contemporary demands of bourgeois educational institutions. Ultimately, the goal was to meet the increasing need among the bourgeoisie for elementary knowledge.[59]

The new ordinance, however, admitted that there was also a certain need for educational institutions for girls, and that instruction in homes and by clergy did not suffice. It pointed out that, assets permitting, schools should be opened to girls for "necessary instruction ... managed by competent persons, also of the female sex." The King in Council simultaneously consented to the use of poor-relief funds to improve teachers' salaries "in order to continue teaching during the vacations and thereby prevent idleness among the children, with its usually harmful consequences."[60]

This, like the 1807 plan, also meant a recognition that the socialization of children was not solely the concern of parents and priests. Teachers and the general public were given real responsibility, even outside the school walls. There was to be some supervision of children's manners and behavior, and they would not be allowed to roam the streets and alleys, visit eating houses, or indulge in objectionable habits. This supervision was the duty of the clergy, the teachers, and the poor-law directorates of the parishes, but other members of the congregations were also expected to watch over such matters. Girls, for instance, were expected to be supervised by married women.[61]

The ordinance was a departure from the fixed organization of control that the former directorate had wished to establish over the socialization of poor children through schooling and other educational activities, by restricting children's leisure time. It meant that the church schools' attempts to prioritize the teaching of poor children, both girls and boys, over that of middle-class boys, had failed. It was made clear that the schools were intended for both the poorest boys and the children who wanted to pursue a longer education. This was a recognition of the needs of a poor school and of a bourgeois educational institute, and the report from the Stockholm Parish Church School shows that the differing background of the pupils led to different patterns of occupation in leisure time: "The poor help their parents. At times they are employed and earn something by plaiting straw or making carders. The more prosperous, when they are not doing something for their parents, or doing their homework, play and amuse themselves."[62] The differences between childhoods were obvious, and shaped the varied relationships to one and the same school.

However, this situation was not acceptable, because rooming children from different backgrounds created tensions that could not be ignored. The headmaster of the same parish described the situation in the schools as follows:

> If school is to achieve its purpose as a *borgarskola* [a secondary school], we should be freed from having to accept children other than those who can read with any ability beforehand. Spelling and reading should be learned either from the parents themselves, or in private schools ... and in children's schools (elementary) established for the purpose.[63]

The statement indicated that the educational institutions had to be restructured to meet the demands of different kinds of childhoods. That problem was addressed and solved by the government in Stockholm in the coming years.

The Proposal of 1817: One School for the Poor and One School for the Rich—from Basic School to Intermediate School

The church schools in Stockholm were open to all children, regardless of social circumstances and class, and pupils (boys) could proceed from these schools to higher stages of education. In November 1816, the Education

Committee was given the task of reviewing the educational system in Stockholm in light of the proposals for a new national system.[64] The unclear status of the church schools was evidently a major reason why the proposal had to be reviewed and adapted to the special conditions prevailing in Stockholm. The Poor-Relief Ordinance of 1812 had made it clear that the church schools should not be designed exclusively for the needs of poor boys and girls.

The Education Committee went much farther. Its proposal, presented in 1817, pointed out the indeterminate character of the educational system in Stockholm. The church schools were to run as a kind of mixture of "pedagogy, commercial school, and school of learning," and there were complaints that they were poorly adapted to the "true" needs of the young people and the requirements of the times. This was why the schools had failed to win the confidence of the parents and the public. The children of the upper classes attended private boarding schools and institutions. The Committee felt obliged to make radical changes in the school system in Stockholm. It suggested establishing a high school ("*gymnasium*"), one higher and one lower school of learning, and two higher and three lower schools of commerce.[65] The church schools had to accept being transformed into "proper schools of learning and commerce at a higher level."

Naturally, this metamorphosis had major consequences for the management of the schools, the teachers' terms of service, salary, calculation of years of service and so on, but also for the recruitment of pupils. The proposal envisaged that the school ordinance was to regulate the conditions for admission to secondary school. Admission normally required a certain level of knowledge. These recommendations, however, were not sufficient, as the Committee states:

> At Stockholm Secondary School even stricter care will be necessary ... The intention can never be to fill these with such poor children as are clearly destined, by virtue of their natural aptitude and other circumstances, to seek their livelihood from manual work in mature age.[66]

The Committee's proposal did not go uncommented upon. The Stockholm Consistory protested vehemently against the way in which the city's educational system was described, and objected to the suggested organization and management. The Consistory argued that the church schools, without ceasing to function according to their original plan, had gradually acquired the role of preparing pupils for higher education. They also claimed that the schools could continue in the future, given better resources, to provide the general education necessary for all classes of society and sufficient for "the great mass." The Consistory also objected to the third kind of school that the Committee proposed, the schools of commerce. It believed such schools would achieve only a pernicious semi-education and an increase in the consumption of society's resources. There was also criticism of the suggested management of the schools; the Consistory felt that it was best suited to supervise the educational system.[67]

The Consistory's view represented a diametrically opposite outlook on education from that expressed in the Committee's proposal. Moreover, it reflected something much more important to the problem discussed here, namely, that the church schools "left it to private charity, and thus to uncertain chance, to provide a scant education to the broad masses."[68]

The Consistory proposed to strengthen the church schools so that they could function better as public institutions and as places of higher education for those who did not enter a trade. On this basis, it questioned the rules and criteria for admission. They argued that the future school staff would not possess the appropriate qualifications to decide who among the poor children should be admitted. Nor did the Consistory understand why those pupils who were "disadvantaged by nature and circumstances" should be excluded from schooling. This rule affected only the poorest pupils. The Consistory's verdict on the proposal was merciless and categorical: comparable educational principles could be found, as far as was known, only in China, where the authorities "acted consistently and systematically to *kill* the disadvantaged immediately after birth."[69]

The Consistory in Stockholm received no support for its views from the archbishop or from the Committee which it attacked. The archbishop said that the commercial schools were obviously needed to satisfy those youths who wished to enter "the military, trade, factories, and other occupations." They needed a knowledge of modern languages, mathematics, geography, and history, which could scarcely be achieved with the present design of the church schools. The admission requirements were reasonable. It was quite natural to exclude those who could not become useful citizens other than as members of the tradesmen's class.[70] In his definition of who should be excluded, the archbishop mocked the kind of pupils supported by the Consistory, stating:

> Disadvantaged by nature and circumstances are those without natural aptitude, deaf, dumb, and unable to speak properly, half-idiotic, afflicted with falling sickness and infectious diseases, so poor that they do not own clothes to cover the body, able-bodied ones who have run away from masters, from the flail and the plow, arriving from other dioceses without valid reasons ...[71]

The archbishop expressed no understanding of the need to arrange schooling for the poorest of the poor, or for those who did not live in a traditional household. He said nothing about the crucial point in the Consistory's statement, that is, about the need to provide "a scant education to the broad masses."[72]

The response from the Education Committee showed no sympathy either for the Consistory's defense of the church schools as schools for all social

classes.[73] The Committee asserted once again that the church schools had
no potential to be educational institutions of that kind. Nor did they want
to forbid private institutions, since such measures would have been against
"civic and personal freedom." The Committee maintained that since the
church schools "are hardly ever attended by any but those from the lower
classes, without plans for their future occupation, who are propelled by the
needs of the moment."[74]

It was thus necessary to separate the education of the bourgeoisie and
the proletariat. This conviction was, of course, closely connected to the
Committee's view of upbringing and education. The duties of the state with
respect to general education must not be mixed up with the responsibility
that rested with the local poor-relief and police authority. The problems in
big cities have a cure, but that "is not among the concerns incumbent on the
Education Committee, but rests with the Police Board, pastoral care, and
poor-relief."[75]

The decision of the King in Council on January 29, 1819, was based on
the proposal from the Education Committee.[76] Poor children were excluded
from the church schools. But the directorate of the education board soon
found that poor schools and craft schools were not sufficient for all the
children of paupers who turned up for lessons. It was therefore suggested
that three "public children's schools" should be established, and this proposal was approved on June 14, 1820. These schools were intended for poor
children "whose circumstances and disposition did not permit or require
any literary education." Instruction was to be given in reading, writing and
arithmetic, using the method of alternating teaching, so that as many children as possible could be taught by one teacher. Public children's schools
were established in the various parishes of Stockholm.[77]

Education—A Community Policing or an Educational Matter? Concluding Discussion

In the changing Swedish society in early 1800s, there was evidently a need
for schools for the new bourgeois strata, the groups of civil servants, and
the lower classes alike. Obviously, some social strata were looking for
skills that were useful for commercial or administrative careers, but also
for participation in the political arenas. The primary school had to address
the problematic situation of the lower-class families' social circumstances
and the traditional organization of church-controlled home education. The
inquiry into poor-relief and the debate about the school system gave some
idea about what people wanted to achieve through the expansion of schooling and different schools.

The poor-relief authority's program for teaching the poorest children was
driven by a desire to reduce begging, but it was no longer, as in the seventeenth century, a matter of regulating begging, but of eradicating it. The
measures proposed were intended to keep children off the streets and find

reliable means to ensure that they were given work. In the view of the poor-relief authority, the parents could not ensure that children observed prevailing norms or acquired sufficient practical knowledge.

The school system took over crucial parts of the educational role that had formally belonged to the households, in accordance with the Lutheran tradition. The schools were regarded as a means to counteract the consequences of the parents' lack of morality and inability to teach their children. The organization of the poor schools meant that they functioned as preparatory schools for the church schools. From 1807, the stricter requirements of knowledge for admission to the secondary schools ("trivial schools") could thus be circumvented. The new school ordinance of 1820, however, meant that the boundary between elementary education and the higher-level schools was emphasized.[78] This public discussion reflected the intentions of those involved in the shaping of the school system, but we have no clear documentation about how things looked in practice.[79]

The significance of the processes, however, lies not in the inability to separate the different social classes in the educational system, but in the establishment of a novel understanding which was separate from the communal Lutheran tradition. The Lutheran teaching was fundamentally the same for all social classes. Now, it was made clear that education was a different matter for children of the poor and the middle classes. The education of the poor was fundamentally a method of policing communities (moral education, keeping children off the streets) and providing social support (food, clothing, protection), while for other social classes it was the content of the education that mattered. A legacy for future debates on education was formed. The Swedish historical experience of urban schooling was a combination of liberalism and authoritarian governance across a spectrum that went from an ambition to create a common, basic school to the creation of separate educational streams, in order to control the population and to create avenues for individual careers.

This chapter has dealt with a formative moment in history that shaped the character of the national school system in Sweden. The policies, developed in the capital of the nation, cleared the path for a parallel education system with different schools for different social classes.

Almost instantly, critical voices against this system emerged from both liberal and traditional religious positions. The discourses about the use of education and the meaning of childhood from different points of views were not readily compatible. The termination of a radical three-year experiment, during which the church schools had been open for all children of all classes and both genders, and administrated by the poor-relief authority, seemed to have shaped the parameters of the discussion. The experiment with a school for all classes was discontinued, but it provided a legacy. It shaped the ideological basis for educational institutions in Sweden. Children of different social classes and gender had fundamentally different relationships to educational provisions. This idea gave birth to an on-going conflict over the role of education in the national narrative that lasted for 150 years and laid bare injustices that were unacceptable to large sections of the Swedish political establishment during the twentieth century but that proved resistant to change until the 1950s.[80]

History demonstrates that a commitment to an egalitarian social system, the creation of equal opportunities for children of all social classes, and the social trust, consensus, and egalitarian values for which Sweden is known are also embedded in a story of segregation, conflict, and a conviction that children of different classes had different social value and different futures. It also demonstrates that such cultures can be reversed and, indeed, can nurture democratic values.

Notes

1 See Chapters 9, 10 and 11by Rørvik, Markkola, and Garðarsdóttir in this volume.
2 Sandin 2012: 110–38, 128–35.
3 See Chapter 3 by Markussen in this volume.
4 Sandin 1986: 141–225; Larsen, Nørr, and Sonne 2013: 109–25, 376–8.
5 Sandin 1986: 141–225.
6 Sandin 1986: 175–261.
7 Sandin 2014: 91–100.
8 Fällström 1974: 3; Sandin 1986: 175–276.
9 Ibid. Stockholm 1805, Gothenburg 1806, and Malmö 1808; Müller 1906: 84–98.
10 Ibid.
11 von Schulzenheim 1801, *passim*; Rönnbeck 1807: 47–60, Ungberg 1840: 3–10.
12 Rönnbeck 1807: 48, 70–80; Fällström 1974: 3, 9, *passim*; *Kongl. majt:s*, 1797.
13 Rönnbeck 1807: 25 (appendices).
14 Agrell 1960: 11–15.
15 År 1724 och 1807 skolordningar, in Hall 1923: 38, 93, 77.
16 Sjöstrand 1965: 53–100.
17 Agrell 1960: 20.
18 Sjöstrand 1965: 70–90.
19 Müller 1906: 95–110.
20 Ibid.
21 Rönbeck 1807: 13.
22 Ibid.: 14.
23 Ibid.: 18.
24 Ibid.: 40–45, at 41.
25 Ibid.: 38–40.
26 Ibid.: 38.
27 Ibid.: 71.
28 Ibid.: 71–2.
29 Ibid.: 72–3.
30 Ibid.: 38.
31 Ibid.: 74.
32 Ibid.: 39–40, 75.
33 Ibid.: 75.
34 Ibid.: 40, 75.
35 Ibid.: 41.

36 Ibid.
37 Ibid.: 76.
38 Ibid.: 40–2.
39 Ibid.: 50–5.
40 Ibid.: 53.
41 Ibid.: 53–4.
42 Müller 1906: 97.
43 Ibid.: 112. The limited parts of the archive that have survived are kept in the National Archives, "Fattigvårdsutredningen 1805 arkiv" (RA).
44 Konsistorii Protokoll 7 and 13 June 1808, 68–72, at 69.
45 Ibid.
46 Uppgifter om skolan 1649–1793 (Klara School), 318.
47 Formulär till målsmansförbindelse i avseende på riktig hemfostran och de växandes ordentliga skolgång, 66.
48 Linge 1914: 23–30.
49 The report for 1811 stated that the plans for industrial schools had been abandoned in view of the economic situation, *Berättelse om fattigvården i Stockholm*: 3.
50 Müller 1906: 131–50.
51 Qvist 1960: 89–90, 325–50; Nyström 1955: 160.
52 Rönbeck 1807: 92–3.
53 "Betänkande om inrättningen af Stockholms fattigvård församlingsvis" (1812), *passim*.
54 Ibid.: 4–5.
55 Ibid.: 4–5, at 5.
56 Ibid.: 5.
57 *Underdånigt betänkande*, 37.
58 Ibid.
59 Silverstolpe 1813: 75–90.
60 *Underdånigt betänkade*, 37.
61 Ibid.
62 Rapport till uppfostringskommittén 1813, 376.
63 Rektors reformkrav och redogörelse 1813, 375–6.
64 Sjöstrand 1965: 70–1; Sleman 1948 (1949): 17–40; Rendahl 1974, *passim*. See also the chapters by Jacobsen and Rørvik in this volume.
65 Uppfostringskommitténs svar, 14 November 1818, 147ff.
66 Ibid.: 153–60.
67 Skrivelse från konsistoriet till Kungl. Majt, 9 September 1817, 157–60.
68 Ibid.: 160.
69 Ibid.: 162.
70 Ärkebiskopens skrivelse med anledning av konsistoriets inlaga till Kongl. Majt (Lindblom, 16 October 1817), 170–80.
71 Ibid.: 171.
72 Ibid.: 172–80.
73 Uppfostringskommitténs svar, 14 November 1818, 176–84.
74 Ibid.: 183.
75 Ibid.: 186–90.
76 Handlingar rörande den nya organisationen av Stockholms stads undervisningsverk (1819), 1–12; Sjöstrand 1965: 71.
77 Linge 1914: 32–3.
78 Linge 1914: 32, note 5; Rendahl 1974: 39–45.
79 Ahnlund and Skoglund 1937: 151–2.
80 Sandin 2012.

9   The Child in the Early Nineteenth-Century Norwegian School System

Thor Inge Rørvik

The Norwegian school system in its current form enjoys high esteem. It rests on the firm principle that elementary education should be uniform for the whole nation and thus bring together children from all different sections of the community. Secondary and higher education should not only be available to all qualified young persons, but also represent a genuine continuation of instruction from the elementary grades. The system as here described was a result of a series of educational reforms beginning in the 1860s, and it has been thoroughly studied by Norwegian school historians. In a book that is no longer new, but is up to now the only comprehensive presentation in English, this development is described as "the uniqueness and importance of the Norwegian social and educational evolution."[1]

Although traditional historical accounts of the emergence of Norway's current school system have provided valuable insights and given us access to an interesting and invaluable material, they have primarily focused on two topics: the school as an institution, and the emergence of a unified and targeted politics of education. When dealing with these topics, this history has often been divided into stages corresponding to the different school reforms, and the period prior to the 1860s has been very much neglected. In addition, by focusing on the school as an institution, these historical works have neglected to focus on the children themselves, those who actually were pupils in the schools.

Given the somewhat narrow scope of traditional approaches to the subject, this chapter will focus on the years between 1814 and 1860, and on what we can learn about the experiences of children in school. The reason for choosing this period is that, although it did not give birth to any school reforms, and scarcely had anything that could be characterized as a politics of education, there is much to learn from the sources about children and their experiences. By examining the history from this unusual angle, this chapter will show that because of the lack of a unified school system, there existed some markedly different conceptions of the child during this period, but also that one of these conceptions can without doubt be regarded as a "model child" for the later school reforms. To explain how this model child was sustained, as well as why other models disappeared, I begin with a sketch of the political and educational landscape in Norway in the decades after 1814. I will then briefly describe the child as pupil, before turning my attention to the different conceptions of the child current during this period. I hope to show that my approach to the topic—focusing on 1814–1860 and on the children in school, rather than on the school system itself—can serve as a valuable supplement to traditional school history.

The Political and Educational Landscape in Norway after 1814

As a result of the Napoleonic wars, the old Danish–Norwegian absolutist state was dissolved in 1814, and Norway was handed over to Sweden in the Treaty of Kiel. Denmark–Norway had joined Napoleon in 1807, whereas Sweden had joined the victorious side and was hence entitled to gain Norway as spoil. Before entering a union with Sweden, Norway chose to proclaim its independence, and in April 1814 a constituent assembly was convened to draft a constitution for the new state. Although Norway entered the unavoidable union with Sweden in the autumn of 1814, its new constitution was respected—which meant that Norway was free to conduct its own national affairs while Sweden handled its foreign affairs. Prescinding from the union with Sweden aside, what makes the Norwegian constitution such an interesting document is that it provided Norway with the features of an emerging democracy—and granted its citizens a degree of political participation hitherto unknown. Although voting rights were conditional on property ownership, the requirements were set low enough to make nearly half of the adult male population eligible to vote.[2] Thanks to the somewhat egalitarian system of landholding, many farmers were enfranchised and were also eligible for election to the national assembly. Given these rather widespread opportunities for a participation in Norwegian political life after 1814, it is worth noticing that the existing school system was "underdeveloped in an absolute sense" and that it would remain so in the decades to come.[3]

To understand the sudden discrepancy between a political system in need of educated participants and a school system unable to provide more than a rudimentary education for the majority of the population, we should bear in mind that Norway was close to bankruptcy in the first decades after 1814. The state simply could not afford to fund educational reform, even if this had been put forward as a political proposal. The fact that such proposals were never made was, however, due not only to economic reasons. The government continued to think in the categories of the old absolutist state, and hence did not regard itself as responsible for offering education on a broader level. Instead, it was content with the inherited school system, which kept alive a social stratification clearly at odds with the egalitarian principles in the new Norwegian constitution. According to this system, there were two kinds of schools: the elite Latin school for the children of higher civil servants, and the commoners' school for the rest of the population.

What is normally referred to as the "Latin school" was not an elementary school. It was a primary and secondary school joined together. The children would normally enter a Latin school at the age of seven, provided that they were already able to read and write, and they would leave the school at the age of eighteen by submitting to the so-called *examen artium*, a final examination arranged by the university, not by the school itself. This was because the Latin school itself was never regarded as an independent education, but rather as a preparatory stage toward further university studies. The most important subjects taught in the Latin schools were the classical languages, Greek and Latin.

Although the "commoners' school" no doubt can be regarded as everything the Latin school was not, we should note that it was not necessarily a school for commoners.[4] Throughout most of the country it was in fact the only educational option, unless the family had the means to have their children privately tutored. Although there were big differences in quality among the commoners' schools, they all faced the same task: to teach children from the age of seven how to read and write, and to provide them with whatever knowledge was considered necessary according to their social standing.

The Latin school and the commoners' school must, however, not be regarded as the twin pillars of a unified system, because such a system did not exist. They must rather be understood as two independent systems or as parts of a fragmented school system. In addition to these two types of school, there existed other less formal kinds of education. One was private tutoring; another was the vocational school or "burgher school." I shall not discuss these here, because the former must be regarded as an education outside of the institutionalized system, while the latter was not a separate school at this period, but was the provision of classes within the Latin school in non-classical subjects, such as mathematics, geography, and modern languages.[5] This narrows the scope down to two types of school and hence two types of children: the child in the Latin school and the child in the commoners' school.

While this short sketch of the Norwegian political landscape and its school system will serve as a background for an understanding of these two types of children, I must emphasize that references to actual children are sparse, both in the sources themselves and in the works of the school historians. When one sifts through the relevant legislation, deliberations, and regulations concerning the school system of the early nineteenth century, one finds page after page about school buildings, discipline, schedules, curricula, and teachers, but very little about the children themselves. No wonder that school historians, who rely heavily on these sources and are able to paint a vivid and broad picture of the Norwegian school system in the decades after 1814, have mostly done so without really including those who attended the schools. Some historians wonder whether it is actually possible to achieve anything more in this research, since the children or pupils are mute in the available sources.[6]

The Child as Pupil

To catch a glimpse of the two types of children in question, we must approach from a different angle than that which is prevalent in traditional school histories. Rather than scrutinizing the school system to find the children, it seems better to start with the children themselves, and regard schooling as an important part—but only a part—of their childhood. Using childhood as a point of departure may make it easier (1) to locate the children at the interface between two somewhat different sites of education—the home and the school— and (2) to pay due attention to the fact that for every child, the transition from being looked after by one's parents to being subjected to an institutionalized school system has always been a profoundly incisive experience. It must be added, however, that my focus here will not be on actual, living children but rather on some prevalent *conceptions* of children.

I take my starting point on a more foundational level than is normally done in more explicitly formulated educational theories.[7] This is all the more necessary, since many educational thinkers seem preoccupied with providing means to an end, that is, with ways or tools of teaching and learning. In what follows, it is not the means, but the end that is most interesting. Regardless of whether the child is struggling with Cicero's speeches in the Latin school or mumbling through biblical history in the commoners' school, they are both in a similar situation in that they are about to enter an alien world, which in the long run, thanks to their efforts, will hopefully not remain so.

Let us for the moment leave aside what children were supposed to learn by entering school, be it arithmetic, a classical language, or biblical history. One basic point is that this learning is something that the children cannot perform on their own, without supervision—they will need a guide. A second point is that the process of learning is, in a broader sense, not only a matter of acquiring knowledge or certain skills, but also a process of leaving something behind, namely the world of the uneducated child. As far as the former is concerned, this was an old insight for educational thinkers of the past. But it turned into a widespread and foundational principle in the Enlightenment, which has been recently described as an epoch with "a powerful drive to bring knowledge to the people, to restore clear sight to those blinded by superstition, to give wisdom to the ignorant—to pave the way for a progress defined as the passage from darkness to light, ignorance to knowledge."[8] Simplistic as this understanding may be, it catches something essential about the Enlightenment. And there is no doubt that this epoch's drive to bring knowledge to those in need of it involved the widespread use of certain ways of thinking that had until then been managed mostly by the church—a thinking that has later been termed "pastoral power."[9]

Pastoral Power and the Objective World

"Pastoral power" is a power exercised for the benefit and interest of those who are subordinate. What makes this power "pastoral" is the assumption that the subordinate lacks knowledge or other resources needed to have the right conduct of life, whereas the superiors are in possession not only of the knowledge required, but also of the means to control and distribute it. This distribution of knowledge is also concerned with how much knowledge the subordinate needs to be able to perform in keeping with his or her social standing. In a still stratified society like Norway in the decades after 1814, a surplus of knowledge was considered potentially dangerous, not only for society in general, but also for those for whom knowing more than what was deemed sufficient might easily prove a hindrance to their proper conduct of life. Pastoral power thus also involved a genuine care for subordinates, by preventing them from knowing things that would be more of a burden than a blessing.

What the children would learn by being subjected to the school's "pastoral power" can thus be described as *sufficient* knowledge of the objective world. Prescinding from the question of what is sufficient, the important thing to note here is that the world the children are about to enter is a world that is not their own—it is a given, *objective world*. And this is the other basic point here: for the children, gaining knowledge of this objective world is tantamount to entering a world that is not of their own making, unlike the world of their childhood, which the encounter with the objective world will ultimately make obsolete. When I speak of an objective world, I do not mean the world of natural phenomena, but a world that is objective in the sense that it is not made by a single individual: it is the social world as such.[10] And this world is not accessible through introspection: it has to be transmitted to new generations through mediators in a process that starts in the home and is intensified in the subsequent schooling. The aim of this process of transmission is to render the objective world transparent to the children and thus enable them to understand the fundamental message: "This is how things are done." One might perhaps, at least in theory, be able to locate the children's basic, formative experience of schooling in the penumbra of this message. But it is one thing to locate it; to actually find a testimony to the fragile experience of a vanishing childhood on the way to maturity is another thing. And to what extent can one expect children to be able to understand what this experience really amounts to?

It is important to emphasize that although the understanding of how things are done may count as *factual* knowledge, it is not theoretical knowledge of how the objective world actually functions. In a given society, theoretical knowledge will in fact be a small, and by no means the most important, part of what passes for knowledge. But this knowledge will be all the more important for those few whose task it is understand how everything hangs together. For the others, it is sufficient to know enough about the appropriate rules to be able to perform one's tasks and thereby fulfill society's expectations. This factual knowledge is limited in two senses: understanding the objective world is the same as understanding one's proper place inside it, and the knowledge necessary for keeping this place is distributed and regulated by those who know what is sufficient.[11] If this sounds harsh, it is nevertheless a perspective that is necessary for a more exact understanding of the Norwegian school system in the decades after 1814—and hence be able to identify the schoolchild in its historical context.

A Fragmented School System

Compared to the Danish and Swedish schools in existence in the early nineteenth century, there was nothing special about the Norwegian school system. This is not surprising, since until 1814, Denmark and Norway had been united in a single absolutist state, so that Norway was subject to an educational politics implemented from Copenhagen. The only difference worth noticing here is that in some commoners' schools, supervised by enlightened members of the Danish nobility, a certain attention seems to have been paid to modern pedagogical ideas and methods.[12] Apart from this, the commoners' schools in both Denmark and Norway were based on the law of 1736 that made confirmation compulsory. Accordingly, the backbone of elementary education in both countries was biblical history and Martin Luther's catechism. This seems to have been the case in Sweden also, both before and after the parliament (Riksdagen) passed a legislation which made elementary education (*allmän folkskola*) mandatory in 1842. In all three school systems, one finds the same wish to provide at least a minimal literacy to the largest possible part of the population. At the same time, the acquiring of this type of literacy, which in itself was regarded as beneficial, was to be properly supervised. It was no longer a question of controlling people by keeping them illiterate, but rather of controlling people by providing them with the proper amount of literacy and knowledge.

What nevertheless made the Norwegian school system special after 1814, was its apparent discrepancy vis-à-vis the new political system. One might have expected that the newly gained political freedom, bringing hitherto unknown possibilities of political participation, would result in a will to rejuvenate the school system to raise the general level of civic competence, but this did not happen. This is all the more puzzling because there seems to be nothing in the political system itself to hinder demands for a school reform. In addition to the economic problems I have mentioned, the hindrances were current ways of thinking—seemingly at odds with the new political system—which affected not only those with the political power necessary to implement reforms but also those with the political rights to demand them.

A characteristic feature of the Norwegian political system until the 1840s was the often passive role played by the state authorities. This was of course partly due to the threat of state bankruptcy, but in matters of education the state did not recognize its responsibility—with a notable exception for the Latin schools, of which there were only four nationwide in the years after 1814.[13] This attitude was without doubt anchored in the thinking of the old absolutist state, where the church had been the traditional cornerstone of mass primary schooling. And if the church was now to be relieved from this demanding enterprise, this was not because this should be handed over to the secular state. Instead, according to several influential spokesmen after 1814, it should be transferred back to the children's family, which was thus considered responsible for providing the kind of education appropriate for commoners' children.

Among these spokesmen was Niels Treschow (1751–1833), philosophy professor at the University of Christiania (now Oslo) and minister of church and education affairs from 1815 to 1825. As part of his administrative duties, in 1821 he drafted a special chapter concerning the commoners' school in a royal proposition for a new church law. In his philosophical writings, however, Treschow made it clear that the family ought to be the site of elementary education and that the schools for commoners that had already been established should be abolished in the near future. They had been erected for a purpose, but in an enlightened society they could no longer be considered necessary.

> Some artifice might be necessary in order to become natural again, or in order to return to the road one should never have abandoned. In this regard, institutions like the commoners' school could be useful; but then they should be only provisional, and by the industriousness of both the state and the church they should, as soon as possible, and with the help of the parents, be deemed superfluous.[14]

What Treschow is actually saying here is that although the commoners' school had already given generations of Norwegian children a basic education, the time had come for them, as adults, to themselves educate *their* children so that they achieve the same skills.[15] Teaching children to read and write, or giving them an elementary knowledge of biblical history and arithmetic, was not considered a duty of the state. Preposterous as Treschow's suggestions might seem to posterity, accustomed as it is to modern egalitarian school systems, they were not completely out of touch with reality. First, the then existing commoners' schools were in many cases a rather sorry sight, with teachers who themselves could barely read or write, and annual terms which in many cases lasted only a couple of months, or even weeks. Another significant problem was absence from school, with or without permission. There were several reasons for not sending one's children to school, but the most important was that they were needed at home as part of the family workforce.[16]

Equality and Difference

Whatever task the commoners' school was supposed to fulfill, and regardless of the degree to which it actually succeeded in doing so, there is no doubt that it was erected and supervised by the bourgeois middle class and thus sustained the values of a certain social level, with the aim of communicating an appropriate measure of these values to the level below. It is also important to remember that the whole idea of compulsory schooling had never been demanded by the commoners or the freeholder peasants: it was a decree from above—as were most decrees back in the absolutist state. It is thus tempting to suggest that, in addition to introducing children into the objective world mentioned above, the commoners' school *per se* represented an alien world to the very group that was supposed to join it, and it remained so for generations to come.[17]

When we reflect on how to catch a glimpse of the children's experiences, we can probably assume that parents' attitudes toward the schooling of their offspring contributed to that experience. In any case, there is no reason to doubt that reluctance to send their children to school was quite widespread; and that the reason for this was the belief the parental home was capable of providing children with all the education they needed. But what the home considered necessary to provide, and the tasks that Treschow, in his argument for entirely abolishing the commoners' school, suggested that the home would be able to fulfill, were two very different things.

Whether with the parents' blessing or despite their reluctance, the children who actually attended a commoners' school in the early nineteenth century and learned how to read by stuttering through the catechism, were at the same time also taught respect for the stratified society in which they were to become fully fledged members. In his explanation of the Fourth Commandment, Luther writes that children should not despise their "parents and superiors, nor provoke them to anger, but honor, serve, obey, love and esteem them."[18] Although the children had probably been told about obedience to their parents before entering school, the scope was now widened: all individuals had a designated place in an order initiated by God, and obedience to the secular authorities was therefore also obedience to God's will. There was, however, another, more egalitarian message in the lower school system. Although it was not so clearly stated, it was nevertheless equally important, because it contained the rationale upon which the school itself rested: all God's children are capable of living an equally Christian life; differences between persons are due only to *human* laws and inventions. For Luther, all believers were equally "priests," and thus all were to be able to read and interpret Scripture and to contribute to the common ground in their various vocations. The only difference in the human beings, in accordance with Luther himself, was a difference in "office and work"—not in "estate."[19]

Although an equilibrium between these two messages was possible in a Lutheran context, it could not be sustained in the long run as a viable position in the political context, which ended with the Norwegian government's acknowledgement of responsibility for the elementary education of its citizens. It was thus necessary to use the message of equality to overcome the traditional view that social stratification was a natural order, since only then could the education *of* citizens be an education of people *in order to become* citizens in a stricter sense—that is persons able to lead a life in society. In 1823, Johan Jørgen Broch (1791–1860), who was later to become a leading voice in the parliament's liberal opposition, stated clearly that the Norwegian political system in all its splendor would be worthless unless the people with the necessary skills and knowledge to maintain it were available. But the ability to lead a life in society was not a natural endowment; it was the result of an educational process that started in one's childhood:

> As is the case with all forms of life, the civic life develops from a germ, which we, though, must not regard as life's absolute beginning; because even if the evolution and its direction first become visible in what we normally regard as a germ, there can be no doubt that it has already developed rather far before reaching the point of attention that we have deliberately chosen. Already the fetus in the mother's womb has its own natural rights; even if the corresponding natural duties emerge only later, with the self-conscious higher life and its peculiar abilities.
>
> The child's life is the germ of life in society. The perfection of life in society presupposes the thorough molding of the child. If the germ rots, if it suffocates from the weed or lacks nutrition, what will the field then look like?[20]

What Broch and other like-minded liberals wanted was the means to form a solid political opposition able to stand up to the dominant class of civil servants. They were all aware that this presupposed a determined and focused education of persons who often belonged to a stratum of society that until then had achieved little more than an elementary schooling. Although they realized that this belonged to the future and hence made no pleas for a reform of the school system, they nevertheless affirmed that the discrepancy between the political system itself and the abilities deemed necessary for political participation was unsustainable.

Whereas Broch spoke from a position within the system, it was voices from outside the established political culture that finally made the state realize its responsibility for a broad elementary schooling. But far from heeding this call for a school reform, the Norwegian state tried to adopt a strategy that could silence threatening voices, whether present or future. To do this, the state aimed to make certain strata of society docile by schooling them. In the eyes of the political authorities, the very presence of social unrest showed that the current system of education was flawed and thus unable to help those most in need of discipline and guidance. The voices that had already been raised could be crushed by sheer power—and this is what actually happened in July 1851 when several members of a movement led by the former schoolmaster and newspaper editor, Marcus Thrane (1817–1890), were arrested. Looking back, it is difficult to see why this movement was considered to be such a dangerous force. But the authorities were no doubt alarmed by the social upheavals that had recently taken place on the European continent in 1848, when workers, artisans, and radical members of the burgher class joined forces and put up barricades in the streets of Paris and several other cities. Be that as it may, what the Thrane movement actually wanted was not to overturn society, but to improve the conditions of the commoners–that is, the underprivileged, the worker, and the tenant farmer.

In a petition signed by 13,000 artisans, tenant farmers, and small farmers delivered to the Crown in May 1850, the movement made several requests concerning the improvement of their conditions, including the improvement of elementary education. Thrane himself wanted the elementary school to be a civic instrument, a "social-political organ, the task of which would be to awaken the citizens to their responsibility and their rights in the social and political sphere."[21] Although the petition was ignored, the movement had made the authorities realize that the current elementary school system was insufficient—naturally, for quite other reasons than those the movement itself had listed. According to the government, the insufficiency was due either to a lack of rigor in the education provided by the existing schools, or to the fact that the school system itself was inadequate. There were too few schools to reach everyone who needed to be taught obedience and docility, and there were not enough qualified teachers. These problems could be solved only by a government that was willing to take responsibility for elementary education and hence formulate a coherent educational politics. This political will was now present, but for the time being, the aims of the entire enterprise were still at odds with the requests for a school capable of molding the children of commoners into the kind of competent citizens presupposed by the constitution. Here, on the threshold of a new (and ultimately loftier) epoch in Norwegian school history, it is time to direct our attention to the children again.

Little Cicero and Little Julius: The Latin School and the Commoners' School

As this brief historical overview has made clear, one should not look for *the* child in school, but rather look for different kinds of children in different kinds of school. Although there are some similarities between the Latin school and the commoners' school, since both are sites of education dedicated to molding children through the use of specific means, there were distinct differences. The aim of the commoners' school was to teach children to read and write; but children were not admitted to the Latin school unless they were already literate. Whereas the Latin school was both a primary and secondary school consisting of five different grades, each grade lasting for two years, the commoners' school was, when compared to later standards, not even a full primary school. And the child who entered the Latin school completed it as an adolescent, while the child who entered the commoners' school at the age of seven completed it as still a child. Given these differences, the questions are: *what* did these two types of children learn, *how* did they learn it—and not least, *why* should they learn it?

Let us begin with the Latin school. Why did this elite education—which it certainly was, at least in the sense that it was the best education available in the existing school system—have two dead languages as its foundation and its backbone? Here one should take into account that the most important thing about learning Latin was not necessarily the language skills. The point was that the skills developed by learning to master the rather difficult classical languages were skills that provided an access to the objective world in a twofold manner. The strenuous process of learning developed the mental and intellectual capabilities of the pupils and gave them a firm character, and their classical curriculum provided them with timeless moral ideals to be imitated.[22]

When they began their Latin exercises at the age of seven, the children entered upon an educational journey that later generations would no doubt find self-alienating. The Latin school aimed at the subjugation of any form of individuality in the pupils' mode of expression, to the advantage of the most homogenous cultural formation possible. It was the exterior, fixed and conventional form—what the great ancient rhetoricians like Cicero and Quintilian labeled *decorum*—that was the primary goal, not personal expression. The process of learning consisted of a strict formal training of memory and the powers of expression, in which the pupil learned to master the rules of classical eloquence to a degree unsurpassed in later times. This process can be divided into three steps: (1) internalization or rote memorization and application of rules and precepts; (2) digestion or mastery of the rules and examples through reading and imitation; and (3) externalization or independent composition and emulation of the models. At some point during this process, the children themselves vanish, and one can only speculate about their experiences prior to the moment when the young boys proudly wrote home to their fathers to show that they were now able to compose letters in the epistolary style of the classics.

Strict as it no doubt was, the educational process of the Latin school must not be regarded as unreasonable. The underlying idea was that if the pupils first learned what was considered the most difficult of subjects, they would no doubt be able to learn by themselves whatever else they might find necessary. And what could be a more adequate training for future civil servants than learning to disregard and suppress their subjective interests, emotions, and expressions in order to become fully fledged citizens of the objective world?

While the Latin school sent little Cicero on a journey to the alien world of classical antiquity, the commoners' school kept the children in their familiar world and tried to consolidate a rudimentary knowledge that the children already possessed. The reason for this procedure was rather obvious: these children were not supposed to achieve knowledge of the structures of the objective world. It was enough for them to understand that their world was part of a broader natural and social order.

The important question about the educational process in the commoners' school is not why the children were to learn to read by reading biblical history, but what else they were supposed to learn by doing so. Although there was no standard curriculum for the elementary education until the 1860s, the first sentence that the children would find when turning over the title page of their textbook, was probably the following quotation from Acts of the Apostles 8:30: "Understandest thou what thou readest?"[23] To provide the children with the necessary understanding, the book provided what the then current educational thinking referred to as exercises of sense. These were short texts with a content already familiar to the children to reflect on: where do we get grain, butter, milk, or linen from? The textbook then moved on to more general and abstract concepts related to moral and social matters:

> Duty is the name of what one ought to or must do. It is the child's duty to do what its parents wants; because that is what the child ought to do. It is the servants' duty to work for the master of the house. It is the duty of the master of the house to pay and feed his servants.[24]

Here the children were confronted with the objective world for the first time, before the textbook introduced the doubtless familiar tales from the Old Testament, beginning with God's creation of the world, Adam and Eve, and Cain and Abel. And what is this last tale about, if not the good child and the bad child? In the way these tales were organized, the protagonists often came in pairs—one good and one bad (e.g. David and Saul) or two bad persons, as in the tale of Ahab and Jezebel, which was presented to the children under the motto: "when two evil people join each other, they both become worse."[25] In this way, the biblical history merged into a more or less coherent picture of the objective world and provided the children with all the moral knowledge deemed necessary to become a responsible member of society.

The Model Child

Unlike the Latin school, there can be no doubt that the commoners' school sustained a picture of the model child to be imitated by its pupils. The Latin school consciously strove to suppress any signs of a still undisciplined or insecure way of thinking and expression, and thus forced its pupils into the adult-regulated world. Similarly, the educational process in the commoner's school aimed to mold the child into a well prepared, precise, obedient, docile, clean, and properly dressed individual—but it did so by letting the child remain a child: clearly a molded child, but still a child. An interesting example can be found in a little book by the pastor Hans Jacob Grøgaard

(1764–1836), who wrote most of the textbooks and alphabet books for the commoners' school until the 1840s. Here, the following tale about little Julius is presented to the reading children:

> Little Julius was a very loveable child. Not only was he obedient to his parents; he was also polite, affable and docile towards everyone else. He reflected on what he heard or read about, whether at school or at home. No one mastered his homework better than he, and his exercises showed diligence. What he did not understand, he inquired about; and he could therefore often answer when asked, even when his fellow pupils remained mute from ignorance. A friend of his parents, who often visited them, found pleasure in conversations with Julius and joy in his reasonable answers. Once the friend said to him: you have now started to learn about religion; if you can tell me where God is, I will give you a pear. Julius answered: if you can tell me where He is not, then I will give you two.[26]

It should be noted, however, that this book was not used in the commoners' school, but was meant as a reward for the clever child—or was given as a Christmas present to one's beloved offspring. In any case, it is clearly representative of what took place in the schools. In short, it was a book for the aspiring model child; and what this child was supposed find in it, was a mirror image of him- or herself. Would such children be able to recognize themselves in little Julius, behind the tale's middle-class coloring? And if they did so, would they realize that they had then made it as far as one could possibly go as a pupil of the commoners' school? Interesting as such speculations may be, they must remain speculations. But one cannot avoid such tales if one wants to look for the children's own experiences.

"I have become what they wanted me to become." If this is the experience of the model child, recognizing itself in little Julius, it would still be the experience of a happy few. Most of the children in the commoners' school would probably have other experiences, for instance the experience of not having to toil on the father's potato field. And perhaps the little girl who was provided with a few weeks of schooling for a couple of years experienced this as a rich and important time that would no doubt be of benefit for her later life?[27] These experiences are just as important and valid as the model child's satisfaction. What makes the tale of little Julius so interesting, however, is the fact that this explicitly stated model child had a long afterlife. If one were to expand the sketch of the Norwegian school system provided here, it would become obvious that whereas the little Cicero of the Latin school simply disappears in the latter part of the nineteenth century, the little Julius remains. Although his shape alters somewhat in the course of changing circumstances, the degree to which he persists should come as no surprise, since he was the model child for the school to educate in the future, regardless of the pedagogical ideas or curricula employed in this process. And he remained the ideal for the children themselves to imitate.

Conclusion

One of the tasks of this article has been to show that even before the Norwegian government acknowledged its responsibility for the schooling of children, the elementary education had already provided a viable conception of a model child. From the middle of the century, the attempt to shape children in this mold is clearly visible in the new textbooks of the elementary school. This suggests that the task of the school was no longer only to provide the children with the knowledge necessary to understand their place in society. They were also to develop a certain understanding of the homeland and hence become valuable citizen.[28] Whereas national awareness had previously not been regarded as a basic element that the school must develop, it was presented to the pupils from now on as an independent topic in the form of appealing narratives from Norwegian history.[29] The elementary school, as an institution, had now become an important part of the nation building project, and the model child, little Julius, was henceforth regarded as a future *Norwegian* citizen and was educated in order to become one. The discrepancy between the principles of the Norwegian constitution and an underdeveloped school system no longer existed.

Notes

1 Rust 1989: xi.
2 Half the adult male population was equivalent to 12 percent of the entire population. In comparison, even after the Reform Act in 1832 had introduced a series of wide-ranging changes to the electoral system, only 2 percent of the population of England was enfranchised. The corresponding number for Restoration France was a fraction of 1 percent. Cf. Valen and Katz 1964: 13.
3 Rust 1989: 15.
4 Until 1889, the expression "commoners' school" (Norwegian: *allmueskole*) was frequently used as a designation of the public elementary school. Later, this was referred to as simply the "public school" (Norwegian: *folkeskole*).
5 It should be noted that there is an interesting portrait of a privately tutored Norwegian child available to English readers in Stubhaug 2000. But Niels Henrik Abel (1802–1829), who was to become a famous mathematician, was not an average child; nor was his father, the pastor and Member of Parliament, Søren Georg Abel (1772–1820), an average father. It is also worth noticing that whereas Abel was tutored by his father until he could attend the upper classes in the Latin school at the age of thirteen, most children in similar situations were taught by hired private tutors who often lacked kindness.
6 Jordheim 1985: 97; see also Tveit 1983: 342.
7 A closer look at the pedagogical ideas circulating in Norway in the decades after 1814, will no doubt reveal that these primarily addressed questions concerning the Latin schools. One of the questions highlighted was which subjects were the best means of education, the classical languages or the more modern subjects (i.e. modern languages or various forms of natural science or mathematics).

And although one will also find in certain instances strains of modern pedagogical theories (philanthropy et al.), these theories were never applied to the other parts of the school system, such as the elementary schools or the commoners' schools.

8 Baumann 1989: 74.

9 This term was coined by the French philosopher Michel Foucault to explain how a certain structure of power, originating inside ecclesiastical institutions, spread to the rest of society at the very moment when these institutions seemed to be losing much of their traditional authority. Cf. Foucault 1982. See also Baumann 1989: 49–52.

10 The notion of the objective world used here is developed by Berger and Luckmann 1991: 59–61 and 129–47.

11 Berger and Luckmann 1991: 88.

12 One such school was the elementary school located at the estate of the Reventlow family at Brahetrolleborg on the island of Fyn. Erected in 1783, it was supervised by Count Johan Ludvig Reventlow (1751–1801), who was a strong supporter of the so-called "Socratic method"—i.e. the idea that elementary education should not be restricted to the work of memorization, but also appeal to the pupils' imagination and judgment. These pedagogical ideas later gained a certain foothold in the educational politics of the absolutist state—but, interestingly enough, not until they were considered relevant also for the teaching in the Latin schools. See also Chapter 3 by Markussen in this volume.

13 The Latin school was an old institution, originally run by the church and located close to the cathedrals—and hence officially referred to as "cathedral schools." Although the church no longer controlled the Latin schools in the period under scrutiny here, they remained located in the cathedral towns in the four Norwegian dioceses: Trondheim, Bergen, Stavanger, and Christiania (Oslo).

14 Treschow 1820: 229. Unless otherwise noticed, all translations are mine (TIR).

15 According to the oldest extant statistics concerning the elementary school from 1837, Treschow was no doubt overoptimistic: Whereas in the countryside 94 percent of the children attended school, 1 percent were privately tutored and 5 percent received no education at all, in the towns 52 percent attended school, 32 percent were privately tutored and 16 percent received no education at all. Cf. Jordheim 1985: 98. Private tutoring appears thus to have been an urban phenomenon. On a more general level, one should of course be careful not to read too much out of these numbers. For example, the fact that 94 percent of children in the countryside attended school may seem impressive, but "school" in this case can mean anything from a regularly schooling to an annual attendance of no more than a couple of weeks at an ambulatory school.

16 Other reasons for keeping the children at home were, according to a study of the school as a part of children's upbringing, that one's child was "at sea," "looking after the herd," "without proper clothing," "lack of food," or simply "bad weather." These examples are taken from commoners' schools in the countryside. Cf. Fauskanger 1989: 169.

17 This point is highlighted in Fauskanger 1989: 71.

18 Quoted from the abbreviated English translation of Pontoppidan *Explanation of Luther's Small Catecism*, 1900, 6. The unabridged Danish edition of Pontoppidan's catechism, originally published in 1737 and still in use in the Norwegian commoners' school throughout the nineteenth century, contained the entire Lutheran doctrine of secular authority.

19 Luther "Open Letter to the Christian Nobility of the German Nation Concerning the Reform of the Christian Estate" [1520], 3. Cf. Rust 1989: 16.

20 Broch, *Politiske Aphorismer* 1823, 50.

21 Rust 1989: 77. A recent study of the Thrane movement has emphasized that the demands for a strengthening of elementary schooling must be regarded as part of

broader program for popular enlightenment. According to Thrane himself, the core of the problem was not a lack of schooling, but the lack of relevant content in the schooling itself. He thus pleaded for an extension of the curriculum, which would include geography, history, and elementary natural science as well as an introduction to the most important parts of the current legislation. Cf. Ringvej 2014: 72–7.

22 The following brief sketch of the educational process of the Latin school is taken from Rørvik 2011.

23 The textbook referred to here is Grøgaard 1843. According to a historical study of the elementary textbook tradition in Norway, Grøgaard's textbook was widely used and had no competitors until the translation into Norwegian of older German textbooks in the 1840s. Sletvold 1971: 49–53.

24 Grøgaard 1843: 16.

25 Grøgaard 1843: 81. The tale of Ahab, the most wicked king of Israel, and his evil queen, Jezebel, is found in 1 Kings 16–22.

26 Grøgaard 1829: 51–2.

27 Fauskanger 1989: 71.

28 In what is probably the most important textbook from the period between 1860 and 1880, P. A. Jensen's *Læsebog for Folkeskolen og Folkehjemmet* [*Textbook for the Elementary School and the Home*] (1863), the content is organized under the following five headings: The Home, The Fatherland, The World, The Church, and "Miscellaneous."

29 For more about the "national" turn in nineteenth-century Norwegian textbooks, see Teilhaug 2012: 195–224. See also Sletvold 1971: 100–4.

10 Negotiating Family, Education, and Labor

Working-Class Children in Finland in the Nineteenth and Twentieth Centuries

Pirjo Markkola

The history of working-class children in Europe, including the Nordic countries, is often told as a sad story. It was shaped in the nineteenth century and retold in the course of the twentieth century. The common notions of working-class childhood brought to the fore the sad life of hungry, dirty laboring children wearing rags, living in urban slums, and smoky industrial neighborhoods. They were the children of the Industrial Revolution, suffering from undernourishment, poor housing, and dangerous work. The famous novels by the British author, Charles Dickens, and the fairy tales by the Danish Hans Christian Andersen, among others, have strengthened the image of suffering children in industrializing societies. However, this is not the whole story of the working-class children in Europe and in particular not in the Nordic countries.

Working-class children are probably the most invisible part of the working classes, not only in Finland but also more generally. This is evident in the historiography of the working classes. Research on working-class children and youth was introduced as part of the so-called "new histories," such as family history, new social history and women's history.[1] The rise of labor history, in particular, made the past of working-class men visible from the 1960s. Their agency, ambitions, and political culture were studied by an increasing number of historians throughout the Western world.[2] Scholars in women's history were soon criticizing labor history for its gender-blind approach and highlighted the experiences of working-class women.[3] Industrial child labor was studied relatively early, whereas other forms of child labor and childhood in general had to wait for scholarly attention.[4] Some scholars emphasize that industrialization did not necessarily, or in the long run, worsen children's lives.[5] They maintain that employment in factories provided lighter work, better nutrition, and increased demand for better education compared to the rural society from which the majority of the industrial working classes were recruited. The fate of working-class children is part of the wider debate on the impact of industrialization. Both the shadow of factories and the light of factories have been present in the interpretations presented by labor historians and social historians.[6]

New insights depend partly on the questions historians ask, partly on the source material. As the Nordic historians of childhood Ning de

Coninck-Smith, Bengt Sandin, and Ellen Schrumpf have stated, "empirical ignorance was not only caused by the priorities of the scholarly world as such, but also because the source material available for the history of child labor was scarce."[7] Current research, however, is relatively well informed on industrial child labor, but other aspects of working-class childhood still need to be analyzed. The gap in particular between rural and urban working classes, established in research, needs to be bridged, as the emerging industrial working classes were not separate from the rural laborers. In the context of the Nordic countries and Finland, in particular, working-class children formed a link between rural society and the emerging industrial society.[8] Children born to agricultural laborers may have grown up in urban working-class homes or become industrial workers themselves.

The aim of this chapter is to study working-class children in nineteenth- and early twentieth-century Finland. The study covers both children whose parents worked as paid laborers or hired servants in agriculture, and children who belonged to the urban working classes. By re-reading old sources and by using a range of new ones, I discuss the ways in which children's lives took shape in rural and urban environments in terms of work, school, and family life. How were family, education and labor negotiated in various settings? The most important old sources, often used in labor history, consist of social surveys. In the 1880s, several social surveys were carried out on rural society.[9] From the late 1890s, an increasing number of social surveys were conducted on industrial workers.[10] The Finnish social surveys deliberately followed British and German models of social inquiry. Focus on families, gave working-class children some visibility; for historians, the surveys provide material on working-class childhood. The household budget study by Factory Inspector Vera Hjelt, published in 1912, is particularly rich in information. Re-reading the Finnish social surveys makes working-class children visible. Other sources consist of ethnographical collections, oral histories, and archival records. If possible, children's perspective and agency are sought.

In terms of approach, I seek inspiration from the Nordic discussions on the child perspective.[11] The child perspective means that scholars focus on children and discuss social conditions from the point of view of children. I argue that some aspects of children's agency can be reconstructed while applying the child perspective to historical documents. By asking how social structures and processes had an impact on children, it is possible to come closer to the children's perspective, too.

Today, child labor and migration from rural to urban areas are topical issues in many countries. This chapter on the history of working-class children provides examples of similar experiences in the Nordic past. Moreover, it illustrates some complexities in the history of childhood. First, urban and rural should not be treated as two clear-cut entities. Intersections of rurality and industrialization shaped the lives of working-class children. Second, this chapter shows that the gender division of labor was not always as rigid as it has been claimed. Third, legislation on child labor, education, and poor relief seemed to impose limitations on children; however, even with labor legislation, children worked long hours. And fourth, child labor, children's education, and leisure depended on family situations. Therefore, to understand working-class childhood, we need to look at family strategies. In this chapter, I will first introduce rural working-class families in Finland and discuss rural children in terms of work, practical training, and learning. Then I will turn to the urban working classes and discuss children's work and education in an industrial setting.

Rural Working-Class Children

Let me first introduce ten-year-old Manta who in 1900 was hired by the wife of a tenant farmer to look after a six-month-old baby. At the age of eighty-five, Manta told her life-story to ethnographers.[12] Her father was a day laborer who often moved from one farm to another, and his daughter had no recollection of their ever having had a home of their own. For Manta, this baby minding marked the end of childhood and a transition toward adulthood, a common experience for rural working-class girls. The young girl, who was forced to go into domestic service in her home village, was first told that she could return to her parents in a couple of days. Manta missed her mother and tried to run away, but there was no return. As the only servant on the tenant farm she had to work, and the mistress of the house trained her in domestic work.

With her rural background, Manta represents the majority of working-class children in nineteenth and early twentieth-century Finland. When she entered the labor market, some 87 percent of Finns lived in rural areas. Agriculture was the main source of income for the majority of the Finnish population, but only less than half of the people living from agriculture gained their livelihood from independent farming. The agricultural population consisted of three major groups: 40 percent were freeholders, 40 percent were agricultural laborers, like Manta's father, and Manta's first employer belonged to the remaining 20 percent, who were tenant farmers (crofters).[13]

Agricultural working-class families formed three categories. The most stable category was formed by tenant farmers (crofters) who paid the rent for their farm in cash, by working for the landowner or in kind, for example, by providing agricultural products to the landowner. Tenant farms were almost always run by families; it was virtually impossible for a single man to gain access to land.[14] The input of children was needed in small-scale agriculture. This was particularly true if the tenant farmer could not afford to hire servants. Moreover, if the farm was too small to provide an adequate living, the children had to earn additional income as day laborers.

The second category, a relatively stable but poor one, consisted of the families of men in contracted annual service. Permanent employment did not guarantee adequate income and all family members were needed to earn extra income. The third and most vulnerable category of agricultural working-class families consisted of day laborers without permanent employment. As their income was extremely sporadic, women, men, and children had to accept whatever work was offered them.[15] These families were quick to send their children into domestic service as soon as the farmers would hire them. Manta's experience was shared by a huge number of children.

Moreover, many mothers of illegitimate children worked as contracted servants or day laborers. Typically, mothers sent their babies to foster care, for example, to their own parents, but some women were allowed to look after their children on the farm. These children were mentioned in some surveys and, of course, in registers of births, but otherwise they are invisible in documents.[16] Some oral histories indicate that illegitimate children followed their mothers, and some mothers have reported having a variety of practices to take care of their babies.[17] Far too often, caring problems were tragically resolved by the death of the child. In the nineteenth century, infant mortality was particularly high among illegitimate children, but death also visited married parents. In the early twentieth century, every fifth child died before reaching the age of five.[18]

In addition to agricultural laborers, such as Manta's family, other working-class families lived in rural communities. According to a survey in 1901, some 60 percent of rural working-class families earned their livelihoods from agriculture, and the remaining 40 percent worked in other sectors.[19] It was typical of industrialization in Finland that industrial communities were formed in the countryside. Not only sawmills but also textile factories and paper mills were founded there.[20] This development increased the number of industrial working-class families in rural areas. When we talk about rural working-class children, we are dealing with the experience of a significant number of Finnish children. To put it simply, there were more working-class children than farmers' children in rural Finland in the early twentieth century.[21]

In oral histories from rural communities, children living on the same farm or in the same village are often described as working together and even playing together, but the living conditions of working-class children and farmers' offspring differed.[22] Although some farming families were of limited means, they were seldom as poor as their laboring neighbors. Moreover, social surveys stated that the parents' social background determined how children were treated. In Eastern Finland, it was common practice for agricultural laborers to live under the same roof as the farm owners. Several families might share one living room. All the children played and worked together, but if something happened, "the children of laborers were always the scapegoats," as one social survey from the 1880s claimed.[23] Middle-class observers used children as examples of social distinctions among the rural population.

Learning to Work in Rural Society

In this section, children's work, practical training, and learning in rural areas are discussed. In the field of primary education, everyone was expected to get the rudiments of learning, and it was the responsibility of the family to provide this education. The grip of the Lutheran Church tightened in the eighteenth century, when confirmation education was introduced. In the nineteenth century, rural parishes established ambulatory schools in which children were to read ABC books and learn the Catechism by heart. Education was further promoted in the Primary School Act of 1866, which decreed that each city had to found a primary school for children between the ages of eight and fourteen.[24]

According to this new legislation it was possible to open primary schools in rural municipalities too, and there was an opportunity to get state support for schools, but the main responsibility for children's education remained with families. In rural areas, the Church continued to organize ambulatory schools.[25] Yet, in 1890, less than 20 percent of rural children attended primary school. In 1898, rural municipalities were divided into school districts and were ordered to establish a primary school in each district with more than thirty children who registered for primary education. However, it was not until 1906 that each municipality in Finland had founded at least one primary school.[26] Those rural children who did not attend primary school were most probably the children of agricultural laborers.

In rural society, it was important to teach all children to work. Both landowning and landless parents shared this norm. In the countryside, children helped their parents not only in their daily chores at home but also in agriculture and forestry. Again, there were differences based on the social status of parents. Insecurity put its stamp on the daily lives of working-class children, including their access to resources and skills. The poorest parents who did not own big animals such as cows and horses were not able to teach their children to milk or to ride and drive a horse. Moreover, parents with limited means seldom had access to the materials and tools needed in carpentry or other crafts. As far as women's skills were concerned, most poor housewives usually owned a spinning wheel, but a loom was a less common piece of property among them.[27] Entering service at a young age was the only chance for working-class boys and girls to acquire the skills needed in farming, animal husbandry, and domestic work.

Childhood in rural society was not only divided according to class and social status, it was also gendered. While everyone was supposed to learn to work, girls and boys were taught different skills. Gender division of labor was a structuring element of rural society, and it was considered important that girls and boys found their proper place in local society. Manta learned women's work, and later, at the age of eighty-five, she recalled that the mistress of the house had taught her important skills: "I was still crying, but then I stopped and started to work and she was a good teacher. She put me to bake with her and she put me to weave cloth and things like that. She was a good teacher but I had to work hard."[28]

Normative descriptions give a very rigid image of the gendered division of labor. Daily practices, norms, and symbols were intertwined in the processes in which girls were raised as women and boys were raised as men. Animal husbandry, in particular milking, was strictly the province of women and girls. Textile production and housekeeping were other feminine skills that girls were expected to acquire. Male children were taught men's work. Young boys had to learn how to cultivate and sow the field, harness a horse, produce and mend tools, fell trees, build, fish, and hunt. Oral histories and ethnographical accounts confirm this normative pattern, but they also reveal some differences between norms and practices.[29] In general, little boys helped their mothers in the cowshed and the kitchen, but they were not expected to learn to spin, weave, or milk cows. It is probable that these skills were rare among rural men, but it was not completely impossible for boys to be trained in women's work. Those mothers who did not have daughters taught women's skills to boys, and those parents without sons relied on girls to do men's work. In some circumstances, if it was possible to obtain extra income, for example, by knitting socks mothers taught their sons to knit.[30] Daily needs, practices, and opportunities shaped the lives of boys and girls.

Manta was a typical example of a rural working-class girl who had to find employment as a servant. From early on, working-class girls and boys were employed by their neighbors, first to help adults in child care or other work in the household, and later in animal husbandry and agricultural labor. Herding animals, for example, was commonly considered suitable work for children. One of the most common tasks allotted to children indicates not only the need for children's work in agrarian society but also the amount of trust involved in their contributions. Herding demanded some skills. Children had to learn how to keep the herd together, how to protect crops from the herd, and how to use the pasture as efficiently as possible.[31] In other words, they had to learn how to manage farming resources.

When it comes to children's skills and ability to work, they lacked physical strength and they lacked training accumulated through long experience. However, they possessed one resource that adults were usually lacking: they had time.[32] Time as a scarce but useful resource in rural society is one of the reasons why children's contributions were needed particularly during the summer season, when adults were busy sowing, harvesting, growing vegetables, and otherwise providing for the coming winter. A combination of many children with rather weak physical strength, some primary skills, and a lot of time, turned into a significant resource in rural society. In addition to herding, this resource was invaluable in picking berries, collecting firewood, fishing, and in helping adults in the field, cowshed, and garden.

From Rural to Urban Working-Class Childhood

Industrial towns represented a promise of a better life for rural working-class children. In this section, I bridge the rural and urban experience by presenting the story of Eeva, born in 1853. Her life story was recorded by an ethnographer in the 1930s.[33] Eeva was the daughter of a tenant farmer, but the farm was small and her family struggled on the edge of subsistence. Despite hard work and industrious parents, lack of food was a daily experience recalled by the eldest daughter. Six children were born; two of them succumbed. More setbacks were to come: "My mam died when I was eleven. The youngest child was in its second year. My mam died around Michaelmas. My dad brought my grandma to take care of the household. Grandma was no longer of any use. I had to look after the animals."[34]

After a year, their father remarried. Eeva and her nine-year-old sister left their home and went begging: "My dad did not force me, but he said it would be good to leave." Eeva's home was some seventy kilometers north-west of the industrial town of Tampere in Southern Finland, and the girls headed to their uncle, who worked in a cotton mill. They stayed a while in Tampere, got some food from their uncle's landlady and supplemented their living by begging in the streets. From Tampere, they continued to the surrounding countryside, then back to Tampere and the following summer they were back in their home village. Meanwhile "two siblings had starved to death." Eeva decided to seek employment in a cotton mill. She had come to know some young female factory workers whom she greatly admired. However, in the town, the first job of the country girl was to herd cows before the factory doors opened to her in the week of All Saints Day.[35] Eeva's life story in which her uncle's landlady was a key person, through whom she was integrated into the urban community, reveals crucial networks and family ties between urban and rural laborers.

Urban Childhood

For Eeva, the factory town and industrial labor represented an alternative to hunger, poverty, and destitution. In the nineteenth century, industrialization gradually widened the differences between rural villages and towns, which had been close to villages in size and economy. Factories came to employ working-class children; moreover, helping parents or running errands for neighbors were other forms of urban child labor. Some children were engaged in the street market, selling newspapers and working as shoe shiners.[36] Furthermore, as Eeva's example shows, begging and agricultural work were other options for children in the urban environment.

Tampere was the Finnish center of industrial child labor. In 1870, 1,480 Finnish minors, that is, children under the age of fifteen, were employed in factories; no less than 1,001 of them lived and worked in Tampere. Later, Tampere was remembered as "the sad fairy tale town of a thousand and one factory children."[37] A relatively large number of factory children is revealing about Finnish society in the 1860s and 1870s. In the late 1860s, a severe famine left many children orphaned. At the same time, soon after the famine, the textile industries recruited intensively. As the number of workers increased rapidly, children were hired alongside adult women and men. Therefore, it is not surprising that the share of minors in the total industrial labor force of Tampere was highest in 1870, some 29 percent. In 1885, their share was 14 percent and in 1900, only 4 percent.[38]

Following the model of other industrial nations, children's work in factories was regulated. In terms of paid labor, workers under eighteen years of age were divided into three categories by the Labor Protection Act of 1889. Those under twelve were not allowed to work in a factory, those aged twelve to fourteen were allowed to work seven hours a day, that is, a so-called half-day, and the daily working hours of young people aged fifteen to seventeen were restricted to fourteen.[39] Thus, in spite of labor legislation, children employed in factories worked long hours.

After the late 1890s the number of industrial child laborers fell and their share of industrial labor force was quite stable, around 4 to 5 percent in Tampere. Industrial child labor diminished but did not disappear. The first decisive turning point in industrial child labor took place before the passing of the Labor Protection Act and the 1890s spelled the second turning point. Yet the proportion of child laborers was relatively high in Tampere compared to other industrial areas in Finland, where the children's share of industrial workers dropped to less than 2 percent.[40]

For a more detailed picture of an urban working-class childhood, we can now turn to the social survey conducted by Factory Inspector Vera Hjelt. She applied the household budget method, well known in the international scholarly milieu of her time. Over a period of twelve months, the families participating in the survey recorded their daily incomes and expenditures. Despite the selective nature of the research method, many family budgets still reveal unemployment, poverty, and child labor.[41]

Parental unemployment sometimes forced children to leave school and seek a job. One working-class family from Tampere exemplifies the need for children's contributions. The family had seven children between one and twelve years of age. Their father was a forty-two-year-old unskilled worker in a cotton mill. The family could not live on his earned income. Vera Hjelt stated: "He must allow his wife and his eldest daughter, although she is only twelve years old, to get additional income for the family."[42] The eldest daughter worked five hours a day in the factory; every second day she attended school in the third class of the factory school. Her brothers, aged eight and eleven, attended primary school, and the parents wanted the younger children also to attend primary school. The eight-year-old boy sold daily newspapers and earned 20 to 30 pennies, which he gave to his mother. The survey does not mention the oldest brother's income, but it clearly emerges that the mother of seven children worked regularly.[43] In addition to occasional jobs, she worked as a bath attendant in a public sauna every Saturday. The earnings of the wife and children amounted to 38 percent of the family's income. It was a high proportion among the working-class families presented in the survey.

Another family of an unskilled worker was bedeviled by unemployment and the father's poor health.[44] The eldest daughter was twelve years old, and in spring 1909 she left primary school, most likely to look after her younger siblings, while their mother worked. Her eleven-year-old brother was due to get a job and leave home the following year. The mother of six children took in washing and sold fruit, flowers, and second hand furniture at the market. In 1909, the father was unemployed for seven weeks, and he reported that unemployment periods of two months were not unusual. The family still had their dreams. The parents told Hjelt that they dreamed of better employment, a more profitable market business, and children's future incomes. The parents reported that the older boys, aged eight and eleven, sometimes deposited their money in the bank. Moreover, the survey stated that the children were allowed to spend their own earnings: "the children often buy cakes and even sweeties with the money they have earned."[45] This family, with obviously limited means, seemed to give their children some freedom. Future expectations, for example, the eldest son's forthcoming job, helped them to survive.

A child of a single parent was more likely to go to work than a child with two adult providers. Among the pupils of Tampere Elementary School in the school year 1906–1907, every fifth child of a single mother earned money for the family. Compared to children whose father was present in the family, this was a high proportion. Only some 13 percent of children with two parents took up paid labor.[46] The family economy of a forty-three-year-old widow who worked as a washerwoman, cleaner, and seamstress, illustrates the life of a single parent. Her three children were not yet at school when their father died, and the youngest one was born soon after the father's death. In 1909, they all lived with their mother: the sons were eight and fifteen, the daughters ten and twelve. The eldest son was old enough to work full days, but he did not have a regular job: in 1909, the children's monthly income varied between 30 marks and 1 Mark. The eldest daughter was an unpaid trainee in a photographer's studio; after a year of training she would become an apprentice, earning 30 marks a month. This meant a vast improvement in the family's subsistence.[47]

The records of the municipal poor relief also reveal the difficulties single mothers encountered in providing for their children.[48] In some cases the combination of mother's factory work and children's earnings was too meagre to lift the family above the minimum level of subsistence. In Tampere, Maria worked in a paper mill and her twelve-year-old son worked half-days in a cotton factory. Matilda, for her part, supported her three minor children by working as an unskilled laborer in the summertime and by taking in washing in the winter, until she got her twelve-year-old son a half-day job at the factory. Josefina's twelve-year-old son also found work at the factory and could help his mother to support the four younger siblings. Their mother did sewing at home. Although their firstborns brought their earnings home, these mothers nevertheless had to seek poor relief. The same records reveal that children who refused to support their parents were clearly condemned by neighbors, authorities, and others involved in the case. This was in line with the Poor Law of 1879, according to which children and parents were to support each other.[49] The common disapproval indicates the norm among the working classes themselves: it was children's duty to contribute to family economy.

Both social surveys and the records of the poor relief indicate a variety of family strategies. First, children gave their earned income to their mother; second, by looking after their younger siblings they helped their parents to go to work. The third practice was found in the six-child family in which the children were allowed to spend their earned income and even deposit some money in the bank. This reveals a more independent position and different role of children in the family economy. The fact that the eldest son was also supposed to move out once he got a job could be interpreted as individualization, but maybe it was after all no more than the previously mentioned rural way of children easing their parents' subsistence concerns by moving out to work.

Children's life was further defined in legislation concerning factory work and primary education. According to the Labor Protection Act of 1889, minor workers without the completed primary school education had to be provided with tuition no less than twelve hours a week. This was reflected on in urban childhood. In 1890 in towns, over 75 percent of children attended primary school.[50] In the school year of 1906 to 1907 a survey on schoolchildren's work showed that many primary school pupils under the age of fifteen worked in the factories in Tampere. Almost all these children were between twelve and fourteen, and they made up about 14 percent of males and 20 percent of females of their age group still at school. Moreover, the number of minor factory workers was increased by the 217 pupils of the factory school.[51] The factory school was designed for those factory workers who were younger than fifteen years, and it functioned as part of Tampere municipal primary school. Children's time in industrial towns was increasingly divided between work and school. In this competition over children's time, entering the labor market gradually shifted toward a slightly older age and school took over the time of minors.

Concluding Remarks

This chapter discusses working-class childhood in rural and urban Finland in the nineteenth and early twentieth centuries, and indicates that rural and urban childhoods were interconnected among the working classes. Not only similar concerns but also a direct interconnectedness shaped the lives of rural and urban working-class children. Industrial work in towns became a realistic option for many rural children, and some of their rural skills, such as herding, could be used in the early industrial communities.

Working-class childhood can be told as a sad story: ten-year-old crying baby-sitter and twelve-year-old beggar walking some 100 kilometers with her younger sister, tell shocking stories of the working-class childhood. Yet, their stories are not without nuances. Both women recall their miseries, but both women also show remarkable agency. Little Manta stopped crying, started to work, and learned useful skills from her first employer.

Eeva decided to take up industrial work. For her, factory work represented a way out from misery, hunger, and begging.

Working-class families in nineteenth-century Finland were negotiating family, education, and labor. Both Manta's and Eeva's parents did what they could to plan the future of their children. Manta's parents found a job in domestic service for their daughter, Eeva's father asked his two daughters to leave home and find their bread elsewhere. In the case of Eeva, the significance of networks becomes obvious. Her uncle and her uncle's landlady helped the young girl to find food, housing, and employment in an industrial milieu.

Family subsistence was a key concern, and children were required to contribute to family economy. However, the ways in which children contributed differed. Rural working-class families had few options: sending children into service or to towns (or out to beg) was part of their survival repertoire. Urban families had better chances to keep their working children at home. Child labor represented a promise of a better future to working parents and their children, just as it did to the rural girls like Eeva.

A new dimension to working-class family strategies was added by the gradually expanding primary education in the nineteenth century. Learning to work was important both in rural and in urban settings, but the skills needed in the labor market were changing. As factory legislation demanded primary education, it became necessary to provide children with some formal education. Reading the ABC book and learning the Catechism by heart was no longer considered sufficient education. At the beginning of the twentieth century urban working-class families still struggled between family survival, children's primary education and child labor, but education was taking up more and more of children's time. In rural Finland, it took longer before school became the proper place for a working-class child. Manta, who stayed in rural areas, did not share the school experience of those working-class children who figured in the social surveys at the beginning of the twentieth century.

Notes

1 See, for example, Parr 1980; Humphries 1981.
2 See, for example, Thompson 1963; for Finland, see, for example, Haapala 1986.
3 See, for example, Tilly and Scott 1978; Kessler-Harris 1983; Roberts 1984; Bradbury 1987; for Sweden, see Wikander 1988; Hirdman 1992; for Finland, see Laine and Markkola 1989.
4 For the Nordic countries, see, for example, Olsson 1980; Bull 1982; Sandin 1986; Schrumpf 1997. On children's work in agriculture, see Sjöberg 1997.
5 For the most famous "pessimist" interpretation, see Thompson 1963: 331–49. For the "optimist" interpretations, see, for example, Pinchbeck and Hewitt 1973; Hartwell 1971. For more recent studies, see Cunningham 1990: 115–18. See also Horrell and Humphries 1995.
6 Haapala's seminal work (1986) was entitled *In the Light of the Factory*, and not "in the shadow of the factory" to summarise his interpretation of the Finnish workers' experience.

7 De Coninck-Smith, Sandin, and Schrumpf 1997.
8 Haapala 1986; Markkola 1994. See also Chapters 8, 11 and 19 by Sandin, Garðarsdóttir and Nykvist in this volume.
9 *Tutkimuksia taloudellisista oloista Suomen maaseudulla* (vol. 1–5, published in 1885–1893).
10 *Työtilastollisia tutkimuksia – Arbetsstatistiska Undersökningar* (vol. 1–16, published in 1903–1914).
11 Söderlind and Engwall 2008; cf. Andresen et al. 2011: 14. See also Chapters 8, 11 and 19 by Sandin, Garðarsdóttir and Nykvist in this volume.
12 University of Tampere. Folklife archives, tape 6667/1975.
13 Markkola 2003: 129.
14 Markkola and Östman 2012.
15 Gebhard 1916: 1.
16 For example, Lilius 1889: 13–14.
17 For oral histories, see, for example, Markkola 2003: 129–54.
18 Haapala 2003: 69.
19 Gebhard 1916: 7. The number of agricultural families was 115,000.
20 Ojala, Eloranta, and Jalava 2006.
21 Haapala 2003: 75.
22 Markkola 2003, based on oral histories and ethnographical collections describing rural life.
23 Lilius 1889: 11–12.
24 Hyyrö 2011: 327.
25 Hyyrö 2011: 328, 337–8.
26 Leino-Kaukiainen and Heikkinen 2011: 20–4.
27 Lilius 1889.
28 University of Tampere. Folklife archives, tape 6667/1975.
29 Finnish Literature Society. Folklore Archives, Ethnological descriptions SKS E 2, SKS E 70, SKS E 72, SKS E 77, SKS E 84a.
30 Markkola 2003: 133.
31 Sjögren 1997: 114–15.
32 Sjögren 1997: 117.
33 Interviews conducted by Unto Kanerva in the 1930s and early 1940s were published in 1946. Kanerva 1946: 30–2.
34 Kanerva 1946: 30.
35 Kanerva 1946: 32.
36 Markkola 1997; Cunningham 1990; Sandin 1986.
37 Markkola 1997: 85.
38 Haapala 1986, Appendix Table 4.
39 Suomen Asetuskokoelma 18/1889; Markkola 1997: 85.
40 Markkola 1997: 86.
41 Hjelt 1912.
42 Hjelt 1912: 127–30, 150–1.
43 Hjelt 1912: 128–30.
44 Hjelt 1912: 124–7, 148–9.
45 Hjelt 1912: 126.
46 Snellman 1908, 30–2.
47 Hjelt 1912: 114–16, 140–1.
48 The records of poor relief are analysed in Markkola 1994.
49 Markkola 1994: 109–11.
50 Hyyrö 2011: 327; Leino-Kaukiainen and Heikkinen 2011: 20–4.
51 Snellman 1908: 33–5.

11 Sheep, Fish, and School
Conflicting Arenas of Childhood in the Lives of Icelandic Children, 1900–1970

Ólöf Garðarsdóttir

Introduction

In 1961, Jónas B. Jónsson, Reykjavík's school inspector, discussed the prevailing views toward children's work in the Icelandic periodical *Menntamál (Educational Issues)*.[1] The article was based on a lecture that he delivered at a Nordic meeting of educators in Copenhagen the same year and was entitled "Leisure and Leisure Activities of Icelandic Youth." Jónsson stressed that the school year in Icelandic schools was considerably shorter than in the other Nordic countries. This was especially true for pupils ten years and older, as their school year was shorter than that of children younger than ten years. This arrangement had been introduced to meet the demand for the helping hands of youth during the labor intensive summer months in the farming sector. According to Jónsson, the short school year put pressure on many adolescents who were not able to meet the growing demands of academic performance in school. Furthermore, he stated that there was little time for leisure activities among Icelandic youth due to hard work. Despite his concerns, Jónsson expressed the pragmatic view that the extension of the school year was unrealistic. Both children and their parents were content with the existing situation and many parents were, according to Jónsson, of the opinion that the school year was too long as it was.

Jónsson's discussion of the short school year in Icelandic schools was by no means unique. I argue that the issue had been a recurrent theme in the discussion of Icelandic schools since the 1920s. Thus, educators and politicians, both at the central and local levels, frequently debated the matter. Normally, they referred to the uniqueness of the Icelandic economy and its great seasonal demand for the labor of youths both in rural areas and in the fishing villages.

This chapter addresses the views concerning school and children's work in Iceland during the period from 1900 to the 1960s. Official documents, such as school reports, legislation and discussions on bills that were introduced into the Icelandic parliament and the Reykjavík City Council are used together with articles in newspapers and periodicals. These sources bring to the fore the opinions expressed on the alleged uniqueness of Icelandic society and the features that were frequently used to explain the positive attitudes toward children's work in Iceland. The chapter deals with the debate concerning the relationship between school and work, a recurrent theme throughout the twentieth century. Although the entire period is taken up, the main focus in this chapter is on the 1960s, a period when child welfare and children's education were intensively debated in Icelandic society.

School and Work – Conflicting Arenas?

Throughout the western world the late nineteenth and the early twentieth centuries was a period when the importance of school in children's lives grew, and concurrently new restrictions were placed on children's opportunities to work.[2] Often these initiatives were met with suspicion by both parents and the children themselves.[3] In the initial stages of mass schooling, schools were generally run in harmony with the local economy, and school vacations were usually planned during the harvest season or other labor intensive periods.[4] Because the demand for the work of young people was generally more significant in the rural settings than in urban areas, the school year was considerably shorter in the countryside than in the towns and villages.

The early twentieth century was characterized by a growing centralization of school systems in the Nordic countries. Thus, attempts to organize schools in a uniform manner, irrespective of the geographical setting, became more common. According to educational authorities, all children should be entitled to full-time schooling, regardless of their social or geographical background.[5] The initiative to change prevailing schooling arrangements was frequently met with suspicion both by local authorities and individual families in rural areas.[6] The view that children's work was important for both the local economy and the moral development of the individual was widespread. The demand for full-time schooling disturbed this arrangement.

Differences in the organization of schools in the urban and rural areas came to be of relatively little importance in the Nordic countries during the interwar period with the exception of Iceland.[7] Even though children, especially children in rural areas, continued to play an important role in the family up until the post-war period, there was a wide-ranging consensus at that time that school was the most important arena for children and youths. However, in Iceland the differences between urban and rural areas prevailed, and even as late the 1990s the length of the school year varied in the countryside and towns.[8]

Schooling Arrangements in a Sparsely Populated Society

At the beginning of the twentieth century, Iceland was the least urbanized society among its Nordic neighbors. As late as 1900, only 20 percent of the population lived in towns and villages with more than 200 inhabitants (see Figure 11.1). With its 6,600 inhabitants Reykjavík was by far the largest

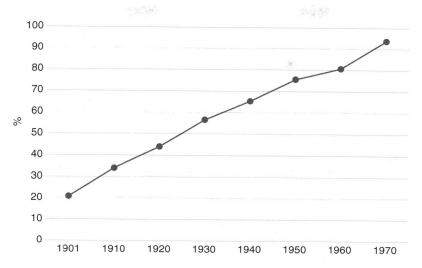

Figure 11.1 Population in towns and villages with 200 inhabitants or more. Iceland 1901–1970 (%).

town in Iceland at the time. The main source of livelihood for the majority of the population was raising animals, sheep farming being of vital importance in most rural areas. During the lambing season, starting in mid-May, there was intensive demand for the labor of children and youth. The fisheries constituted an important subsidiary source of income in rural areas, even in remote upland areas. A large fraction of farmhands in the southern and western part of the country spent a few weeks each year in coastal areas in late winter. The seasonal demand for surplus labor both in rural areas and coastal towns and villages caused a relatively intense seasonal migration between urban and rural areas. Temporary migration continued to be of importance well into second part of the twentieth century. Children and youths were an important part of this movement.

The settlement pattern outside the coastal towns and villages was characterized by isolated farms, and most often there were several kilometers between individual households. It goes without saying that under such conditions there were limited possibilities for the operation of schools in permanent school buildings. Contrary to many other sparsely populated societies in the Nordic countries (for example, northern Norway), boarding schools were not seen as an option in rural areas in Iceland until the late 1930s.[9] So-called "ambulatory schools" came to be the main school form in the rural setting until the second part of the twentieth century.[10]

The ambulatory school system was by no means unique for Iceland. When schooling was made compulsory in the Nordic countries, ambulatory schools were an important form of schooling in remote, sparsely populated areas. This was the case in Sweden, but less so in Norway where boarding schools were established at a relatively early date.[11] Iceland presents an extreme case in this respect, and ambulatory schools were still common in rural settings as late as the 1950s.[12]

The organization of the ambulatory schools differed from one school district to another. Most frequently ambulatory schools were operated on a temporary basis, moving between households in each school district. The schoolmaster travelled between the households where the school was operated. The school was generally held in the wealthiest farms in the community, and often a large fraction of the school children would stay in the household where the school was operated. During the first part of the twentieth century, the school year in the ambulatory schools for individual children was generally not longer than two months, as compared to a school year of between six and eight months in the permanent schools in towns and villages.[13] There was also a large difference in the organization and the curricular content of these different types of schools.

The early twentieth century was characterized by rapid population growth and a shift in the settlement pattern in Iceland as the fisheries increased in importance. Consequently, the share of the rural population declined, and the coastal towns and villages expanded. Between 1901 and 1930, the share of the population living in towns and villages with 200 inhabitants or more grew from 20 percent to more than 50 percent. By 1960 more than 80 percent of the inhabitants lived in towns and villages (Figure 11.1). This shift had important bearing upon schooling arrangements. With a denser settlement pattern, preconditions were created for running schools on a more permanent basis. There was thus a continuous decline in the proportion of children attending ambulatory schools.

More than half of all Icelandic children went to ambulatory schools in the beginning of the twentieth century. The same was true for one third of children in the 1930s, and in the 1950s the share fell below 10 percent (Figure 11.2). At that time, boarding schools had replaced ambulatory schools in the most remote rural areas to a large extent and during the late 1960s only a handful of Icelandic children went to ambulatory schools. It is, however, evident that traditional patterns with a clear division between schooling arrangements in urban and rural areas prevailed until the postwar period. This was especially true regarding the length of the school year. However, it must be borne in mind that, although the school year was considerably longer in towns and villages than was the case with rural areas, up until the 1990s the school year in urban areas in Iceland was considerably shorter than in the other Nordic countries. Another difference between town and countryside was school age. Until the 1930s, the compulsory school age in Iceland was ten to thirteen years. Parents were thus responsible to teach children to read before they started school at the age of ten. In Reykjavík and other larger towns, a large proportion of children under the age of ten attended school at the age of seven or eight as early as the outset of the twentieth century. As regards the rural areas, there was no radical

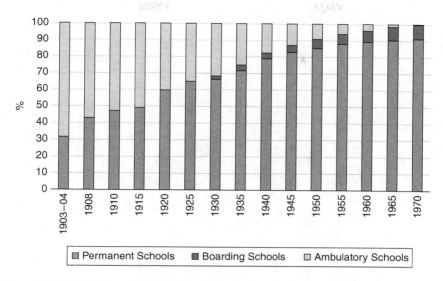

Figure 11.2 Distribution of school children by type of school 1908–1970 (%).

shift when school age was lowered to the age of seven in 1936, as individual school districts were allowed to apply for an exemption from the principle of school start at the age of seven.[14]

It was noted that during the early twentieth century, the Nordic countries were marked by an increased attempt to organize schools in a uniform way, irrespective of the geographic and economic setting.[15] Here Iceland was an exception. Thus, the first decades of the twentieth century were a period when prevailing structures were consolidated and ambulatory schools continued to be the main school type in rural areas. The decline in the proportion of children attending ambulatory schools was thus mainly because the rural population declined both in absolute numbers and as a proportion of the total population of Iceland. A comparison between Figure 11.1 and Figure 11.2 shows that the increase in the proportion of children going to permanent schools is almost identical to the share of the population living in towns and villages with more than 200 inhabitants.

Continuities and Changes and in the Views on the Role of the School

The discussion on the length of the school year was a recurrent theme in the Icelandic school debate from the 1920s until the 1990s. Initially the debate was chiefly restricted to the urban setting, as it was seen as self-evident that the school year in rural areas would be shorter than in towns and villages. To have a full-time school year was not seen as a feasible option in urban areas,

Figure 11.3 Feeding the animals. Dýrafjörður in the Vestfjords, North-Western Iceland 1962.
Source: Reykjavik Museum of Photography (Photographer: Gunnar Rúnar Ólafsson, (1917–1965).

not even in the capital of Reykjavík. In spite of the rapid urbanization during the first half of the twentieth century, the ties with the rural areas remained of great importance, and during the post-war era a large proportion of the inhabitants of towns and villages still had close relatives in rural areas. It was common for the people living in urban areas to work part of the year in the rural areas during labor intensive periods, in particular during the lambing and haying seasons.[16] A large majority of children living in towns and villages spent their entire summer holidays working in rural areas (Figure 11.3).[17] In the newly urbanized society, most children had close relatives in the rural areas, and it was seen as important that children had the opportunity to work in the rural areas during summers. Educators, such as Jónas B. Jónsson, who was referred to in the introduction of the chapter, and members of parliament often referred to the distinctiveness of the Icelandic economy when discussing the length of the school year. The tradition of sending children to work in rural areas during summer was an important reason for the long summer holidays in Iceland. An example from Reykjavík in the 1920s shows that even school authorities in the largest primary school in Iceland saw it as impossible to prolong the school year. In a school report dating from 1924, the extension of the school year in Reykjavík was said to be unrealistic for the following reasons:

> Many school children who stay in rural areas during the summer would in any case not come to school until the end of September and some

even later. Children working in rural areas would thus not return to the urban areas until after the sheep from the highlands were rounded up. Moreover, school girls helping out in homes in urban areas would be busy until the female servants came back from their work in the rural areas.[18]

The issue of the length of the school year was also raised in the parliamentary debate on a bill on education during the mid-1930s. Despite relatively important changes in the Icelandic school system, there was a consensus about the importance of work in the lives of young people.[19] According to the School Act that was issued by the parliament in 1936, there were notable differences in the length of school in rural and urban areas and among different age groups in the urban setting.[20] Children in boarding and ambulatory schools were supposed to have at least twelve to thirteen weeks of schooling each year. In the permanent schools, children below the age of ten were supposed to have at least thirty-three weeks of school a year, whereas children ten years and older were only offered a school year of twenty-four weeks.[21]

Children, ten years and older, thus did not start school until late September and ended in the beginning of May. It was apparently regarded as self-evident that a large majority of children that had reached the age of ten would leave the city when the lambing season began and not return home until the sheep had been collected from the highlands. Others, in particular those who had reached the age of thirteen or fourteen, were able to find work in the towns and villages. During the post-war era, few children in rural areas went to school for more than seven months a year, and as late as the 1980s the school year in rural areas rarely exceeded this figure. Even in the large urban centers, summer holidays were as long as three months until 1990.[22] The positive attitude toward children's work in Icelandic society is also reflected in the fact that young teenagers in fishing villages were occasionally exempted from school when there was a need for surplus labor in the freezing plants.[23]

In the mid-1940s, there was an extensive reorganization of the school system in Iceland. At that time, an effort was made to prolong the school year. According to the 1946 School Act, the school year in rural areas was to be seven months and in towns and villages "close to nine months."[24] The implementation of this rule proved more unrealistic than anticipated. As a matter of fact, the law gave individual school districts the right to determine the actual length of the school year. Furthermore, headmasters could exempt individual pupils from school from mid-May, if they were going to work in rural areas. In reality, the difference in the length of the school year for children ten years and older and those below ten years prevailed at least until the 1960s. This was even true for schools in Reykjavík where the school year for pupils ten years and older started at the end of September and ended in May until 1964.[25]

A few years after the 1946 Act was passed in the Icelandic parliament, Iceland was faced with an economic recession. How did educational authorities in Reykjavík react in a situation where flocks of children and youths went idle during the long summer holidays? At this point, authorities did not propose an extension of the school year. The solution to the problem of idle youths was the so-called "work schools." Work schools were established in most towns during the late 1940s and 1950s with the aim of meeting the demand for work for children and youths during the summer holidays.[26]

Despite a prevailing positive view toward children's work, the late 1950s and the 1960s came to be a period of growing interest in the reform of the Icelandic school system. At this time, the operation of the ambulatory schools in rural areas gradually came to an end, and the school year in rural areas was increased in length. The increased interest in school reforms was also reflected in the establishment of the Department of Educational Research and Development (*Skólarannsóknardeild*) within the Ministry of Education.[27] The early 1960s were also characterized by lively debate on educational issues, and the problem of children's work was raised several times in the parliament and the Reykjavík City Council, culminating in the passage of a new Act on Child Protection in 1966.[28] Contrary to other Nordic countries, there had been stipulations on children's work in the child protection legislation in Iceland since the 1930s. In the parliamentary debate of the bill on child protection in 1965, it was noted that as long as there was no labor protection legislation in Iceland, it was necessary to retain the stipulations on the limitations on children's working hours and the ban against children working in factories in the Child Protection Act.[29]

In the parliamentary debate on the limitations on children's work, it was pointed out that both youths and parents strongly opposed the limitation on working hours of children below the age of fifteen. It was maintained that for employers it proved hard to send the children home after eight hours work in the freezing plants.[30] A memorandum on the proposed bill on child protection in 1964 discusses numerous incidences of accidents involving children who had worked on dangerous machines (Figure 11.4). At the same time, it was pointed out that pragmatism was important when making laws regarding restrictions on work among children and youths. Both parents and children had positive views toward work and voiced demands to work long hours during their summer holidays.

There was a clear conflict between the views of left-wing and right-wing politicians in the discussions on children's work both in parliament and the Reykjavík City Council. In the parliamentary debate on the child protection legislation, Einar Olgeirsson and Alfreð Gíslason, both members of the Labour Party (*Alþýðubandalag*), brought up the question of children's work in freezing plants, pointing out that it was highly paradoxical that freezing plants were not defined as factories. Children as young as eleven or twelve years worked long hours in freezing plants without any opposition from their parents or the local authorities.[31]

Figure 11.4 Women and teenaged girls working side by side in the herring Industry. Seyðis-fjörður, East Iceland 1963.

Source: Reykjavik Museum of Photography (Gísli Sigurðsson, 1930–2010).

Similar criticism toward children's work in Reykjavík Harbor was expressed in the left-wing press in July 1965. A substantial proportion of the dock workers consisted of children and youths, and the youngest workers were, according to the workers' union *Dagsbrún,* eleven years old (Figure 11.5).[32] The left-wing newspaper *Þjóðviljinn* criticized the employment of young children in such dangerous working conditions and pointed out that a young boy had died in the summer in an accident at the harbor.[33] The conservative press was more positive toward the work of youths. It caught the attention of the press that a number of the workers were female. The girls interviewed by the conservative newspaper *Morgunblaðið* expressed a positive view toward the work in the harbor. "It's great," one of them said, "and much better pay than in the work school." Another girl commented, "[The boys] try to show their strength when we look at them."[34]

The introduction of this chapter presents the views of the educator Jónas B. Jónsson about the lack of feasibility in extending the school year for children above the age of nine. Jónsson's statements, made in 1961, must be viewed in light of the economic boom and dire need for seasonal reserve labor in the fishing industry in the early 1960s. In this respect, it is somewhat contradictory that only three years later, in 1964, it was decided by school authorities in Reykjavík that from then on, the school year in Reykjavík's compulsory school was extended to nine months.

Figure 11.5 Dock Work. Thirteen-year-old boys working in the Reykjavík harbor in 1964.

Source: Reykjavik Museum of Photography (Photographer: Jóhann Vilberg Árnason, 1942–1970).

This was met with suspicion by the children. Newspapers interviewed school children on the first day of school in September. The children who had worked in the rural areas during summer expressed their discontent with the new arrangement. They had been forced to leave the countryside before the sheep were rounded up from the highlands, which, according to the children, was the most exciting part of the work on farms. And next spring they would miss the lambing season.[35] "We are planning to go on strike!" one of the girls declared. "Yes we're going to march with banners," her friend replied. When the reporter asked them what they would put on the banners, a boy instantly replied: "We request a shorter school year!"

The extension of the school year in Reykjavík in 1964 was preceded by an inquiry on children's work. The inquiry was initiated by the Reykjavík School Board, and its objective was to evaluate the need for summer activities for children and youths. The 1962 inquiry was carried out in all schools in Reykjavík and included 89 percent of all children, aged twelve to fourteen, who were asked about their work during the previous summer (when they were eleven to thirteen years old) (Figure 11.6). The concept of work was by no means defined narrowly, and the inquiry was directed far beyond

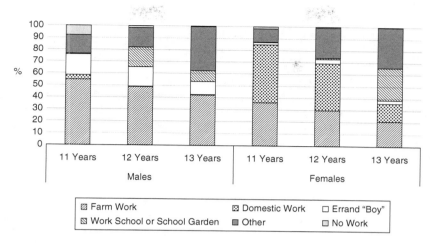

Figure 11.6 Summer jobs of Reykjavík youth by sex and age 1962 (%).

the scope of traditional labor. Thus, it included, for example, information on housework in the parental household.[36]

The study revealed that a tiny minority of all children maintained that they did not work during summer. Figure 11.3 shows that eleven-year-old boys were least likely to work, 8 percent reporting that they had not worked during preceding summer. The same was true for only 1.7 percent of the girls the same age. The older children were more likely to work than the younger ones; only 0.5 percent of fourteen-year-old boys and 0.3 percent of fourteen-year-old girls had not worked during the summer. Most children started working shortly after beginning the school break in May and stopped when school started in September. According to the children's own estimates, they had long working hours. More than two thirds maintained that they worked in excess of eight hours a day during the summer.

Conclusions

The period between 1900 and the early 1960s was a period of fundamental changes in Icelandic society. In the beginning of the twentieth century, Iceland was one of the least urbanized countries in the western world, where a large majority of the population lived in sparsely populated rural areas. During the first decades of the twentieth century, urbanization proceeded rapidly, and by 1930 more than half of the population lived in towns or villages. The same was true for more than 80 percent of the population in the 1960s.

These changes had an important bearing on the everyday life of children and youths in Iceland. In the beginning of the century, the playground of Icelandic youths was the rural setting, and most children attended ambulatory

schools that were operated only a few weeks each year. With modernization this changed, and schools became an increasingly important arena in
most children's lives. However, this chapter shows that up until the 1960s,
work continued to be of central importance in children's lives, even in the
large urban centers. The school year was thus organized with regard to the
needs of rural society so that, even in the capital area, school ended when
the lambing season started and began when the sheep had been rounded up
from the highlands. Thus, a large fraction of youths living in urban areas
was able to take part in those important events in rural areas. Other youths
would remain in the towns and villages working in the fishing industry.

The chapter shows that the 1960s were marked by growing concern about
the extensive work of school children. As indicated in the introduction of
this chapter, this was also a period of growing discussion on the importance
of extending the school year, at least in urban areas. Interestingly, these concerns were expressed during an economic boom when there was demand for
the contribution of the labor of children and youths. Thus, despite the dire
need for the reserve labor of youths, the school year was extended to nine
months in the compulsory schools in Reykjavík and in other large urban
areas. This was criticized by many children and their parents who regarded
work as important for the individual development of young people. Despite
this change, the school year in Iceland continued to be shorter than in the
other Nordic countries, and until the 1990s children in compulsory schools
continued to be able to find work during the long summer holidays.

Notes

1 Jónsson 1961: 237–44.
2 Cunningham 1995; Boli 1989.
3 de Coninck-Smith 1997: 129–59. See also Chapters 9 and 12 by Rørvik and
   Hansen in this volume.
4 Sjöberg 1996; de Coninck-Smith 1997; Schrumpf 2007; Garðarsdóttir 2009:
   173–85; Garðarsdóttir and Guttormsson 2014: 7–20.
5 Nissen 1973; Gjerløff and Faye Jacobsen 2014: 72–5.
6 Nissen 1973; Sjöberg 1996; de Coninck-Smith 1997.
7 Gjerløff and Faye Jacobsen: 72–5; de Coninck-Smith 1997.
8 Garðarsdóttir 1997: 160–85.
9 In many areas in northernmost part of Norway, boarding schools were relatively common in the early twentieth century. See, for example, Edvardsen 1989;
   Minde 2003: 121–46; Jensen 2005.
10 Guttormsson 1992; Garðarsdóttir and Guttormsson 2014; Kjartansson 2008b:
    44–63.
11 On ambulatory schools in northern Scandinavia, see Guttormsson 1992;
    Johansson 1992; Florin www.lararnashistoria.se/sites/www.lararnashistoria.
    se/files/artiklar/Fr%C3%A5n%20folkskola%20till%20grundskola_0.pdf.
    Folkskolorna redovisningsåret 1929–1930: 10–11.
12 Guttormsson 1992.
13 Garðarsdóttir and Guttormsson 2014: 8–11.
14 Garðarsdóttir and Guttormsson 2014: 11.

15 Edvardsen 1989; de Coninck-Smith 1997; Nissen 1973: 335–45; Sjöberg 1996: 123–4; Gjerløff and Faye Jacobsen 2014: 72–5.
16 Gunnlaugsson 1988: 153–4.
17 Garðarsdóttir 2009; Guttormsson 2008: 284–98.
18 *Skýrsla um Barnaskóla Reykjavíkur skólaárið 1923–1924* (Reykjavík 1925, 1) cited in Garðarsdóttir 2001: 424–5.
19 See Garðarsdóttir 1997.
20 Interestingly, there is only mention of boarding schools in rural areas despite the fact that only a small fraction of children in rural areas went to boarding school. Guttormsson 1992 has argued that the ambulatory schools were at the time seen as an archaic arrangement that was to be replaced by boarding schools.
21 *Lög um fræðslu barna* nr. 94/1936, article 7.
22 Garðarsdóttir 1997.
23 *Ibid*. For a discussion on the positive views toward work, see also Ólafsson 1996.
24 *Lög um fræðslu barna* nr. 34/1946.
25 Bernharðsson 1998: 209–10. See also Jónasson 2008: 114–17.
26 On the work schools, see Garðarsdóttir 1997.
27 Kjartansson 2008a: 90–98.
28 See Garðarsdóttir 1997.
29 *Alþingistíðindi* 1965, A-deild: 191.
30 *Ibid*.
31 *Alþingistíðindi* 1964, C-deild, 83–158. See also various legislative proposal by parliamentarians of the labour party (Margrét Sigurðardóttir and Lúðvík Jósefsson) on the right of children to rest during summer holidays. (Margrét Sigurðardóttir, Alþt. 1962, D, d351–357) and 1963 (Lúðvík Jósepsson, Alþt. 1963, D-deild, 786).
32 Dagsbrún mótmælir barnavinnu við Reykjavíkurhöfn (*Tíminn* 21 Júlí 1965: 16). Online at http://timarit.is/files/12014287.pdf#navpanes=1&view=FitH.
33 Unglingavinnan við höfnina, Þjóðviljinn 23. maí 1965: 1 and 12. Online at http://timarit.is/files/14289234.pdf#navpanes=1&view=FitH; http://timarit.is/view_page_init.jsp?issId=218382&pageId=2807501&lang=is&q=uppskipun. Barna- og unglingavinna við Reykjavíkurhöfn eykst enn, Þjóðviljinn 18. Júlí 1965: 1. Online at http://timarit.is/files/14291085.pdf#navpanes=1&view=FitH; Barnavinnan við höfnina til umræðu í borgarstjórn: Starfskilyrði barnaverndarnefndar verða að batna, Þjóðviljinn 23. September 1965: 2. Online at http://timarit.is/files/14293315.pdf#navpanes=1&view=FitH.
34 Þeir reyna að sýna kraftana, þegar við horfum á þá! Unglingsstúlkur og piltar í uppskipunarvinnu við höfnina, Morgunblaðið 17. Júlí 1965: 3. Online at http://timarit.is/files/16100262.pdf#navpanes=1&view=FitH.Unglingsstúlkur komnar í uppskipun, Tíminn 16. Júlí 1965: 16. Online at http://timarit.is/files/12014063.pdf#navpanes=1&view=FitH.
35 See Bernharðsson 1998: 209–10.
36 See Garðarsdóttir 2009.

12 Educational Policy and Boarding Schools for Indigenous Sami Children in Norway from 1700 to the Present

Ketil Lenert Hansen

Introduction

The Norwegian authorities began to take a serious interest in teaching and missionary work among the Sami at the beginning of the eighteenth century, at a period when the church had the responsibility for all education throughout Norway. A Missionary College was set up in 1714 with the task of organizing the missionary work among the Sami. Mission and education went hand in hand, and it was taken for granted from the very outset that the activity should be conducted in the Sami's own language, Sami.[1] Thirteen Sami mission districts were established in Norway, from Femund in the south right up to the Russian border in the north. At that time, the church had the responsibility of training teachers and missionaries, who were to preach the Christian message and teach Sami children.[2]

The Norwegian Parliament decided as early as 1822 to set up a "seminar for teacher training" in northern Norway, principally to cover the need for missionary work and the spread of information among the Sami people. The teacher training institution began its activity in 1826. It was founded in the northern coastal town of Harstad (68'N) and in 1848, moved further north to Tromsø (69'N), which is the largest town in northern Norway today and continues to offer teacher training at The Arctic University of Norway (UiT—The University of Tromsø). This seminar was intended not just to train Norwegian teachers who spoke Norwegian, but also to train Sami teachers who were fluent in Sami and could preach and teach among the Sami in their native language.[3]

There was a national political consensus in the first half of the nineteenth century about a fundamental presupposition: namely, that the education of each people must build on its own language, culture, and identity. If the intellectual development of the Sami was to be improved, it was necessary to elaborate a good Sami written language and translate teaching materials and the Bible into Sami. Pastor Nils Vibe Stockfleth (1787–1866) was a powerful advocate of giving the Sami a thorough instruction and education in Sami; this would make it possible to promote Christian knowledge, culture, and civilization among the Sami in the North.[4]

This view about education in the mother tongue was, however, replaced in the second half of the nineteenth century by the view that Sami children should learn the Norwegian language in school.[5] This meant the abandonment of the idea that education in their mother tongue was the best for Sami children and young people in school.

In this chapter, my focus will be on the boarding school system and the school policies toward the Sami people in Norway from 1700 to the present, and how the developments in this school system reflect changes in the views and policies of the national authorities. This is a history that has until recently been little known and studied. I shall first give a very brief overview of Sami living conditions, language, and history, and then present Sami thinking and practices regarding the formation of children. Building on various research projects—both old and new—and on the experiences and narratives of many Sami, I will give a presentation of the boarding school system and how it affected the lives and self-perceptions of Sami children. My focus will particularly be on Norwegian material, since the majority of Sami live there; however, I shall offer some side glances to the other Nordic countries.

The Sami Population

The Sami are the indigenous inhabitants of Scandinavia. They live in the northern regions of Fennoscandia, in what today comprises the northern areas of Norway, Sweden, Finland, and Russia's Kola Peninsula.

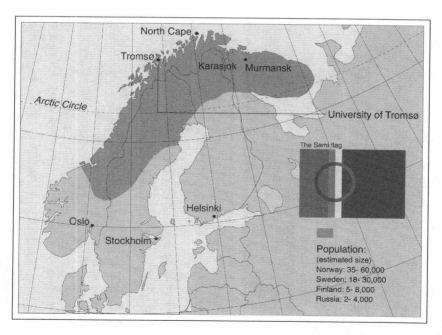

Figure 12.1 Map of the area of the Sami (called Sápmi).
© Ketil Lenert Hansen.

The Norwegian government has confirmed that the Sami are the indigenous people in Norway.[6] The Sami include several subgroups stratified by different geographical areas and dialects.[7] The size of the Sami population has been calculated to approximately 70,000–100,000, but estimates vary in accordance with criteria such as genetic heritage, mother tongue, and the personal sense of ethnicity. The largest population of Sami is believed to reside in Norway (60,000–70,000), followed by Sweden (20,000) and Finland (8,000), and with the lowest proportion residing in the Russian Kola Peninsula (2,000).[8] A lack of information about ethnicity in public registers makes it difficult to operate with minimum or maximum numbers, since there are no current demographic numbers that indicate the size of the Sami population.[9]

Sami engage in a variety of livelihoods today, including farming, fishing, trapping, sheep and reindeer breeding and herding. Although reindeer herding is considered to be "traditional" and a cultural marker of the Sami, it is in fact of relatively recent vintage: it developed in the sixteenth century. In Norway and Sweden (but not in Finland), semi-nomadic reindeer herding is an occupation strictly reserved to Sami by law.[10]

In Northern Norway, the population grew from 79,100 people in 1801 to 452,500 people in 1970. This growth was due to a surplus of births over deaths and to migration to this part of the country.[11] In 1970, Norway's northernmost county, Finnmark (where most of the Sami live), had a fertility rate of 3.2 children per woman, while the rate in the capital Oslo was 1.8 children.[12] At the end of the 1950s, the infant mortality rate in Finnmark and Troms, the two northernmost counties, were 28.0 and 32.3 per 1,000 living births respectively, and 16.7 in Oslo. Today, 5.6 and 6.4 children per 1,000 living births die in Finnmark and Troms, and 4.2 children per living births in Oslo.[13]

The Sami Language, and the Kven Population and Language

The Sami language belongs to the Finno-Ugric branch of the Uralic language family. The closest linguistic neighbors of the Sami are the Finns, the Karelians, and the Estonians.[14] There are ten different Sami dialects or languages, and the "borders" between them cross nation-state boundaries. Today, approximately 25,000 Sami individuals in Norway are proficient in the Sami language. About half of these can speak, read, and write Sami; for the others, Sami is primarily a spoken language only. It is difficult to present an exact distribution of the different dialects, but Northern Sami is clearly the most common of the Sami languages in Norway.[15] In addition to the Northern Sami, who constitute the largest Sami group, there are also smaller groups of Sami in Norway: the Southern Sami, the Skolt Sami or Eastern Sami, and the Lule Sami, with their own dialects that are partly very different from Northern Sami. The distinct linguistic traits are specific to the geographical regions where the groups live.[16]

The Sami language has had, and still has, a natural role in the traditional Sami community as an integral part of Sami social and cultural life.

The language has played a central role in the upbringing of Sami children, thanks to its value as mother tongue and bearer of culture. It is completely central to the transmission of Sami culture, values, identity, and knowledge from one generation to the next.[17]

In addition to a large Sami population and the majority Norwegian population, Northern Norway had, and still has, a third ethnic group, the Kvens, who migrated from Finland. The early eighteenth century was a period marked by war between Finland and Russia. The Finnish people were so impoverished that almost all who could do so fled to Northern Norway and Northern Sweden. Kvens speak their own language, which is an old Finnish language. They were granted minority status in Norway in 1996, and Kven was recognized as a minority language in Norway in 2005.[18] Kven and Sami children share a common history of strong linguistic and cultural assimilation at boarding schools.[19]

Perceptions of the Sami and their History

The Sami have a long, continuous historical relationship to the High North, which includes parts of contemporary Norway, Sweden, Finland, and Russia, where they developed viable trades as well as multiple distinct languages, culture, and identity. This goes back to the time before the area was colonized and before the formation of nation states on partially Sami soil. Until the 1970s, Sami history was mostly not deemed to belong to the field of historical studies.[20] The Sami were therefore commonly regarded as "a people without a history," and attitudes of this kind found expression when the national histories of the Nordic countries were written. The reason for neglecting the Sami people in historical accounts seems to be that the notion of "settlement" was made synonymous with the permanent farming settlements of the Norse peoples. The Sami adhered to a nomadic lifestyle, and their living areas were often marked on maps as "uninhabited."

In the nineteenth century, the origin of the Sami people was put on the scientific agenda, partly because of European social and scientific trends such as the growth of nationalism and the emergence of the theory of evolution. The nation-state ideal would affect how the Sami were regarded, and inevitably came to influence Sami living conditions. The view of the Sami "origin" changed considerably during the second half of the nineteenth century. Scholars had previously believed that the Sami were descendants of the populations that inhabited Scandinavia and northern Europe during the Stone Age. But this idea was dismissed, and the Sami were ascribed the more limited status of the indigenous population of northern Fennoscandia.[21]

This status was further marginalized in the early twentieth century, when several scientists began to question whether the Sami had a genuinely indigenous presence in the Nordic region: it was argued that they had in fact migrated to the Nordic region from the East, long after the current majority population had settled there.[22] In public discourse, the Sami were described as inferior, uncultured, and partly lacking material rights, and the goal became to assimilate the Sami and to make them change language and culture.[23]

This policy was inspired by nationalism, social Darwinism, and rationales of national security, and its goal was the cultural disintegration of Sami society. The gaining of Norwegian independence in 1814 did not immediately lead to a negative view of Sami language and culture, but from the mid-nineteenth century onwards, the national romanticism that flourished in Europe also spread to Norway, where "the love of one's country" was expressed primarily through idealizing the rural—settled—farming lifestyle.[24]

Toward the end of the nineteenth century, cultural researchers began to apply Darwin's tenet of the survival of the fittest to the increasing rivalry in human social development, thereby founding what we today call "social Darwinism." In its essence, it is a way of arranging ethnic groups according to the level of development that the peoples of the world are considered to have attained. On this model, the most "primitive" peoples are placed last, and the most "civilized" or "urbanized" first. In this thinking, the Sami and Kven were regarded as lagging behind the ethnic Norwegian population in terms of development.[25]

In relation to national security policies, the government worried about the potential for Finnish or Russian expansion into northern Norway. The fear of Finland and Russia was central to the wide-ranging Norwegianizing measures that were implemented: Norwegian policies in the 1860s found it necessary that the Sami and Kven should feel closely associated with Norway.[26] Finnish nationalism was seen to be growing strongly around this time, adding to the urgency of imposing the Norwegian allegiance on Finnish immigrants to northern Norway.[27]

These attitudes toward the Sami and the Kven populations had serious consequences for Sami and Kven children and the generations following in northern Norway. This was particularly the case in the schools and also the boarding schools, where the demand came to be made that these children should change their language, culture, and identity from Sami or Kven to Norwegian. Before dealing with this, however, I shall briefly present some central features in the Sami upbringing and formation of children.

The Education of Sami Children and Young People in the Sami Context

Sami children and young people received their education by sharing in adult life together with their parents. Knowledge was transmitted between the generations as children learned important skills and knowledge from their parents and grandparents. This was a great contrast to the modern Norwegian school system, where Sami pupils were taken away from their parents' everyday lives and placed in boarding schools to acquire education and knowledge in a culture that was unknown to most of the Sami, namely, Western culture and identity.[28]

There are considerable differences between the Sami and the Norwegian educational methods. Sami parents have traditionally been concerned with toughening their children: they often allow them a greater freedom and self-determination. The methods of control also differ. Parents can often tease and trick their children, or frighten them by means of supernatural beings, so that, for example, they will not go down to the water or expose themselves to other dangers. Sami parents have traditionally emphasized internal control rather than external control. The goal has been a child that is autonomous and hardy, and has inner strength. It is still customary in Sami families, for instance, that the children themselves decide when they shall eat and sleep. Sami parents have, in general, fewer rules and restrictions about games, mealtimes, and sleep. On the other hand, Sami parents' methods of control are often rougher than in Norwegian families, although this does not involve violence.[29]

The Sami education of children is often based on tactics that are more indirect than in Western culture. The child is coaxed and tricked into doing what one wants. The Sami education is also based on a high level of physical and psychological closeness. There is thus a balance between care and love, on the one hand, and the rough, free interaction, on the other—an equilibrium that makes this education well-suited for their future lives.[30]

The Sami pedagogue Asta Balto (b. 1948) emphasizes that the distinction between traditional and modern Sami knowledge and fundamental values lies in the contrast between informal socialization and acquisition of knowledge in the home environment—the traditional context, and socialization and education in formal educational institutions—the modern context. Traditional Sami knowledge is developed in daily routines, with a low level of socially imposed functional differentiation and specialization.[31]

Historically, the Sami have been a "people of nature" who lived both "in" and "off" nature. Since Sami society had

> habitual educational processes in regard to traditional knowledge, one may emphasize that this took place in a social and cultural context characterized by Sami primary industry activities and sustenance husbandry in a rudimentary, external and natural environment. It is commonly and widely believed that this setting has affected socialization, shaped how children were raised, and influenced educational processes for traditional knowledge in Sami society.[32]

The Sami regarded the school as of little profit to them. This is why many parents failed to send pupils to school or to boarding school even after attendance was made compulsory by law in 1739, and this was the case until World War II. Not only was the language of instruction foreign; the content of the schooling was very remote from the lives of the parents and grandparents in their local society. The school did not give the Sami pupils what they needed. From the perspective of the school, the pupils were

Figure 12.2 Sami Children were sent to boarding schools where they spoke only Norwegian. Here are nomadic Sami children from Karasjok, Finnmark, in 1950.

© Scanpix. Sverre Børretzen.

poorly prepared and were not motivated to learn the matters laid down by the curriculum and the law.[33]

Many Sami today say that the school is important—but there are other things that are more important. The school represents what is modern, while their work represents what is traditional. Most agree that education is important if one is to get a job in Norwegian society, but in Sami society much of the transfer of knowledge still takes place between the generations, especially within the primary Sami industry, reindeer herding. One can have the impression that the school is less important for Sami boys than for Sami girls. Nor are the boys as strongly motivated as the girls to attend secondary school for between three and five years, and then go on to further studies at college or university. The boys take a year off, work a little, or attend shorter courses at secondary school to establish a freedom vis-à-vis the school. For some, the school can be used for training within the primary industry or in other occupations.[34]

The School Situation for Sami in Northern Norway (1700–ca. 1900)

In the period from 1700 to 1850, Sami school and church history are two sides of the same coin, because it was the church that took on the responsibility for teaching the Sami in northern Norway. School attendance was difficult in southern Norway, but it was much harder in northern Norway.

Sami children encountered a school that was very different from their own culture, language, and identity. Even today, linguistic and other cultural presuppositions have made it difficult for the Sami as a minority and an indigenous people to get the same advantages from their schooling as the majority population.[35]

The law of 1739, which made school compulsory for all, also applied to the Sami. These were first and foremost confirmation schools. The teacher traveled around and gave about twelve weeks' instruction during the year, primarily to teach the children to read. This was known as the *omgangsskole* ("half-school"). We are told that at the end of the eighteenth century, there were few Sami and Kven children who were able to read a "Danish" book. Danish was the written language in Norway at that time, since Norway was subject to the Kingdom of Denmark. This meant that when Norway became independent from Denmark in 1814, the schooling of Sami and Kven children in northern Norway was in a bad condition.[36]

Teacher training was established in northern Norway at Trondenes in Harstad by means of a royal resolution of May 4, 1822, and it began to operate in 1826. Given that the Sami were so different in their education and lifestyle from the majority of Norwegians, the intention was to meet the urgent need to train Sami teachers and develop an educational program for the Sami population that would be sensitive to their culture. There was a consensus that it was almost impossible for the Sami to learn the Norwegian language, culture, and civilization.[37] This view, however, changed from the mid-nineteenth century, when the authorities took the view that it was necessary to have teachers who spoke the Norwegian language and had a Norwegian culture, since Sami teachers were considered unskilled and lacking the adequate education to be teachers of the Sami population.

This assertion was given support in 1867 by Nils A. Aall, pastor in Nesseby (in eastern Finnmark, on the Russian border), who pointed to nine Sami teachers in Finnmark who had attended the seminar in Tromsø with grants for Sami, and who—in his opinion—had failed totally. He affirmed that they all drank too much and were incompetent. He held that the Sami were incapable of being teachers because they "lacked the necessary gifts of mind and body. It goes without saying that even the best of them can scarcely have any notion of what discipline is."[38] Many other clergymen and professionals shared this view, and the authorities proclaimed that "the best thing was to send Sami teachers in whose mouths the Norwegian language rang out with full life and resonance, and who, as far as their own state of life was concerned, were full participants in the Norwegian civilization."[39]

Between 1850 and 1880, Sami-speaking areas from Ofoten (around Harstad, 68'N) in the south to the Russian border in the north were divided into seven districts called "transitional districts." The intention was to get the Sami and Kven children to go over from their mother tongues to the Norwegian language. Most of the population in these areas was Sami- or Kven-speaking, with little ability to speak Norwegian. It became clear toward the close of the nineteenth century that the school system was envisaged as a chief instrument in the work of "*fornorskning*," literally "Norwegianization." An instruction to teachers in the transitional districts in 1880 entailed a wide-ranging prohibition on the use of Sami and Finnish in the schools: it specified that Sami could be used in teaching only where it was absolutely unavoidable. The instruction has been called the Magna Charta of Norwegianization.[40]

Great hopes were placed in one particular instrument at the service of Norwegianization: the foundation of boarding schools. Plans were drawn up in 1899 for building boarding schools in Finnmark, where several state schools of this kind were constructed from 1905 onward. The first boarding school in Finnmark, Strand Internat in South Varanger, opened its doors in 1905.

Boarding Schools and the Policy of Assimilating the Sami

The policy of assimilation in Norway, "Norwegianization," had already begun with the proselytizing of the Sami in the seventeenth century, and continued with the same earnest momentum in the schools from the second half of the nineteenth century.[41] In the context of the educational system, the policy envisaged the "school as the battlefield and teachers as the frontline soldiers."[42] Boarding school experiences were considered the context in which the assimilation process could flourish, but integrated public schools with both Sami- and Norwegian-speaking children could be equally problematic for indigenous children who may face forms of racism and be subject to culturally irrelevant curricula. In parallel to the experiences of indigenous children worldwide, boarding schools were set up in Norway to adapt the Sami and Kven pupils to Norwegian ways of knowing and being.[43] This included speaking Norwegian as their first language. It was unavoidable at this time that some Sami and Finnish were still being used in the learning environment, but this was discouraged, since the predominant language of instruction was Norwegian. In 1880, the requirement for instruction exclusively in Norwegian was reinforced throughout the educational system. Sami and Kven now only had the status of secondary languages that were not to be taught. They were seen as "useless" languages.[44]

It was assumed that the teachers would follow the instructions about Norwegianization in the school, so that the regulations of the boarding school could be an effective instrument in this process.[45] The 1880 instruction served as a basis for further Norwegianization. It was consolidated by an instruction in 1898, which stated: "The school's teaching is conducted in the Norwegian language. The Lapp (Sami) or Kven language is employed only as a help to explain things that the children cannot understand." This instruction was named the "Wexelsen Program," after the Minister for church affairs.[46]

The Wexelsen Program guided the development of the public-school system. From 1851, the Norwegian Parliament allocated money to target the assimilation of the Sami and Kven people, in the form of the "Finnish fund." This was the start of more than 100 years of assimilation of the Sami and Kven. Most of the schools built until World War II were boarding schools, especially in northern Norway. By the start of the war (1940), there were fifty boarding schools in Finnmark, attended by 2,800 out of a total of 7,900 schoolchildren. Of those, 1,500 lived in state boarding schools, 950 in boarding schools run by the local authorities, and about 300 lodged in private households.[47]

In the fall of 1944, the German army burnt down almost everything in the region of Finnmark, as far to the south as Lyngen in Northern Troms, and the inhabitants were moved to the southern parts of mid- and northern Norway. After the war, people moved back and had to rebuild everything. This was another big loss to Sami culture and also a historical trauma for all the people in the North.[48]

The Sami language was deemed "useless" because of the dominant view of the Norwegian elite nearly 100 years earlier that the Sami children had to be rescued from their "primitive" cultural backgrounds. Formally speaking, this 1898 instruction was valid for schools and boarding schools until it was abolished by the school law of April 10, 1959. It ordered the teachers in strong terms to be bearers of Norwegian culture.

Swedish and Danish Policies in the Schooling of Sami Children

In Sweden, the view was taken at the close of the nineteenth century that the Sami were on a low developmental level, and a school system based on segregation was established—unlike the system in Norway, which aimed at assimilation. The definition of "Sami" in Sweden was closely linked to the herding of reindeer; and to ensure that this nomadic group would neither die out nor mingle too much with the Swedish population, so-called "nomad schools" were set up, with a level lower than that of the Swedish primary school. The principle was: "Let a Lapp be a lapp" ("*Lapp skall vara lapp*"), and very few hours were set aside for teaching. The School Reform of 1913 brought some educational benefits, albeit segregated and of modest scope. This, however, did not extend to the use of the Sami language in schools, since the medium of instruction remained Swedish, although the first three years of schooling were provided at itinerant schools, and only subsequently at schools on fixed sites.[49]

Like the Norwegian state, the Danish authorities too wanted to make their indigenous people on Greenland, the Inuit, good fellow citizens in the national state of Denmark by means of assimilation. One example is the social experiment in the 1950s, when a group of twenty-two children were taken from their families on Greenland to be educated as model Danish citizens. This was a part of the assimilation process of the Inuit People on Greenland. Denmark wanted to improve conditions in its Arctic colony, and the Danish authorities decided that the best way to modernize the island was to create a new type of Greenlander. With the help of Save the Children Denmark, they sent Inuit children between the ages of six and ten to foster families in Denmark, so that they could be re-educated as Danes. Twenty-two children were sent from Nuuk on Greenland to Copenhagen in May 1951. Although the attempt was a failure, the children were never allowed to return to their families. They ended up as a small, rootless, and marginalized group on the periphery of their own society, and more than half of them died young.[50]

The Situation and General Experiences at the Boarding Schools

For much of the twentieth century, more than a third of Sami school pupils in Finnmark lived in boarding schools, which many scholars have described as "the abuse of children by the public hand."[51] In the boarding schools, they were alienated from their original identity, culture, and language. Johan Turi (1854–1936), the first Sami author to publish a secular work called *Muitalus sámiid birra—My book about the Sami people* in 1910 (published both in Sami and in Danish), formulated the paradox in the Sami schooling as follows:

> It is good that they (the Sami) learn to read and write and count, so that they will not be hoodwinked everywhere by merchants and people with a settled abode, who have cheated many in the past in matters of invoices and drink. Nevertheless, the school is destroying the Sami children now. They acquire a good knowledge, but they also learn many useless things. And then they acquire so much of the nature of those who have a settled abode, and they are away from the Sami in the period when they can learn best. All they learn is the farming life; they do not at all learn the Sami life. And nature changes too, the Sami nature is lost and is replaced by the farmer's nature. And many of the children in the King's school have bad chests. But when there is no school in the Sami's own region, they must go where the schools exist, even when that is not so good.[52]

Without doubt, many more of the Sami children had experiences of the kind described by Turi. One woman who was at a boarding school in east Finnmark (Strand Boarding School in Sør-Varanger, 1951–53) related: "The worst thing about the years in the boarding school was that they made me such a stranger to my own family. The homesickness was terrible, but it was also hard to come home. Looking back later, I realized that I became a stranger to my mother and to the others in my family. The long absence made me shy toward my own relatives."[53]

Lill Tove Fredriksen, Associate Professor in Sami literature at The Arctic University of Norway, has spoken about her mother, who was one of many children who were sent to boarding school in the 1950s. She began her schooling at the age of seven. She lived in a village on the eastern shore of the Porsanger fjord, fifty kilometers from Børselv, where the boarding school was located. She went home three times a year. She did not know Norwegian when she began at school, and the teachers did not speak Sami, which was her mother tongue.[54] Fredriksen also says:

> My mother's experiences put a face to the many who suffered under the policy of Norwegianization ... In Porsanger, my mother's generation did not necessarily lose the oral Sami language. But that is what happened to us, the next generation. My mother spoke Norwegian with me. The Sami I learned as a child, I learned from my grandparents. When I was to begin school, we moved to Lakselv, the local district center. My mother wanted what was best for me. She did not want me to go through what she had experienced.[55]

Fredriksen emphasizes that the transmission of the Sami language was not the result of an unbroken tradition. The attempt was made by the Norwegian authorities to destroy this tradition. This meant that when she was an adult, she had to endeavor actively to take back her Sami family language, and that she had to work hard to ensure that her children, who attend primary school today, shall learn the Sami language.[56]

Everyday Life and Cultural and Social Challenges at the Boarding Schools

Many of the children who went to the boarding schools grew up in homes where only Sami was spoken. This meant a big transition for them when they went to school in the mid-twentieth century, and started to speak Norwegian only when they started school at the age of seven. One such case is Anton, who started at boarding school around 1950, and has the following to say about school: "It was hard. You know, the school was in Norwegian, and we couldn't speak Norwegian. I did not learn to speak Norwegian well until I was sixteen or seventeen. That was when we were evacuated ... and I then learned to speak Norwegian." When he was asked what it was like to go to school when he could not speak the language, he replied: "It was hard at school ... And the teachers were not allowed to teach us in Sami, at least not at the beginning ... In the breaks, we talked Sami."[57]

As for the diet at the boarding schools, it has been claimed that the food was better than in many poor homes in Finnmark. One former boarder said: "If it hadn't been for the boarding schools, surely a lot more children in Finnmark would have died before the War."[58] Fish and herring for dinner on weekdays and meat on Sunday were customary. The children at boarding school usually got gruel for breakfast and porridge for supper. Later, the gruel was replaced by a slice of bread, but porridge remained the evening meal, even when the standard of living rose somewhat in the 1930s.

However, the diet in the boarding schools was alien to many Sami children, who were accustomed to eating Sami food at home, where reindeer meat was customary. They encountered a completely different diet in the boarding schools.[59] The pupils were weighed, to document that they were growing and were content with the food.[60] The teachers were given better and more varied food than the children, some of whom reacted against this. But the diet in the boarding schools was on the same level as what the children got at home; and there were many who envied the boarders their food.[61]

A study of bullying and discrimination carried out among adult Sami who were born between 1924 and 1974 shows that many Sami were bullied when they attended school and boarding school.[62] A follow-up study shows that adult Sami say that the school is the place where most have experienced hurt at the hands of fellow pupils and of teachers.[63] Sami report having been bullied at school (including boarding school) far more frequently than majority Norwegians.[64]

Recent research shows that Sami have been exposed to emotional, physical, and sexual violence to a greater extent than the majority population in Norway. Many of those who were interviewed state that the assaults took place in their childhood.[65] There has been no study of what happened in the boarding schools, but we know that some of these Sami attended them. It is, therefore, likely that some of those who report violence in their childhood experienced this in the boarding schools.

Many Sami with disabilities have strong experiences linked to school, including negative experiences. For the older, adult interviewees, it was very hard to be sent to a boarding school and be denied access to one's own language; their disability made this an additional challenge in their daily life. Although young and adult Sami with disabilities were mostly allowed to go to school in their local environment, we can see that, despite the law establishing the right to learn the Sami language, getting access to this right can still be a struggle for many. All age groups relate that bullying at school is widespread. Sami with disabilities were bullied both because of their Sami background and because of their disability. And they were bullied by both Norwegian and Sami fellow pupils.[66]

The Post-War Period: A New Public Policy Vis-à-Vis the Sami Population

A direction in public policy gradually developed that put an end to the active policy of Norwegianization. Important international currents were connected to the United Nations Declaration of Human Rights in 1948; these found expression in many countries in the political consciousness of the equality of the various cultures.[67] This may have played a role when questions of Sami education were treated for the first time in an official position paper in Norway. A "Coordination council for the educational system" was set up in 1947, and its report in 1948 marked a breach with the

Norwegianization policy.[68] It proposed that the solution to questions of the Sami school and language was a task for the state itself.

The parliament debated a number of concrete measures, and a more positive interest in Sami questions grew. In 1956, the Sami Committee discussed both fundamental questions and concrete measures for the Sami; its proposals were presented in 1959, including statements and proposed measures that would make it easier for the Sami to live in their own culture within the framework of Norwegian society.[69]

Social-Psychological Consequences of Norwegianization at the Boarding Schools

The fact that the Sami children at the boarding schools were not taught in Sami, their own mother tongue, signaled to the children who spoke a minority language that the Sami language, identity, and culture were not equal in value to the Norwegian majority language and culture.[70] This led many Sami children to believe that they were of less value, and that this was their own fault, resulting in a low self-esteem and self-appreciation in many Sami children and adolescents.[71] And there is no doubt that experiences at the boarding schools have left their mark on many adult Sami. Many cannot write and speak Norwegian well. They feel that they are losers in society, that their schooling prevented them from developing their full potential, and that they carry with them the negative childhood experiences from their time in the boarding school.[72] Jens-Ivar Nergård (b. 1947), Professor in Cultural Pedagogics at UiT, says:

> The boarding school experience created in many a pain and a situation of powerlessness that most likely could be dealt with only by suppressing it – as depth psychology understands this term. The parents felt a deep guilt vis-à-vis the children, but they had no choice. The children felt abandoned; they felt that their parents had handed them over. Many experienced the boarding schools as internment camps. We can well imagine that they laid the foundations for damage in children similar to the damage we see in today's internment camps in regions of conflict and war around the globe.[73]

In this context, Nergård says that whenever conflicts arise in the children between the identity attributed to them in the school and the identity attributed at home, the children must be able to extricate themselves from this conflict, either by rejecting the school and its identity ascription, or by rejecting the home environment and its ascription. Another possibility, of course, is that the children reject both ascriptions of identity, that of the school and that of the home—and find themselves in a marginalized position.[74] Because of these processes, many Sami have abandoned their Sami language and culture, and many of them experience this as a great loss.[75]

Sami Childhood and Sami School Policy Today

Sami children grow up today in a society in which the Sami culture and language enjoy a completely different status from the society in which their parents grew up. For Sami children who possess a sure linguistic and cultural Sami competence, the definition of their own "Sami-ness" will be freer and less politicized than for many in their parents' generation.

The school plays an important role in the work for strengthening and developing Sami culture and social life. If a genuine equality is to be attained, it is important that Sami pupils are taught within the framework of the common school. The choice between the Sami or the Norwegian language does not have to be taken today. Instead, it is an ideal to be functionally bilingual and to have bicultural competence; this is also a presupposition for active participation by Sami in society.[76]

Many young Sami experience their identity as composite, both Norwegian and Sami—and some experience themselves as Kven or Finnish. Among Sami children and young people, where the family has been exposed to assimilation during Norwegianization in the boarding schools, this has led to passionate intergenerational discussions of ethnic identity, especially where individuals with the same background have chosen different solutions in dealing with their Sami–Norwegian identity.[77]

A report from the Children's Ombudsmen in the Nordic countries shows that Sami children are still being bullied in Norway because they are Sami. However, most are proud of their culture and identity, even if it is not always easy for Sami children and young people to be open about their background. Some children also experience prejudices within Sami society, since they do not always feel that they are accepted by others as "good enough Sami," if their families, for example, no longer speak the Sami language.[78]

In the school year 2014–2015, 2,116 students aged from six to sixteen years were learning the Sami language in primary schools in Norway. Of these, 812 use Sami languages as the main language in the school day, and 1,201 as a second language in the school day. In college, 452 students have the Sami language as their first or second language, and 899 Sami children attend Sami kindergartens, 127 of whom are learning the Sami language in their kindergarten.[79]

Organized distance learning in Sami was established in Norway in 2004, against the background of an increased need for alternative forms of teaching in Sami after most of the Sami boarding schools had been closed.[80] These courses are designed to allow Sami children and young people to take back the Sami language, identity, and culture.

The Norwegianization process with the boarding schools has left deep traces on the Sami population. Many have lost the "language of their heart," their Sami mother tongue, their culture and their identity.[81] However, the Norwegian authorities have committed themselves today both in international law and in national law to establish the conditions that will allow the Sami ethnic group to preserve and develop its language, its culture, and its social life. The boarding school system in Norway has seen shifts from what started out as pro-Sami culture and later became a political means for assimilation. Today, however, as we have seen, many Sami parents choose Sami boarding schools to help teach their children Sami language and culture.[82]

Notes

1 Jensen 2015: 17.
2 Ibid.: 17–18.
3 Jensen 2005.
4 Jensen 2015: 18–19.
5 Dahl 1957.
6 International Labor Office. *Indigenous and Tribal Peoples' Rights in Practice: A guide to ILO Convention No. 169*, 2009.
7 Jernsletten1993, and Fyhn 2013.
8 Pettersen 2015.
9 Pettersen and Brustad 2015.
10 Bjerregaard 2008.
11 SSB [Statistics Norway] homepage: www.ssb.no/a/histstat/tabeller/3-2.html.
12 SSB, Økonomisk analyse 2/2013 – Befolkningsutvikling, by Helga Brunborg and Marianne Tønnessen, online at www.ssb.no/nasjonalregnskap-og-konjunkturer/oa/_attachment/109883?_ts=13e3bd8cc80, 3–14.
13 SSB—Anne Gro Pedersen, Samfunnsspeilet, 2003/3 100 år med redusert spedbarnsdødelighet, online at www.ssb.no/helse/artikler-og-publikasjoner/100-aar-med-redusert-spedbarnsdodelighet.
14 Hassler 2005.
15 Hansen 2011.
16 Ibid.: 21–2.
17 Hjertespråket—Forslag til lovverk, tiltak og ordninger for samisk språk, 2016.
18 Hyltenstam 2003.
19 Minde 2005.
20 Hansen and Olsen 2006.
21 Ibid.: 18–51.
22 Ibid.: 18–51.
23 Jernsletten 1993.
24 See, for example, Chapters 9 and 14 by Rørvik and Olsen in this volume.
25 Ibid.: 115–32.
26 Eriksen and Niemi 1981: 333–8 coined the term "the Finnish threat" (*den finske fare*) for what the Norwegian authorities decreed in 1860.
27 Jernsletten 1993: 115–32.
28 Nystad 2003.
29 Javo, Ronning, and Heyerdahl 2004.
30 Javo 2010.
31 Balto 1997.
32 Bergstrøm 2001.
33 Høgmo 1989. See also Chapters 3, 5 and 11 by Markussen, Lahtinen, and Garðarsdottir in this volume.
34 Nystad 2003.
35 Lund et al. 2005: 36.
36 Reiersen 1915: 2–4.
37 Jensen 2015: 22.
38 Dahl 1957.
39 Ibid.

40 Jensen 2015.
41 Minde 2005; Todal 1998.
42 Minde 2005.
43 Martin et al. 2014. Boarding schools as a means of assimilation of indigenous people in Norway has had a parallel in the treatment of Aboriginal children in Canada, see http://nctr.ca/assets/reports/Modern%20Reports/canadian_public_opinion.pdf (as seen Jan 27, 2017). There are presently discussions within Sami milieus in the north about establishing a similar Truth Commision.
44 Jensen 1991.
45 Ibid.: 1–117.
46 Jensen 2015.
47 Meløy 1980.
48 Todal 1998.
49 Kent 2014: 147.
50 In 2009, Save the Children Denmark apologized for this treatment of the children. Many of the survivors and their families now demand that the project be recognized as an assault. See BBC News – "The children taken from home for a social experiment." June 10, 2015; see www.bbc.com/news/magazine-33060450.
51 NRK Dokumentar – "Internatskolene var barnemishandling i offentlig regi." Retrieved Jan 10, 2017 from www.nrk.no/dokumentar/-statlig-barnemishandling-1.11298675.
52 Turi and Lindbach 2011.
53 Tjelle 2000: 88.
54 Fredriksen 2016: 3, online at http://nordnorskdebatt.no/article/fornorskningspolitikken-et.
55 Ibid.
56 Ibid. Today her working language at the university is Sami.
57 Melbøe, Johansen, Fedreheim, and Hansen 2016.
58 Tjelle 2000: 21.
59 Lund et al. 2005: 268–84.
60 Meløy 1980.
61 Tjelle 2000.
62 Lund et al. 2007; Hansen et al. 2008.
63 Brustad et al. 2014.
64 *Sámi logut muitalit 9: čielggaduvvon sámi statistihkka 2016.*
65 Eriksen et al. 2015.
66 Melbøe, Johansen, Fedreheim, and Hansen 2016: 42–54.
67 Morsink 1993.
68 *Tilråding V om opplæring for born som treng serskoler 1948: 5.*
69 Lund et al. 2005.
70 Skutnabb-Kangas 1981.
71 Nergård and Mathiesen 1994.
72 Sárgon 2007: 73–6.
73 Nergård and Eriksen 2006: 242.
74 Nergård 1979.
75 Dankertsen 2014.
76 Javo 2010.
77 Thuen 1995.
78 Barneombudene i Norden, 2008.
79 Slaastad 2016.
80 *Sámi logut muitalit 8: čielggaduvvon sámi statistihkka 2015.*
81 Bjørklund 1985.
82 Javo 2010. The chapter is translated from Norwegian by Brian McNeil.

13 Children and Their Stories of World War II

A Study of Essays by Norwegian School Children from 1946

Ellen Schrumpf

Introduction

In 1946, Norwegian schoolchildren participated in a national competition in which twelve- to thirteen-year-old pupils, boys and girls, were invited to write essays about their experiences from World War II, which in Norway dates from April 9, 1940 to May 8, 1945. Children throughout Norway participated in the competition, and two essays from each school were submitted to the national jury by the local school teachers.[1]

These essays have been kept for posterity and, so far, they have scarcely been studied by anyone. The uniqueness of this source is the access it gives to children's own voices. So far, most of what we know about childhood during World War II is narrated in retrospective and from adult's perspectives.[2] We know very little about children's experiences and perspectives on the war. The aim of this chapter is to give Norwegian children who lived through the war a voice. How did children in Norway experience World War II, and how did they remember and narrate the war? My analysis of about 100 of the essays on "A Memory from the War" aims to answer these questions.

We know that the war was an extraordinary situation, which caused children to suffer.[3] Accordingly, many of the essays tell about dramatic war incidents and reflect exceptional childhood experiences. Childhood is, however, a social and cultural phenomenon, characterized by continuity.[4] Hence, it is an assumption here that the essays will not only tell us about exceptional childhood during World War II, but will also reveal general characteristics of Norwegian childhood at that time.

However, not only Norwegian children were affected by World War II. Children from all the Nordic countries were involved in the war in different ways.[5] In Finland, the Winter War from November 1939 to March 1940 was followed by the Continuation War in the years between 1941 and 1944. Both wars inflicted severe strains on the Finnish people. Denmark, like Norway, was occupied by German troops. Both countries capitulated, Norway only after some months of hard military resistance. Sweden kept neutral during the War, but was influenced by the war in the neighbor countries. Inter alia,

Sweden hosted thousands of refugees from the neighbor countries at war, including many children.[6]

Children in all the Nordic countries lived through and experienced, in different ways, the hardship of World War II. Further, Nordic childhoods in general had much in common in the ways education, family, and work were practiced and organized in the nineteenth and twentieth centuries.[7] Despite social and political differences, Nordic childhoods shared cultural values.

The hypothesis of this chapter is that in a situation of marginal and harsh living conditions for both children and adults, it was required that children should act as responsible social agents who executed extensive duties within and outside the families. Children's actions and experiences made them perceive themselves as social agents and "human beings."[8] They acted in an "adult" way and as adults' co-workers. The borders between childhood and adulthood were blurred.

Historical knowledge is a construction based on the researcher's selections and interpretations of the reminiscences from the past.[9] The actual reminiscences from the past are the essays, which are interpreted as children's narratives and contribution to a collective and social production of memories.[10] Four themes appear in the essays written in 1946 about "A Memory from the War." These themes inform the reader about how children experienced and remembered the war. The most obvious themes in the essays are the following: (1) The adventurous war; (2) resistance and participation; (3) the brutality of war–wounding, killing, and death; and (4) patriotism, heroism, and humanism.

The essays cannot be understood as exact records of what happened in the past. Rather, they are expressions of recollections of emotional experiences.[11] Besides this, they must be read and understood as narratives in which experiences from the past are selected elements in constructed and meaningful stories. In fact, the acts of recalling and retelling consist in *taking up* certain aspects of lived experience.[12] Read as narrative constructions, we can see the essays as expressions of cultural codes and keys to understanding collective beliefs and notions, and as expressions of norms and values in post-war Norway (1946), the specific collective culture at that time.[13] The stories were narrated in specific genres, which were defined by the cultural context in which the essays were written; the place (post-war Norway), time (1946) and the school assignment ("A Memory from the War"). This specific context sent an unspoken but clear message to the children about both genre and plot.[14] The children themselves, however, were the narrators and masters of these stories.

How can we then read and understand children's memories from the past? When children in 1946 wrote about "A Memory from the War," they were looking back at a past that was close in time. The events they referred to happened in a recent past: from one to six years earlier and together they cover all the five years from 1940 to 1945. The children were from six to twelve years old at the time when the event they remembered and wrote about occurred.

The essays must be read as a combination of factual (facts) and narrative (fiction) elements. The factual elements are descriptions of children's living condition and experiences during the war. It is probable that the more dramatic and exciting the adventures, the more exact the children's description would be, because children would have no problem with recollecting such events. We can then expect that information about facts such as time, place, and people involved is reliable. On the other hand, dramatic war incidents inspired the children to dramatize and color the narratives in favor of their own, or their family's role and importance. Traumatic incidents may have been repressed. At any rate, the narratives tell us about children's minds, their attitudes and their values at the moment of narration (1946) and about the events to which they refer.

The essays, which were submitted for participation in the national competition, were selected by the local teachers for different reasons. It is probable that they selected the formally most correct essays with regard to such matters as handwriting, spelling, and grammar. We can, however, assume that the teachers chose those essays that were ideologically correct, as well as essays that fitted into the post-war discourse and collective memory at that time (1946). The collective memory divided Norwegians into two separate groups: the good Norwegians who had participated in the resistance and fought against the enemy, and traitors who were on the "wrong side"— those who had collaborated with the enemy.[15] All members of the political party that had collaborated with the Germans—Nasjonal Samling (NS)— were perceived as the enemy and as one homogenous group, regardless of their specific actions during the war.[16]

We can assume that children on the "wrong side" did not write essays from their perspective. Children of parents who had supported the NS felt ashamed and although they themselves were not responsible, they brought themselves to silence.[17] Since the post-war discourse was one-dimensional and not open for alternative voices and "problematic" narratives, the children were exposed to censorship from within and from without.

As a whole, the essays express an "airbrushed" presentation of children's experiences and everyday lives in Norway 1940–1945. We have to be critically aware of these circumstances when analyzing the source material. The essays tell neither the whole, nor the true story about Norwegian childhood 1940–1945. In what follows, children's stories are presented and structured according to the four themes presented above.

The Adventurous War

Some of the children seem to have experienced the war as an adventure, and they describe the events with excitement rather than fear. These essays contain expressive elements such as bright colors, flashlights, reports, dull sounds, stamping, and so on. In one essay, Karen Margrethe Bjelland from Arendal (south Norway) writes about an air raid. It was winter and the family had supper. Then they heard an air raid and looked out of the window:

> Searchlights swept across the sky, and sometimes they managed to spot the aircrafts. The aircraft looked like small silver shining moths ... Missiles flew up in the air and glowed in yellow, green and red colors. The sight was beautiful in the dark winter evening, like a firework.[18]

Margrethe saw all kinds of colors and glowing and silver shining objects, and she found the sight beautiful. Suddenly, it was as if "a torch was fired" and sank at high speed to the ground. An aircraft was hit and crashed into an ice-covered lake. The next day, Margrethe went to the scene of the accident, and a dreadful sight met her. The ice was painted red and she saw blood, hands, feet, and intestines spread out everywhere. Margrethe felt sick and she was upset and deeply sorry for the death of the young English pilots and for their parents who had lost their sons.

Margrethe's memory of war was imprinted on body and mind, and was accordingly easily brought back to mind and dramatized later. Her close exposure to the sounds and sights of the brutality of war made Margrethe feel sorrow, but also excitement. The memory was narrated like a true story that had been portrayed on the stage.

The adventure and beauty of war was also a theme in other essays. Edith Gjerde lived in Mosterhamn, in Sunnhordaland. In her essay, she describes a beautiful evening in January 1943.[19] The moon was shining and the snow on the trees glittered. Edith was at home alone together with her younger siblings, and then she heard load booms from aircraft, cannons, bombs, and anti-aircraft fire. She looked out of the windows and watched a spectacle:

> It was like a firework. The bullets from the vessels and from the fortress on Tittelsnes crossed each other in all kinds of colors ... and from the anti-artillery cannons the bullets went straight into the air. It was at the same time creepy and beautiful.

A mixture of feelings—both fear and excitement—was fixed in her memory from the war. Edith was living close to a war target and she was directly confronted with the consequences of war. So did Eva Steenberg, who lived near Slagentangen, a military area. Eva remembered the day when Slagentangen was bombed on April 25, 1945. Because of the bombing, she had to go down to the cellar in the middle of the night and it was from there that she watched the bombing:

> We ran from one window to the other to see it all. An ocean of flames increased and the bullets dashed everywhere ... The aircraft rushed and the bomb dropped, doors opened and windows clinked, shell splinters dashed through the air and the night was illuminated. Then the aircraft

vanished and all fell silent. The flames, however, were bigger than ever. The sky was lighted up red and the smoke rose to the sky, thick and black.[20]

Eva was eleven years old when the bombing happened and she was excited when she watched the spectacular sight outside the windows. She ran from one window to the other to make sure that she would not miss anything. In the description given six years later, she uses vivid and expressive terms such as colors, sounds and sight of flames, smoke and aircraft in the air.

From these essays, we learn that children sensed the war incidents through their hearing, sight, and smell, and that they did not always connect their experiences to the negative and destructive perception of war.

Resistance and Participation

Children's wish and need to participate in the resistance is an important theme in many of the essays. This theme reflects the children's perception of themselves as "human beings" and social actors who played a role in the situation of war. To take part in the resistance might, however, be a dangerous mission, and this was first and foremost a "boy" theme. Arne Kinserdal (twelve years old) writes about his brother, whose age is unknown; but since Arne was twelve years old, the brother was probably some years older than Arne. The incident took place in Arendal in 1942 and concerned the transportation of guns and ammunition to the home front. The mission was indeed dangerous, and the parents did not allow Arne's brother to go. He did not, however, obey his parents and together with his comrades, he loaded rucksacks with ammunition and guns, which they transported on a ferry to Arendal. However, the situation was hazardous, since German soldiers too were on board:

> My brother and his comrades stopped breathing. The Germans approached the boys and they opened their rucksacks. The Germans, however, saw nothing else other than a wool blanket on top, and they thought of course that the boys were workers from the military construction site.[21]

The boys succeeded with the operation and were able to hand over the equipment to the home front.

What is this story about? First, it is about independence and protest. Arne's brother acted in accordance with his own will and conviction. He disobeyed his parents and decided to take part in a dangerous action. Second, the story is about a young boy's participation in the resistance during the war. Arne and his comrades were responsible for a mission, which we can assume was important. The supply of guns and ammunition was decisive for the home front's capacity to fight against the Germans. The boys acted like mature grownups and the hard realities of war affected childhood in a way that blurred the factual and mental borders between childhood and adulthood. We must, however, bear in mind that the story was constructed according to the heroic war narrative, which had a strong hold on general opinion in 1946, and that it was an admiring brother who wrote the essay. The essay must be read as a story in which factual incidents and fictional devices are combined, and the main plot was the heroes' fight against evil.

Other essays likewise illustrate children's keenness to participate in the resistance and conflicts between children and parents. Jann Beckmann, who was eight or nine years old at the time of the incident, was walking with his father in the woods in the Modum area when he discovered a drop load from England. The home front was the recipient of the drop load. The Germans were all around and Jann was not allowed to take part in picking up the drop load the following night, since his father thought it was too dangerous. Jann argued that he had a right to come along, since he was the first to discover the drop load. But it was his father and uncle who picked up the container and handed it over to the home front. When his father returned that evening, he had a chocolate bar for Jann. The bar was a gift from the home front leader who wanted to give Jann a reward as a sign of recognition. Humiliation and disappointment then turned to pride:

> [B]ut I can almost still not forgive my father for not letting me join in when collecting the drop load, but now I know how dangerous it was, and then it was understandable that my father said no. The chocolate paper hangs on the wall in a frame and glass as a memory from the war.[22]

Jann experienced the restoration of his self-esteem, and the chocolate paper on the wall signaled the importance of his discovery to the parents and to Jann himself. Thanks to the chocolate bar, the story could be written as a heroic story in which Jann played the role of the hero who had made an important effort for the resistance.

Children were, however, also deliberately involved in their parents' resistance. Children were messengers who brought illegal papers and messages. Such work was usually carried out by girls in urban areas, like Henny from Trondheim, Else from Bergen, and Kari from Stavanger.[23] Henny was aware that the work was important and involved both risks and responsibility, and accordingly that she "could not tell anyone, not even her best friend, because even if she was trustworthy she could make a slip of the tongue." Henny was, however, happy to be involved because "it could be fun but also risky." The two dimensions—fun and risk—are central elements in the story. One evening, Henny went out with papers and a message to "Mrs Hansen." It was dark and suddenly two Gestapo men stopped her. They smiled "maliciously" and pointed at her bag. She explained that it was her schoolbag and they let her go. "Mrs Hansen" turned out to be a young man and Henny ran the whole way back home "since everything was so creepy after she had met the 'two big guys.'"

Henny took part in missions, which she executed with courage and accuracy. It seems from the essay that her parents trusted her and that they regarded Henny as a responsible co-worker. Henny's memory from the war expresses the experience of being included and useful. After the war, she could write a story about participation and about how she was involved in a struggle to serve a higher cause. Her mission was to get back to those days when "we had enough food and no Germans devastated our country."

Sometimes children were involved in dangerous situations, which they had to deal with on their own. It was summer in 1944 and Gunnar Wagtskjold (eleven years old) from Bergen spent the summer holiday with his uncle who lived on an island in Sognefjorden, on the west coast of Norway. Gunnar and his cousin spent a hot summer day by the sea, swimming and sunbathing. Then the war was suddenly visible above their heads: English and German airplanes in a dogfight, like "in a witches' dance":

> An aircraft was hit, set on fire and exploded, another aircraft fell into the sea with a smoke-tale behind. Then, suddenly, we felt a rush above our heads and we bent down instinctively. Another aircraft was hit and fell into the sea with an enormous splash, a short distance from the bathing place.[24]

Soon after, the boys recognized something white colored floating in the water. They swam out and found an English pilot who had managed to escape from the plunging plane. The boys helped the pilot ashore, and he turned out to be uninjured. The two boys knew they had to hide him before the Germans arrived. Two hours later, the Germans appeared. Every house on the island was inspected, and the boys were cross examined. They kept their mouths shut, however, and after a while the Germans left. Then the boys hurried down to the potato cellar where the English soldier was hidden in a trunk covered with mold. Two weeks later, the English pilot was picked up by an English submarine at night. After the war, the pilot returned to the island, and Gunnar and his cousin received a watch, which, according to Gunnar, they "appreciated very much."

This story is about young boys' independence and energy in a dangerous situation. It seems as if the two boys acted on instinct, without reflecting about the danger they put themselves and their uncle into. The way Gunnar describes that particular day on the island indicates that the boys were able to act bravely, and resourcefully, when necessary. Gunnar tells the story as a drama that contains no traces of fear and horror. He presented himself in a modest way without much fuss about the rescue of the English soldier or the watch he received after the war.

Randi Ophaug from Trondheim was another child who entered unexpectedly into a dangerous situation. She spent the summer holiday at her aunt's cottage together with her family. One night, she and her brother were at home alone when a stranger knocked on the door. He was pale and skinny and about twenty-five years old, and he told the two children that he had escaped from German captivity. He asked for food, and the two children invited him in and served him food. The refugee knew that the Germans were chasing him, and he instructed the children to say nothing if the Germans turned up:

> Then I heard voices from down the road. First, I thought it was my mother and father but as they approached, I could hear that they were not Norwegian. I was so scared that I shivered. The stranger crawled under a bed in the bedroom. Then somebody knocked on the door. I opened the door and outside two Germans and one Norwegian were standing.[25]

Randi declared that they had seen no one, and the refugee escaped later that evening. Afterwards, Randi learned that the man had reached Sweden safely.

This story is about two children who entered into a situation that required courage, energy, and empathy. The children handled the situation as any grownups would, and they saw that their efforts to feed and protect the refugee might have been decisive for his safe arrival in Sweden. Such experiences must have marked children for life.

The essays also tell about children who had the ability to keep secrets, either because they feared for their own lives or because they wanted to protect others. Eiler Villmones lived in Korgen in Nordland, close to a prison camp.[26] His family had to pass the camp on their way to the summer farm, and there they observed how the Germans tortured and terrorized Serb prisoners. One day, something awful happened. Two prisoners brought food to fellow prisoners who were building a road across Vesterfjellet. A German guard was following them. Suddenly, one of the prisoners hit the German so that he fell on his face, and then the prisoner stabbed him with a knife. Soon after this, Eiler returned from the summer farm and he came across the dead German lying in the middle of the road:

> I was frightened to death and ran the whole way home. While I was running, I thought that no one must ever know what I have seen. We might all die, or father or mother might be sent to a prison camp.[27]

Later, forty Serb prisoners were shot dead by the Germans as a reprisal. But Eiler kept his promise; he told no one about what he had seen that day, as long as the war lasted. After the war, he told the story to his parents, and then he was no longer frightened.

Eiler acted both courageously and in a responsible way when he decided not to tell anyone about the horrifying incident. The decision to keep the terrible story secret had consequences for Eiler's wellbeing, since he was constantly frightened as long as the war lasted. The essay reveals how a child can act with courage and responsibility in a very demanding situation.

Children had different experiences concerning resistance and participation; some children were involved in parents' activities while others were not allowed to do so. Some children acted on their own despite their parents' will, and some entered accidentally into situations that demanded courage and responsibility. Boys were more directly involved in resistance missions, while girls were messengers. The essays tell about co-work between children and grownups, and about children's courageous and independent agency.

The Brutality of War: Wounding, Killing, and Death

According to the dominant perception of childhood at that time (the 1940s), children should be protected from seeing and being close to experiencing death and destruction. This idea can be dated back to the turn of the nineteenth century. Then, as child mortality in Western countries declined, a change took place in the attitudes towards children and death. The phenomenon of death, which traditionally took place in the private sphere and within the family, was gradually silenced, institutionalized, and hidden from neighbors, family, and children. The dying were taken away from the home and the nearest environment and placed in hospitals. "A heavy silence has fallen over the subject of death," writes Philippe Ariès in his book on Westerners' changing attitudes to death.[28]

During World War II, children experienced the brutality of war and were exposed to killing and death. The brutality of war aroused strong emotions and left deep traces in the children's memories. What worried children most was the possibility of losing their parents.[29] Losing family members and beloved ones is one key issue in the essays. Oddlaug Sletta lost her cousin.[30] It was a beautiful summer day in 1942 in Foldfjorden near Kristiansund. A fishing boat, which had transported many Norwegians across the North Sea to England was in port, and suddenly two aircrafts rushed over the house roofs and headed towards the fishing boat. Suddenly, Oddlaug heard a cry and she saw her cousin, Asbjørn, writhing in pain. A bullet had hit his arm and cut the artery. When the doctor arrived, he just shook his head:

> Everything was at once dark and unpleasant. Outdoors, the aircrafts droned with those scary noises, murmuring and roaring with a stir that bore witness to death, creepiness and war. Indoors lay a young boy who was strong and healthy just a while ago and then was sick and dying.

Asbjørn died, and thereafter Oddlaug always associated aircraft with "this sad and sinister memory." From that day she looked at all Nazis with hate and horror; they were to blame for her dearest cousin's death.

Some children saw dead bodies and body parts. Alfred Koppervik was six years old in 1940.[31] On the morning of April 25, a troop of Norwegian soldiers had arrived at the summer farm in Bagn, Sør-Aurdal in Oppland, where Alfred and his family lived. That afternoon, they were warned about a German soldier who was on his way to the summer farm. As soon as the German soldier opened the door, he was shot dead, and he lay in a pool of blood.[32] Both Alfred and his sister Sigrid were exposed to the shooting, killing, and death. It is hard to say whether and if so how children were traumatized by such experiences; but Alfred narrated the story in a straightforward and sober way, without adding dramatic elements. The narrative indicates that after all, he managed to keep dramatic war experiences at a distance.

Other children narrated their experiences about the brutality of war as something horrifying. Bjørg Wiik lived in Byåsen in Trondheim. She was seven or eight years old in 1941 when the sirens blasted and her family rushed down to the cellar. In the cellar was a young student (the University of Technology was located in Trondheim), and his face turned white as they heard German boots above their heads. The student went upstairs to see what the Germans wanted. Soon after this they all went upstairs, and an upsetting sight met them: "The sight could make us faint, all of us. We were, however, so upset that we managed to keep conscious." There, on the floor the student lay unconscious while a young Gestapo man kicked him with all his strength. The German accused the student of hiding illegal papers. He did not find anything and the student survived. But Bjørg adds that he did not survive the war.[33]

The sight of the tortured student was inscribed on Bjørg's body and mind for a long time, probably forever. Kate Villmones had a similar experience with Serbian prisoners. Kate lived in Korgen in Nordland County, close to a camp for Serbian prisoners.[34] She recalls in detail how the prisoners starved, were shot for minor offences, had all kinds of deficiency diseases, and were tormented by vermin. Once, forty prisoners were shot, and Kate remembered that she heard the shots while she was sitting on her grandfather's veranda. "I will never forget these memories," she writes.[35]

Torbjørn Johansen lived in Finnmark in the northern part of Norway, and he recalled "all the sad memories from the years of war in Finnmark."[36] It was a summer day in 1944, the sun was shining and a gentle breeze was coming from the southeast. Torbjørn was making hay and since lowering clouds were approaching, they worked quickly. Then they heard the "sad, whining and moaning siren," which they had become used to. However, "the nerves were brought to a boil of fear and anxiety," for Torbjørn knew from experience that civilians would either be hurt or killed, or their houses would burn down. At that time, the German warship *Tirpitz* was in port in Kåfjord, twenty kilometers from the rural village where Torbjørn lived, and the allies were hunting the *Tirpitz*. According to Torbjørn, thirty English bombers crossed the village that day and "blaze, thunder was in the air and bombes and grenades poured down." The damage was enormous:

"Windows and doors were broken, dead sheep and cows were thrown across the fields. German cars and medical service were busy driving hurt soldiers and 900 young Germans soldiers were buried." Living in Finnmark and close to the war target, the *Tirpitz,* Torbjørn experienced the horror of war. He also experienced the scorched-earth strategy and the terrorizing of Russian prisoners: "Close to 1,000 Russians starved and they were beaten and tortured to death." From Torbjørn's essay, we see that children in Finnmark experienced the brutality of war at a very close range.

Patriotism, Heroism, and Humanism

War threatens individual safety in all its forms: safety of life, health, means of living and home. War also disrupts individual, familial, and communal everyday life. Insecurity, change, and fear become bearable if one is supported by the tightening of communal ties in the name of a collective enemy. The negative feelings projected onto the enemy may have helped to perpetuate an enemy image that served communal unity in times of hardship.[37]

From the essays, we learn that children were well aware of what the war was about: a struggle between good and evil. Further, the war divided the "world" into two opposite spheres, which consisted of patriots and traitors. All Nazis were considered traitors and excluded from the grand, national "We." They were the "Others." It is significant that none of the selected essays expresses a Nazi perspective or sympathy with the Nazis. In one of the essays, Nazism is presented as expression of evil. Egil Hope was probably from a rural place in the region around the city of Bergen, and he writes about a Nazi family who lived in the same rural area. The daughter in the family was, according to Egil, "dating the Germans" although she had yet not finished school. Furthermore, the girl did not say hello to the other children when she arrived at school in the morning. Egil also writes about how she once met their teacher and reached out her hand, saluting him with "Heil Hitler." The teacher did not answer, and from then on, the girl refused to greet the teacher. At the end of the spring term, the girl left school, but she got bad marks for her behavior, while all her fellow pupils got good marks. She complained to the Germans and the teacher was arrested by the local Nazi policeman. The teacher was sent to Espeland prison camp in Arna outside Bergen, a prison camp set up by the Germans in 1943. On the day when the teacher was sent away, a lot of people met on the quay to say goodbye. Later, the local pastor was arrested too. The school children hoped and waited for the teacher to come back. One day before Christmas, he suddenly turned up and "everybody was happy to get our teacher back."[38]

Egil's essay is a patriotic and anti-Nazi story in which the teacher, the pastor, the school children, and the local community were "the good guys," while the girl, her Nazi family, and the local Nazi police were the "bad guys." All the "wrongs" were ascribed to the girl, such as dating Germans at a young age, being rude to the teacher, and being a traitor who was responsible for the arrest of the beloved teacher. The "facts" in Egil's essay might be correct, but they are embedded in a patriotic narrative, which dominated at the time of writing (1946) and in which the teacher, his resistance, and the pupils are the heroes, whereas the girl, her family, and the Nazi police are the enemies, and consequently demonized.

Generally, the Germans are portrayed in the essays as the "bad guys," and some children said that they did not pity the Germans if they died. Else-Marie Gjertsen was sitting on top of a hill in Mosterhamn with a friend. It was a nice sunny day and they were watching the ferryboat *Austri* heading into the fjord from Stavanger. Then they heard loud sounds, and soon they noticed smoke from the ferry. The two girls screamed and ran home "stricken with fear." From the window, she and her family could see the *Austri* sink. The ship was hit by British aircraft, which had bombed it because Germans and German war equipment were aboard. Else-Marie assumed that both Germans and Norwegians went down together with the boat:

> People did not talk much about the Germans, since there had to be fewer Germans if there was going to be peace. I felt however sorry for the poor Norwegians who had lost their lives and for those who were left alone because they had lost a father, a mother, a brother or sister, a husband or wife.[39]

Else-Marie's empathy with the dead ones included Norwegians only. Nevertheless, some children were able to see that even the enemies were human beings, and children's ability to act and think about the enemy as humans is obvious in a number of the essays. Harald Solberg from Setskog in Aurskog-Høland (Akerhus) went to the local shopkeeper for his mother, to pick up the weekly ration of bread. When he arrived at the shop, Harald noticed many German soldiers, one of whom was guarding the door. It was a young boy, hardly older than fifteen years, Harald thought to himself. He noticed that the gun reached from the soldier's legs to his head and Harald remembered his reflections concerning the young German soldier:

> Maybe he did not have a mother or father, sister or a home. He was just a tiny boy hated and despised everywhere he arrived. I felt deeply sorry for him. Now, every German child attends proper elementary schools where they can learn not to make war against other nations.[40]

Harald hoped that education and enlightenment would prevent war in the future. He empathized with the German soldier, probably because the soldier was a young boy who was far from home. Harald ascribed human feelings to the soldier, such as longing, hardship, and loss. The meeting with the German solider in 1944 and the image of him was so vivid that two years later he chose to write about it and about the empathy he felt for him. Harald expresses humanism and atonement in his essay.

The children told stories with strong emotions of both honor and contempt in the essays, and they contributed to the collective memory about the war at that time (1946). Hence, they participated in the formation of moral values and national discourse in post-war Norway. However, they could also express compassion towards people who suffered in the war, even if they belonged to the enemy.

Conclusions

What do the essays tell us about childhood experiences in Norway during World War II, and how have the essays informed us about Norwegian and Nordic childhood at that time? First, they show us something of how the war was experienced from children's perspective. Their senses experienced events such as bombing and air-raids spontaneously, and sometimes they described the incidents as fun and as spectacular adventures. Second, we see that children did not want to, be protected from the consequences of war; nor could they be protected from these consequences.[41]

Children experienced all the negative effects of war; they lost family members, they were on the run, they were forced to evacuate and they experienced huge material damage to the houses and places where they lived. We have also learned that children experienced how insecurity and fear became bearable if they were supported by the tightening of familial and communal ties, in the name of a collective enemy. Third, we have learned that children were eager to take part in the resistance. Girls and boys accomplished different tasks; girls were messengers, and boys had independent duties for the home front. Through participation, children experienced being co-workers of the adults in their families, and they experienced being included in a broader and age-integrated community. When children proved to themselves and their families that they mattered and that they mastered demanding and dangerous situations, and probably saved themselves and others from all kinds of danger, they experienced their own sense of importance, and their pride and self-esteem increased. Children proved that they were competent agents who made a difference during the war.

Participation, independence, and responsibility are accordingly main constitutive elements of Norwegian childhood at that time. Children participated and mastered situations that demanded responsibility, independence, and vigorous actions, and they were social and cultural actors who contributed to and influenced both the realities and the perceptions of Norwegian childhood at that time.

Participation, independence, and responsibility characterize Norwegian childhood, as well as Nordic childhood in general, and not only in time of war. In time of war, however, these characteristics become more obvious and more important.

Notes

1 The Norwegian publishing house Ariel announced the competition in the Norwegian Journal for School Teachers. Two assignments were given: "A Memory from the War" (*Et minne fra krigen*) or "When Peace Came" (*Da freden kom*). One hundred and eighty-six essays were selected by the local school teachers and submitted to the national competition; 101 of them were entitled "A Memory from the War." The essays are registered in the National Archives of Norway.
2 For example, Ericsson and Simonsen 2005; Olsen 1998; Nøkleby and Hjeltnes 2000.
3 We know that as many as 500 Norwegian children were killed during the war. It is also a fact that every fourth Norwegian who lived through the war was a child and that children participated in every single part in the history of war and occupation; see Nøkleby and Hjeltnes 2000: 11.
4 See Schrumpf 2007: 16ff.
5 While in Norway, 10,000 people were killed during the war, in Denmark the number was 3,600. See Gustavson 2007: 264. See also Chapters 11, 14 and 19 by Garðarsdóttir, Olsen and Nykvist in this book.
6 Gustavson 2007: 260–5.
7 See de Coninck-Smith, Sandin, and Schrumpf 1997; Schrumpf 2012.
8 For the concepts of "human beings" and "human becomings" cf. James, Jenks, and Prout 1999: 289.
9 Eriksen 1999: 10.
10 Eriksen 1999: 14.
11 See Junilla and Jalagin (unpublished working paper): 2.
12 Merleau-Ponty 2012: 132. Merleau-Ponty sees in "the taking up," *la reprise*, an articulate assumption of existence and maintains that "The acquired ... is only truly acquired if it is taken up in a new movement of thought, and a thought is only situated if it itself assumes a situation. The essence of consciousness is to provide itself with one or many worlds, to make its own thoughts exist *in front of* itself like things, and sketching out these landscapes and abandoning them indivisibly demonstrates its vitality."
13 Cf. Lorås 2007: 436; and Kaldal 2003: 96ff.
14 Cf. White 2003: 126.
15 Eriksen 1999: 108.
16 The political party, Nasjonal Samling, which collaborated with the Germans, had at the most 43,000 members in 1943; cf. Furre 1991: 177. In the trial after the war, 55,000 members of the Nazi party were accused of "unpatriotic behavior." See Borge 2014: 476.
17 Cf. Borge 2012.
18 Et minne fra krigen. Karen Margrethe Bjelland. Arendal. File 1, National Archives of Norway.
19 Et minne fra krigen. Edith Gjerde. Skimmeland skole. Mosterhamn. File 3, National Archives of Norway.
20 Et minne fra krigen. Eva Steenberg. Klokkeråsen skole. Slagen pr. Tønsberg. File 5, National Archives of Norway.
21 Et minne fra krigen. Arne Kinserdal (12). File 1, National Archives of Norway.
22 Et minne fra krigen. Jann Beckman. Bygeløy skole. File 1, National Archives of Norway.
23 Et minne fra krigen. Henny Grande. Lademoen skole Trondheim. File 5. Else Hansen. Bergen. File 1 og Kari Bø. Nylund skole. Stavanger. File 5, National Archives of Norway.
24 Et minne fra krigen. Gunnar Wagtskjold (13). Bergen. File 1, National Archives of Norway.

25 Et minne fra krigen. Randi Ophaug. Lademoen skole. Trondheim. File 5, National Archives of Norway.

26 Eiler was brother of Kate, cf. above.

27 Et minne fra krigen. Eiler Villmones. Korgen. File 3, National Archives of Norway.

28 Ariès 1991: 570, 614.

29 Cf. Junilla and Jalagin: 10.

30 Oddlaug Sletta. Et minne frå krigen. Foldfjorden pr. Kristiansund. File 3, National Archives of Norway.

31 This essay was copied by Alfred's teacher.

32 Et minne fra krigen. Alfred Koppervik 12 år. Bagn, Dølven skole. File 1, National Archives of Norway.

33 Et minne fra krigen. Bjørg Wiik. Lademoen skole. Trondheim. File 5, National Archives of Norway.

34 Et minne fra krigen. Kate Villmones 13 år. Korgen. File 3, National Archives of Norway.

35 See Eiler Villmones, cf. above.

36 Et minne fra krigen. Torbjørn Johansen, Moan skole. Børsa. File 1, National Archives Norway. In Finnmark and northern Troms, the civilians were forced to evacuate and the Germans effectuated the scorched earth strategy. Accordingly, around 70,000 people were forced to evacuate. Thousands of people escaped, however, and lived in the mountains until this part of the country was liberated by the Russians in winter 1945.

37 Junilla and Jalagin: 6.

38 Et minne fra krigen. Egil Hope. Vestlandet. File 5, National Archives of Norway.

39 Et minne fra krigen. Else-Marie Gjertsen, Skimmeland skole. Mosterhamn. File 3, National Archives of Norway.

40 Et minne fra krigen Harald Solberg. Grasmo skole. Setskog. File 4, National Archives of Norway.

41 In 2014, children in 23 different countries lived in war areas, and in Syria alone 10,000 children have been killed because of the war. See www.aftenposten.no/fakta/innsikt/6-fakta-om-barn-i-krig-7682271.html.

14 "In Song We Meet on Common Ground"

Conceptions of Children in Songbooks for Norwegian Schools (1914–1964)

Eiliv O. Olsen

Singing has a long and very strong tradition in the Nordic countries. From the Middle Ages, people have often made songs and dances to remember special events and preserve memories for future generations. Singing was a common activity in everyday life: songs to call the cattle, to calm babies, and to express love. Hailing songs and drinking songs used in social contexts were common, and children too had their own oral social repertoire of songs and dances, developed through generations. The Norwegian Constitution of 1814 stated that "The Evangelical-Lutheran Religion shall still be the official Religion in Norway," which meant that hymns and other religious songs were to be learnt and sung both in churches and in schools, together with secular songs.[1] Choir singing continues to be a widespread and important activity in all the Nordic countries—whether in local communities, universities, high schools, or compulsory schools. Many choir competitions are arranged. Nordic people are indeed "a singing people," both musically and socially.

Given the strong tradition of singing in the Nordic countries, one important source for conceptions of children in Norway is to be found in school songbooks. As early as the eighteenth century, hymn collections were used in schools as part of the Lutheran education, and during the nineteenth century, many songs belonging to the cultural heritage were included along with the hymns. Songs with texts from a child's perspective did not appear until the twentieth century.

Although songbooks for children play an important role in school, little attention has been paid to the role of school songbooks in the history of childhood in Nordic countries and to what the songs tell us about the conceptions of children. Even though there has been a lot of sociological research into lyrics, music, and youth in general, there has been little interest in school songbooks, despite their contribution to a common song repertoire for all Norwegian children.

The aim of this chapter is to contribute to the history of childhood and especially conceptions of children in Norway and the Nordic countries by exploring the selection of songs offered to children in the most widespread school songbook in Norway—the *Skolens Sangbok*. This highly influential songbook was edited by the school teacher and amateur singer Mads Berg (1865–1955) and was published in many editions, from 1914 to 1999.[2] Thus, a great number of Norwegian children have sung and been influenced by these songs through most of the twentieth century.

I will have a closer look at three editions of the *Skolens Sangbok*—from 1914, 1949 and 1964. My chapter first provides a background to the songbooks by underscoring the significance of the Norwegian Constitution of 1814. It then highlights the significance of singing as stated in the introductions to the three selected editions of the *Skolens Sangbok*. The next parts of the chapter analyze central themes in the 1914, 1949 and 1964 editions respectively, providing a frame of reference for understanding elements of Norwegian notions of childhood and conceptions of children. Then I will review the songs that were included in all three editions, forming a "Norwegian Canon." In the last part, I compare the Norwegian songbook with one much used Swedish songbook and one Danish, and then discuss similarities and differences within a "Nordic Canon."

By closely examining the three editions of the *Skolens Sangbok*, we can observe some characteristic features: (1) grounds for the important role of singing in childhood; (2) overall conceptions of what it meant to be a "good Norwegian child" in a quite homogenous, mainly rural, Lutheran society, for example, appreciate freedom, love nature and the seasons, especially winter sports, be helpful and industrious, love mother and father, and believe in God; and (3) a wish to present artistic quality to children by singing songs made by renowned poets and composers, especially from Norway and other Nordic countries.

The Norwegian Constitution of 1814 and Its Background for School Songbook Lyrics

From 1387 to 1814, the old Kingdom of Norway was a Danish province. During the Napoleonic War in Europe, the king of Denmark/Norway, Frederik VI, chose to support Napoleon who, however, was defeated in the battle of Leipzig in 1813. During the ensuing negotiations in Kiel in January 1814, Denmark was forced to give Norway to Sweden as booty. However, the Swedish king, Karl Johan, did not follow up the situation, and during the next couple of months, Norwegian men from the upper dynasties decided that a number of elected citizens from all over the country should gather at Eidsvoll (a mansion in the central southern part of Norway) to craft a constitution.[3] The constitution was signed by 112 delegates from different parts of Norway on May 17. It was based upon ideas from the constitutions particularly of the United States and France, and many songs in the later Norwegian school system were strongly influenced by it, thereby promoting national ideals to children. Some of the most important ideas expressed in the Constitution included the following: The Kingdom of Norway is a free, independent, and indivisible State; every man has the right to life, freedom and property; knowledge and sciences will show the way, eliminating superstition and prejudice; tradition must be respected and changes must be conducted with caution; equality and freedom are for everyone; in the future, peace shall reign in the Nordic countries.[4]

The creation of the constitution in 1814 is celebrated still today on May 17, the Norwegian National Day. This holiday has been, and still is, the most important celebration day in Norway, much more so than national days in the other Nordic countries. Around 1870, the holiday started a new and very special tradition—processions of children parade through the streets in towns across Norway, carrying Norwegian flags and singing national songs. May 17 is also called "Children's Day," and there are no signs of weapons or soldiers in the parade. Many songs in *Skolens Sangbok* are used on this day, and the celebration of the National Day has always been one of the most important features in the lives of Norwegian children.

The *Skolens Sangbok* Editions: Singing People with a Common Ground

The prefaces and introductions to the various editions of the *Sangbok* say much about Norwegian views of the importance of singing and music and the role that music should play in the lives of children. In the 1914 edition, Mads Berg points to the old folk songs, from the time when singing in the Nordic countries was alive among the people. He wishes that Norwegians once again will be "a singing people," as in the old days when it was as natural to sing as to talk. At that time, folk songs were learned by ear and "the song treasure" was actively used and highly appreciated among people. Berg argues that although all children must learn to read in school, we must not forget the joy and relaxation of singing. He trusts that the songbook will contribute to this, especially because all the melodies are printed with music and therefore easier to learn, if the children have learned to read music. He also stresses the importance of encouraging children to sing solo, facing the class, so that they get used to singing as a natural activity.

In the 1949 edition, the preface (also written by Berg) points to the "normal curriculum" from 1939, a curriculum based upon the ideas of "child-centered" or "activity-centered" school. Two sentences from this curriculum say much about the significance of music—training the children's voices is one of the most important tasks in singing lessons, and such training must be connected to the singing of hymns and secular songs in the classroom. The preface ends with the following statement: "Our song treasure is the nation's common property. In song we meet on common ground."

In 1961, the Norwegian Council for Experimental School Programs made a curriculum for a planned nine-year compulsory school. The songbook preface from 1964 (written by Åse and Arnfinn Klakegg) refers to this curriculum where the subject of song and music has a more prominent role than earlier. The number of songs has increased: there are almost a hundred new songs, but "the good old songs" are still there. This edition also gives importance to recorder playing, an important activity in the music curriculum. Training in note values and intervals is also implemented in this book.

The three prefaces state very clearly that the significance of singing is closely linked to the aim of integrating the children in the—positive—traditions of Norway and also of the other Nordic countries. The children should fully participate in the common ground of singing.

An important sign of the egalitarian thinking within the school system in Norway since 1865 was the fact that all children had to read and write two official Norwegian languages because the authorities decided that both "riksmål," the language based upon Danish language used by the official bureaucracy and in most of the cities, and "landsmål," constructed by the linguist Ivar Aasen (1813–1896) around 1850, based on rural dialects mainly from the west coast of Norway and some inland valleys, should be used equally. The aim of singing in both languages was for children to get used to both, but in fact children from cities in the eastern part of Norway sometimes found the western "landsmål" somewhat unfamiliar. To them, "landsmål" was not part of the "common ground."

The 1914 Edition and Its Repertoire for Norwegian Children

The 1914 edition of the songbook contains 185 songs, and I have divided most of them into thematic groups as a way to highlight important elements of what the book reveals about the ideas of what should be in the common ground of songs for Norwegian children. In some cases, a song may belong to more than one group; in any case, however, the main tendencies are clear. The five most interesting groups are: (1) songs about the people of Norway and Norwegian nature; (2) hymns, Christmas songs, and other religious songs belonging to a common Nordic Lutheran tradition; (3) lyric songs about nature; (4) songs about family life and the rural home; and (5) songs from other countries. These divisions will also be followed in this chapter.

Songs about Norway and its People, Nature, and Seasons

This is by far the largest group with almost fifty songs. Many of them express patriotism in some way or another. Patriotic feelings are often linked to the Norwegian nature: the far north, with bare, wild mountains and eternal snow, steep hillsides and peaceful valleys, forests, waterfalls and lakes. Offshore are the ocean and the fjords, sometimes calm and smooth, sometimes with strong winds and dangerous waves. The Norwegian peasant living in the valleys is often described as steady and safe, while the Norwegian sailor and fisherman are portrayed as heroes, gambling with their lives in the struggle to earn their living or to save other people from drowning. The coastal pilot is one of the greatest heroes, saving many lives from storms and sinking ships. Shores are mostly depicted as rocky and wild. Walks in the high mountains are described as peak experiences, in contrast to narrow and dark valleys. But in the valleys, there also grow beautiful flowers. There are calm ponds, small creeks and peacefulness. In general, these songs describe a kind of Norwegian "map of landscapes and the people living there" to the children—a conception of the common ground for children. Many of these songs are written by Bjørnstjerne Bjørnson (1832–1910), winner of the Nobel Prize in Literature in 1903.[5] Several of his poems in this book have melodies composed by Bjørnson's cousin, Rikard Nordraak (1842–1866).[6] Within this group of songs, Bjørnson and Nordraak's works form a distinct canon.

The seasons most frequently described are winter and spring. Spring is often depicted in agricultural terms: "The spring is here, and all of us must clear the fields, plow and sow, to make life grow in Norway." The symbol of spring is also used to describe the gift of independence and freedom from 1814. On the other hand, a number of songs have words like "winter," "sleeping," and "darkness." Such words are also used as symbols to describe the 400 years of Danish rule. But winter is also described as a season of sport and freshness. Norwegian children seem to love skiing, often down steep hills at the highest possible speed, with a feeling of freedom. In the *Gymnastics March*, Norwegian boys are urged to endure hard work, frost, and heat because "Old Norway really wants that sort of boys." But when he skis down the steepest hillsides, the girl follows right behind! Maybe she will overtake him one day? Nobody can be a champion without training, and boys and girls are equal when it comes to winter sports. One line goes: "That kind of boys old Norway will have"; there is, however, a long tradition in the Norwegian school that all girls sing as loud as possible: "That kind of *girls* old Norway will have." This twist has made the song very popular in the classroom, and underscores conceptions of equality between boys and girls, and the love of winter sports.

There is only one song with warlike lyrics in this book: *Hr. Sinclair dro over salten hav.*[7] The song is based on a true event in 1612 when Scottish troops disembarked on the west coast of Norway. They intended to march through the valley of Gudbrandsdalen and into Sweden, where they were meant to join Swedish soldiers in war against Denmark. But in a narrow part of the valley, the Scotsmen were assaulted and massacred by Norwegian peasants. The song ends with a warning—it is dangerous for soldiers to visit the people who live in the Norwegian mountains.[8] The message for the children is—we shall not be aggressive, but we have the right to defend ourselves.

Other songs tell us that Norway must be built in peace "to give to our children," and the word "freedom" is present in many of them: "We claim a free nation, and we do not gamble with freedom. We claim a nation for you and me, and the nation's name is Norway." Per Sivle (1857–1904), who wrote this song, was an ardent spokesman for Norway as a free and independent country, and several of his songs are included in this songbook.

A variation on this theme is a picture of Eidsvoll as a monument of the Norwegian 1,000-year-old "saga" when freedom was something natural: "A life in freedom, a death in happiness was all the Norwegians required," wrote Olaus Arvesen (1830–1917) in the song "At Eidsvoll Stands a Saga-Hall." The song is included in all three editions of Mads Berg's songbook featured in this chapter.

Henrik Wergeland (1808–1845), often described as a leading pioneer in the development of a Norwegian literature, contributes a poem often called "The National Anthem of the Children"—"We, the small children are also members of the nation."[9] The song is still used in the children's parade on May 17. Another of his songs, which is very popular in school, is "Gnomes and Dwarves are Building in the Mountains."[10] This text is a good example of Enlightenment ideas: the gnomes and dwarves build societies inside the mountain, in darkness, but "we," the new generation of children, will chase them out—with dynamite! Here, Wergeland expresses an important conception of children as the future hope for their country.

The Norwegian flag, with its cross in red, white, and blue, is mentioned in several songs: "We raise our flag, because we are one united people."[11] The flag is a symbol of freedom and of Christianity, and almost every child carries a little flag during the National Celebration Day. The keyword for the children to remember is "Freedom," both as members of a free nation and by overcoming obstacles in nature, by God's help. However, freedom is never obtained by aggression, but, if necessary, by defense, as in the Sinclair song. Another keyword is the love of Norwegian nature and winter sports. Freedom, Christianity, and nature are "common grounds" that play a significant role in the conception of children.

Hymns, Christmas Carols, and Other Religious Songs

There are more than forty songs in this group. The songbook opens with the hymn "We are Going to Work in Thy Precious Name," presenting a typical Lutheran way of living, based on his understanding of vocation—we work together in order to utilize and take care of our country given us by God, as best we can, and to contribute to the common good, trusting in Him.[12] The song states that Norwegians must have faith in God, if He refuses to be the builder, our attempts to build the country will be hopeless, and if He will not defend us, no guard can help. "God Bless our Precious Homeland" says: "So please, watch over us, that we can live here in peace!"[13] This song is sometimes called "Norway's National Hymn" and is sung every May 17.

There are six Christmas hymns and songs, all of them also used in Denmark and/or Sweden, and often sung when walking around the Christmas tree. One of them, "Silent Night," is of course known in all the Nordic countries, as it is in many parts of the world. "Oh, Christmas with Thy Joy" is based on a Swedish Christmas song.[14] It is called "The children's Christmas Song" because of the refrain: "We clap our hands, we sing and laugh and turn around." In the last verse, everyone must take the hand of the person next to him- or herself, "and promise to love each other." This song, together with a couple of other Christmas songs, show a conception of Nordic children allowed to be free, merry, and physically active, as in, for example, the "Gymnastics March."

"Lovely is the Blue Heaven" was written by the Dane, Nikolai Frederik Severin Grundtvig (1783–1872), as are several other religious songs in the songbook.[15] Many of his songs are translated into other Nordic languages, and belong to a Nordic "common ground" of religious song tradition both in churches and at home.

Lyric Songs about Nature

This group comprises more than thirty songs. Of course, many songs hailing Norway also include descriptions of nature, but the poems in this group mainly describe nature without linking it to patriotism, but from a purely aesthetic point of view. It seems that the main point here is to present the best Norwegian nature lyricists and composers (like Grieg) from the nineteenth century to the children. The most renowned, besides Bjørnson, is Johan Sebastian Welhaven (1807–1873), who strongly disagreed with what he called a boasting and rude patriotism. His poems describe nature in various ways, like "The Wild Duck" and "I Listened to the River where Nøkken Sings."[16] The bishop Jørgen Moe (1813–1882), too, wrote beautiful poems about nature, such as "I Will go to the Mountains above the Parish."[17] Bjørnson is of course also represented here. Some of the songs are from his *Peasant Tales*, novels describing rural life in Norway in a rather romantic but also lively and colorful manner. Examples are "I Wonder what there is to see Behind the High Mountains" and "The Fox Lay Under the Birch."[18] It is obvious that such songs are included to give the children examples of aesthetic poems on a high level together with "good and beautiful" music. This seems to stem from a conception of children being able to appreciate good poetry and music. Therefore, the authorities emphasized the important task of offering aesthetic quality to the children in compulsory school.[19]

Two additional songs from this group should be mentioned: "The Bridal Journey in Hardanger" and "Solveig's Song." The first is a three-part composition for a male choir. It was originally performed, together with a painting of the same title as a tableau, at an exhibition in Kristiania (Oslo) in 1849. The painting was made by the famous Norwegian artists, Adolph Tidemand and Hans Gude, and pictures a rowboat with wedding guests on a sunny and calm Hardanger fjord. The lyrics include: "It is a shining summer's day at the waters of the Hardanger Fjord." The music is partly inspired by Norwegian folk music. Both the painting and the choir song are still among the most iconic national Romantic artistic works in Norway. The second song, "Solveig's Song," is one of the very few lyrics written by Henrik Ibsen, from the play *Peer Gynt* (premiered with Edvard Grieg's music in 1876). Obviously, these two songs cannot have been meant for singing in the classroom. The main purpose seems to have been to give the children experiences of some iconic national artistic works, as part of their cultural heritage.

Songs about Family Life and the Rural Home

There are about twenty songs in this group and only one is about a father. Curiously enough, that song describes a bourgeois home, where a mother watches "three sweet children" standing by the window, waiting for father to come home from work (maybe at the office).[20] Almost every other song describes scenes from a rural environment, most of them written in "landsmål." Mother works very hard, the sweat runs like blood, but still she wipes away tears from the children's cheeks and kisses them with love. At the farm, a little sparrow finds grains and straws to eat and has a good time, but he must be aware of the cat and of the hawk high up in the air. Ivar Aasen, the "father of landsmål," remembers the good time when he grew up at the old farm with big trees, green grass, hills and valleys, flowers and berries. There were magpies and starlings, and as a boy he could visit every home in the neighborhood, he knew everyone. He expressed a strong sense of belonging![21] Aasen also wrote many songs describing wisdom of life, for the children to remember, for example "No one can please everybody."[22] There is always someone who does not like your food and drink. And many people laugh at others, but they do nothing good themselves

A rather humorous description of rural family life is "Anne Knutsdotter" ("Anne, daughter of Knut"), told from a young girl's point of view. The little family lives on a rocky slope where nobody would believe anyone could live. Her father is a peddler, traveling widely around, her mother cleans the house, and Anne works at the spinning wheel, but her little four-year-old brother does nothing. They have a goat eating the grass on the roof, and sometimes during winter they do not see people for more than fourteen days, due to snow and wind. They only just manage to feed one cow and one pig. This sounds pretty sad, had it not been for the very cheerful folk melody. It seems that in spite of the dramatic nature surrounding them, Anne and her brother feel quite happy and safe within their small family. These two songs, among others, point clearly to an idea of how children's lives should be—filled with a feeling of safety and affiliation.

Labor movement songs are not included, despite the growing labor population in many towns. The "common ground," therefore, is mainly rural.

Songs from Other Countries

The national anthems of Sweden, Denmark and Finland are included. There are two more Finnish songs, both hailing the Finnish woods—the Song of Suomi. One song praises Iceland, where the Old Norse culture still lives.[23]

The children must learn to know their Nordic neighbors, but except for the *Marseillaise*, other national anthems are not included in this edition.

The 1949 Edition: New Songs

There are no significant changes of repertoire in the edition of the song-book from 1949. The understanding of children and the "common ground" seem to be much the same as in 1914. However, we find some examples of songs aimed more directly at children. One example is "Dance, Dance, My Puppet!"[24] The editor comments: "In primary school, the girls occasionally bring their puppets. If so, they must be allowed to sing the Puppet Song." Another example is "The Skating Song," where children are urged to practice skating.[25] Maybe one day they will be better than the three times Olympic champion Sonja Henie (figure skating) or Oscar Mathisen, five times World Champion (skating). But in 1949, Mathisen was sixty-one years old and Henie forty-eight, so maybe children had new skating idols at that time. Another song is about children picking blueberries. Some songs are about domestic animals: cows giving milk, the old horse, and the dog that must be caressed, not beaten.

There are also some examples of song plays for children and some more folk songs. Three songs should be mentioned because they tell something about how children ought to behave at that time. One song states that the children must come to school merry and light footed, greet each other, and sing a morning hymn. During the day at school they must work hard, read, sing, draw, write, do arithmetic and play in the fresh air during breaks. They must be honest and righteous. Nobody must cheat or be negligent if they want to be good, reliable Norwegian citizens in the future. They must also try to please their mother and father. Another song is about the little girl Lotte and the little boy Herman. They are nicely dressed and have clean hands when they walk to school, and they are polite. A third song (translated from Swedish) is about the little girl Lise. She knows nothing, is constantly in the way, and does things wrong. When she grows up, she will be helpful. But until then, the only thing she can do is to love her parents. Ideals like this belong to the notions of children in the Nordic Lutheran upbringing tradition.

There is only one song about father in this edition: "My father's hand was worn and grey," but it was helpful and steady. When the poet feels his power fail in the storm at sea, it feels as if his father's hand steers the boat to the shore.[26] To the children, father's role as a savior is close to God, as He is described in the patriotic songs about Norway.

We find more songs about winter and the importance of skiing, songs describing Norwegian landscapes, and an increased number of hymns and songs with religious content. This may be due to experiences with the Nazi occupation of Norway during World War II: "Please watch over us so we can live here in peace."

Iceland's national anthem has been added to the other Nordic Anthems (Iceland became an independent nation in 1944), and generally the bonds between the Nordic countries are emphasized. More Swedish folk songs and song plays are included, six of them in Swedish, the others in translation. In this way, Norwegian children may learn to sing in Swedish language, so the Nordic "common ground" seems to be extended in this edition. Surprisingly enough, there are no songs in English, although English became a subject in compulsory school as early as 1936. "The common ground" for Norwegian children still means the Nordic countries. There are no labor movement songs in this book either.

The 1964 Edition: New Songs

The editors of the 1964 edition of the songbook write in the preface that almost 100 new songs are included. A look at the songs tells us that the word "new" does not mean newly made songs. In fact, few of them were composed later than 1950. Examples of the more newly made songs are some that can be categorized as "hits." For instance, the most recent song is "Eventyrvisa" ("The Fairytale Song") from the Norwegian movie *Toya* (1956), which was a "hit" for a couple of years. The movie was based upon the story *Toya, The Refugee Girl*, written by Norwegian children and presented on the radio.[27] In 1956, many Norwegian children met refugee children from Hungary in the classrooms. Their families had left Hungary, because of the revolt against Russian authorities, so the story was quite realistic. All the fairytales mentioned in the song were of course Norwegian, and this is a good example of how the Norwegian Broadcasting Corporation supported the concept of children's potential as artists.

Another "hit" is the patriotic, march-like song "Norway in Red, White and Blue."[28] The song was written in 1941 when Norway was occupied by the Nazis. It was supposed to be performed in a cabaret in Oslo but was forbidden by the Nazis. During the occupation, though, the song became well known among the people, and when a new cabaret was set up in May 1945, a time of celebration of freedom and peace, the song was presented again with great success. The colors of the flag are linked to Norwegian nature— the snow and the birch trunk are white, red is the color of the evening sun and of the little cottage by the road, and blue is the color of the glacier and the bluebells. In the next verse, colors are linked to future generations, a boy and a girl. Her dress is white, her cheek is red, and her eyes are blue like the violet. His forelock is white, his cap is red, and he has a blue-eyed trust to his country. The last sentence goes like this: "You are ours; you are ours, old Norway! We will dress you in red, white and blue!" The song expresses both the love of Norwegian nature and the belief in new generations.

Two relatively new Christmas songs are included. These are among the most beloved songs ever in Norway. One is "The Christmas Eve Song," written by a very popular singer and songwriter, Alf Prøysen (1914–1970).[29]

He grew up in a small cottage in a rural environment in eastern Norway, and many of his lyrics describe children's everyday life written from a child's perspective. In 1951, he was asked to write a song about the Christmas Gospel "in a way that everyone can understand," and he begins the song like an address to children: "We have cleaned the floor and carried wood for the stove. We have set up a sheaf of grain and we have decorated the Christmas tree. Now we will take a rest, and I will tell you about the Christmas star." The star shone over the stable where Jesus was born, and after having described some of the Gospel events, the song ends: "You still can see the star over the roof where midwife Matja lives." In this way, the stable of Bethlehem is linked to a little Norwegian hamlet, and the song is written in a simple language that every child can sing and understand. The other song, "It is Light in Quiet Hamlets this Evening" from 1931, was written by the west coast poet Jacob Sande (1906–1967).[30] He describes how thousands of children's hands raise lightened candles to the sky, celebrating the little child in Bethlehem who had a pillow of hay. Both these authors locate the story of Christmas Eve among children and "common people" in a good Lutheran tradition.

The really new element in this book are the many songs in English—twenty in all. There are the national anthems of England and the United States; three Negro Spirituals ("Go down Moses," "One more River," and "Nobody Knows the Trouble I've Seen"); the Scottish traditional songs "Auld Lang Syne" and "Loch Lomond"; "The land of my Fathers" from Wales; and two English soldier songs ("It's a Long Way to Tipperary" and "When Johnny Comes Marching Home"). And finally, twenty-six years after the Disney movie *Snow White and the Seven Dwarfs* came to Norway, the children could sing "Heigh Ho" and "Whistle While You Work." Probably, the children had great pleasure singing in English.

Another remarkable change is the increased number of Norwegian, Danish, and Swedish folk songs. Some of the lyrics are in Swedish, as in the 1949 edition. Several of these songs have been included into the Norwegian "common ground" repertory, for example "The Girls from Småland," "Into our Garden," and "The Värmland Song."[31] "The Oats," a song written by the Danish poet Jeppe Aakjær (1866–1930), is also among often-sung songs in Norway.[32] And finally, in this songbook we find two labor movement songs. One is "A Young Boy is Weeding in the Fields." His dream is to earn enough money to buy himself a Ford.[33] The other is "Jens Vejmand," also written by Jeppe Aakjær. Jens Vejmand worked as a road worker cutting stones during his whole life, but they never gave him a stone on his grave. There is also an increase in children's songs. However, religious songs and hymns including Christmas hymns, Norway and its nature, and the family in the (rural) home are still dominant themes, as they were in the edition from 1914. Lyric songs about Nature have become less numerous than in the 1914 edition. Instead, the editors have included some contemporary poets like Alf Prøysen, writing for and to children, but at a high artistic level.

In general, then, the "common ground" of songs is expanded in the 1964 edition in four ways: more Nordic songs; more folk songs; more songs based on children's own lives; and more traditional songs from the United States and Great Britain. The conceptions of children, however, seem to be much the same as in earlier editions.

Songs Included in All Three Editions

The 1914 songbook contains 185 songs, the 1949 songbook 249, and the 1964 edition 305. Many new songs have been added, and many are excluded, but I think it is particularly interesting to have a look at the ninety-nine songs included in all three editions of *Skolens Sangbok* during these fifty years. Which songs and poets are "canonized?" What seems to be the core of "common ground" for children throughout this period? And what can we learn from this "common ground" about the Norwegian concept of children?

One poet stands out, and consequently merits special attention: Bjørnstjerne Bjørnson, who wrote sixteen of the ninety-nine songs. During his lifetime, Bjørnson was a very prolific author. He wrote plays and novels, poems, and songs with themes from the past and from his own times. Many of his songs have a strong moral appeal, and that may well be the reason for the "canonizing." Furthermore, many of his songs are very melodious and pleasant to sing, thanks to composers like Grieg, Nordraak, and others.

The sixteen songs show his diversity as a poet. Seven of them are about Norway, its people, and nature: the Norwegian seaman, our country in the far north by the eternal snow, the duty to defend our free home, a strong and healthy youth, and the need for human compassion instead of war. A scene from the Viking Age is described in the song "Grand Sails Cross the North Sea," when the Norwegian king Olav Tryggvason, who was a very good sportsman, was in the year 1,000 defeated and killed at sea by Norwegian rivals with support from the Danish and the Swedish kings.[34] Some lyrical songs from his *Peasant Tales* are also included: "I Wonder What there is to see Behind the High Mountains" and "The fox Lay Under the Birch." Another song is "Ingerid Sletten," a song about a girl who owned a little knitted hat that her mother had given her. It was her most precious piece of property, and she saved it for special occasions in life. But the occasions never took place. As an old woman, she wanted to look at the hat once more, but "there was no thread left." The moral is: do not hesitate to use your gifts! Another song is "Raise Your Head, Brave Boy!"[35] If you are disappointed, there will be new hopes! A deep trust in God is expressed in "Lord, Take the Playing Child into your Strong Hands."[36] Of course the national anthem is among the sixteen songs. Most of the melodies are composed by Edvard Grieg and other well-known Norwegian composers.

Other songs included in all three books are written by "canonized" Norwegian poets: Ivar Aasen, Henrik Wergeland, Johan Sebastian Welhaven,

Aasmund Olavsson Vinje (1818–1870), Elias Blix (1836–1902), Jørgen Moe, Arne Garborg (1851–1924) and Per Sivle—some of these songs have already been mentioned. Henrik Ibsen's "Solveig's Song" is also among these, as is his merry mountain hiking song.[37] Thus, the editors maintain that a canon of poets from the nineteenth century is still valid in a school songbook in 1964. The songs still belong to the main categories mentioned earlier, and they represent examples of artistic poetry on a high level. The "common ground" for the children seems to be the same throughout the whole period, and so are conceptions of children as human beings in need of artistic experiences on a high level. The experiences of World War II in Norway seem to have strengthened the focus on God, nation, and the king. In 1964, the songbook begins with the national anthem, and continues with "Song for the King." The third song is "The Second National Anthem" by Elias Blix.[38]

The prefaces in these three songbooks (and many other songbooks used in Norwegian schools) have the following message: Singing is important! Singing together is important for a variety of reasons. First, and perhaps above all, it is important for a child's education and intellectual development. Songbooks claim, for example, that singing together gives children "a strong impression that singing, like the other arts, is a means to lift the mind above the daily struggle." And further: "Beautiful music has ... a profound effect on people's minds ... it helps open up for what is beautiful and good, and also to promote togetherness and friendship."[39] Even the *Læreplan for Forsøk med 9-årig skole* (*Curriculum for Experiments with 9-Year School*) (1960), published by The Norwegian Council for Experimental School Programs states that music has great educational value. Listening to good music may help children to open their minds for the good and beautiful, and may promote a feeling of togetherness.[40] Second, the songbooks emphasize that singing is also important to develop a good voice and clear pronunciation. A third reason offered for the importance of singing, whether for religious or national education, is that it introduces children to a country's common cultural heritage. Finally, the art of singing is also seen as a goal in itself.

Comparison with a Swedish and a Danish Songbook

From Sweden, I have chosen *Nu ska vi sjunga* ("Now we will sing"). This book was meant for primary school and was first published in 1943. The initiator, Alice Tegnér (1864–1943), was a music teacher, often acknowledged as the best writer of children's songs in Sweden during the first half of the twentieth century. The songs were selected by school children and teacher. New editions have been published periodically, and by 2004 two million copies had been sold. The songs are divided into seven themes: seasons, songs about animals and flowers, song plays, songs about hiking, Christmas songs, canons and "other beautiful songs."

Mads Berg's songbook was meant for both primary and secondary schools, and it will not be fair to compare the two books in everything. Still, some significant differences should be mentioned, since *Skolens Sangbok* also aims at children in primary school. First, Mads Berg does not divide the songs into themes. *Skolens Sangbok* has songs covering all the themes in *Nu ska vi sjunga*, but they are not systematized, and it is difficult to get an overview. *Skolens Sangbok* begins with simple songs, while more advanced songs are presented toward the end of the book. Second, it is natural that most songs in *Nu ska vi sjunga* are "childish," much more so than in *Skolens Sangbok*, because children themselves were allowed to choose the songs. The Swedish book has songs about a great variety of animals and flowers—lambs, nestlings, swans, bluebells, roses, and more. In Mads Berg's book, animal songs are mostly about domestic animals, and there are almost none about flowers. There are also more children's song plays in *Nu ska vi sjunga*. Third, both books have many songs about walking in nature, but most of the Swedish songs are about woods and meadows, while Norwegian songs often describe mountains. Furthermore, *Nu ska vi sjunga* has fewer songs about Sweden as a nation than *Skolens Sangbok* has about Norway. There are also fewer songs by "canonized" authors in the Swedish book. Some of the lyrics in *Nu ska vi sjunga* have examples of old-fashioned upbringing. When little Maja sings to her doll, she tells her to sleep and be kind, because otherwise the chimney sweep will come and take her, and father will bring the rod.[41] None of the songs in *Skolens Sangbok* have that kind of threat. Generally, conceptions of children in *Nu ska vi sjunga* seem to be "let children be children."

It may be relevant at this point, to draw attention to the fact that Sweden has a long and strong tradition of female authors writing for and about children, from Nobel Prize winner Selma Lagerlöf (*Nils Holgersson's Wonderful Journey Across Sweden*) to Astrid Lindgren's *Pippi Longstocking*.

In Denmark, by far the most commonly used songbook is *Højskolesangbogen* (*The Folk High School Songbook*).[42] The first edition, called *Sangbok udgivet af foreningen for højskoler og landbrugsskoler*, was published in 1894, the most recent in 2006. The collection of songs started in 1876, when three folk high schools published 700 songs, mostly written by Grundtvig, founder of the *Folkehøjskole* in Denmark.[43] This songbook has played a very important role in the Danish song tradition both in compulsory school, in the "folk high schools," and in common public singing. From 1940, when Denmark, like Norway, was occupied by the Nazis, some of the Danish songs were used as a silent opposition, and the songbook became even more popular after the end of the war.

From the very beginning, *Højskolesangbogen* has represented a strong Danish cultural canon, including songs written by the hymn writers N. F. S. Grundtvig, Thomas Kingo (1634–1703), and Hans Adolph Brorson (1694–1764), and by literary authors Jeppe Aakjær, H. C. Andersen, and others. Carl Nielsen (1865–1931), the renowned Danish composer, is the most frequently represented composer. Maybe in contrast to a book such as *Skolens Sangbok*, this Danish cultural canon seems to have had a unifying effect upon the Danish people, both adults and children. One explanation can be that the book has been constantly revised in accordance with the development of the Danish society; the selection of songs has gradually changed. In 2006, for example, several Grundtvig songs were omitted, while contemporary poets like Kim Larsen (1945–) and Suzanne Brøgger (1944–) were included. This is justified by the wish to keep the very strong Danish song tradition alive. Another explanation can be the strong liberal tradition in Denmark of many so-called "free compulsory schools."[44] An example of this is *Arbejdersangbogen* (*The Workers' Songbook*) from 1926, used in compulsory schools and emphasizing the rights of workers and citizens. There have been no equivalents to this in Norwegian compulsory schools. Today, *Højskolesangbogen* includes 572 songs and about 2.4 million copies have been sold. As in *Nu ska vi sjunga*, the songs are divided into themes, such as morning, evening, faith, life, freedom, community, the seasons, and the Christian holidays.

It seems that *Højskolesangbogen* as well as *Skolens Sangbok* offer a similar "common ground" based upon cultural canons, but the Danish editors seem to have been more aware of the importance of renewing the repertory.

Conclusion: The Songbooks and Conceptions of Children

The most striking finding represented in the school songbooks is the conception of children as future members of a homogenous and unified Norwegian nation with a common cultural tradition. The selection of songs supports and emphasize the spirit of the national constitution of 1814 in many ways. As I have pointed out, many songs are about equality and freedom for all. And despite several songs describing traditional gender roles, there are examples of songs hinting at equality between boys and girls, as in the "Gymnastics March." Another important point is peace: "Peace shall reign in the Nordic Countries," as affirmed in the Constitution. In fact, none of the songs describes war or similar aggression of any kind, except for the Sinclair song. The songs emphasize that Norwegians should not be aggressive, but ready to defend their country.

Many songs express a strong belief in God and that children should trust in God. Both the national anthem (*Ja, vi elsker*) and the national hymn (*Gud signe vårt dyre fedreland*) express faith that God will protect Norway. In the national hymn, Blix also sends up a prayer: "Let Thy peace shed light from mountain to shore and winter flee from the sunshine of spring."[45]

Home and family are almost exclusively described in rural environments. Mother and father are honored, often together with a description of the hard work they do. The traditional roles are mostly retained: the father is steady and strong, and the mother wipes tears from her children's cheeks and sing for them. Per Sivle's "The First Song I Heard was Mother's Song by the Cradle" in the 1949 and 1964 editions is one example.[46] People are depicted as honest, hardworking, peaceful, and modest, and these characteristics are expressed as important for Norwegian children. A typical statement is: "We don't need castles, just a poor but cozy cottage under the glacier."[47]

A majority of the songs describe the nature and climate in Norway, together with some historical traits from the Viking Age. A keyword for Norwegian nature is the great variation—mountains, glaciers, woods, deep valleys, stony shores and the sea. Sailors and coastal guards are heroes, struggling for life and saving others. Walking in the mountains gives a feeling of joy and freedom, and Norwegian children of both genders love to do outdoor sports. In winter skiing on the heaths or, better still, down steep hills. So, winter is described as a fine season, especially for children's sports, but spring is the most beautiful season. Then the sun shines and the winter darkness give way to hope and expectations. As mentioned earlier, spring is also used as a symbol of freedom, from Danish or Swedish supremacy and from the Nazis during the World War II. Norwegian children are told this story every May 17.

In summary, the songs reveal many elements of a Norwegian conception of children. Children are depicted as having a close relation to nature and an intimate relationship to parents and to the home; living in a nation that values freedom, equality, and peace; trusting in God and working hard for the common good; and having a proud memory of a Viking past, but without any aggressive slogans. The selection of songs also reveals a conception of children as having aesthetic and artistic sensibilities that need to be honored and cultivated. The *Skolens Sangbok* has a relative absence of songs purely for children, such as we find in *Nu ska vi sjunga*. It was obviously important to offer the children the experience of artistic and aesthetic quality through the songbooks, less important to use "childish" songs. As *Læreplan for forsøk med 9-årig skole* states: "The aim of Music teaching is to make pupils love good music."[48] Mads Berg's *Skolens Sangbok* was clearly regarded as an instrument providing valuable education of this kind through singing (and recorder playing), but rock and pop music disturbed old attitudes. While singing in compulsory schools up to 1960 mainly meant the adoption of common traditions from the adult world, easy access to new music intended for teenagers changed the repertoire of school song dramatically for the years to come. From about 1970 songbooks were also published with more songs for and to children.

Given the long-time and broad dissemination of songbooks such as *Skolens Sangbok*, *Nu ska vi sjunga*, and *Højskolesangbogen*, and the strong impact they have had on children and their later adult lives, this is a field that clearly merits much more study. Let me finally, then, offer a couple of suggestions for future research. First, a fruitful area of research would be to compare more closely conceptions of children in Nordic songbooks from different times and to explore what might be their "common ground" today. Second, the study of the Norwegian songbooks raises a number of intriguing research questions related to the labor movement. For example, given the strong growth of the labor movement in Norway and other Nordic countries during this period, why are labor movement songs practically nonexistent in the songbooks?[49] Were working-class children alienated? Were conceptions of children mainly rooted in a traditional, rural society? Did every child recognize the "common ground?" Finally, the study of conceptions of children in Norwegian songbooks can also prompt further research into the conceptions of children found in school songbooks from other parts of the world and from different historical periods.

Notes

1 See § 2 of the 1814 Constitution. Alnæs 2013: 505.
2 During these years, more than 900,000 copies were printed.
3 In 1837, Eidsvoll became the first official national monument in Norway. On this period, see Chapter 9 by Rørvik in this volume.
4 Alnæs 2013: 203–10.
5 Bjørnson is by far the most represented poet in the songbooks, see below.
6 Bjørnson and Nordraak also produced the national anthem of Norway, *Ja, vi elsker dette landet*.
7 "Mr Sinclair travelled across the salty sea."
8 In the songbooks from 1949 and 1964, this song is omitted. But the same kind of spirit can be traced in some of the reactions to the Nazi occupation of Norway during World War II. See also Chapter 13 by Schrumpf in this volume.
9 In Norwegian *Vi ere en nation vi med, vi smaa, en alen lange*.
10 In Norwegian *Nisser og dverge*.
11 In Norwegian *Me heiser vårt flagg for me er eit folk*.
12 In Norwegian *I ditt dyrebare navn*.
13 In Norwegian *Gud signe vårt dyre fedreland*.
14 In Norwegian *Å jul med din glede*.
15 In Norwegian *Deilig er den himmel blå*. See more about Grundtvig and his hymns in the chapter by Bunge in this volume.
16 "Nøkken" is a Norwegian and Swedish folkloristic being, living in ponds, rivers and creeks, and luring people into the water to drown them.
17 In Norwegian *Til fjells over bygden står min hu*.
18 In Norwegian *Undrer meg på hva jeg får å se*, and *Og reven lå under birkerot*.
19 Probably this conception is rooted in John Dewey's philosophy of aesthetic education. On the Norwegian national romanticism, see also Chapter 12 by Hansen in this volume.
20 In Norwegian *Tre søte småbarn med øyne blå*.
21 In Norwegian *Tidt eg minnest ein gamal gard*.
22 In Norwegian *Til lags aat alle kan ingen gjera*.
23 In Norwegian *Ytterst mot Norden lyser en ø*.
24 In Norwegian *Danse, danse dokka mi*.
25 In Norwegian *Skøyteløpervise*.
26 In Norwegian *Handa hans far min var sliten og grå*.
27 From 1953 and for many years afterwards, the Norwegian Broadcasting Corporation (NRK) arranged an annual competition for children where they were invited to write new chapters to a story every week. The best chapters were printed and became "The Book of the Children's hour."
28 As mentioned earlier, the Norwegian flag is red, white, and blue.
29 In Norwegian *Julekveldsvisa*.
30 In Norwegian *Det lyser i stille grender*.
31 In Swedish *Flickorna i Småland*, *Uti vår hage* and *Värmlandsvisan*.

32 In Danish *Havren*.
33 In Norwegian *Det lå en pjokk og lukte*.
34 In Norwegian *Brede seil over nordsjø går*.
35 In Norwegian *Løft ditt hode, du raske gutt*.
36 In Norwegian *Herre, ta i din sterke hånd barnet som leker ved stranden*.
37 In Norwegian *Vi vandrer med freidig mot*.
38 See note 13.
39 Lund 2010: 5, www.journals.uio.no/index.php/adno/issue/view/114.
40 Forsøksrådet for skoleverket, 219–20.
41 *Maja's Song*.
42 This title is from 2006. From the eleventh edition, circa 1925, the book was called *Folkehøjskolens Sangbog*.
43 "Folkehøjskole" is a high school without any degrees open to all citizens; such schools were developed by Grundtvig and are thriving still today; for more on the Folkehøjskole, see Chapter 7 by Bunge in this volume.
44 The "free compulsory schools" represent a multitude of ideological, religious, and pedagogical ideas, and work for the right of each family to choose the sort of education they want.
45 In Norwegian *Lat lysa din fred frå fjell til strand og vetter for vårsol røma*.
46 In Norwegian *Den fyrste song eg høyra fekk*.
47 The title in Norwegian *Brøyte seg rydning i svarteste skog*.
48 *Læreplan for forsøk med 9-årig skole*, 2. edition (Oslo: Aschehoug, 1964), 219.
49 This fact may be explained by Pierre Bourdieu's theories of battles between "cultural capitals" within a "field," *in casu* school songbooks as part of the official education system. The Labor movement had no valid cultural capital there.

Part III

Literature

Children's Books, Fairy Tales, and Novels

15 Children, Dying, and Death
Views from an Eighteenth-Century Periodical for Children

Merethe Roos

In the final decades of the eighteenth century, Denmark experienced an explosion of new periodicals and newspapers that sparked vivid debates and a high degree of openness in Copenhagen's public sphere. This rich variety of print materials introduced a diversity of opinions and a broad range of voices to the public, which also got its first exposure to writers who were women and members of the lower social classes. The diversity of the new periodical culture grew as an increasing number of periodicals targeted audiences from particular professions and guilds. All of this amounted to a revolution of the written word, and contemporaries even used the term "epidemic" to describe the new climate.[1]

This atmosphere of unprecedented public debate was the legacy of total press freedom under the government of Johann Friedrich Struensee. Struensee rose to power in Denmark–Norway in 1770 and rapidly introduced radical reforms and liberal attitudes throughout society. The public at large viewed the liberal attitudes and reforms brought to the country by a German physician as a provocation, and in January 1772, Struensee and his closest aide, Enevold Brandt, were overthrown in the so-called "Palace Revolution." But although strict press regulations were then re-installed by Struensee's successor, the conservative theologian Ove Høegh-Guldberg, Denmark–Norway nevertheless continued to see an increasing variety of publications throughout the final decades of the eighteenth century.

A New Audience: Children

Some of the periodicals and newspapers of this time targeted a new audience: children and adolescents. Many of these publications were translated from foreign languages; for example, Mme Beaumont's French *Magasin des Enfants* and *Magasin des Adolescents* appeared in Danish in 1763–1764. Others were originally published in Danish, including *Avis for Børn* (*Newspaper for Children*), which hit the streets of Copenhagen every Wednesday from 1779–1782.[2] *Avis for Børn* had a relatively high number of young subscribers—in the last issue of 1779, 223 names were mentioned on its final pages. The subscribers' list increased by ten to twenty names every year and included children who were to become famous as adults in the public sphere.[3] The newspaper was most likely published by a group of three publicists: the journalists and writers Emanuel Balling, Hans Holck, and Niels Prahl, all well-known names in Copenhagen at that time. Their tasks in relation to publishing the paper may have overlapped, although Hans Holck was the owner of the publishing house and therefore responsible for distribution.[4] *Avis for Børn* had several similarities to contemporary international publications for children.[5] Thus it included, inter alia, moral lessons, geographical essays, letters, stories, death notices, obituaries, and tragedies. Like its international counterparts, the journal positioned itself to address something previously lacking—reading material expressly intended to enlighten and stimulate young readers.[6]

Avis for Børn has been the focus of previous research. The Danish literature scholar, Nina Christensen, has read it as a magazine that abolishes the distinction between fictional and non-fictional literature and gives the child a role equal to that of adult readers.[7] This perspective can be seen, she argues, not least in the formal structure of the magazine: its different columns, lost and found reports, and miscellany of notices give it a structure resembling that of an adult newspaper, such as *Københavns Adresse-Contoirs Efterretninger* (*Information from the Newspaper's Office in Copenhagen*), which had a monopoly role in bringing short notices to readers in Copenhagen.[8] Because the magazine invited the child into an adult world, addressing role playing and independent learning skills, it serves as an important source for understanding how childhood was perceived in the Nordic countries in the late eighteenth century. As Christensen has shown, many of the texts in this newspaper depict children as equal partners to adults and as individuals with imagination and creative abilities.

Although some research has focused on *Avis for Børn*, little attention has been paid to texts about dead or dying children, whether stories from the sick bed, death notices, obituaries, or didactic texts aimed at children. These texts may give important glimpses into both the child's role in the family and child-parent relationships. Harald Bache-Wiig, a Norwegian literature scholar, has written about one piece that appeared in the magazine, a drama thematising children and death, in which two thoughtless and disobedient boys pay for their bad behavior by nearly dying from self-inflicted injuries.[9] The overall point of the piece is to warn young readers that death is a possible consequence of failing to meet behavioral expectations. The text resembles other cautionary tales in the magazine in which children are presented with fictional characters who suffer the consequences of straying from behavioral norms. However, the periodical's texts about dying and dead children also provide positive perspectives on the qualities and attributes of children as they confront issues such as sickness, grief, and loss. These aspects of the texts aimed at children in *Avis for Børn* add new and valuable insights to the research by Christensen and Bache-Wiig.

The aim of this chapter is to use this rich source material of texts about and for children to further our understanding of childhood in the Nordic Countries in the eighteenth century. The focus will be on challenging established theories on the family about the eighteenth century on the basis of these texts about dead and dying children. In his well-known book *The Fall of Public Man*, the sociologist Richard Sennett identified the movement of affluent eighteenth-century people away from the urbanized public sphere toward a private, natural realm that emphasized nurturing and the family. According to Sennett, the family sphere was an arena for natural maturation where every family member received love and was accorded value and importance. This shift to the family, placed children in a special position and emphasized their need for, and right to, nurture and protection. Both parents had the need and right to meet the moral and emotional needs of their children, who were dependent upon their parents' care, love, and consideration.[10]

Drawing on Nina Christensen's findings about the adult status ascribed to the juvenile readership of *Avis for Børn*, it is worth studying the roles given to children in the texts it published. Sennett describes this era as one characterized by the shifting roles of adults, who increasingly defined themselves in relation to the family setting, where they saw themselves as caregivers demonstrating devotion, love, and comfort.[11] Through a close examination of texts about dead and dying children in *Avis for Børn*, and with a particular focus on the language used by and about children in these texts, this chapter analyses the corresponding changes in the child's role in the family and in the child-adult relationship in Denmark–Norway at this time. The idea of the "competent" child, an expression that often appears in present-day discussions of modern childhood in the Nordic countries, and which describes the child as a social and cultural being who acts, reflects, and interacts in society, appears to have its eighteenth-century roots in precisely the kinds of texts we will examine from *Avis for Børn*.

This chapter will create a window onto the family and the perceptions of children in late eighteenth-century Denmark–Norway. As this era is generally regarded as anticipating the defining aspects of our own time, it provides an important background for understanding children's status and role in the Nordic countries in the present day.[12] This chapter highlights the importance of looking at the study of childhood within a historical perspective, and it also points to the role of periodicals and newspapers for understanding children, childhood, and the conception of family both in a Nordic eighteenth-century context and in different parts of the world at different times.

The following presentation will comprise three parts. The first part will give a thorough introduction to *Avis for Børn*, its content and audience. The second part will focus on how the texts studied here depict children as they confront dying and death. This part will examine how the texts emphasize children's roles in the family and present the relationship between children and adults. The chapter will conclude with a third part that summarizes the findings and draws upon them to arrive at a model for understanding how the modern conception of the "competent" child applies to eighteenth-century Nordic society

What Was *Avis for Børn?*

Avis for Børn must be seen in the context of Northern-European Enlightenment and the expansion of the public sphere that typified that era. Improving literacy and education among people at large meant an expanded pool of readers and writers.[13] With *Avis for Børn*, as with other periodicals for juveniles, children were now included as legitimate voices in the public sphere, first and foremost as readers, but also as potential writers.[14] Juvenile magazines appeared in several European countries. In Sweden, for instance, the weekly *Wecko-Blad til Barns Nytta och Nöje* (*A Weekly Magazine for the Benefit and Pleasure of Children*) was published between 1766 and 1774, while children in Germany could read *Der Kinderfreund* (*The Friend of Children*) between 1775 and 1783.[15] The expanding print culture in the eighteenth century multiplied the number of publications devoted to educational matters, and this was paralleled by an increasing amount of general texts written for children. Reading was seen as a crucial educational tool, not least for girls.[16]

The Nordic countries had the best possible conditions for including children in this enlarged public sphere. In Denmark–Norway, as well as in Sweden, literacy among young girls and boys was exceptionally high thanks to the "Catechism policy" maintained by the orthodox Lutheran church. While religious books dominated children's as well adult's reading lists in Scandinavia well into the eighteenth century, a range of secular literature aimed at a differentiated audience from all strata of society increased markedly toward the nineteenth century. Periodicals of various kinds played an important role in this new print and reading culture. The establishment of *Avis for Børn* was part of the expansion of this culture, although there was also an economic motivation behind its publication. As the owner of a publishing house in Copenhagen, Hans Holck was constantly occupied with establishing new markets and new audiences, as well as with other activities that provided an income.[17] This led to a number of different periodicals adapted to different groups of audiences.[18]

The journal's imitation of an adult paper strikes the modern reader immediately in the title page of the first volume. Underneath the magazine's masthead is a statement that it is published by the newspaper agency *Avise-Contoiret* (The Newspaper Office). This is most likely a play on the name of the agency of Holck's publishing house, which was the home of the previously mentioned *Kiøbenhavns Adresse-Contoirs Efterretninger.* Thus, beginning with the front page, where the magazine presents its style and concept, children are invited to use their imaginations and enter a fictional mock-up of adult publications. This play on the adult publishing world continues throughout the introductory part of the magazine, in which the editors explain the composition of the periodical.

It becomes clear from the introduction that just as *Kiøbenhavns Adresse-Contoirs Efterretninger* has different types of texts, so too does *Avis for Børn*. The juvenile magazine includes short notices on trade and shipping, lotteries, travelers' reports, announcements, a lost and found section, and reviews of various books adapted for children. There are also different forms of literary fiction, crisscrossing the genres that we know today. One important genre comprises dramas that often extend over several issues after initially presenting the different characters. All these texts have children in central roles. As the editors point out in the foreword, other minor items are also included, such as announcements of rentals and vacancies as well as ads by job seekers.

As the variety of this list implies, *Avis for Børn* covers a broad range of text types, spanning from bone-dry columns thematising the different institutions of the absolutist state; to information on trade, shipping, and politics; to fables, myths, and fictive letters. Harald Bache-Wiig has argued that many of the items appear as fictive prose that simulates the characteristics of non-fictive texts.[19] Just as non-fictional prose can be expected to illustrate real-life issues, so the texts in *Avis for Børn* serve as expressions or images of reality at a particular point in time. In this way, they invite the child into an adult world.

Behind their playful self-presentation, many of the journal's texts have a clearly pedagogical aim. A good illustration of this can be seen in the lost and found columns, many of which use fictive and humorous stories to teach children the necessity of being orderly and tidy. One such story tells of a little girl who lost her gloves and had to go to school without them. The short story depicts the girl as negligent with her belongings, despite having been taught by her mother to keep her things in good order. As a consequence of losing her gloves, she fears her mother's wrath and promises that anyone who finds them will be rewarded with three of her morning pretzels. Directly underneath this text is a report of a pair of gloves that was found, presumably by her brother, in the trough in the kitchen. Covered in flour, the gloves were ready to be retrieved by their owner in exchange for a suitable reward.[20]

A pedagogical aim can also be seen in the so-called "cautionary tales," through which the children are taught to behave properly by witnessing the negative examples set by fictional characters. I have already mentioned the tale of the two thoughtless boys; another similar text is the story of little Lovise, who used to hold a needle in her mouth when dressing or sewing, despite her mother's warnings and reproaches.[21] This habit caused the little girl's death. One day when she was standing with the needle between her lips, her brother came into the room and teased her, whereupon little Lovise swallowed the needle. She was then overwhelmed by fear and immediately called out to her mother. But although the mother immediately called in the doctor, there was no hope for the little girl. The needle had lodged in her breast, and poor Lovise died after fourteen days of pain. The lesson of this story is that children should always listen to their parents.

In sum, *Avis for Børn* is a typical magazine of its time, adapted to a particular group of readers: children. Its aim is education and enlightenment, and it uses different types of articles to communicate its message to young readers. It stages dramas in which the child is invited to participate in an imaginative re-enactment of the adult world.

Dying and Dead Children: Views from *Avis for Børn*

I now turn to the texts that will be under particular consideration in this chapter. Several texts about dying and dead children are found in *Avis for Børn*. They vary in type and genre. Some are written as traditional obituaries, in which a child is portrayed in the same way as a deceased adult. Examples are the obituaries of Frederica Elisabeth Christiane de Levzov, who died in her tenth year, and a six-year-old, Johan Bøchman from Laurwigen (today's Larvik), in Norway.[22] For the latter child, no information about the date of his death is provided. Both texts use metaphors taken from nature to describe the deceased child. Examples include descriptions of a child as a flower, comparisons of a child's life to a straw, and the image of God transplanting a plant into hallowed ground as a metaphor for the death of a child.[23] The use of metaphors from nature is particularly striking in the text about Frederica Levzov. The text starts by describing the child as a wonderful rose and continues with a description of death as the fading of the flower before it has had a chance to fully bloom.[24] Both obituaries use the deceased child as a role model for young readers. The author warns that it is essential to be virtuous and pious, as both these children were. The readers are exhorted to follow the examples of these unfortunate children so that they too can approach God with honor when their time comes. These examples underline the rich variety of text types in this periodical, as well as the way it plays with adult genres.

Other text types thematising children and death in *Avis for Børn* play on children's fantasy and imaginative abilities. Examples include epitaphs such as that for Johanne Friderica Syberg and visions that illustrate the transition stage between life and death.[25] One example of the latter type of text is the story of Menalkes, a young shepherd who is gravely ill and in great pain.[26] In a vision, he sees and speaks with an angel. Menalkes sees his dead father and begs the angel to stay by his father's side. The angel, however, exhorts the young shepherd not to give up living and to go back to the "innocent" Signe, presumably his girlfriend. The epitaphs quoted in *Avis for Børn* are texts of unknown origin. It is hard to know whether Johanne Friderica Syberg was a real person and the piece has no accompanying information about where the epitaph is located. These texts pretend to refer to incidents in real life, but it is impossible to say whether they are real.

Another noteworthy text on the subject of children and death depicts children on their deathbeds adopting a nurturing and comforting role toward their parents, family, and friends. The tragic drama *De døende Brødre* ("The Dying Brothers") appeared over five issues (75–79) in 1779. It relates the story of two dying brothers, Christian and Friedrich, surrounded by their friends and family before their untimely deaths. In all, the drama unfolds over twelve scenes in which the readers are introduced to the young boys and see them expressing both their fear of dying and their confidence in God while repenting their sins, making their confession, and expressing forgiveness. All the while, they give comfort to their parents, their sister, and visiting friends. Thanks to their incredible strength of will and their ability to be reconciled with friends and with God, the boys become the heroes of their own deaths.

The usual parent-child role, in which the parent provides comfort and moral support to the child, is strangely reversed here. The dying boys are the ones who display fortitude and seek to restore the moral order. For example, on the boys' own initiative, their parents bring their friends from school so that the dying youths can thank them for their friendship and ask for forgiveness. One of the three boys who are brought to them even confesses his own sins and seeks forgiveness for having stolen a couple of rix-dollars from his father.[27] Assuming that his father will not reject the prayers of a dying child, the school friend seeks help in bringing about his father's forgiveness, but he also promises to improve his own behavior. In this way, the example of the dying boys helps to restore moral order by inspiring repentance and forgiveness in others.

Another aspect of the child-adult role reversal in this drama is the strange maturity of the two boys, who face the reality of death despite their parents' expressions of false hope and promises of recovery. One example of these switched roles can be seen in a dialogue in which the father, using a positive and optimistic tone, brings good news from the doctor—the doctor has given the assurance that the boys will recover from the illness as long as they stay calm and warm.[28] The boys, however, are more realistic and accept the reality that their symptoms are signs of immanent death. They believe neither in their mother's assertions about the doctors' optimism nor in the efficacy of medication.[29]

The boys not only model adult behavior on their deathbeds, they actually surpass the surrounding adults in their achievement of the moral and religious ideals of that era. Their extreme piety and moral fortitude are on display in a dialogue with their aunt in which she promises them her fortune and predicts them a long life.[30] The boys, however, are focused on the eternal wealth of heaven and argue that thanks to the last six weeks of illness, they have been released from this world's craving for money. Earlier, says little Christian, he counted his money daily, but now he is able to banish these earthly concerns at the thought of their joyful afterlife.[31]

The boys' position of moral leadership in relation to the adult world is enhanced during an encounter with their grieving parents, when they express theological and eschatological thoughts about the future. Comforting their mother and father with the hope of an everlasting reunion in heaven, they place their trust in God to take care of their parents after their own deaths.[32] Here in Richard Sennett's description of the family as the state of nature is turned upside-down, it is the strong and rational child who cares for the parents, while the parents themselves are frail and emotional. The dramatic form and the emotional dialogue between the boys and their relatives strengthen the impact of this flipped family hierarchy—the textual form and wording intensify the text's topic.

Other, shorter texts in the magazine offer similar perspectives. In a short narrative about "little Charlotte," who suffered from a serious case of pox, the sick girl comforts her mother, who sits at her daughter's bedside crying.[33] The text includes a detailed description of the child's symptoms—the illness had glued her eyes shut, and she is not able to see her mother. Nevertheless, the girl is the one who displays moral strength, drying her mother's tears, she comforts her mother by reaffirming her belief in God and God's love, and also proclaims her faith in the final judgement.[34] The dialogue is intense, and it is easy to imagine that this is a story about life and death. The decisive point and the reason for the mother's grief is not primarily the impending loss of her daughter, but rather her inability to follow her child to heaven. Charlotte focuses on this point in her comforting words to her mother, and the story ends with her assurance that her mother will soon follow her to heaven. Stammering and repeating her words, the girl dies while praying for her mother's release from this world. During Charlotte's final moments, she is a strong soul, full of love for her mother, and convinced that they will meet in the afterlife.

Another text that is similar but written from the perspective of a mother looking back, is the story of a wise man's son.[35] The text's setting is familiar, with a conversation between a mother and her daughter framing the narrative. The deceased boy, "little Carl," has just died of the pox at the age of nine. After having seen him lying dead in the coffin, his sister remarks to her mother that Carl's peaceful look has given her comfort. The reader is left with an image of his death that focuses not on the grief and sorrow it caused, but rather on the feelings of gratitude and harmony that accompanied the deathbed scene. Carl experienced peace of mind while patiently awaiting death; this could clearly be seen from the peaceful look on his face. He willingly took his medication, often praying or singing hymns he had learned earlier in life.[36] Moreover, he comforted his parents and demonstrated affection and humility until the very end. This text can thus be regarded as a modern *ars moriendi*—the boy's death is depicted as an ideal death, and he dies in peace and harmony with God and surrounded by his closest family and friends. The dead boy is the hero of the story and thus constitutes an ideal for his sister, who at the very end of the narrative states her own desire to die in the same way.[37]

As previous research has underlined, the texts in *Avis for Børn* reflect important aspects of how children and childhood were perceived at that time. The magazine presupposes and depicts children who are curious, inquisitive, and sometimes thoughtless, and the texts it publishes aim to entertain while enlightening young readers. However, when it comes to texts on dead and dying children, the writers appear to have found inspiration in older sources. One of the most read children's books in the seventeenth and eighteenth centuries was *A Token for Children*, written by James Janeway (1636–1674), a British Puritan minister and author. In this book, Janeway depicts the exemplary life and joyful deaths of thirteen children.[38] This book, which was originally published in English in 1671–1672, appeared in subsequent editions and was translated into many foreign languages, including Danish.[39] *A Token for Children* inspired several other books on the same theme, many of them also available on the Danish market.[40]

One of the texts in the book is the story of Susannah Bicks, a fourteen-year-old Dutch girl who comforts her parents while lying on her deathbed. The story portrays Susannah consoling her parents with quotations from the Bible and expressions of hope in the resurrection. In many respects, this text shares an ethos with the pieces from *Avis for Børn*, but despite the similarities, there is an important difference—the texts from Janeway's book have the rhetorical aim of preaching the Christian *ordo salutis* to a juvenile, whereas those in *Avis for Børn* have at their core the relationship between children and their parents, friends, and relatives.[41] The theological aspects that were central in Janeway's era played a subordinate role by the late eighteenth century, when most of the focus was on the child's role in the family circle.

The texts about dying and dead children in *Avis for Børn* also express certain expectations of children's behavior. As social and reflective beings, able to interact with adults, they are expected to base their actions upon sound and rational choices. The cautionary tales in the collection have a clear pedagogical aim, but they also serve as a source of information about what was expected of children at this time and about children's ability to function as rational human beings. A clear example, related to the story of the needle-swallowing Lovise, is the tale of "little Christian," who was suffering from the flu.[42] It seems that Christian was to blame for his illness because he had been running about the house undressed and in bare feet. The narrative voice appears to adopt the perspective of truisms of that time—the boy bears responsibility for his illness because his thoughtless behavior had caused it.[43] Christian's flu soon led to further complications in the form of a rash over his whole body. The doctor reassured the parents that this might well be the boy's rescue, because it might induce him to calm down and stay in bed until he had fully recovered. However, Christian continued to follow his own unruly nature, sleeping without covers and leaving the windows and doors open. This had fatal results, and as a consequence of his own foolishness, according to the authorial voice, he died in great pain and torment.

Conclusion

Avis for Børn is a typical eighteenth-century juvenile newspaper published in Copenhagen between 1779 and 1782. It serves as an example of how the public sphere had opened up at that time to include young people as writers, subjects, and readers, and it also underlines how children were viewed in Nordic society toward the end of the eighteenth century. Some of the new kinds of texts that appeared at this time imitated genres one could find in adult papers. This chapter has focused in particular on texts about dead and dying children, as a way of studying how these texts depicted children and defined their roles in relation to the family.

The idea of the competent child is often discussed in our own time, not least with regard to children in the Nordic countries. In particular, sociologists and educationalists have argued for the child as a "being" more than a "becoming"—in other words, the child should take an active part in society in the same way as adults.[44] This view regards children as reflexive and autonomous human beings. This concept has historical roots. Researchers have recognized the concept of the competent child as a part of Nordic rural tradition; however, it is also clearly influenced by Rousseau's Romantic view of the child. According to the Scandinavian social scientists, Brembeck, Johansson, and Kampmann, the child was considered as a competent worker in the eighteenth century too, engaging in "chores considered appropriate for their age and gender."[45] But, they continue, "The generational relations were however far from democratic. Children were expected to show unconditional obedience to adults and to keep out of their way."

The texts from *Avis for Børn* show that children in the last decades of the eighteenth century were regarded as bearers of competencies far beyond practical issues. They were, besides being competent readers, also competent in caring for their relatives and friends in vulnerable situations of life. This view of children transgresses the generational hierarchy that is traditionally considered the underpinning of the family structure, as Richard Sennett visualizes it in his work on the public sphere versus the private sphere. In some respects, the flipped moral-religious hierarchies found in the pieces on dead and dying children in this late eighteenth-century journal come closer to the contemporary conception of the competent child than to earlier depictions of idealized children facing death. In certain situations, they show themselves able not only to interact with adults on equal terms, but even to take their place as caretakers, as we see in some of the texts which have been under consideration above.

Notes

1 The word "epidemic"—and other metaphors for illness—originates in international periodical literature, for instance in the British periodical *The Spectator* in 1714. See Krefting, Nøding, and Ringvej 2014: 188–9.
2 The original Danish title will be used hereafter.
3 These include Otto Horrebow, who himself became a publicist and newspaper editor (born 1769), and Jacob Christlieb Schandorff, who later moved to Norway and became a well-known pharmacist in his adult life. There were also children of well-known families in Copenhagen, such as the Pelt family scions and the

daughter of the editor Niels Prahl. The Pelts, of Dutch origin, were wealthy sugar refinery magnates, several of whom held esteemed positions in Danish society.

4 According to a note by Frederik Thaarup, written in 1795, the magazine was edited by Emanuel Balling. See Thaarup 1795: 29. Bibliotheca Danica mentions Niels Prahl as the publisher of the magazine. During Struensee's removal of press restrictions, Niels Prahl became an editor of independent magazines, many of which supported Struensee's political ideologies and practice. See Horstbøll 2005: 371–414.

5 See Bache-Wiig 2014.

6 See, for instance, Dawson 1996: 217–41.

7 See Christensen 2012; see also Bache-Wiig 2014.

8 Already in 1770, *Avis for Børn's* predecessor, *Ungdommens Ven* (*The Friend of Youth*), had launched an idea about imitating adult papers. See Christensen 2009: 192.

9 The text is published in four subsequent issues, nr. 20–23, 1781. See also Bache-Wiig 2014.

10 Sennett 2002: 95.

11 Harald Bache-Wiig has already challenged Sennett's understanding of a distinct public sphere in the eighteenth century to which the children did not belong. Sennett regarded this public sphere as an exclusively adult one that involved only adult play. However, Bache-Wiig argues that *Avis for Børn* invites the child into an enactment of the adult world, where the child is allowed to adopt theatrical roles and explore the assertion of individual will and pleasure as a fictional member of the adult world. This created world, in which the child is allowed to play at adulthood, has strong affinities with Sennett's public realm. See Bache-Wiig 2014: 458.

12 This is emphasized by a number of scholars in different fields, such as literature, history, history of ideas, gender studies, and church history. I have also thermalized this point elsewhere. See Roos 2013.

13 See Appel and Fink Jensen 2013.

14 Christensen 2009.

15 Bache-Wiig 2014: 454.

16 According to M. O. Grenby's findings from England, girls seem to have owned much more of the new children's literature than boys toward the end of the eighteenth century; see Grenby 2011.

17 Christensen 2012: 192. Christensen mentions Holck's diverse activities—in addition to publishing newspapers, he developed the national lottery, was active in forming public societies aimed at improving and advancing the state, and established an auction company as well as a newsstand, which also sold *Avis for Børn*.

18 See Krefting, Nøding, and Ringvej 2014: 202. Among other periodicals, from 1777 onwards Holck also published *Forsvars-Journal for fornærmede Skribenter* (*A Magazine in Defense of Insulted Writers*), which printed authors' replies to reviews in various periodicals, including the patriotic *Magasin for patriotiske Skribentere* (*Magazine for Patriotic Writers*) (from 1771).

19 Bache-Wiig 2014: 455.

20 *Avis for Børn*, January 27, 1779, 40.

21 *Avis for Børn*, January 20, 1779, 28.

22 The text on Frederica E. C. de Levzov was printed on August 18, 1779, while the text on Johan Bøchman appeared on May 5, 1779.

23 The text on the six-year-old boy from Norway informs us about his big heart and good intellect, for which he was loved by his parents, and even more by God. God took this noble plant and replanted it in a holier land, in which a cleaner climate was present, to be raised there in the company of angels from earth.

24 In describing the child as a flower and using nature metaphors, the texts show strong commonalities with eulogies being printed in theological magazines at the time, such as Nikolai Lorenz Fallesen's *Magazin for Religionslærere med Hensyn til Vore Tider*, which was published in Copenhagen between 1793 and 1803 and was particularly directed toward rural pastors.

25 The epitaph for Johanne Friderica Syberg is printed on August 25, 1779, 279. See also Chapter 4 by Aavitsland in this volume.

26 The story on Menalkes is printed on May 19, 1779.

27 "Ah, how will I end up, I have to confess to you, that I, fourteen days ago, took some Rix-Dollars from my father, he will surely get to know it, whereupon I fear the consequence." September 15, 1779, 302.

28 September 8, 1779, 292–293.

29 See, for instance, scene 9, where the father asks one of the sons (Christian) if he is allowed to give him the strong "English medicine" that the doctor has brought, whereupon the son replies that if his father wants, he is allowed to give it to him, but, says Christian, "at 11 o'clock in the evening I will not any longer be amongst them." September 22, 1779, 311.

30 Again, the adult voices in the dialogue utter optimistic bromides, while the boys themselves accept death as the consequence of their illness. This optimism is demonstrated rhetorically through the short, exclamatory sentences of the aunt: "You must not die! Cheer up! You will become rich!" The boys reply that a heavenly inheritance is one million times better than all the wealth on earth. September 15, 300.

31 Christian states: "Dear aunt, a while ago I counted my money that my parents gave me, at least once a day, and at that time, I could not lose a half-penny, but in the span of six weeks, my heart is completely released from this desire for money, so that I even don't care about seeing it. It is possible to lean the heart to earthly desires in such a way that you forget God, and even if you live a long life, it will remain in the world. However, heavenly riches will never be taken away." Ibid.: 301. See also Chapter 9 by Rørvik in this volume.

32 Friedrich says: "We will reunite in a little while, my dear Father. The years will pass quickly, until we meet again and will be together forever." September 8, 1779.

33 This text appeared on March 15, 1780, 88.

34 "Ah, my sweet mother, don't cry, I will come to God Father and my Saviour in heaven, who has always loved me: he has loved me more than both you and my father here." Ibid.

35 January 6, 1779, 14–15.

36 "He was so patient in his illness, so thankful for every favour he was given, he willingly took his medication, folded his small hands and prayed the prayers he had learned in his healthy days. He even sang beautiful songs that were proper in his situation." Ibid.

37 "Ah, Mama, I would also like to die in this way." Ibid.

38 The full title is *A Token for Children: Being an Exact Account of the Conversion, Holy and Exemplary Lives, and Joyful Deaths, of Several Young Children.*

39 The Danish version was published in 1729 and was entitled *En liden Aandelig Exempel-Bog for Børn; Det er en udførlig Beretning om adskillelige smaa Børns omvendelse, hellige og exemplariske levnet, samt glædelige Død.*

40 One of these was *Opbygelig Haand-bog for Børn* (1740), originally published in German by the clergyman Johann Jacob Weinreich six years earlier. See Weinrich 2004: 57.

41 The term *ordo salutis* refers to a series of conceptual steps in the Christian doctrine of Salvation. The order of these steps differs among the various Christian traditions and denominations.

42 Published on April 28, 1779, 143.
43 "Little Christian was suffering from the flu: this was a consequence of his behaviour: even if he was sweaty, he got up from bed, running about the house undressed and in bare feet. Even if he was admonished, he did not give up this behaviour. No wonder, then, he became ill." Ibid.
44 See, for instance, James and Prout 1990; Tufte, Kampmann, and Hassel 2003; and Brembeck, Johansson, and Kampmann 2004.
45 "Introduction," in Brembeck, Johansson, and Kampmann 2004: 15–16. See also Chapters 17 and 18 by Widhe and Ommundsen in this volume.

16 Incandescent Objects and Pictures of Misery

Hans Christian Andersen's Fairy Tales for Children

Maria Tatar

"He was a perfect wizard," August Strindberg declared in a tribute to the author whose stories had captivated him as a child.[1] The Swedish playwright was not alone in his enthusiasm for Hans Christian Andersen (1805–1875). According to UNESCO, the United Nations Educational, Scientific, and Cultural Organization, Andersen ranks among the ten most widely translated authors in the world, along with William Shakespeare and Karl Marx. His stories have become collective cultural property, operating almost like folk tales rather than literary works. Children in Beijing, Calcutta, Beirut, and Montreal have wept over "The Little Match Girl," admired the child in "The Emperor's New Clothes," and identified with the abject baby swan in "The Ugly Duckling."

Walt Disney Studios has done much to sustain and extend the global reach of Andersen's fairy tales, first with its animated film *The Little Mermaid* (1989), then with *Frozen* (2013), inspired by Andersen's "Snow Queen." That Andersen is not just for the young becomes quickly apparent from the many adult adaptations in the United States of his tales, from Kathryn Davis's novel *The Girl Who Trod on a Loaf* through Sandra Gilbert's "The Last Poems about the Snow Queen" to Joyce Carol Oates's short story "You, Little Match Girl." These contemporary writers, along with a host of British and European authors—among them Henry James, Hermann Hesse, W. H. Auden, and Thomas Mann—grew up with Andersen's stories and then grew into them, admiring their imaginative force and allowing it to seep into their own art.

Many remember Andersen for the beauty of his images—for the shiny red shoes that captivate Karen, the golden slipper hung around the neck of the melodious nightingale, and the chunks of ice dancing for joy in the palace of the Snow Queen. In "The Little Mermaid," the sun looks like a "purple flower with light streaming from its calyx"; the eleven brothers in "The Wild Swans" write on "golden tablets with pencils of diamond"; and the soldier in "The Tinderbox" enters a hall where "hundreds of lamps" are shining. The bright wonders and vivid marvels in Andersen's stories go far toward explaining what drew British and Continental artists like Arthur Rackham, Edmund Dulac, and Kay Nielsen to illustrate the fairy tales.

This chapter aims to show that there is more to Andersen than beauty and that the incandescent objects in his works are deeply connected with the grotesque pictures of misery that unfold in his narratives. It will chart Andersen's move from a preoccupation with beautiful objects, with all their seductive power to lure us into the aesthetic pleasures of other worlds, to a mania for suffering that is equally compelling. Andersen discovered early on that language can produce both heat and light, turning the ordinary (shoes, peas, and tin soldiers) into the extraordinary. And he quickly applied the lessons learned to scenes of suffering, creating a poetics of pain as incandescent as the beautiful objects constructed in the stories. Today, we can align him with a literary tradition that recognizes the emotionally gratifying satisfaction of feeling bad in order to feel good.

To understand the full consequences of this double orientation toward pleasure and pain and the resulting complex entanglements of aesthetics and ethics, I will situate Andersen's works in the literary traditions of his time, showing how he turns his back on the cautionary tale, with its behavioral messaging, to embrace the redemptive power of beauty and suffering. Capitalizing on an aesthetics of misery, Andersen inaugurates a new era in children's literature, turning away from the flat morals of nineteenth-century writers and promoting an ethics of empathy that remains a hallmark of children's literature today. We not only witness the suffering of characters like the Little Mermaid and the Little Match Girl, we also get inside their skin, empathizing with them and experiencing what they feel.

Beautiful Surfaces and Emotional Power Surges

Andersen's paper cuttings, sketches, and collages remind us that he was supremely dedicated to the visual, a painter of images as much as a poet of words. C. S. Lewis once described how *The Chronicles of Narnia* were inspired by visual cues: "Everything began with images: a faun carrying an umbrella, a queen on a sledge, a magnificent lion." Drawn to the fairy tale because of its "brevity, its severe restraint on description, its flexible traditionalism, it inflexible hostility to all analysis, digression, reflections and 'gas'," Lewis instinctively recognized the value of surface beauty in the fairy tale.[2]

Unlike Lewis, Andersen came to be deeply invested in both surface and depth. He was committed to everything that glitters, dazzles, and shines, yet he was also deeply concerned with what lies beneath appearances. If Andersen's magic lies in his ability to combine beautiful surfaces with emotional power surges, critics have been reluctant to dwell on it, focusing instead on autobiographical features of his stories. In *Hans Christian Andersen: The Life of a Storyteller*, Jackie Wullschlager begins by declaring that her subject is a "compulsive autobiographer" and proceeds to document in superbly comprehensive ways how the art charts the stations of its author's troubled soul. In the fairy tales, we discover, the truest self-portraits are etched in generous and fulsome detail. "He is the triumphant Ugly Duckling," she declares, "and the loyal Little Mermaid, the steadfast Tin Soldier and the king-loving Nightingale, the demonic Shadow, the depressive fir tree, the forlorn Little Matchgirl."[3] Reginald Spink, author of a classical study on Andersen, writes: "Andersen never stopped telling his own story ... Sometimes he tells it in an idealized form, sometimes with self-revelatory candor. In tale after tale ... he is the hero who triumphs over poverty, persecution, and plain stupidity, and who sometimes, in a reversal of the facts, marries the princess ... or scorns her."[4]

By reducing the art of the tales to "self-revelatory candor," critics attribute the emotional power of the stories to a confessional mode that makes us commiserate with the author more than anyone else. Missing the opportunity to explore the link between surface beauty and emotional depth, they also fail to interrogate the techniques Andersen uses to create an immersive reading experience, one that enables us to see and feel what his characters see and feel.

How do authors get readers hooked in the first place? How do they trap us into suspending disbelief and passing through portals into fictional worlds more alluring and compelling than reality? How do they animate spaces constructed by mere words to create cozy patches of warmth and luminosity? In what follows, I will identify Andersen's strategies for making readers feel at home in fictional worlds. What is the bait and how do we get "gut-hooked and dragged down overboard," as one writer puts it?[5] And why do we linger in those precincts, intoxicated by the air we breathe in them and affectively attached? Readers are capricious, idiosyncratic, contrarian, and inventive, and there is no predicting how individuals will react to a given work. I will nonetheless theorize a reader who is constructed by the effects in Andersen's text. That reader will, to be sure, remain something of an abstraction, but I follow the sociologist, Michel de Certeau, in imagining anything but a fixed ideal type in that role. In what follows, the reader of Andersen will be "like a hunter in the forest [who] ... spots the written quarry, follows a trail, laughs, plays tricks, or else like a gambler, lets himself be taken in by it."[6]

Beauty and Incandescent Objects

Let me turn now to fairy tales and to Andersen's literary intervention in a hallowed oral tradition. Johann Gottfried von Herder and the Brothers Grimm told us over two centuries ago that simplicity, artlessness, and spontaneity are the chief features of fairy tales, stories that are homespun rather than ornate, sophisticated, and complex. Yet in recent years, critics have revisited the notion of the fairy tale's artlessness and identified its highly stylized features and how they are foregrounded. As Jessica Tiffin writes in *Marvelous Geometry*, the fairy tale shows "an awareness and encoding of itself as *text*, the classic opening 'Once upon a time' signaling a precise relationship with reality which makes no pretense at reality, but which is continually aware of its own status *as story*, as ritualized narrative enactment." Participating in the pleasures of fairy tales depends "entirely on recognition of the artificiality of that universe, the fact that it is a work of art." Formulaic structures, repetitions, rhymes, embedded songs, stereotypical names, the formulation of explicit morals—all these devices underscore the degree to which fairy tales are fictional artifacts. Anti-mimetic, they are, in the realm of prose, "as artificial as possible," lacking real-world referents.

Paradoxically it is the artificiality and constructed quality of fairy-tale other worlds—and Andersen was among the first to recognize this fact—that makes them so deeply absorbing. The very lack of texture and detail challenges readers of all ages to co-create with the author, to become active participants in the construction of the fairy-tale universe. In *The Uses of Enchantment*, Bruno Bettelheim declared that fairy tales *simplify* situations: "details, unless very important, are eliminated."[7] As a result, whatever particulars do appear have a heightened significance. Objects become fraught, loaded, and charged in ways that are symbolically weighty. They may not be sacred but they are treated with a form of reverence that invokes associations with Walter Benjamin's concept of the aura that surrounds unique works of art.[8]

"Aura" is a highly contested term with a certain conceptual fluidity that has generated much debate. On the one hand, Benjamin, as an expert in aesthetics, invoked it to describe the authenticity and authority that radiate from original artworks. But he also recognized a more profane and (somewhat) vulgarized form of aura in the sense defined by the critic Miriam Hansen, as an "elusive phenomenal substance, ether, or halo that surrounds a person or object of perception, encapsulating their individuality and authenticity."[9] In some ways, Benjamin finds himself in the odd situation of being unable to divorce the term "aura" from the discursive field he is seeking to disavow. The halo—what Benjamin once described as a "profane illumination"—not only facilitates perception but also, in a miracle of aesthetic alchemy, dissolves the boundary between subject and object, enabling a fundamental reciprocity as one gazes at the other.

Somewhat surprisingly, though perhaps less so given the German philosopher's deep interest in children's books, Benjamin describes a passage in a story by Hans Christian Andersen and uses it (without for a moment alluding to the concept of aura) to illustrate the merging of beholder with work of art. "The Wild Swans" is the tale that captured his imagination. In it, Elisa, whose brothers have been enchanted and turned into beautiful swans, has a book that costs "half a kingdom." The picture book comes alive: "Birds were singing, and people stepped out of the pages of the book and talked with Elisa and her brothers." When Elisa turns the page, the characters and objects leap back into the book. Benjamin was convinced that Andersen had it wrong: "The objects do not come to meet the picturing child from the pages of the book; instead, the gazing child enters into those pages, becoming suffused, like a cloud, with the riotous colors of the world of pictures." Note how the phrase "like a cloud" and the word "suffused" suggest a phantasmagoric merging of subject and object, a union of the two as the agent of perception joins in to animate and become animated through the perceived world. Benjamin may have it right, but it is also possible to think in terms of reciprocity: the characters exit the book and enter the reader's world even as the reader is invited to dwell in the "riotous" world of *word pictures* in the book. The "picturing" child is a reader who also succeeds in becoming part of the picture. "Ink, with its powers of alchemistic dyeing, its colorative life, is capable, if it but finds its dreamer, of creating a universe," as Gaston Bachelard tells us in one of his philosophical meditations.[10]

Incandescent is the term I shall use to describe Andersen's luminous things of beauty, objects that operate magically in his universe of make believe. They are often the trigger for the shift from word to image and from image to world. They will be familiar to readers of fairy tales, who have marveled over glass slippers, golden spindles, and silver trees—even red riding hoods and red apples. Objects are aestheticized and fetishized in ways that endow them with rich symbolic meaning. Small wonder that writers like Oscar Wilde, who endorsed beautiful surfaces in fresh, new ways, was completely at home in the genre of the fairy tale. The flat metallic surfaces, reflective mirrors, and sparkling glass that Max Lüthi finds so prominently featured in fairy tales become the armature of the narrative universe in *fin-de-siècle* fiction, not just in Wilde's works but in fiction ranging from Joris-Karl Huysmans' *A Rebours* to Rainer Maria Rilke's *Notebooks of Malte Laurids Brigge*.[11]

Fairy tales have always placed a premium on beauty, but Hans Christian Andersen gave us moving objects—moving in the double sense of the word in that many come alive and are also endowed with the power to evoke an emotional response. These cult objects have singular beauty and transformative energy. They are not always easy to identify and locate, for they engage in remarkable disappearing acts, playing sly games of hide-and-seek with the reader. Take the case of the pea in the celebrated "Princess and the Pea," and it becomes evident that even the most ordinary objects can come to be invested with a special aura. The pea, hidden under a thick pile of mattresses, becomes, by the end of the story, an authentic museum piece on display in the Royal Museum. Contained and placed on a pedestal, it is revered as a thing of beauty that has secured the proper succession in the kingdom.

A second object is even more elusive. The invisible cloth woven by the two swindlers in "The Emperor's New Clothes" captivates, making us do the imaginative work of seeing something beautiful even when it has no material reality and is constructed from mere words—the cloth from which the Emperor's clothes will be cut is "light as spider webs" and "exquisite." Here we are in the realm of a self-reflexive allegory about how verbal art is both beautiful illusion and ludicrous fraud. It takes us in when we are willing collaborators and co-conspirators but it is also easy to mock as a mirage with no grounding in reality.

Consider also the two birds in Andersen's "The Nightingale." They are both enchanting, but the real nightingale, as opposed to the jewel-encrusted mechanical one, sings with a voice "so lovely" that tears roll down the Emperor's cheeks. Beauty moves the Emperor to tears, and the scene of his emotional release enables us to see a possible link between beauty and suffering. In this particular story, the beauty of song has a healing power, but in tales like "The Red Shoes," the protagonist's love of beauty is shadowed by sadistic punishments that lead to suffering that is anything but transcendent. The magic of the beautiful new shoes made for Karen turns against her, taking possession of her, compelling her to dance endlessly in a frenzied spectacle that ends with the amputation of her feet. For Andersen, beauty has transformative energy, but its link with pleasure arouses profound fears about excesses both evil and dangerous. And it can easily tip into the unsightly and grotesque.

Situating Andersen's Fairy Tales Historically

Before turning to the poetics of pain, I want to situate Andersen's fairy tales historically, at an important juncture in literature for children. What did the landscape look like before Andersen? In the centuries before fairy tales, nonsense, and adventure stories made their way into entertainment for children, there was a premium on spiritual uplift, moral education, and behavior modification. James Janeway's *Token for Children, Being an Exact Account of the Conversion, Holy and Exemplary Lives and Deaths of Several Young Children* (1672), which packaged the benefits of salvation in deathbed scenes with precociously spiritual children as young as six, remained a bestselling volume for several centuries, in England as well as in the United States. Cotton Mather added some examples from New England a century later to make the volume spiritually relevant at the local level. In the same era, John Bunyan and Isaac Watts aimed to produce docile, well-behaved children with verse that condemned the disobedient child to perpetual torment in the afterlife. In this kind of climate, the fables of Aesop and LaFontaine seemed downright playful and cheerful.

In eighteenth- and nineteenth-century European and Anglo-American cultures, salvation began to take a back seat to good behavior. Heinrich Hoffmann's *Struwwelpeter*, published in 1845, is emblematic of the rise of the cautionary tale, with its tableaus of torture bent on civilizing the child, turning what Freud called a "cauldron of seething emotions" into something less turbid, amorphous, and messy. Moving in the mode of "Or Else!" instead of "What if?", the stories in *Struwwelpeter* warn children about the consequences of disobedience and curiosity, along with all those other traits that deviate from adult agendas for civilizing and taming the young and the restless. Despite the fact that most of the protagonists in the self-contained vignettes end up in the graveyard (Pauline perishes while playing with matches and Caspar dies after failing to eat his soup), the volume has endured—perhaps in part because children are contrarians who embrace the fear factor and find the volume's excesses entertaining.

Andersen inserted himself into an alternative tradition, a folkloric register that famously staged spectacular punishments, but nearly always reserved for ogres and other evildoers. In fairy tales, the adult villain perishes, but the child hero nearly always survives. The witch from "Hansel and Gretel" burns in the oven; the evil stepmother in "Snow White" dances to her death in red-hot iron shoes; and like a latter-day biblical David, Jack vanquishes a giant and slides down the Beanstalk. Andersen's stories rarely indulge in enacting revenge fantasies or deserved punishments. Instead we have scenes of suffering, tableaux designed to evoke compassion rather than to celebrate triumphant victories over villains.

Empathy and Pictures of Misery

Fairy tales value wealth, power, and romance, and "happily ever after" often translates into marriage and a kingdom. Prolonged scenes of suffering and the promotion of compassion were a new twist, added by Andersen to a genre that, in its literary form, enabled readers to slip inside the minds of characters and learn something about them. In his notes for tales translated from the Brothers Grimm, Philip Pullman pointed out that it is something of a stretch to use the term "character" for a genre that gives us figures resembling cardboard cut-outs with virtually no interior life. Action trumps character, and we rarely have the nuanced interiority and complex representation of minds at work, as in, for example, the novel. "There is no psychology in a fairy tale," Pullman declares.[12] The characters are all surface with no real depth of feeling. Things just happen to them. And here is where we suddenly hit a brick wall when it comes to assigning Andersen's stories to the category of fairy tale. While they share with traditional tales an anti-mimetic position, they also take us inside the heads of their characters and let us get inside their skin. If anything, digression, reflection, and gas take over and go wild. Language does not run dry when it comes to describing pain, contrary to what Virginia Woolf stated, and Andersen's fairy tales offer hard evidence for that truth.[13]

Take the Little Match Girl, a character (and I use the term with all due deliberation here), whose story begins as follows: "It was bitterly cold." Already we are plunged into a world of painful sensation. "Poor mite, she was the picture of misery as she trudged along, hungry and shivering with cold." We swiftly move into the girl's head, feeling the sharpness of her pain: "She knew that her father would beat her and, besides, it was almost as cold at home as it was here." Suddenly we have shifted from a gaze that takes in externals to a place inside the girl's head. "Ah, but a little match," she thinks, "that would be a comfort." All that follows is focalized through the little match seller, and, as readers, we see what she sees, feel what she feels. "No one knew what lovely things she had seen," Andersen writes at the end of her story. That may be true for those who find her corpse on the cold sidewalk, but certainly not for those who read about and share her New Year's Eve visions.[14]

The Little Match Girl's discovery of beauty in impoverished material circumstances mirrors the burst of beauty created by Andersen's descriptive powers. The words used to describe the girl's visions and her suffering create luminous effects that provide readers with the same warmth, light, and comfort that comes when the girl lights her matches. And presto! Beauty turns us into generous readers, compassionately attuned to what the little match seller sees and feels. Illustrators have long been attuned to this mirroring effect, and they often surround both the girl and her visions in a warm glow.

In "The Little Mermaid," Andersen moves us almost immediately into the consciousness of the youngest of the Sea-King's daughters. She is the one who loves to hear about the human world, who longs to rise to the surface, and who cannot take her eyes off the young Prince and his ship. And we witness her suffering when she loses her voice and feels as if her heart is breaking "for grief." When she drinks the potion of the Sea Witch, we feel the "sharp pain" that courses through her body as well as the "two-edged sword" slicing through her and the "sharp knives" on which she walks.[15] This tale, like "The Little Match Girl" shows how a curious transvaluation takes place as Andersen struggles with the cruelty of those who enjoy a cult of beauty and pleasure (the *bon vivants* celebrating New Year's Eve at home in "The Little Match Girl" and the royals feasting and dancing in the Prince's palace in "The Little Mermaid") while others suffer in silence. The two "pictures of misery" draw our notice more powerfully than the warmth and light of interior scenes. We gaze and empathize more than we admire and wonder.

In "The Ugly Duckling," Andersen works hard to restrain himself from wallowing in the sorrows of the "strange" and "nasty" duckling. "It would be dreary to describe all the misery and hardship the duckling endured in the course of that hard winter." Of course, Andersen has done nothing but give the reader a steady barrage of vivid details about the insults and injuries to which the title figure is subjected.[16] We recoil from the cruelty of those who persecute the duckling, empathizing with the downtrodden figure caught in the ice but also rejoicing in a transformation that takes place while the sun is shining "bright" and "warm" on the overjoyed swan.

Empathetic Readers

We live in what Steven Pinker has called an age of empathy, with dozens of books on why empathy matters, on the neuroscience of empathy, on the empathy gap, and so on.[17] Cognitive neuroscientists have discovered mirror-neurons that they refer to as "empathy neurons" in part for their capacity to connect us with others and how they feel and behave. Pinker points out that empathy has come to be associated with several mental states: projection (putting yourself in the position of another person), perspective taking (visualizing how another person sees things), and mindreading or mentalizing (figuring out what someone is thinking or feeling). He believes that sympathy, rather than an immersive form of empathy, is a more accurate term for capturing the productive altruistic impulse that enables us to understand the pleasures and pains of being someone else. Whether we bring that sympathy to real people or to fictional characters, he adds, we end up feeling greater compassion for the entire category of people that that individual represents.

Pinker's conclusion rests on studies offering evidence for the capacity of reading to promote empathy and emotional intelligence. Experiments conducted by Emanuele Castano and David Comer Kidd show that subjects who read extracts from sophisticated literary works score higher than those who read non-fiction on tests measuring the ability to imagine the lives and understand the mental states of others. The headline here is not so much that reading fiction makes us more compassionate than that witnessing the sufferings of both real people *as well as* fictional characters animates our sense of sympathy.[18]

The historian Lynn Hunt told us long ago that fiction promotes "new forms of empathetic identification with individuals who are now imagined to be in some fundamental way like you."[19] She confirms what George Eliot told us back in 1856—that "art is the nearest thing to life." "It is a mode of amplifying experience," the novelist added, "and extending our contact with our fellow-men beyond the grounds of our personal lot."[20] Walking in someone else's shoes," "getting inside someone's head," "feeling their pain"—these phrases illustrate just how easy it is for us to slide into a relationship of sympathetic identification with others. Fiction sharpens our interest in their lives and quickens our desire to decode the cognitive puzzles of their minds.

And how do we react? With rapture and wonder about those we admire and envy, but also with anxiety and empathy about the fate of those trapped in toil or in pain. And that is especially the case when a Hans Christian Andersen comes along, a writer who understands supremely well how to aestheticize suffering and to pull us into the luminous orbit of the pain of others.

Today, this turn in Andersen's work seems less than radical. Young Adult fiction has eagerly hijacked the dark side, amplifying jolts of horror in dystopic fictions ranging from *The Giver* to *The Hunger Games*. It has given us the vampires, werewolves, and ghouls that were once strictly cordoned off in the arena of adult entertainments. Even the younger crowd yearns for titles like *Goosebumps* and *A Series of Unfortunate Events*. To be sure, children are, from the get go, sensation seekers. But these days we also give them books like R. J. Palacio's *Wonder*, Sharon Draper's *Out of My Mind*, and Cynthia Lord's *Rules*. Each of these volumes turns on the drama of *looking* different, giving us characters who are defined by the inability of others to fix their gaze on them. In *Wonder*, Auggie Pullman feels ordinary, but "ordinary kids don't make other ordinary kids run away screaming on playgrounds."[21] "People stared. Some pointed. Others looked away," Melody tells us in Draper's *Out of My Mind*.[22] A child with cerebral palsy, she is describing a tantrum thrown in the grocery store because she cannot speak and communicate some vital information to her mother. David in Lord's *Rules* fails to *see* "the looks people give us," as his sister reports to her deep chagrin.[23] These novels all feature protagonists who are different in some ways, divergent because of a disability. Their stories remind us that today we have traded in a grim fascination with misery for deep engagement with those who fail to conform to conventional appearances. Beauty is no longer powerfully harnessed for its redemptive force, and instead we seek to normalize what was once designated as grotesque.

Andersen's fairy tales may begin with "What if?" and move us to ask "What's next?" but they are also unusual in inspiring us to ask "Why?" Causation is no longer random and arbitrary as in the folk genre, but psychologically motivated and realistically portrayed. In both "The Little Match Girl" and "The Little Mermaid," beauty coexists with suffering in ways that create a new aesthetic, one that turns from radiant objects to a commitment to widening the gaze to include scenes that inspire compassion as much as wonder. We may enter the tales through the gates of Beauty but we linger in the precincts of the unsightly and grotesque, in places that lead us to look in horror rather than to gaze in pleasure. As compensation, we exit these narratives with a renewed sense of compassion and connection, and as importantly, with a more capacious sense of what beauty is.

The US novelist and essayist, Roger Rosenblatt, once remarked on the complex nexus connecting beauty to suffering, evil, and justice. The point of writing is to "make suffering endurable, evil intelligible, justice desirable and love possible."[24] Like Andersen, he has faith in the redemptive power of words—words so beautiful that they enable us to fix our gaze on things not so beautiful and to seek the justice that will repair the suffering and evil that lingers on in pictures of misery.

Notes

1 Strindberg 1920: 443–5.
2 Lewis 1994: 36.
3 Wullschlager 2000: 3.
4 Spink 1981: 10.
5 Wynn-Jones, online at www.azquotes.com/quote/618690.
6 de Certeau 2011: 173.
7 Bettelheim 1976: 8.
8 Benjamin 2008.
9 Hansen 2008: 340.
10 Bachelard 1989: 49.

11 Lüthi 1986.
12 Pullman 2012: xiii.
13 Woolf 1967: 184.
14 "The Little Match Girl," in Tatar 2008: 214–22.
15 "The Little Mermaid," in Tatar 2008: 119–55.
16 "The Ugly Duckling," in Tatar 2008: 98–118.
17 Pinker 2011: 571.
18 Comer Kidd and Castano 2013: 377–80.
19 Hunt 2000: 13.
20 Eliot 1992: 264.
21 Palacio 2012: 3.
22 Draper 2012: 17.
23 Lord 2008: 2.
24 www.pbs.org/newshour/bb/entertainment-jan-june11-rosenblatt_01-31/.

17 Inventing Subjectivity and the Rights of the Child in Nineteenth-Century Nordic Children's Literature

Olle Widhe

At the close of World War I, the Scandinavian peace and women's movement fought to ensure that society would protect children against oppression and discrimination. Only six months after Eglantyne Jebb had founded Save the Children in England, writers and pioneers of women's rights, such as Elin Wägner and Anna Lenah Elgström, founded Rädda Barnen in Sweden in the fall of 1919. When the altruistic approach that was characteristic of the nineteenth century gave way to a politics that took account of children's own interests, this entailed a new way of looking at children. Previously, they had been an object of benevolence and kindness on the part of adults, but now the new ideas were an invitation to a perspective that allowed children to be a subject to a higher degree.[1]

It took more than fifty years before various declarations about children's human rights were replaced by the more or less legally binding Convention on the Rights of the Child (1989), which affirms that children, just like adults, have a full and equal human dignity. It also accommodates the children's own will and their right to express themselves on every question that concerns them. The ascription of a human dignity thus means that one is allowed to be a subject to whom the surrounding world must relate in a particular manner. Against this background, it is not surprising that the idea of children's rights was linked in the late twentieth century, not only with the question of what is good for the child, but also with the question of how the child experiences its world. The Convention on the Rights of the Child underlines how important it is that adults relate to the child's perspective, and in this way, it has influenced perceptions of how one should work children in psychological, pedagogical, and political praxis.[2]

It is, of course, true that an ideological and normative text like The Convention on the Rights of the Child helps to shape the way in which adults relate to children. But one can also turn this argument around and see this development from the opposite direction, pointing out that the act of making visible the perspective and subjectivity of the child is an essential presupposition of the elaboration of the conventions about children's rights and of the construction of a world where the child too can take his or her place. The Scandinavian countries are particularly interesting in this context, and Sweden above all, both because of the active role it played in the foundation of the United Nations Children's Fund (UNICEF) after World War II and because it has long been held up in the international sphere as a model country of how one can work on children's rights.[3]

Naturally, there are many difficulties involved in answering the question of how one should describe a child's perspective on his or her own situation.[4] Can one say that all children have a special perspective that is clearly different from that of adults and that is linked to their biological quality of being children? Or is it the case that our ideas about what a child's perspective on reality entails, precisely like our perceptions of children and of childhood, has a history? In this chapter, I shall investigate how the child's perspective emerges and is described in Scandinavian children's books, and shed an historical light on what adults say about how children experience the world. I believe that this is a fruitful approach to which insufficient attention has been paid, at least if we want to understand how the presuppositions about childhood take shape and are altered in the Scandinavian context. In this way, I shall present a picture of how adults' attitudes to the child as subject are connected with the changing view of the child's rights and duties.[5]

When a children's book shapes relationships between adults and children, it formulates affirmations about how they behave, and should behave, toward each other. This is why children's literature is regarded as an important starting point for the reading child's understanding of his or her own rights and duties.[6] But we can also say that when writers in the second half of the nineteenth century attempted more systematically to depict children's specific way of experiencing, there emerged an idea of the child as subject with experiences and a will to which the adults had to relate both with reason and with feelings. It has been pointed out that the view (which became increasingly widespread in the eighteenth century) that each individual is autonomous, with reason, feelings, and a will of his or her own, established an essential premise for both the American Declaration of Independence in 1786 and the French Declaration of the Rights of Man and of the Citizen in 1789.[7] However, the Scandinavian children's books show that it took until the mid-nineteenth century before children as a group were described with a subjectivity that, in its turn, could function as a premise for the view that they had a right to their own way of experiencing the world, and a will and a moral judgment of their own.

Scandinavian authors of children's books have long taken on the responsibility of molding how children see the world. Although this perhaps applies most strongly to those writers who were active during the second half of the twentieth century, children's supposed experience and perspective were given a special place already in nineteenth-century. The authors of children's books are often regarded as a group with a particular closeness to children, and they tend to be ascribed an ability, either natural or trained, to think with the same logic as a child. We often hear of their ability to recall how it is to think, feel, and experience as a child.

Today, the link between the child's perspective and the child's right is more or less taken for granted as a starting point for many Scandinavian authors of children's books. When the Swedish writer Pernilla Stalfelt (born 1962), who has written books such as *Hurray!!! The Rights of all Children* (2009; *Hurrraa!!! Alla barns rätt*), spoke relatively recently about her own work in an interview, she did so in a manner that illustrates with unusual clarity this tradition in Scandinavian children's books: "I want to communicate the child's own voice. Adults often want to take the child's place. They are nostalgic when they look back to their childhood. It easily happens that the adult takes over the space."[8] There is thus surely no real doubt that the authors of children's books have influenced, and continue to influence, our perceptions of what a child's perspective and a child's rights are.

If one wants to investigate the emergence of the idea of a child's perspective, however, it is useful to look back to Scandinavian children's literature in the mid-nineteenth century, since it seems that the child's perspective appears at that date in children's books that were published in Sweden, Finland, Denmark, and Norway. In comparison with other European countries, this seems to happen at a relatively early date and in one specific way. The group of authors who are discussed here also had a decisive influence on the development of children's books in the Nordic countries. I shall pay particular attention to the Danish author Hans Christian Andersen (1805–1875); the Norwegian folklore researcher, bishop, and author Jørgen Moe (1813–1882); the Swedish pastor and author Olof Fryxell (1806–1900); and the Finland–Swedish journalist, historian, and author, Zacharias Topelius (1818–1898).[9] Their importance for twentieth-century children's books can be seen not least in Astrid Lindgren (1907–2002), who in many ways is in their literary debt.

Astrid Lindgren: The Perspective of the Other

Astrid Lindgren has become the very embodiment of what we mean by a child's perspective in literature for children and young people, and this makes her especially important in this context.[10] Her *Pippi Longstocking* (1945; *Pippi Långstrump*), which was published in November 1945, two months after the end of World War II, comes at the close of the history of Scandinavian childhood that is portrayed in this book, but it is the clearest expression of the fact that something was happening to the power relationships between adults and children in Scandinavian children's literature. Its unconventional description of children's subjectivity and will attracted considerable attention, but also extensive criticism on the part of leading cultural figures of the period.[11]

Scholars tend to highlight Pippi Longstocking's unexpected actions, her cheeky attitude, and her lack of respect for authorities as a radical example of how Lindgren reformulates the world of the children.[12] In Lindgren's fictitious universe, the reader encounters a narrator who attempts to take children's experiences and feelings with genuine seriousness, while at the same time establishing a humoristic sphere that reverses the power relationships between adults and children. In this way, Pippi often actualizes the question of what adults are entitled to do to children.[13] But Lindgren's defense of a child's perspective on existence was not limited to the fictitious portrayals of relationships between children and adults in her children's books. It also found a more immediately political expression that makes her a shining example of how the assertion of the child's perspective on existence by the authors of children's books could have a real political influence.

Before we turn to the mid-nineteenth-century predecessors, I shall give a short example that illustrates how Lindgren makes herself a political defender and interpreter of the child's perspective, and of how she links the idea of the child's perspective with that of the child's rights. In her 1978 speech "Never Violence!", held on the occasion of receiving the German Booksellers' Peace Prize, we find a moving anecdote about a young mother who feels that she has to give her little child "a good hiding" as a punishment for something naughty he has done.

> She told him to go out and find a suitably supple stick or rod for her to use. The little boy was away for a long time. He eventually came back in tears and announced: "I can't find a rod, but here's a stone you can throw at me."
>
> At which point his mother also burst into tears, because she suddenly saw the whole situation with the child's eyes. He must have thought: "My mum wants to hurt me, and she can do that just as well by throwing a stone at me." She threw her arms round him, and they spent some time crying together. Then she placed the stone on a shelf in the kitchen, and it stayed there as a permanent reminder of the promise she had made to herself at that moment: never violence![14]

The turning point in the narrative is the mother's insight that the child does in fact have a right to a life without violence. But it is equally important to note that this insight is borne of her sudden ability to see "with the child's eyes." The anecdote thus formulates a special concept of the child and indicates how important it is that adults are able to see the world from the child's perspective. The speech "Never Violence!" was certainly controversial, and it was regarded at the time as provocative. Nevertheless, it made Astrid Lindgren one of the more important opinion formers in the campaign against corporal punishment in Sweden. The debate about the corporal punishment of children had raged intensively in the 1970s both in Scandinavia and in the rest of the Western world. Many were worried about what would happen if adults were deprived of the possibility to inflict corporal discipline on children. In 1979, however, Sweden—the first country in the world—was enriched with a law prohibiting corporal punishment in the home (followed by Norway in 1983 and by Finland in 1987). Norway was the first country in the world to prohibit corporal punishment in schools in 1936 (followed by Sweden twenty-two years later, in 1958).

At the close of the 1970s, the Cold War and the balance of terror between East and West was an obviously present threat that was experienced strongly in northern Europe. The terrifying world situation, where it was thought that the definitive atomic war lay just around the corner, is also clearly highlighted in Lindgren's speech. She told the German audience that, to change the world as we now see it, we must "start from the bottom," with the child. If we succeed in bringing up children without violence, we can perhaps hope for a more peaceful world when they have grown up. But her anecdote also indicates that it is the adults who have to change. If only they could see with the child's eyes, show them respect and give them an upbringing with dignity, it would surely then also be possible to create a better society. It was natural for her, as a children's books' author, to say that children's books would be able to make a contribution here.

The fact that Sweden was the first country to forbid the corporal punishment of children can be linked to the welfare state's responsibility for the individual child. Lindgren's endeavors in various contexts to defend the child's perspective were thus in the spirit of the age. It was also based, to no little degree, on her desire to defend the lonely and exposed child against a world that displayed no compassion with the small and the weak. This makes the cheeky and recalcitrant Pippi Longstocking a representative spokesperson for the human rights of those who have no power to affect their own situation. But she is also a defender of what, at least since Romanticism, has been linked to children and childhood, namely, playfulness and imagination, naturalness and freedom, delightful disorder and boundless enjoyment. The central place of the child's perspective in Lindgren's books finds perhaps its most striking formulation in the stories about Pippi Longstocking, which not only relate how she visits the candy store and uses her gold coins to buy the children as much candy as they want, but also contain criticism of the adults' abuses and the little "squiggle" pill that means that one never needs to leave the land of childhood and grow up.[15] The playfulness and the resistance are not only a motif in the portrayal of the children; they also find their way into the treatment of language itself, where multiplication becomes "plutification" and new words like "squeazle" see the light of day.[16]

From the perspective of the history of childhood, it is not surprising that play and playfulness should have such a prominent role in Astrid Lindgren's attempts to write from a child's perspective. To be a child and to have a childhood have long been associated with play and imagination. But this was not always the case. It was only in the nineteenth and twentieth centuries that the place, the time, and the manner of play were clearly and positively anchored in the concept of childhood and its presuppositions. Industrialization not only meant that the child in the bourgeois social class was gradually freed from working; in parallel to the increasingly well-ordered leisure time, with free evenings and weekends, work gradually moved from the home to factories, offices, and other specialized workplaces. This made the home a more clearly appropriate place for family life and relaxation. Industrialization both widened children's possibilities for play and aimed the time and the place of play more directly at children.[17] By using the motif of play, the authors of children's books at that period shared in the creation of a specific view of children and of their way of experiencing and feeling.

H. C. Andersen: The Play Motif and a Child's Way of Seeing Things

A link between childhood and play can be identified as a constant element in the Scandinavian children's books that were published in the last 200 years. In a Scandinavian context, it is particularly important to underline the motif of play and its relationship to various perceptions of children and childhood. One may perhaps state quite simply that the early popularity of the motif of play in Scandinavian children's literature is connected with the attempt to approach childhood as something special and valuable; or, as one Norwegian literary scholar puts it, "If children are taken seriously, it is only right that play too acquires a very central position."[18]

The shape given to play by the Scandinavian children's books tells us a great deal about how children and childhood were seen in various periods, but also about what being a girl and a boy was thought to entail. If one follows the descriptions of play across the history of Scandinavian children's books, one also sees how they help to create ideas about boys who are to become men, and about girls who are to become women. To make a wide-reaching generalization: one can say that the description of girls' childhood play often anticipates, historically speaking, the orderly home that they are to help to create as grown women, while the description of boys' play creates something that seems, on the surface, to be a boisterous questioning of rules.[19]

But one can also follow the way in which the play motif in children's books creates various ways of seeing and experiencing. One celebrated Scandinavian author who often employs the play motif to shape this is the Danish writer H. C. Andersen, who is best known for his literary fairy tales. He played an important role in the development of Scandinavian children's literature, not least through his direct influence on the Finland–Swedish author Zacharias Topelius.[20] Astrid Lindgren too was strongly influenced by Andersen, whose stories were a recurring and important element in her own childhood reading. These authors are largely united in their attempts to construct a child's perspective on existence.[21]

It is often held that the child's perspective becomes clear in children's books only in the second half of the twentieth century, since it is believed that it was then that the authors of children's books began to invite the readers to take part in credible psychological processes on the child's level.[22] This is undeniably a perfectly reasonable claim; but every claim of this kind is dependent on what one actually means when one thinks that a child's perspective is found in the one children's book, but not in the other. The answer to the question of what a child's perspective is, is ultimately connected to one's own perceptions of a child's qualities, emotional life, and psychology. Accordingly, one way to study the child's perspective is to examine impartially the way in which ideas about the child's qualities, emotional life, and psychology emerge in the text. For example: to what extent is the reader allowed to take part in the events of the story via the child characters' senses and their specific logic? We shall see several examples from the long history of adult authors' attempts to describe children's point of view and their experience of the world. These attempts can be said to have their starting point in the changing perception of what a child is.

As is well known, a more markedly subjective and emotional perspective on reality emerges with Romanticism at the end of the eighteenth century. In the course of the nineteenth century, there is a higher appreciation of both the child and childhood as the child's way of existing in the world.[23] This was also the century in which clearer attempts to articulate a child's perspective can be seen in Scandinavian children's books. H. C. Andersen is often presented here as a comparatively early example of an author who gives a special space to the child's experiences and emotions. By addressing his readers like an oral narrator, he establishes a special contact between the one who narrates and the one to whom the story is narrated.[24] The oral and direct address on the part of the narrator is a technique that Astrid Lindgren was to take further, many years later. This not only allows her to place the reader in the events she relates; in both Andersen and Lindgren, this technique establishes a special perspective on what is narrated, since the narrator draws close to the reader and to his or her assumed way of seeing things.

It is not easy to know how best to describe the construction of the child's perspectives in H. C. Andersen's stories. It cannot even be taken for granted that his literary fairy tales are actually addressed to children; in some instances, they must be regarded as too complex and ironic to permit classification as children's literature.[25] It is, however, striking that his narratives tend to depict a world that has its starting point in the notion of the child's everyday life and play. To take one example: his well-known short story "The Steadfast Tin Soldier" (1838; "Den standhaftige Tinsoldat") is a playful but sensitive narrative about a boy who is given a collection of tin soldiers as a birthday present. One of them is one-legged, and the narrative centers on him. The fairytale portrays either a special world or a special way of looking at reality, because the one-legged tin soldier, who cannot move, takes part in a number of various adventurous events, and the reader is allowed consistently to feel what is happening from a perspective that appears to be close to that of the tin soldier himself, but is not limited to this.

After the boy picks up the tin soldier from his box, the soldier sees a paper doll that portrays a ballerina, and he is immediately smitten by what he sees: "Now she would be just the right wife for me, he thought."[26] From this point on, his love for the paper doll is at the center of the story, but after a sequence of events, it finishes wretchedly. The one-legged soldier is thrown into a tile stove and is dissolved in a scene that expands to become an ambivalent image of love's consuming fire:

> And then a strange thing happened. One of the small boys picked up the tin solider and threw him into the stove. He had no reason for doing this; it must have been the fault of the snuffbox goblin. The tin solider stood framed in a blaze of light. The heat was intense, but whether this came from the fire or from his burning love he could not tell.[27]

The story of the steadfast tin soldier, which has been claimed to be the first literary fairy tale with a non-human protagonist, was originally published in a context addressed explicitly to children, in the second part of *Fairy Tales Told for Children* (1838; *Eventyr fortalte for Børn*). Bearing in mind the envisaged reader, one is tempted to regard the narrative as the staging of everyday experiences in the home of a bourgeois, middle-class boy. The course of events is not necessarily related from the tin soldier's perspective; rather, it establishes a child's experience. One can say that the narrative is filtered through an idea of how a child sees—that is to say, it reports the story from the outside, through what can be assumed to be the imaginative perspective of a child at play. The fact that the narrative can be read as an articulation of a child's (rather than an adult's) perspective on existence is already indicated by the sharply circumscribed description of existence: it is the toys and their adventures that occupy centerstage, while the adult word is almost totally absent. If one were to see the story through the eyes of the adult characters, one would suspect that the toys in Andersen's narrative have no life of their own. From such a perspective, the soldiers, the jack-in-the-box, and the paper doll are dead, exactly as *things* normally are. But from the perspective of the child and of his play, they are alive. They can move, think, and feel.[28]

Nothing in "The Steadfast Tin Soldier" indicates that what happens to the living tin soldier is a fantasy by one of the children in the story. But although the tin soldier is not explicitly given life by means of the common literary motif of the fantasy of a child who is at play or dreaming, there is much that supports the view that the text is to be understood as configuring the way in which a child at play relates to the world. This means that the contrast between the supposedly adult way of experiencing the things of the world and the child's supposedly imaginative world of play is generated by the relationship between the text and the reader; it is not present in the fictional world itself.

Although it is difficult to determine, strictly speaking, whether what happens in the fairy tale is happening in reality, or is instead a reflection of a child's supposed experience, the description of the child's toys and feelings already entails a higher appreciation of children and of childhood. Here, therefore, we are relatively far away from the literature which was common at that period and addressed children with advice and information to teach them how to behave, so that they would become sensible adults as quickly as possible. Instead, the short narrative concentrates its portrayal of reality on the playful imagination, thereby portraying what it would be like to experience the world like a child. The notion of the child is thus linked to the idea of a subjectivity that is specific to the child.

Jørgen Moe: Girls and Boys at Play

A closer examination of nineteenth-century children's books makes it plain that the child's subjectivity is given a special space in this period, not only in Andersen, but also in other writers. Around the middle of the century, a number of books were published where the child's perspective is a central element in the narrative. Many times, as in Andersen, this is done in connection with the description of the child's play—dolls in the case of girls and battles in the case of boys. In what is regarded as Norway's first children's book, Jørgen Moe's *In the Pond and on the Hill* (1851; *I Brønden og i Kjærnet*), much of the plot is concerned with two children and their games.[29]

Moe is best known for his collection and publication of Norwegian folk tales in the 1840s, together with Peter Christian Asbjørnsen (1812–1855). In the context of research into Scandinavian children's books, it has been claimed that Moe presented in a completely new children's way of experiencing things, and that when he wrote for children, he investigated what it meant to be a child with the same sensitivity he employed when he collected folk tales in order to discover the soul of the Norwegian people.[30] The comparison between the people and the child points to the link between the emergence of the Scandinavian national states and their people, on the one hand, and the historical coming into existence of the idea of childhood as a specific land separated from the world of adults, on the other hand.[31]

The protagonists in *In the Pond and on the Hill* are siblings, the five-year-old Beate and the seven-year-old Viggo. In their play, they bring to life dolls and other dead things in their surroundings. As in "The Steadfast Tin Soldier," events are related by an external narrator and the perspective is close to that of a child. This invites the reader to look at reality, and at the events described, in a particular way.

Unlike Andersen's story of the tin soldier, Moe's narratives create a perspective that moves between being a description of the game as a game and a description of the game as reality. In other words, the narrative shows the disconnect between what is portrayed as the child's imaginative way of looking at reality, and the reality that is not animated by the child's imagination and thus appears indirectly as the adult way of relating to one's environment. We find one example of this kind of duality in the first part of the book, which begins with a description of Beate's birthday presents: a hat, a pair of yellow shoes, and a doll. The narrator draws close to the envisaged reader by means of a direct address and a language that already in its simplicity is generated by a notion of what a child is. After describing the straw hat Beate receives from her father, the narrator turns to the reader and says: "And believe you [*singular*] me, it was lovely."

This is the narrator's opinion, but it almost appears as a formulation of how Beate herself can be thought to experience the gift. The narrator sees and records what happens through the child's experience, while at the same time inviting the reader, through the direct address, to see from this perspective; and this is intensified in the following description of Big Beate and her doll Little Beate:

> Big Beate – it is true that she was only five years old, but she was much bigger than the other Beate – and Little Beate quickly agreed that they should pluck pussy willows [*Gaasunger*, literally 'goslings'] from the tree and drop them into the well, so that they would have a good time, just like the big goslings [*Gaasunger*] they had seen swimming around. It was actually Big Beate who made the suggestion, but Little Beate made no objection, because she was always incredibly nice and accommodating.[32]

The doll Little Beate comes alive when Big Beate plays. But the narrator also points out that the doll itself does not reply when Big Beate makes her suggestion that they should pretend that the pussy willows on the tree are really geese and that they should throw them into the well. Indeed, he adds that the doll is always "nice and accommodating," indicating that it is precisely in Big Beate's imagination and play that Little Beate comes alive. This technique is applied several times, for example, when Big Beate asks Little Beate whether she should lean over the edge of the well. This allows the narrator to present the child's perspective, while at the same time showing that this is, precisely, the *child's* perspective: "Little Beate did not reply; but her left eyebrow shot up in a remarkable manner and she really moved her right arm, as if she wanted to say: 'Please don't do that, dear Big Beate'."[33]

Big Beate's play invites the reader to take a child's perspective in relation to her doll; her brother Viggo's play invites the reader to take a child's perspective in relation to reading. In the book's second chapter, Viggo is inspired by reading an old chronicle and plays at being a Viking. Unlike his sister, he does not generate a loving and healing idea when he plays. Instead of giving Little Beate life with his imagination, he takes the life from her by simply cutting off the doll's head with his little ax. In short, his play stages the ideal of masculinity that, according to the narrator, he has just read about in his books: "but he had read in an old chronicle about a terrible bearded Viking who had the same name; he sailed from land to land and killed people, and he took with him on board his ship all the gold and silver that he found, and all the pretty girls."[34] Moe's *In the Pond and on the Hill* thus formulates an inclusive child's perspective that stages the stereotypical way in which the girl and boy characters look at reality.

Olof Fryxell: The Important Perspective of the Community of Boys

To construct a child's perspective by letting the boy character in the narrative play at war under the inspiration of his reading is not a completely unusual motif in nineteenth-century Scandinavian children's books. We find one of the earliest examples in the Swedish author Olof Fryxell's *Snow Castle. A Story for Countryside Boys* (1830; *Snöfästningen. En berättelse för Landt-gossar*). Fryxell was studying theology at the time the book was published, and he was ordained in 1831. It was relatively common in Sweden in the first half of the nineteenth century for pastors to write literature that was specifically addressed to children. Pastors in general had a prominent place in public discourse, and church law laid down that they were to oversee children's upbringing.[35]

The book stages several ideas that were current at the time of its publication. The description of the children not only links young boys' becoming men with a nationalist winter game that is inspired by sagas about Vikings of the past, it is also explicitly addressed to boys and illustrates the idea of the important community of boys. *Snöfästningen* tells the story of three aristocratic boys who build a snow castle in order to invite the neighboring peasant boys to take part in a snowball fight. Despite their membership in different social classes, it all takes place amicably, and their mutual comradeship is underlined when the boys confirm their friendship with each other after the game. The short narrative is rounded off when Major von *** (the name is missing), the father of the aristocratic boys Ferdinand and Wilhelm, who has observed the fight from his window, comes into the boys' castle. The narrator informs us that he has the noble figure of an old warrior, and he preaches to the boys about human conflict, the beauty of nature, and the eternal peace of heaven.

Like "The Steadfast Tin Soldier" and *In the Pond and on the Hill*, *Snow Castle* is related by an external narrator. But he has a tendency to take on the collective perspective of the boys in his description of their game. He begins by depicting a broad perspective, describing how large snowflakes fall from the clouds over woods and fields, how children in the countryside play with the snow, and how happiness spreads both inside and outside the houses. He then zooms in on the three aristocratic boys who are the main characters in the story. They stand on a level place with spades in their hands, building the snow castle that is announced in the title. The introduction to the narrative separates the boys from the rest of the world's throngs and gives them a specific position in the course of events. This is followed by a detailed account of how the snow castle takes shape. When the structure is finished, the boys select Gustaf, the pastor's son, to be their opponent and invite him to be the enemy, together with the five peasant boys, and to try to take the snow castle by storm.

The narrator describes how Gustaf approaches the peasant boys, taking a path that is not completely straight. But although it is the external narrator who speaks, the course of events appears to be narrated from a perspective that lies close to the collective experience of the three aristocratic boys inside the walls of the snow castle. It is not only the narrator's field of vision that is restricted by means of a perspective that lies close to the characters' own experience of what takes place. The perspective is also restricted by the fact that neither the narrator nor the aristocratic boys hear what Gustaf and the five peasant boys in the approaching enemy troop are planning together. The narrator tells us what happens:

> He (Gustaf) spoke quietly with his company, and then began to roll a snowball on the ground, until it had become a big sphere of snow. Now he spoke at length with the soldiers, and probably told them how they were to conduct themselves. Then they spread out around the castle, and each one began to roll a mighty sphere of snow for himself.
> "I wonder what Gustaf intends to do now," said Karl. "I bet it is something to do with us."[36]

It is the word "probably" that both creates tension and indicates that the reader is offered a viewpoint close to the viewpoint that the aristocratic boys have from inside their castle. Compared with the narrative space that is given to the aristocratic boys in the introduction, this perspective-defined aural and visual impression is generated by a child's perspective on the course of events. In addition, it offers scope for the reader to take sides and get involved in the text.

It is interesting, in the context of the history of childhood and of literature, that Fryxell employs the form of the narrative to portray the experience of the child at play. This makes him an early exponent of the Romantic current's higher appreciation of the child's experience, and of the emphasis on childhood as a special way to see, think, and feel.

Zacharias Topelius: Taking One's Place Inside Children's Play

Zacharias Topelius is regarded as one of the more important innovators in Scandinavian children's books in the second half of the nineteenth century. It has been said that his story "The Adventures of Walter" (1855–1856; "Walters Äfventyr") depicts for the first time in Swedish "the piece of everyday drama that an imaginative and active child experiences uninterruptedly."[37] This description is correct, although we have seen that the child's perspective and experience can also be found in other authors of children's books at that time, both in Sweden and in the other Scandinavian countries. As in Andersen, Moe, and Fryxell, it is often in connection with the depiction of play that Topelius creates the child's subjective reality. Unlike his predecessors, however, he links play more systematically with the child's perspective, as well as more explicitly giving an ethical dimension to his depiction of the child's play.

When Zacharias Topelius' writings are presented as a turning point in the history of Scandinavian children's literature, his explicit endeavor, as author and educator, to locate himself inside children's own circle tends to be mentioned.[38] He said in 1866 that it is important for one who writes for children to be able to take on "childhood's outlook" and to let morality clothe itself in a "living form" instead of "being poured on from a ladle or stuck on like a signpost."[39] Topelius had a much greater influence than Olof Fryxell on the perception of children and childhood in Scandinavia. It is also relevant to note how Fryxell approaches "childhood's outlook" by means of his subjective description of the battle for the snow castle and gives its adult-defined ideology a "living form" seventeen years before Topelius himself makes his debut as an author of children's literature with his collection *Sagor* (1847).

Children appreciate it when the narrator "takes his place among them," explains Zacharias Topelius, when he formulates his view of the task that awaits the author of children's literature.[40] One who writes for children must not speak "in the well-known *condescending* tone," as if one were "sinking down into things of a lower order." The more equal relationship between adults and children that Topelius expresses here is based on a view of the child inspired by Romanticism. He states that the child fashions a noble unity between "belief and conviction" that "only the highest wisdom possesses in conjunction with the innocence of childhood." But childhood is not only an exalted state that deserves the highest veneration; the child must also be protected from growing up too fast:

> Innumerable parents, teachers, and writers cannot rest until they have brought the snake into paradise, until they have succeeded in igniting the premature reflection that destroys everything. The dear children are not left to grow in peace with their happy faith in life, their happy unity with nature and with their own selves. The school all at once becomes so perfectly rational. They hear every day that the blue sky is merely empty air, and the golden cloud of morning is merely a hazy cloud formation; they hear that the king in their game is wearing a paper crown and that the boundless world of the nursery is merely an antechamber to the school.[41]

The idea of childhood that Topelius formulates accords a higher value to the child's way of experiencing, thinking, and feeling. The child's own world is given a special value, and is not regarded first and foremost as a stage that must be passed as quickly as possible. The child has a right to be a child. The difference between being a child and being an adult is thus particularly important for Topelius. But while these two stages are in many ways regarded as antithetical, the one also presupposes the other. A "withered" childhood in which one is "a little old person" can never be made good. It becomes a dried-up root and leads to an unhappy life later as an adult.

This means that the writer's ability to take on "childhood's outlook" (to borrow Topelius' phrase) is not only an endeavor to get away from the didactic or moralistic children's literature that wants to tell its young readers how they are to behave, so that they can become rational and adult as quickly as possible. Instead, the most important task of the children's book is to protect childhood. It must allow the child to be a child—or, to put it differently and more critically, it must show the child reader what it means to be a genuine child and what it means to see and experience the world as a genuine child. At the same time, the children's world is clearly divided by gender, and so we must add that Topelius' children's books do not show what it entails to be a child, or to have a child's outlook, independently of ideas about what it entails to be and to experience as a boy or as a girl.

The Adventures of Walter is a story about the six-year-old Walter, whose pranks recall the much better known Emil in Astrid Lindgren's *Emil in Lönneberga (Emil i Lönneberga)* (1963). Walter can break plates, kick a ball through a window, pull the thread from a spinning will, and trample down the backyard. But Topelius' narrator (like Lindgren's) also underscores that he does not do his pranks out of badness: "Otherwise, he has a good heart, but he is bad at remembering Papa's and Mama's admonitions, and this is why he encounters so many adventures."[42]

We find one example among many in the second story in *The Adventures of Walter*, which tells how he gets a new sled as a Christmas present. Walter takes his sled, and goes to the precipice above the slope where the others are driving their sleds. Scarcely even the most courageous dare to drive up on this height. No path has been trampled up to the top, and the reader understands that Walter is setting out on a reckless adventure. The trip ends when he crashes into a big tree, faints, and has to be carried home. When he finally wakes up in his bed, he hears his father saying that he was driving his sled "like an idiot head-first down the high slope."[43]

This (one might think) makes the narrative an example of what happens if one is an excessively careless and unrestrained child—ultimately, the narrative would then be establishing the perspective of adult reason. But it certainly cannot be taken for granted that the function and the moral teaching of the narrative lend support to the adult way of doing things. At the beginning of the story, Walter is presented as an example of a healthy and spry boy. Unlike those children who (like the reader) sit at home before a warm fire, he is outside in good spirits, despite the cold. After berating the reader for being a "namby-pamby boy" who sits indoors instead of being out, the narrator defines what seems to be the moral teaching of the adventure: "There is something worse than frozen fingers, and that is to remain a weak wretch all one's life."[44]

The narrator addresses his readers and formulates a moral maxim, which is then concretized through the exemplary narrative's description of Walter's reckless ride on his sled. But the exemplary narrative not only establishes a contrast between the namby-pamby calm of the home and the freshness of the outdoor world: it also stages the child's perspective on what happens. This is particularly prominent when Walter hurtles out over the precipice on his sled Pukki. Initially, the reader takes part in what happens from the perspective of the astonished children, and then from Walter's own perspective:

> All the boys and girls looked on in astonishment. Walter climbed up, and Pukki followed him like a dog ... At first, all they saw was Walter's head, and then only his cap; finally, they saw nothing ... Pukki and Walter had disappeared in the snowdrift.
> Walter closed his eyes when he disappeared. He felt himself sinking and sinking, just like a crow that is shot in its wing and falls from the top of a birch tree, and then there was a mighty jerk. When Walter looked up, Pukki and he stood in front of a huge castle of ice, with glimmering high pillars and vast rooms of brightest silver.[45]

There is a clear transition from the perspective of the group of children to Walter's own perspective. The child's experience is thus presented through the shaping of the game. After this, however, Walter's experience glides imperceptibly over into a dream-like description of how he lands in the realm of the Snow King, and the reader is shown what happens to Walter there. The narrator indicates that this is a dream-like journey into an imagined foreign land, when he tells us that Walter suddenly wakes up from his unconsciousness and realizes that he is lying at home in his bed. Although Papa says that he is talking "in his nightcap" and that he has been "dreaming," Walter, "who could scarcely believe what he was told," remains doubtful until the close of the story, which thus ends in a kind of ambivalence—since it is not completely clear whether Walter has really experienced what he experienced, or whether it was all a dream. This technique was used by Lewis Carroll ten years later in *Alice's Adventures in Wonderland* (1865). But both Walter's and Alice's adventures, like many children's books written at a later date, show that dreams and fantasies are an experience that must be taken seriously, if one looks at them from the child's own perspective.

Conclusion: The Child's Perspective and the Child's Rights

Historians of culture identify a link between the development of the novel in the eighteenth century and the emergence of human rights. From this perspective, human rights were developed not only through philosophical arguments or altered material presuppositions, but also as a consequence of new discoveries about what it means to be a human being. Lynn Hunt, the North American historian, has been the foremost researcher into the modern novel's significance for the invention of human rights and for a right that builds upon empathy and identification. She holds that the novel's potential for developing the reader's empathy is central to the humanitarian sentiment and subjectivity that are necessary, if human rights are to take form: "I believe that social change and political change – in this case, human rights – comes about because many individuals had similar experiences ... through their interactions with each other and with their reading and viewing, they actually created a new social context."[46]

We have seen how ideas about the child's perspective, and about what it entails to be and to experience like a child, are formulated in Scandinavian children's literature in the mid-nineteenth century. One could go on to make a similar affirmation that the idea of children's rights is generated by a changed picture of children and of how they experience their world. Just as Samuel Richardson's *Pamela* (1740) and Rousseau's *Julie* (1761) made possible the very idea of human rights by allowing wider strata of readers to feel empathy beyond the boundaries of class and nationality, children's literature made it possible for adults to relate to the child as a subject with experiences of his or her own. In this way, the basis was laid for the discussion of children's rights that took place in the second half of the twentieth century. The children's books that we have discussed here all bring out children's subjectivity and will in connection with various discussions of play. Via Astrid Lindgren, the link between children and play later acquires great importance for the development of the child's subjectivity in the second half of the twentieth century.

This chapter has shown that a special attentiveness to what was thought to be the child's way of living and experiencing emerged in a number of Scandinavian writers in the first half of the nineteenth century. In their books, they give a clear space to the child's subjectivity, while at the same time creating narratives that transform children, from being an object of the predetermined upbringing by adults, into subjects with their own experience, feelings, and will. When writers at this period held that childhood was characterized by an important and specific way of being and experiencing, they were thus inviting the adults to acquire a new moral attitude to children. But one can also argue that children's literature at this period functioned as a discourse that supported children's rights by showing them their own place in the world, and showing what rights they had. To take one example: already in the nineteenth century, a writer like Topelius could have the adults in his stories refrain from disciplining their children in a violent way.[47] Such a view means that literature is regarded as a source of law for children, and that children's literature can teach them about their rights.[48] Accordingly, children's literature can also show how morally significant power relationships between adults and children have emerged and changed in the Scandinavian context.[49]

Notes

1 Hammarberg 1991: 18.
2 Qvarsell 2003: 101–3. This article points out the problematic aspects of various applications of the child's perspective as a theoretical concept in relation to the

question of human rights. On children's rights, see also Chapter 6 by Jacobsen in this volume.

3 Fass 2011: 24.
4 Sommer, Pramling Samuelsson, and Hundeide 2009; Hedenborg 1997.
5 The emerging field of Literature and Human Rights is interdisciplinary and deals with a diversity of topics. For a comprehensive overview, see McClennen and Moore 2015.
6 Widholm 2012: 45; Todres and Higinbotham 2013: 5. See also Saguisag and Prickett 2016.
7 Hunt 2007: 20 and 26ff.
8 Lindén 2013, online at http://na.se/bloggar/forfattarbloggen.
9 See Chapter 16 by Tatar in this volume.
10 Lundqvist 2007: 6.
11 Bak 2011: 10–12.
12 Asplund-Carlsson 2003: 6; Nikolajeva 2010: 9. On the child's perspective in post-modern Swedish picture books, see Österlund 2009: 19–33.
13 Several examples of how children's rights are presented in relation to adults' abuse of power can be found in Astrid Lindgren, *Pippi in the Seas* (trans. Turner 2012), especially chs. 1 and 4.
14 Lindgren, *Aldrig våld!* (2011/1978: 28); following the English trans. by Thompson 2007: 2, modified; online at www.swedishbookreview.com/article-2007-2-never-violence.asp.
15 Lindgren, *Pippi in the South Seas*, 109.
16 Lindgren, *Pippi in the South Seas*, 67 and 23.
17 Cross 2013: 270.
18 Bache-Wiig 1996: 75.
19 Widhe 2015: 37.
20 Von Zweigbergk 1965: 120.
21 On the relationship between Andersen and Lindgren, see, e.g., Grum-Schwensen 2007: 104. On the relationship between Topelius and Lindgren, see Svensson 2008: 128. See also Chapter 16 by Tatar in this volume.
22 Rhedin 1999: 95; and Rhedin 2013.
23 O'Malley 2003.
24 Weinreich 2006: 210.
25 Weinreich 2006: 211.
26 Andersen, *Tales of Hans Christian Andersen*, 87 (trans. Lewis 2004).
27 Andersen, *Tales of Hans Christian Andersen*, 92.
28 MacLean 2004: 28.
29 Moe 1851. It was translated after Moe's death into English as *In the Pond and on the Hill. Stories for Boys and Girls,* by Young 1883. See also Chapter 18 by Ommundsen in this volume.
30 Hagemann 1963: 184 links Moe's research into ordinary people's lives with his relationship to children.
31 On the comparison between the emergence of the modern national states and the interest in childhood as a foreign land, see Palmenfelt 2013.
32 Moe, *I Brønden og i Kjærnet*, 13.
33 Moe, *I Brønden og i Kjærnet*, 14.
34 Moe, *I Brønden og Kjærnet*, 19.
35 Hedenborg 1997: 229–30.
36 Fryxell, *Snäfästningen: Berättelse för Landt-*Gåßar, 25.
37 Von Zweigbergk 1965: 120.
38 Orlov 1999: 345.
39 Topelius, *Läsning för barn 1. Lekar*, 8.

40 Topelius, *Läsning för barn 1*, 4.
41 Topelius, *Läsning för barn 1*, 5.
42 Topelius *Läsning för barn 3. Visor och sagor*, 12. See also Klingberg 1998: 93.
43 Topelius, *Läsning för barn 3*, 21.
44 Topelius, *Läsning för barn 3*, 19.
45 Topelius, *Läsning för barn 3*, 20.
46 Hunt 2007: 34.
47 Topelius, *Läsning för barn 3*, 35.
48 Todres and Higinbotham 2013: 5ff.
49 The chapter is translated from Swedish by Brian McNeil.

18 Competent Children

Childhood in Nordic Children's Literature from 1850 to 1960

Åse Marie Ommundsen

One important source of knowledge about childhood is children's literature. Studying how childhood is constructed in children's literature, that is, texts written by adults for children, is interesting not only from a literary perspective, but also from a sociological and historical point of view. The fact that at a certain time in history, children were considered worthy, deserving and in need of their own literature is a clear indication of a new perspective on children and childhood.

Nordic children's literature started, as children's literature commonly does, with didactic stories written to children to teach them the right values and virtues. Typically, few if any of the early moralizing stories have survived up to the present. Alongside the educational path, there was another path, in which stories, songs, and adapted folklore were published to entertain. Canonized children's literature often belongs to the latter category. The first Norwegian picturebook for children, *Norsk billedbog for børn* (*Norwegian Picturebook for Children*), is a good example. It was first published in 1888, and is a collection of children's songs that are still used today, with illustrations depicting Norwegian landscapes and children joining in the family's work either as farmers or fishermen. The connection between child and nature has been an important concept in Norwegian children's literature from the beginning, in which childhood was linked to the conception of childhood in the countryside, in a close relationship to nature. In the poem in Figure 18.1 we can see that the boy is taking care of the animals on his own. The poem is written by the influential Norwegian author Bjørnstjerne Bjørnson (1832–1910), who also wrote the national anthem, and is a national icon himself.

A number of authors of the first golden age in Norwegian children's literature wrote children's stories and books that would enter the canon. Some of these books are known internationally, but in contemporary society, Nordic children's literature is probably most known abroad for Astrid Lindgren's (1907–2002) anti-authoritarian heroine *Pippi Longstrump* (*Pippi Longstocking*, 1945) and crossover books like Jostein Gaarder's (1952–) *Sophie's World* (1991), the world's best-selling book in 1995.[1] We will see that Pippi can be called a distant relative of one of the competent

Figure 18.1 Elling Holst: *Norsk billedbog for børn* (1888). Text by Bjørnstjerne Bjørnson. Illustration by Eivind Nielsen.

characters to be discussed in this study, namely Inger Johanne, who was already questioning adult norms and authority in 1890.

In Norway, the first national children's literature evolved in a nation-building phase in the second half of the nineteenth century, in a period in which Norway tried to emancipate itself both politically and culturally from Denmark and Sweden. This first literature published exclusively for children was used to build national identity and a notion of Norwegian childhood.[2] In the twentieth-century popular children's literature authors from the neighboring Scandinavian countries, such as Elsa Beskow (1874–1953) and the already mentioned Astrid Lindgren, also had a great influence in Norway. In examining children's literature from 1850 to 1960 it is thus pertinent to ask whether such a thing as a "Nordic childhood" exists, or whether childhood will always be closely linked to the nation, in this case Norway.

Farming was for a long time the main occupation in Nordic countries, and children took part in farm work alongside their parents. In the studied material, I find children working, taking care of siblings, and guarding animals during long days spent on their own. A change in terms of the construction of childhood began in Norway around 1850 and continued throughout the second half of the century. The construction of childhood in Norway was closely linked to the development of a public-school system and public child protection, which gave society the instruments to limit parents' rights. The Norwegian school system was regulated and standardized through the new school law of 1860, *Lov om Almueskoleværket på landet*, which aimed to provide a minimum of schooling for all children. Norway was the first country in the world to introduce public child protection, secured through *Vergerådsloven* the child protection act, in 1896.[3] The 1915 *Castbergian Children's Act* guaranteed equal juridical and economical rights to all children, including children born outside marriage. Norway was also the first nation in the world to inaugurate legal prohibitions against corporal punishment of children (1972), and the first nation to establish *Barneombudet*, an ombudsman exclusively for children (1980).

Research on Nordic Children's Literature

Two important and common motifs in Nordic children's literature that have been explored by several studies are the notions of children as competent and close to nature.[4] In the material discussed in this study we can find children who are competent in different ways, depending on their age, gender, and class. The competent children depicted in children's literature act as autonomous, active, robust, and responsible figures, taking care of animals or younger siblings, or playing outdoors on their own and mastering nature alone without adult supervision. This picture of the competent child contrasts with the notion of children as innocent, inexperienced, powerless, vulnerable, ignorant, dependent, and immature human beings.

Several studies of Nordic child culture and pedagogy have dealt with the concept of the competent child.[5] The Nordic child is considered competent as a family member, a pupil, a consumer, and a citizen. But maybe this view upon children is not always for the best of the child?[6] The responsible and competent children depicted in children's literature from the nineteenth and early twentieth century anticipate contemporary institutions such as the "negotiating family" and "dialogical pedagogy" in school and kindergarten. Nordic countries have an international reputation as welfare states in the vanguard of developing high quality standards for safeguarding the child as an individual with rights of its own, making today's competent child a reasonable, responsible, and reflective child, a child who accepts responsibility, who is a critical and conscious consumer, and who is able to take part in democratic processes, in school students' councils as well as in family discussions.[7]

Within research on children's literature, the concept of the competent child has been especially prominent in recent decades alongside the phenomenon of crossover literature, and both concepts have been linked to the Nordic child.[8] In the Nordic countries, boundaries between literature for children and adults have been blurred and partly erased since the beginning of the 1990s, a phenomenon that apparently occurred earlier and more frequently in the Nordic countries than in other parts of the world.[9] The tendency to erase borders between literature for child and adult reflects changed power relations and erased boundaries between children and adults in society. The new, more horizontal relationship between children and adults has been pointed out by scholars since the early 1990s; one of the concepts involved is "the sibling society."[10] The concept of the competent child has been on the agenda in research on childhood from the early 1990s. Children's status as "beings" or "becomings" has been raised as a topic and discussed, and the new childhood studies have sought to establish a new paradigm within childhood research: The child as an "agent."[11]

Although research has been devoted to the motif of competent and free children in Nordic children's literature post 1960, less attention has been given to this motif in children's literature prior to 1960 and to nuances in the construction of "competent" and "free."[12] The aim of this study is to go back to three classic children's books from three periods prior to 1960—1851, 1890 and 1941—and to explore various dimensions of constructions of "competent, free and close to nature" children. These books are, respectively, *I Brønden og i Tjærnet. Smaahistorier for Børn* (*In the Well and in the Mere. Small Stories for Children*, 1851), by Jørgen Moe (1813–1882); *Vi børn, af Inger Johanne, 13 Aar gammel* (*We Children, by 13-Year-Old Inger Johanne*, 1890), by Dikken Zwilgmeyer (1853–1913); and *Duktiga Annika* (*Talented Annika*, 1941), by Elsa Beskow (1874–1953). These three classics can provide three snapshots of Nordic childhood from the respective periods. I have chosen classic books written by popular, innovative and influential authors. The three books have appeared in several editions up to the present and have been translated into English and other languages including German, Dutch, Spanish, and Danish.

All three books show active girls and boys in daily life and play, presenting a picture of childhood at a particular period. Children's literature is closely linked to national identity, but also to regional identities.[13] I will examine how the notion of a specific national (Norwegian) or regional (Nordic) childhood is constructed through Nordic children's literature from 1850 to 1960. The three selected books have a common characteristic, that of "the competent child." The children are competent in different ways depending on their gender, class and education, but they all prove active, independent, robust, and responsible, working or playing in a setting seemingly free of adult supervision.

Although these early children's books express notions of "competent" and "free" children who are active, responsible, and robust, the children in the books are competent in different ways, and constructions of competence vary in the texts depending on the child's gender, class, and education. My main findings are that the notion of the competent child is an important motif also in early in Nordic children's literature, but this competence is nuanced, has many dimensions and is colored by notions of class, gender, equality, education, nature, and the nation. The competent child in this period is different from the virtuous child in earlier literature, and also different from the contemporary "equal and competent consumer and citizen child" and the blurred lines of adult and child in literature of the new millennium.

This chapter contributes to the history of childhood with a complex view of the competent child found much earlier than what is recognized by most studies on childhood and children's literature. Hopefully, it may help contemporary readers to re-examine their own pre-conceptions about children as "competent" and "responsible" and how our notions of "competent" might be colored by many factors. The chapter raises some questions about the relationships between adults and children and about the responsibilities of children and adults in any period, including today.

1851: The First Norwegian Children's Book by Moe

At the beginning of the nineteenth century only a few people in Norway could read and write, and the books were only affordable for a small upper class with strong connections to the political capital, Copenhagen. Consequently, most of the literature for children was published in Danish. In the cultural conflict between the two dominant theological positions of the time, Grundtvigians and Pietists, children's magazines were used on both sides to teach children the right ideas. In the following period, children's magazines dominated the reading scene for children.[14] The magazines mostly consist of typical contemporary genres like the exemplary story, spiritual songs, and sermons, the moral usually clearly expressed with an adult admonition. The cultural conflict between Grundtvigianism and Pietism is clearly visible, and can be linked to the two almost diametrically opposing views upon children, as "Devil seeds and little angels."[15]

Norway gained independence from Denmark in 1814, but it took some time before the first genuine Norwegian children's book was published. In 1851, the Norwegian fairy and folk tale collector Jørgen Moe (1813–1882) published what is considered to be the first original Norwegian children's book, *I Brønden og i Tjærnet* (see Figure 18.2). *Smaahistorier for Børn* (*In the Well and in the Mere. Small Stories for Children*).[16] The book consists of four chapters containing six interlinked stories. In the three first stories five to seven-year-old Beate is the main character, and in the three last stories her older brother Viggo (aged eight to ten) is the main character. This shift in focus makes it relevant to study the gender perspectives in the book. To what extent can the childhood of a girl and of a boy be seen as one common or two different childhoods?

As typical examples of Norwegian children, the children play outdoors in nature, seemingly free of adult supervision. The simple, realistic depictions

Figure 18.2 The Beheaded Doll. Jørgen Moe: *I brønden og i tjærnet* (1877). Illustrator Erik Werenskjold.

of the main characters represent a new approach. The children are portrayed with psychological insight and with respect for their personal feelings and integrity. The typical idealization of the time is missing, as well as the period's typical openly moralization/didacticism. Moe's book represented something new as it was told in the same direct, oral style as in the folk tales Moe collected with P. Chr. Asbjørnsen (1812–1885), which were published from 1842 onwards. All the six stories in the book have a Norwegian setting, with a Norwegian landscape and climate, and were considered Norwegian by contemporaries. Even though the book is written in Danish, which was still the written language in Norway at the time, it also has some Norwegian words relating to the Norwegian environment and nature.

As the children's literature scholar Gunvor Risa (1997) points out, words like "Tjørnerose," "Gaasunger," and "Sokkebrønden" situate the action in a Norwegian environment, and make the book Norwegian. The book shows the contemporary view upon the upbringing of children, in which the children are expected to be obedient and honest. Beate is presented as a "wise and good little girl," while her brother Viggo, who is eight years old in the first story, is presented in that story as "Viggo the Viking," a "wild, unruly boy."[17] This foreshadows the second story, in which Viggo kidnaps and beheads Beate's best friend, her doll Little Beate (Lille-Beate), so that the story ends sadly with grief and the funeral of the doll. Even though Viggo is depicted as a mean boy in the story, he is apparently not punished for his evil actions. The reader is only indirectly told that the adults also regard Viggo as a mean boy. Beate tells him: "You are a mean boy, and never cause anything but trouble, as mother said the other day."[18]

At the age of five, Beate acts autonomously and is capable of saving her own life. In the first story, she is introduced on her birthday, when she is given the doll, which she treats from the beginning as a living being and her best friend. Even though the narrator states that Beate is "a wise and good little girl," she plays near the well, ignoring her mother's warning. When she falls into the well and nearly drowns, it is her doll, Little Beate, who saves her life by stretching out her arm so that Beate can grab it and lift her head above the water. Both Beate and her doll thus act as competent children, and with the help of her doll, Beate is able to save her life. Still, Beate is not totally independent, as her parents are close enough to hear her shouting and come to her rescue.

Viggo clearly shows development throughout the book. In the third story, Beate "has grown two years older," and her brother Viggo is said to have grown "bigger and more reasonable."[19] In the third story he even helps his sister and her friends to get out to the floating island. The children live in a wealthy family that employs a nanny, which was unusual at that period, as the middle and upper classes were small. The nanny is important in the third story. One day the nanny tells Beate that if she manages to hold the egg of a white-breasted guillemot at the floating island, she can wish for whatever she wants, for example, to become a princess, and it will come true. Beate asks her father if he can help her to get out to the island without telling him the real reason. This makes her feel terrible: "She felt she had been untruthful to her father, and she had never been before." The story ends rather sadly. Beate loses the egg, which breaks, and her wish doesn't come true. Her wish had not been to become a princess, as the nanny suggested, but that her beloved doll "Little Beate" should be hale and healthy again, and still sitting where she had left her before she became the victim of Viggo the Viking in the second story. As the beheading incident took place two years earlier, her wish emphasizes how much the doll meant to Beate. Beate cries and confesses everything to her father:

> She said that she knew why her wish didn't come true, that it was because she had told lies and hadn't been honest with him, but she promised faithfully that it would be the first and last time that she was such a bad girl. And her father said it was a beautiful promise, she should always keep it, and then her wishes would come true.[20]

Beate's regret and strong feeling of guilt may reflect a religious upbringing in which the individual's determination to avoid sin plays a crucial part. She asks for forgiveness and is forgiven.

Viggo shows courage and strength in playing the role either of a Viking or a soldier, and the three last stories are about him. One important role model, and his main friend, it seems, is the old soldier, Hans Grenadier, who lives on one of the family's crofter's farms. Viggo's development is not linked to inner, spiritual promises, but to his courage and strength and the way he acts according to what the old soldier, the Grenadier has told him. His Viking role and his hunt for the doll, Little Beate, and his words "Now I will rob girls!" can be seen as an indication of this development.[21] Viggo gets a dog called Allarm from Hans Grenadier. In the fifth story the boy has to save his dog from being eaten by four wolves. He has to be brave when attacking the wolves. It is a dangerous situation, but he succeeds because he remembers the old grenadier's words: "One thing is shameful, and that is to show your back before you retreat."[22]

Ice skating on the lakes is a typical wintertime activity for Norwegian children. In the last story, the dog Allarm proves competent as he saves Viggo's life when he is ice skating and falls through the ice. The episode may imply that ice skating was an activity mainly for boys at that time, as no girls join in. It also shows that Viggo is willing to take chances and forget his promise to his father, not to go too far out on the small forest lake, as the ice is not safe further out on the mere. Challenged by a boy called Per Friskfant, Viggo wants to show all the boys how brave he is and what a good ice skater he is, and he goes exactly where he promised his father not to go. His punishment, aside from almost freezing to death in the cold water, is to be dressed up in the grenadier's old clothes, which—symbolically—are much too big for him. The Grenadier approves of him by saying: "You are still a child ... But who can know what you will become. You have a heart, and the water wouldn't take you."[23] The book ends with the narrator telling us that Viggo has become a lieutenant and, "If war would come," he could become a general.[24] The writer Jo Tenfjord argues in her epilogue to the 1973 edition that Viggo actually became a teacher for officers, a writer and a bishop, as she takes Viggo to be the author Jørgen Moe himself. The stories are based on Moe's own memories of his childhood with his sister, Beate, events that took place at their big farm at the beginning of the century. The headless doll is said to have been dug up from its grave under the rosebush, and was in the family for 150 years.

The universe where children are free to play outside in natural surroundings without adult interference is a common motif in Norwegian children's literature, and opens up for competent children who are active, free autonomous and robust.[25] An adult comes to help Viggo only after the last wolf has left. As the literary historian Åsfrid Svensen has pointed out, the moral duties are different for the girl and the boy. Svensen argues that the girl's upbringing involved strict discipline, and when Beate realizes that her hopes don't match reality, she adapts to the norms and gives up, while Viggo's dream becomes part of a great future.[26] The literary critic Birgitte Furberg Moe argues that the different reactions of the two siblings may also be

Figure 18.3 Viggo. Henrik Sørensen. Illustration from the book *I brønden og i tjærnet* by Jørgen Moe (1928, 1939, 1963, 1972, 1987).

© Henrik Sørensen / BONO 2016.

explained by the fact that Beate is five to seven years old, while Viggo is eight to ten years old.[27] I find it interesting that even though their virtues vary depending on the sibling's gender, neither of the two siblings is actually heavily disciplined throughout the book. In fact, they seem to have a rather free childhood, and they both take responsibility for their respective best friends, Little Beate and Allarm.

Both children play apparently without much adult interference in their childhood universe. Even though Beate is presented as a dutiful child, she is also competent, and when her doll and best friend Little Beate is murdered, she does not tell the adults, but buries the doll herself. Likewise, Viggo is said to work hard at school, which his parents expect, but he is also presented as a competent child with the courage to attack the four wolves that are about to kill his dog, Allarm, an unexpected act on his part.

Extracts from the book were published in Nordahl Rolfsen's much-used ABC, *Lesebok for Folkeskolen* (1892–1950), and thus the stories became canonical. Moe's book has been published in several editions under the titles *I Brønden og i Kjærnet*, *I Brønden og i Tjærnet*, and *I brønnen og i tjernet*.[28] The book was published in English in the United Kingdom as *In the Pond and on the Hill. Stories for boys and girls* (1883), in German as *Im Brunnen und im See* (1885) and in the United States as *Viggo and Beate* (1915).

Birgitte Furberg Moe shows the extent to which the story has been changed in the various translations.[29] In the English edition, published in London in 1883, the story no longer takes place on a Norwegian farm but

Figure 18.4 Jørgen Moe: *I brønden og i tjærnet* (1898). Cover by illustrator Lars Jorde.

among the British aristocracy. As Norway doesn't have an aristocracy, this change is rather striking. Beate no longer falls into the well but into the pond, and she doesn't play in the courtyard but in the "garden." In short, she is not depicted as a competent Norwegian child anymore. She has lost some of her competence and has turned into a little lady instead. Whereas in the Norwegian book, she washes, dresses, and plaits her hair herself, in the English edition "she hardly gives the servant time to wash and dress her, and to plait her hair." The translator has also put in moralizing elements, as in the inserted sentence: "and I am happy to say that by the help of God she was able to keep her promise." These moralizing elements distance the English edition from the innovative way of writing in Moe's original text, in which he leaves to the child reader to draw his or her own conclusions.

In the American edition, the story is more radically changed, as the most violent and emotionally touching scene is censored. The doll, Little Beate, is no longer beheaded by Viggo's axe; instead, she is lost, taken away by Viggo. This change leads to several other changes. In the American version, Beate's greatest dream comes true as she finds Little Beate on the floating island. Instead of the tragic ending of the narrative, there is a happy ending, and Beate is rewarded for not telling her father the truth. *Viggo and Beate* is mentioned in many American reading lists for children, and the first chapter, "The Doll under the Briar Rosebush," was a school classic in American culture. In the Norwegian edition, as I have said, the chapter ends with grief and a funeral, while in the American version it ends happily in bed, where Beate and her doll fall asleep.[30]

1890: The Golden Age and the Work of Zwilgmeyer

Toward the end of the century the book gradually became a more important medium, and Norway gained its own publishers and bookstores. Children's literature played a major part in the nation-building phase and in the creation of a national identity. The period around the turn of the century has been called a "golden age" in Norwegian children's literature.[31] In this breakthrough phase a wealth of children's literature suddenly appeared as an expression of a children's culture created by adults. At the turn of the century a new generation of authors writing for both children and adults ("cross writers") appeared in Norway. The cultural struggle in the nation-building phase opened the way for a new kind of children's literature. What was new was that the new authors wrote from a child's perspective, from the viewpoint of children.

A new kind of girl emerged in Norwegian children's literature—active, determined, and independent girls such as in the books by Dikken Zwilgmeyer (1853–1913) about the thirteen-year-old heroine, Inger Johanne (1890–1911). As pointed out by Harald Bache-Wiig, the title of the first of the twelve books, *Vi børn*, subtitled *af Inger Johanne, 13 Aar gammel* (*We Children. By 13 Year Old Inger Johanne*) (1890), already creates a shared "we" that includes and involves the reader. Inger Johanne is a first-person narrator who speaks directly to her child audience, "to you who reads this," and the narrator, Inger Johanne, became so real for her child readers that they sent her masses of fan letters. Inger Johanne writes, by her own words "for no reason," which is radical for 1890 when almost all children's books were written for a didactic purpose.[32] She introduces herself in a humorous, direct way:

> I have always heard grown people say that when you meet strangers and there is no one else to introduce you, it is highly proper and polite to introduce yourself. Uncle Karl says that polite people always get on in the world; and as I desperately want to do that, I will be polite and tell you who I am.
>
> Everybody in our town knows me; and they call me "the Judge's Inger Johanne," because my father is the town judge, you see; and I am thirteen years old. So now you know me.
>
> And just think! I am going to write a book! If you ask, "What about?" I shall have to say, "Nothing in particular," for I haven't a speck more to tell of than other girls thirteen years old have, except that queer things are always happening to me, somehow.
>
> Probably it isn't easy to write a book when you have never done it before, especially when thoughts come galloping through your head as fast as they do through mine. Why, I think of a hundred things, while Peter, the dean's son, is thinking of one and a half! But, easy or not, since I, Inger Johanne, have set my heart on writing a book, write it I will, you may be sure; and now I begin in earnest.[33]

The real author's name is not mentioned, but was later added to the book at the library, written in pencil: Hendrikke Zwilgmeyer. Zwilgmeyer's book is, like Jørgen Moe's, canonical, and was published in several editions, as *Vi Børn* and as *Vi barn*. It was published in English in the United States as *What Happened to Inger Johanne. As Told by Herself*.[34]

The cover illustration for *Vi Børn* (1890) is by Gerhard Munthe (1849–1929), and the same illustration is also on the title page. The picture gives the story the setting of the small coastal town, Risør, in the south of Norway, with typical wooden houses. It illustrates one of the episodes in the book, namely an episode from the chapter "War" in which the upper-class boys hunt down the working-class children to take over their tobogganing slope. We can see the boys depicted in the picture as active, fighting or running, all in movement, some of them stretching out their arms to hit other boys.

In contrast, the three girls in the forefront of the picture are watching the boys, but only passively, not taking part in the activities. They are dressed in upper-class clothing, and as they are all wearing dresses, coats, and hats, they are not really dressed for fighting or tobogganing, even though the story tells us the girls sledge just like the boys. Tobogganing and playing in the snow are typical winter activities for Norwegian children, due to the cold snowy climate and the hilly landscape. The verbal text stresses that all the children, boys and girls alike, are tobogganing and having fun. But the picture depicts the girls as passive spectators of the "war," and the gesture of the girl in the middle shows she is shocked by what she sees. The girls apparently do nothing to stop the fight, even though they could. We learn from the chapter, which this episode belongs to, that one of the girls is Inger Johanne, the main character and narrator of the story. The illustration contradicts the text, in which Inger Johanne proves to be the active leader of her friends, Peder, Karsten, Ezekiel, Nils, Massa, and Mina: "all of us boys and girls who play together, and whom I am going to tell about in my book."[35]

Inger Johanne not only plays the role of the leader amongst her friends, she is also smart, quick, and funny, and the boys admire her immensely. But the barrier between the children from the upper class and those from the

Figure 18.5 Inger Johanne (Dikken Zwilgmeyer). *Vi børn* (1890). Cover by illustrator Gerhard Munthe.

lower class seems impossible to surmount. The class difference is a strong theme in this book, but written from the view of the thirteen-year-old daughter of the urban district court judge. Her friends are sons and daughters of other officials in the town, and the boys and girls all play together.

Inger Johanne describes the children from the other parts of town as "poor people," as when she describes the people who live by the best tobogganing slope in the town: "There are only poor people who live on Tangen, pilots and sailors and workers. The small houses are placed spread out and erratic ..." (32). The slope is full of children, boys and girls, laughter and fun when they arrive, but when the "poor children" discover the upper-class girls in their slope, they are surprised. One of the "seaboys" says: "Come on, why do you stop, we are allowed to sledge in our own slope even if there are some fine Townflies watching" (33). After the "battle," Inger Johanne recognizes little Tollef, who is crying. He is the son of their laundry-woman, but his mother is not at home to console him. Tollef's neighbor says: "Will they now even take that small pleasure from poor people's children?" Inger Johanne sees an anger in his eyes that frightens her. "And suddenly, at that very moment, it hit me: what a shame, what a terrible grand shame we had done when hunting those poor children from their slope" (37). She destroys the last snowballs, and goes home to cry. But she doesn't tell her mother why she is crying.

Inger Johanne and her friends seem to live a very free childhood without adult supervision. The children are competent in the sense that they take active parts as citizens in society, they master their own universe, and don't need or ask for adult interference or action. They derive their competence and power from the social class Inger Johanne and her friends belong to, as part of the small upper class in the coastal town of Risør. They live close to nature, and also prove to be competent in saving two working-class children from drowning in the sea. Despite the overall impression of a light book, written in a humorous tone, read from today's perspective the children's arrogance toward the lower classes and poor people are rather shocking. The two grimmest chapters are the one about their new teacher and the one about their fight to win the tobogganing slope from the poor children of the city.[36]

Inger Johanne often ridicules and questions adult norms and adult authority, and tends to make fun of other people, both from the upper and lower levels of society. Her favorite butts for ridicule are the dean and his rather slow son. She questions everything and characterizes everyone. Her characterizations of the people around her are fun for the reader, but maybe not always fun for the characters she ridicules. The cruelest example is when the children bully their new teacher Eiebakke, who seems to be their victim because he is poor and poorly dressed, and thus placed lower than them on the social ladder. Inger Johanne is spearheading the bullying of the teacher, until she discovers—too late—what they are about to do to the poor man. When she finally feels regret it is too late to ask for forgiveness. The ambiguity of Inger Johanne's humorous storytelling and the underlying criticism of society may be one of the reasons Zwilgmeyer's books have survived.

1941: Influences from Sweden and the Work of Beskow

At the beginning of the twentieth century, in addition to popular Norwegian authors, Norwegian children also read books by a popular Swedish author, the writer and illustrator Elsa Beskow (1874–1953). Beskow's numerous picturebooks have been part of the Norwegian canon since the beginning of the century, and still are today. The combination of children, animals, and nature are typical in idealized picture books of the time, and popular among adults who buy books for children based on nostalgic memories of their own childhood. But Beskow's books are not only simple idealization, as she also introduces fantastic elements like pixies and other miniature people. Several of her child characters behave like competent children.[37]

As an important part of the Nordic canon, Beskow's books have constructed not only a Swedish childhood, but also a Nordic childhood, probably more than any other picturebooks have done. While the other books mentioned above are illustrated by popular illustrators and painters of their time, Elsa Beskow illustrated her picturebooks herself in an innovative, colorful style. The relationships between text and images are stronger, and this makes it meaningful to talk of a picturebook in the true sense of the word, with interplay between text and image. Beskow was a pioneer in creating picturebooks in which the pictures tell the story.

As in the other books of the first half of the twentieth century, the ideal child depicted in Beskow's book *Duktiga Annika* (*Talented Annika*, 1941) (see Figure 18.6) is a kind, well-behaved, clean and neat girl, who spends her day helping her mother:

> Annika was very kind and clever. She could wash herself and comb her hair, get dressed and button up all the buttons on her blouse. She could help her mum with everything, set the table, do the dishes and keep flies away from Mairos [the cow] when her mum was milking.[38]

From a gender perspective, it is interesting to note that Annika appears more competent than the older boy, Skryt-Olle, who brags about great deeds he can do, but never does them, while Annika actually does things without bragging about it. Annika is not only a dutiful, clean, and neat child, she also proves to be highly competent in more than washing herself. Like Beate a century earlier, Annika is a dutiful little girl capable of "washing herself." But as a representation of the rural child, she also acts as a competent member of her family, helping out in daily life at their small farm. She is only a small, pre-school girl, but brave enough to look after their cow, Majros, alone, and stop her from fleeing through the damaged fence. She even makes sure that the fence is fixed with the help of her friends. As in the fairy tales,

Figure 18.6 Elsa Beskow: *Duktiga Annika* (1941).
© Elsa Beskow. Heirs of Elsa and Natanael Beskow, 2016.

Annika helps others and in doing so, gets friends who will help her when she needs it.

But the most interesting thing from a gender perspective is her courage and determination. She encounters several obstacles on her way to the enclosed pasture, but none of them prevent her from following her plan. First, she meets a big dog, but she is not frightened. Then she meets Skryt-Olle who always boasts and brags.[39] He boasts about the big fish he will catch for Annika if she follows him, but she refuses. Then she meets an angry old man who turns out to be the person who can help her open the gate.

As in several of the other Beskow books, this book contains fantasy elements like small pixies, which are important in Nordic folklore. Annika helps the pixies, and they help her to fix the fence. When she meets the older boy Skryt-Olle again later, she give him her opinion of his bragging: "You said you would catch a fish that was double the size of Mairos, but I don't think that fish is that big," she says. Traditional power relations are reversed when the little girl can put the big boy in the right place and make him change his behavior. The book's happy ending is that Olle decides to stop his bragging activity: "He didn't want to brag anymore, because he thought himself it sounded stupid." The happy ending is that the two children can be on an equal level, having a "great time together feeding the rabbits," and Olle gets back his Christian name, without the disparaging "skryte" attached to it. The younger girl has been a role model for the older boy, and indirectly taught him how to behave if you want to win friends.[40]

Duktiga Annika, like the other canonical books I have discussed, has been published in several editions.[41] Even though Norway had just gained independence from Denmark (1814) and Sweden (1905), and Norwegian children's literature was important in the nation-building phase as a builder of national identity, Norway did not exist in a vacuum. Beskow's book is a fine example of how translated literature from other countries has always influenced Norwegian children, and children's literature from Sweden more than literature from any other country.

Conclusion

Even though the concept of the competent child is often linked to crossover literature of the new millennium, my material proves that we can actually find the competent child much earlier, and even in what is considered the first, original Norwegian children's book. In Nordic children's literature, children are competent and deal with nature by themselves, sometimes in a universe seemingly free of adults. In all the discussed canonical classics—*I Brønden og i Tjærnet* (1851), *Vi Børn* (1880), and *Duktiga Annika* (1941)— we find competent, autonomous, and robust children coping well with their environment. Maybe childhood is more individualized in children's books of the new millennium, but in the discussed classics the individual children have to confront their own challenges by themselves.[42] Child labor and children helping their parents were the norm in earlier children's literature (dependent on the social class of the characters), whereas children's litera- ture in the new millennium may portray a new kind of society in which parents are absent and the children therefore have to cope with challenges themselves.[43] When Beate falls in the well in the book from 1851, she can expect her parents to come running when they hear her shouting. While the child could rely on the collective for help in earlier children's literature, this is not always the case in children's books of the new millennium.

Although the concept of childhood may have appeared later in the Nordic countries than in other parts of Europe, Nordic children's literature of the new millennium often depicts a more competent and free childhood than what is commonly seen in most other parts of the world. The celebration of the concept of the competent child raises questions about the relation- ship between child and adult, and about the responsibilities of children and adults in any period, including the present: should the relationship between child and adult—at home and in school—be horizontal? Does the notion imply that adults can abdicate responsibility, and thus force children to take responsibility for their own lives and challenges, as is the situation presented in many contemporary crossover books? Alongside children's competence, several new challenges appear, such as the lack of parents willing to behave as parents.[44]

Nature plays an important role in children's literature as a builder of national identity, but what is considered nature varies in different regions and countries. A common motif in British children's literature is children playing in beautiful rose gardens behind safe fences. In Norwegian children's literature, the gardens would probably be wilder, often with direct access to the woods, as we can see in both Moe's and Zwilgmeyer's books. Playing in the snow, skiing, and sledging are common motifs in Norwegian children's literature, and depicting what could be seen as the ideal Norwegian child‍hood and Norwegian identity.[45]

Nature is a common motif in Nordic children's literature as a whole, but children's games in nature vary among the Nordic nations due to differ‍ent landscapes and climate conditions. For example, would the children's sledging in Zwilgmeyer's *Vi børn* probably be considered a rarer activity by a Danish audience, as the Danish landscape has few hills and little snow. Similarly, the temperature in Denmark is seldom low enough to allow safe ice-skating on lakes, as is the case in Moe's *I brønden og i tjærnet*. Also, the motif of children fighting wolves or bears in the woods would be unu‍sual in Danish children's literature, whereas this is a motif Norwegian chil‍dren's literature shares with Swedish and Finnish children's literature.[46] The Danish scholar, Nina Christensen, points to a more harmonious coexist‍ence between children, animals, and nature in Danish picturebooks, much like the harmonious relationships depicted in Beskow's picturebooks.[47] Still, childhood in the different Nordic countries seems to have one important concept in common: The concept of the competent child.

Nina Christensen poses the question whether it is meaningful to talk about a specifically Nordic idea of what childhood is and how it can be rep‍resented. She argues that "negotiations of the limits of childhood are more explicit in these [Nordic] countries than in other countries. Such books are indeed a sign that a number of authors, editors and other professionals think of the child as a robust, curious and perhaps even 'mature' individual."[48] The strong tendency toward publishing crossover literature in the Nordic countries also shows that the boundaries between children and adults have been partly erased in the new millennium.[49]

Childhood will always be closely linked to the idea of the nation, as sev‍eral studies on children's literature have pointed out.[50] National identity is connected to representation of the landscape, as we can see in the discussed books. Landscape representations can also be linked to a regional identity, even though landscapes in the different Nordic countries do have some strik‍ing variations. Still, it may be meaningful to talk about a Nordic childhood, as the Nordic welfare states seem to share a concept of childhood based on a competent, autonomous, free, robust, and responsible Nordic child.

Notes

1 The highly competent girl heroine Pippi has had a great impact on Nordic chil‍dren's literature as well on children's literature in general, and is one of the most translated children's books. The subversive and independent girl has influenced Norwegian children's literature as well as children's literature in other parts of the world, as is also the case with several of the subversive and anti-authoritarian children's books by Danish authors such as Ole Lund Kirkegaard (1940–1979).

2 Ommundsen 1998.
3 This was almost a century before the ratification of the United Nations Convention on the Rights of the Child (1990). By 2015, the Convention on the Rights of the Child had been ratified by all the members of the United Nations except the United States.
4 Christensen 2013; Goga 2013; Ommundsen 2012; 2013.
5 Ehn and Løfgren 1996; Eide and Winger 1996; Sommer 1998; Frykman 1998; Juul 1998; Juncker 1998; Tufte, Kampmann, and Juncker 2001; Tufte, Kampmann, and Hassel 2003; Brembeck et al. 2004; Kjørholt 2010.
6 Kjørholt 2010.
7 Brembeck et al. 2004: 7, 21–2.
8 Christensen 2013; Goga 2013; Ommundsen 2012, 2015.
9 Ommundsen 2010. International scholars have pointed to the international success of the novel *Sophie's World* (1991) by the Norwegian author Jostein Gaarder (1952–) as a "pre-Potter-crossover hit." Lacking an English term, they borrowed the Scandinavian term "allalderlitteratur"; see Beckett 1999.
10 Bly 1996.
11 Qvortrup 1994; James, Jenks, and Prout 1998. Lee 2001 argues that there are no "beings" in the sense of complete, autonomous, and independent individuals: Adults and children alike are all "becomings."
12 On the motif of competent free children, see Christensen 2013; Goga 2013; Ommundsen 2012.
13 Ommundsen 2013a.
14 Between 1875 and 1910, more than 165 different magazines for children and young adults were published in Norway; see Ommundsen 1998. See also the chapter by Roos in this volume.
15 Ommundsen 1998.
16 See also the chapter by Widhe in this volume.
17 "en klog og god liden pige," Moe 1851: 9; "en vild, uregjerlig Knægt," Moe 1851: 14.
18 The Norwegian word for "boy"–*gut*—is used instead of the Danish *dreng*; Moe 1851: 15.
19 "han var nu større og forstandige," Moe 1851: 23.
20 J. Moe 1851: 25–6.
21 "Nå vil jeg røve piker!"
22 "Én Ting er Skam, og det er at vise Ryggen, før der er slaaet Retræt," Moe 1851: 40.
23 Moe 1851: 48.
24 Ibid.
25 Ommundsen 2012.
26 Svensen 2001: 228.
27 Moe 2009: 18.
28 *I Brønden og i Kjærnet* was published in 1851 and 1877; *I Brønden og i Tjærnet* was published in 1880 and 1898; *I brønnen og i tjernet* was published in 1914, 1928, 1939, 1954, 1963, 1964, 1972, 1973, 1987, 2009, and 2013.
29 Moe 2009.
30 Moe 2009: 18.
31 Hagemann 1970.
32 Bache-Wiig 1999.
33 Translation from the 1919 edition, published as a Gutenberg's e-book at www.gutenberg.org/files/32502/32502-h/32502-h.htm.
34 The editions of *Vi Børn* were published in 1890, 1893, 1900, and 1910); under the title *Vi barn*, the book was published in 1915, 1929, 1943, 1950, 1955, 1967, 1972, and 1990. The English translation was published in 1919.

35 Zwilgmeyer 1919: 26.
36 Both chapters are left out of the American version.
37 Including Pelle in *Pelles nya kläder* (Pelle's new clothes) (1912), in which Pelle has to work in order to get new clothes as a reward.
38 Page 1–2, not paginated, my translation.
39 *Skryte* means "boast" or "brag."
40 The "ideal girl" is later questioned by other influential authors like Thorbjørn Egner (1912–1990) with his Lille Kamomilla and Astrid Lindgren's Annika from the Pippi-books.
41 Nine editions have appeared in Sweden (1941, 1951, 1955, 1960, 1965, 1970, 1983, 1994, 2006) and four editions in Norwegian translation under the title *Annika* (1974, 1985, 1994, 2000). The book has also been translated into Danish, *Dygtige Annika* (1975), Dutch, *Annika* (1994), English (*Emily and Daisy*, 2009), Spanish (*Ana en la granja*, 2007), and Japanese (*Orikō na Anika*,1986).
42 Ommundsen 2008.
43 Kåreland 2006; Ommundsen 2010, 2015.
44 Bly 1996.
45 Ommundsen 2013b.
46 As in the first Norwegian children's book from 1851, the main character in Swedish author and illustrator Pija Lindenbaum's (1955–) *Gittan och gråvargarna* (*Bridget and the Grey Wolves*, 2000) also meets real wolves alone in the woods. But as a child playing alone in the deep woods is not realistic in the new millennium, Gittan is portrayed in the setting where she gets lost when her kindergarten is out for a walk. She becomes friendly with the wolves, and they never threaten her, thus the plot resembles the classic Norwegian story "Lille Alvhilde" from 1829. Wolves and bears are a common motif in children's literature from the nineteenth century, and often represent a threat or danger the child protagonist needs to protect his or her domestic animals against. Gitte represents the new institutionalized childhood that occurred in the Nordic countries after the World War II. Daily life for Nordic children has changed dramatically since 1945, mostly due to day care. Long playful days at home have been replaced by the kindergarten project of creating good citizens.
47 Christensen 2006.
48 Christensen 2013: 193.
49 Ommundsen 2010.
50 Meek 2001; O'Sullivan 2004; Kelen and Sundmark 2013; Ommundsen 2013a.

19 The Small People in the Big Picture

Children in Swedish Working-Class Novels of the 1930s

Karin Nykvist

When the story of Scandinavian literature is being told in an international context, the Swedish proletarian novels of the 1930s are frequently held up as the more important of the regional canon.[1] In these celebrated novels, childhood and children are at the center—so much so, that I would suggest that the child is one of the more prominent motifs of Swedish literature between the two World Wars. Narratives on childhood were not new in any way in the Swedish or Nordic context during this period, but these novels told of childhood at a pivotal moment in history, when the child figure and the role played by childrearing in the forming of the nation were the subjects of animated discussion.[2] And they told of childhood in a new way, from the unprivileged point of view of the child. Many titles were published, but among the more widely read—and therefore the scope of this text—were Ivar Lo-Johansson's *Breaking Free* (1933), Eyvind Johnson's cycle of four novels named *The Novel of Olof* (1934–1937), Harry Martinson's *Flowering Nettle* (1935), and Moa Martinson's trilogy about Mia, *My Mother Gets Married* (1936), *Church Wedding* (1938) and *The King's Roses* (1939).

The authors of these novels had no formal education, and would later come to be known of as the "autodidacts" of the 1930s. They were striving to find new forms of narration while introducing new themes into the narrative of childhood, and they were quickly established among the most important in the nation. Two of them, Eyvind Johnson and Harry Martinson, were elected to the Swedish Academy and later awarded the Nobel Prize for Literature.[3] As their books were published over the course of a few years, the narrative of working-class childhood came to the foreground in Swedish public debate.[4]

In the scholarship on these novels, scholars tend to choose one of two directions. Either they adopt an individualist view, regarding the texts as narratives of the authors' childhoods, important to understanding the development of the individual author, or they adopt a political view, turning the children into vehicles, symbols of the working class.[5] I argue that both ways of reading are fruitful but reductive. As I see it, the scope is much wider. These novels are political, their children symbols of a whole category of people. They are also somewhat autobiographical, and as such testimonies of childhoods lost. But more than that, they are paradigmatically important: they took part in a Nordic reshaping of the notion of childhood at a point in history where the very concepts of "child" and "childhood" were being renegotiated. Thus, their portrayals of the child and of childhood are part of a larger discussion, crossing the boundaries of fiction, biography, and political debate. In them, the portrait of the child is thoroughly ambivalent. The children are naive as well as achingly mature, innocent as well as experienced. They are acting subjects and they are objects of action. These complex and ambivalent constructions of childhood are intrinsically bound to another ambiguous and complex construct that emerged at the same moment in history—the master narrative of the *Folkhem*, of the nation as a home for the people. It is my intention to highlight the relationship between the narratives of these novels and their ideological and political counterpart, the *Folkhem*, and their joint importance to the construction of on the one hand the Nordic child, and on the other, Nordic twentieth-century self-understanding.

Narrating the Nation

As has been pointed out by many scholars, children are often used in the telling of a nation and its history. The child figure may signify change as well as continuation, not to mention it being a powerful symbol of the future and its possibilities. As such, the figure of the child and the family can be viewed as important props to national self-understanding.[6] From this perspective, it follows that the child that can be found within representations of children and childhood in art and literature must not necessarily be taken for a historical one. Rather, it should be understood as a theoretical category, a construct formed by adult desire and ideology. This construct, however, is closely linked to the discourse of childhood within which it takes shape, a discourse that is anchored in real practices toward children. The arts both mirror and alter the notion of the real world in complex ways, thus depicting as well as changing how we deal with children and regard childhood.

In the first half of the twentieth century, the construction of children and childhood were the subjects of renegotiation in political and ideological debate.[7] When these novels were published, children, childbearing, and childhood were emerging as important political issues, with questions of education, child care, and child protection being brought to the fore in Swedish and Nordic public and political debate, most famously by the influential economist Gunnar Myrdal and by the sociologist Alva Myrdal, who were both active Social Democrats. They jointly published *Crisis in the Popular Question* in 1934, advocating social support for families with children.[8] Child education and protection had, however, been part of an ongoing discussion in the region for decades, following Ellen Key's bestselling *The Century of the Child* (published in Swedish in 1900), while more traditional values regarding child rearing and discipline were the defining features of the practice surrounding childhood at the time.[9]

But the child was also important as a *symbol*; in the emerging welfare state, it came to stand for acknowledging the value and the potential of every member of society, no matter how small and insignificant he or she may seem. This welfare state ideal would soon come to be known as *Folkhemmet*: a home for and of the people. Although this metaphor was not introduced by the Social Democrats it became intimately associated with them during the decades following World War II. The future Prime Minister Per Albin Hansson used it in a in a speech in 1928 when, in words that are often repeated in the history books, he elaborated on the *Folkhemmet* metaphor:

> The good home does not recognize anyone as privileged or misfavoured; it knows no special favourites and no stepchildren. There no one looks down upon anybody else, there no one tries to gain advantage at another's expense, and the stronger do not suppress and plunder the weaker. In the good home equality, consideration, cooperation and helpfulness prevail.[10]

The *Folkhem* metaphor's importance to Swedish national self-understanding cannot be overestimated. The ideology that it was meant to signify aimed for a society where everyone was taken care of and kept safe, while the individual was given means to develop and thrive. This was to be accomplished through a combination of a market economy and an expanding public sector with universal health care, unemployment benefits, and old age pensions.[11] It certainly played a part in turning the novels of this study into national monuments; they told the story of a state of affairs left behind that many could relate to, a story of a rural nation governed by poverty, where the weaker members of society were left to their own devices.[12]

Storytelling presents a form of narrative knowledge, and in the modern era ancient myths have given way to newer forms of stories that explain history and historical change.[13] In a Swedish and Nordic context, the story of the advent of the *Folkhem* plays that part, and the novels discussed here are included in the makeup of its powerful story. While telling stories of childhood and of children, they simultaneously and symbolically told the story of the adult citizen who was doomed by class, poverty, bigotry, and bad luck to remain outside of society, who had nothing and was treated without respect.

Adding to the force of these novels in the grand narrative of the people's home is the fact that their plots are quite similar; one could say that they share a master plot. This plot tells the story of an intelligent child of small or no means, let down in different ways by grown-up society, very often literally or symbolically orphaned, and his or her strife to break free in order to find a new life. The end of childhood is an important motif in all the novels, and the ending points toward an unknown future. There is, however, an important note to be made about gender. While the three novels depicting the lives of boys all end with the boy leaving everything behind, alone, heading for the great unknown, Moa Martinson's (1890–1964) trilogy about Mia ends with her returning from her attempt at a modern, urban life of independence, making her narrative circular instead of linear. At the end of the third novel, she is unmarried with many children, poor and used up, and lives with an alcoholic man in a small, rural cottage. The child figure that is successfully making the transition to a modern future of possibility is, for the time being, a boy.

The idea of a master plot may also be used when interpreting events in real life.[14] In the reception of these novels, the story of the autodidact's personal journey from a childhood in poverty to an elevated position in society has played an important part. The biographical legends of these authors are thus added to the national grand narrative, giving it an element of a rags-to-riches story.

This story is also the story of something seemingly insignificant growing to its full potential. Thus, the biographies of these authors mirror the idea of the Swedish nation maturing into an adult, responsible state. And in this storyline, the imagery of the child growing up is a powerful device. Childhood is, after all, commonly regarded as a period of "becoming." More often than not, childhood is regarded as the time period that passes *before* the important events of a person's life take place. To be a child is to *wait*, to stand on the threshold of something new. And this is what Swedish society as a whole did in the 1930s, at least if regarded from the point of view of Social Democrat historiography.[15] They had already been in power for a few years in the 1920s, but after winning the election in 1932, the Social Democrats did not lose again until 1976. During this time, the story of the nation's becoming a *Folkhem* became a national staple.

In Eyvind Johnson's (1900–1976) novels about Olof, the notion of symbolically waiting on the threshold is a prominent theme. His protagonist Olof—who at the end of the novel will leave the manual labor of the north for a new life in the south—forgets the present while waiting for the future to arrive, the words "one day," being a mantra in his mind: "'Sometime when I'm really grown up,' he thought, 'When I've found myself properly. Then …' But he did not really know what it was he was going to do."[16] This is life before the opportunities of the new society, one that is so new it is almost impossible to imagine. When Olof, and the children like him, pick up and leave, they will, however, carry with them the memories of the way things were, as a reminder, giving the narrative of the birth of the *Folkhem* in its opening scene.

The Child in Need of a Family

The image of the *Folkhem* provides every citizen with a family, the prime minister after all being the father of the land, and the provider of safety, care, and inclusion. In the novels studied here, however, the figure of the orphan is prominent. Olof is denied the care of his living parents, and

Martin is reluctantly cared for by the parish. Mia is an illegitimate child, and thus fatherless. The title *My Mother Gets Married* has lost the somewhat scandalous air that surrounded it when it was published—in the 1930s it was a given for every woman to be married when becoming a mother, even if the real world was full of unwed mothers. Johnson's Olof has a family but does not live with them for reasons of poverty, and he clearly feels abandoned by them. In a symbolically loaded scene, he visits his family, and notices how his hat is not put on the nail in the wall with the others, but on the windowsill—he does not belong. Later in the novel he dreams of "a mother, a father, a sister or a brother, a friendship, a love, a feeling of fellowship with someone and something."[17] Martin's experience of family is also one of want. After foolishly driving the family business to bankruptcy, the father dies, upon which the mother leaves for America and the children are scattered among foster families, or earn their keep as farmhands and maids. Martin goes through foster families who expect him to work to earn his keep, and when he proves to be difficult to like, he is let go. His mother sends him unintelligible letters, underscoring her desertion. In the novel, quotation marks are used whenever the word "home" is mentioned.

All in all, these children are deserted by the adult world, and their physical and/or existential loneliness makes for a strong theme. All the child protagonists in these novels are victims in one way or another—to social injustice, poverty, physical abuse, alcoholism, or disease. Child mortality is a real threat; Mia's mother is constantly pregnant, but none of the babies live. Neither do all the babies born in Lo-Johansson's *Breaking Free*. Older children die from malnutrition, or poor housing that leads to mortal disease, or simply from neglect or lack of supervision. When the parents are forced to work for survival, the children are left to fend for themselves. The death of Mikael's sister is mentioned in passing—they are only two brothers in the family, "after his sister had died in an accident at the river one summer morning," the narrator laconically reports.[18] All in all, it is conspicuous how the families of these novels do not live up to the traditional image of the family and how that is portrayed as lacking. These broken families and parentless children all point toward the need for a people's home, a *Folkhem*.

Paradoxical Children in the *Folkhem* Paradox

The grand narrative of the *Folkhem* is a somewhat paradoxical one. It combines the ideas of the good of the many with that of individual freedom. While the nation cares for all, social and geographical mobility of the individual is a desired given.[19] Furthermore, it clearly advocates the development of competence and agency for everyone, while its social safety nets and standards of norms can sever agency among its citizens, as has been shown at its harshest for example by the forced sterilization laws that were in effect from 1935 to 1975, practically throughout the history of the *Folkhem*.

Mobility—social as well as geographical—is encouraged while the idea of a classless society where social mobility would have no point and be impossible is the official norm.

These paradoxes are played out in the lives of the novels' protagonists in different ways. Social and geographical mobility is, for one, an important theme shared by all of them. All the protagonists dream of leaving the environment and circumstances they were born into, loathing their own poverty and lack of education. This could open a discussion on class betrayal.[20] Even though, for example, Lo-Johansson uses many different voices and point of views, his novel celebrates Mikael, the loner and artist at heart who will leave it all behind.[21] And although Eyvind Johnson tells the story of destitute laborers in the northern Sweden at the beginning of the twentieth century, his main focus is Olof, who will break free as well. In this, the political collectivism and the modernist ideal of the individual, original artist clash. When Olof regards his colleagues at the lumber mill he knows "that his life would not be like theirs."[22] Harry Martinson's Martin is also existentially alone, and even though children in his predicament were common in Sweden at this time, and the novel can be read as bearing witness to their plights as a collective, its main concern is the telling of individual experience, and of an individual dreaming of his way out.[23] Viewed from the point of view of the welfare state, this is, however, part of the paradoxical mythology of the *Folkhem*, where the collective was to benefit from individual strife and fulfilment.

It is, however, worth noting that Moa Martinson's trilogy does not fit into this pattern of individualism. *My Mother Gets Married* opens with a poem called "Our Mothers," told by a collective "we,"—"for we were illegitimate children / our mothers were unwed women."[24] Mia is a mere representative of this collective. As mentioned earlier, Mia is the only protagonist who does not succeed to break free: true to the collective stance of the novel, her story is not of the celebrated artist's but of every woman's.

Another paradox is that of innocence and competence. This mirrors the discussion on childhood at the time—were they innocent, natural victims of a brutal "civilization," or were they competent and able to make good choices that would turn them into mature citizens of a modern state? Put in another way: are children agents—subjects who take action—in the grand narrative of the welfare state or are they the objects of action, acted upon by family and society? Thematically, the children of these texts are trapped in the confinements of poverty and the power structures of class, age, and gender. They are acted upon by adult society: parents, schools, employers, parishes. Adult neglect, however, makes wiggle room possible, when left to their own devices these children become quite resourceful. The master plot of the stories also shows that the struggle for agency is achieved in the end, at least for the male protagonists.

This thematic ambivalence concerning the status of the child as object or subject is mirrored and underlined in the very form and narration of the texts.

Even when the child is conveyed as powerless, it is given the perspective; the power of what is usually called the "focalizer." Instead of a traditional, omniscient narrator that sees and knows everything, these novels follow the perception of their children protagonists, often reporting solely what they see and feel. When the point of view is granted to a child, that child is given the power to define its story. The romantic notion of children as "truthsayers" lingers in this way of presenting the story to its reader, giving the texts an air of authenticity and testimonial. The child becomes a witness to an individual story as well as to a defining moment in Swedish history. Through foregrounding the child's point of view in this way, the very form of the text turns political, making the child the subject, not the object, of these stories, thus testifying to a new way of regarding children and childhood.

Focalization can be cognitive, emotive, ideological, or optic, conveying the understanding, feelings, ideological convictions, and sensory impressions of the person given the perspective in the text.[25] In these novels, the emotive and optic focalization of the small child is in the foreground, thus constructing these children as having fresh eyes and strong feelings. "Why were grown-ups like this?" Mia wonders. "Why did they torture themselves and others? Why did they say they loved each other, gave each other gifts, hugged each other after they'd hit each other and quarreled and fought? They were just like us children."[26] The child sees and reports, although she might not always understand.

This supposed lack of cognitive and ideological maturity is turned into an efficient literary device, where the implicit author is able to make points of ideological or political value to the implicit reader by letting the child's perception and lack of understanding highlight the absurdity of their predicament. The cognitive interpretation and evaluation of the injustices reported by the child is left to the adult reader to work out—or to the adult voice of a visible narrator.

Playing with Innocence and Experience

An effective example of where this discrepancy between focalizer and narrator is used, is in the depiction of class. To the child protagonists of these novels, poverty is shameful. It is dirty, cold and full of lice, bedbugs, cockroaches, and vermin, and the children turn their ugly feelings concerning their situation inwards and toward their families, and loathe themselves for being dirty, sick, and infested. Mikael, Mia, and Martin all despise their own class and admire the rich, because of their finery. Thus, the righteousness of class inequality is internalized within them.[27] There is a clear distinction between the implicit and sometimes explicit political stance of the adult narrator and the non-political gaze of the child who is the victim of the many economic, social, and ideological injustices of these narratives. The child Mia is told by the narrator to be an impossible proletarian, as she is too taken with the nice things of the upper class. In this, the children mirror the apolitical stance of the still unenlightened laboring class: they are still in the dark.

This ambivalence in the narration of the books between focalization and narration, give them an elusive, eerie quality. The apparent childishness and naivety of the child is made part of the narrative—the child does not understand what she sees, but reports on it, and suffers the consequences. A bond between the adult narrator and the adult reader is forged, an understanding where the child clearly turns into an object that illustrates an ideological point in an exchange to which the child protagonist is not always invited. This ambivalence mirrors the debate regarding children at the time, but it also problematizes the very act of historical writing and the question of whose story it tells—in these narratives, the point of view is granted these small members of society while the power of narration still is given to someone else.

Also in the presentation of religion, the clearly anti-religious stance of the writer is contrasted by the naive perspective of the child protagonists. The social democratic project of the welfare state was a secular one, and the books mirror that ideology. In this respect, these children are a far cry from the romantic child construct, where the child is closely connected to deity. In the Mia-trilogy, Mia's step-grandmother goes through a period of great piety, which is treated with an offhand irony by both the narrator and Mia's mother. *Flowering Nettle* is filled with Biblical intertexts, but this intertextuality is clearly invoked by the child focalizer, and is part of characterizing Martin as naive. Martin views himself as the lost son, and in one of the more famous passages of the novel he accidentally kills a calf with an axe, inverting the biblical scene of triumphant homecoming and belonging. The gap between the implicitly adult narrating voice and the child focalizer makes it quite evident that the implicit author is to be regarded as secular. In a passage depicting Christmas Mass, the archaic language used by the narrator underlines that Christian beliefs are remnants of times passed: "As in the olden days, the congregation passed into the ante-room of the church, the weapon-house; but they had no longer any swords to hang there. Olden days had been over for too long."[28]

In Johnson's novel, Olof reads about how man is descended from monkeys, and makes a note to remember that for his confirmation in church, turning his childish musings into a joke between the implicit author and reader, who both know that the local priest will not appreciate Olof's autodidactic learnings. Thus, religion is conveyed as belonging to a naive sphere, underlining the child status of the protagonists, but not in a metaphysical, Romantic way.

The depictions of the child at play in nature are Romantic, however, and put to good use in many of these texts, and the experience often borders on the metaphysical. The child's experience of small insects, flowers, pieces of moss, of mud, sunrays, and puddles of water keep returning, especially in the novels by Harry Martinson (1904–1978), and Ivar Lo-Johansson (1901–1990), a take that makes the child *natural* and authentic, placing it in a discourse of civilization discontent. In Lo-Johansson, the child's experience of life and its body is immediate:

> Nothing gave as much pleasure as peeing or doing your business. Nothing was as nice as eating your fill. Getting dirty in the mud puddles near the barracks turned into a major event. First the children stuck in a foot, a hand, or a finger. Then they were seized by dizziness, a kind of intoxication. They rolled around in the filth, smearing it on their pale, questioning faces. ... Their mothers were in despair.[29]

In this passage, children are getting dirty while their incorruptibility and purity are underlined—they behave as if they were still in Eden. "Sun, mud, water and animals filled his childhood," writes Lo-Johansson about his protagonist.[30]

Childhood as a period of innocence is invoked in other ways as well. In the Mia trilogy, the illegitimate girl Hanna—the name, by the way, means *grace* in Hebrew—is described as an apparition of light, marked by starvation. Mia's first meeting with her is described almost as an epiphany:

> Her hair was nearly white and so tightly braided that it struck straight out from her neck. Her face gleamed white as a flower the sun shines on, a flower that soon will be cut. Her face shone with light, a thin little face. ... Her bare feet stuck out, small and white. ... I remember that her hands were folded so tightly that her knuckles were white. She was maybe three feet tall.[31]

As such, she is more than a child, she is the idea of the small and weak human being who cannot fend for herself and is forced to rely on the whims and good will of others for her survival. She is stigmatized for the sins of the adult world—irresponsible adultery and abuse, and the contrast invokes the imagery of the child as victim. The metaphor of the flower forebodes a short life.

But the idea of the innocent child can also be mocked. Harry Martinson's Martin is not innocent—the romantic idea of the pure-hearted child is thoroughly rejected in Martinson's novel. The difference between children and adults is that children are more vulnerable, and sometimes that vulnerability can be mistaken for purity. This is what happens when Martin is forced to leave one of his foster families, and at the awkward moment of goodbyes, blurts out a tearful "God bless you" that is anything but sincere—and almost makes them cry.[32]

Old School and Modern Education

In the Social Democratic-value system, school and education played an important part in that it offered social advancement to the individual, but also because education was highly valued as a means to acquire true democracy and societal progress.[33] In the 1930s, however, less than 4 percent of the country's youth completed their A-levels, a fact that in the 1940s would lay way for the coinage of the expression *the gifted reserve*—the idea that the country was full of citizens who would benefit from a higher education they were not offered or did not have the economic means to acquire.[34]

The children of these books belong to this category of students—they are gifted learners, often described as too intelligent for their station in life. In her influential work, *The Century of the Child*, Key presented ideas for a school system where the individual talents of the child and the child's desire to learn were to be preserved and cultivated. Key's interest in the child rested upon the conviction that childhood determines adulthood. That makes childhood important to the individual, but also to society as a whole, since the responsible citizen is shaped while growing up. The way to bring about a new nation of inclusion was to bring up the children of the country as independent free thinkers, able to take on the full responsibility of citizenship. These ideals, seem, however, to be far off in the schools depicted here—except for in the ideology of the novels' undertexts, where, as Mischliwietz has shown, they can be unveiled.[35]

To Harry Martinson's Martin, early school is a refuge where he enjoys being a part of the child collective, but as he grows older, he is mocked by fellow students as well by the narrator of the novel for doing so well. Moa Martinson's Mia experiences many different schools and teachers. Some schools are places of learning, others are places where the class, status, and income of the children's parents are mirrored inside and outside the classroom, and the hierarchy of the adult world is reproduced. In that setting, an intelligent child-like Mia does not fare well—in one instance, her teacher "hates" her, in another, she is shamed for using language considered above her station. In Lo-Johansson's *Breaking Free*, the children are taught the family pedigree of the local baron, and learn to admire the blue-blooded family that own their land and despise their own situation in life. School becomes an institution of control where social power structures are reproduced, rather than a place of learning.

All in all, the children do not recognize their own world in the imagery and stories presented to them. Mia does not feel any proximity to the history of the royals, and the Norrköping that they learn about in school is not the Norrköping that she lives in and knows. The images of Sweden presented to young Martin in school and in popular culture are images he cannot recognize—they are the picturesque images of the folklore of Dalarna and the national romantic imagery of Jenny Nyström. There is another Sweden, the novel implicitly says, and the text that we are reading is finally telling it.

School and education are not necessarily linked, however. Education can be found elsewhere. The poor child's hunger for learning and search for reading material is a topos within these texts, showing Maxim Gorky's autobiographical novels as an important precursor and intertext; in Gorky's novels, the yearning for education and the quest to find reading materials are important themes.[36] Eyvind Johnson's Olof does not go to school, but the novels are filled with accounts of his working on a literary education for himself. He reads everything he can get his hands on—odd pages of papers on the wall of the outhouse, and later, books he lends from a local library, for example, Homer's *Odyssey* is mentioned. Mia also reads whatever books she can find. Bunyan's *The Pilgrim's Progress* makes an impression, as well as cheap stories about lords and fantastic travels.

The scarcity of literature, art, and music that these children experience only seems to heighten their sensitivity to it. Their fantasy is triggered by brief and strong experiences of art, more often than not being of the poor man's variety—organ grinding, oleographs, cheap novels and chapbooks—art that stands in stark contrast to the high-brow novels themselves.

Art is, however, not automatically a good thing. To Martin, the world is a place where fairy tale and reality mingles in an unsound way. He escapes his dire life situation and makes sense of the world around him with the help of Icelandic sagas, poetry, and Biblical myths. To the narrator, this is questionable, there is strife for the real in these narratives, and the experience of the real is missed through the immersion into dream and fiction.

Literature is not necessarily printed matter. The books are filled with oral literature such as songs and rhymes and storytelling, in scenes that foreshadow the protagonists as future writers. In a joyous passage, Mia meets a man who "wrote poems, too, just like me," and revels in the experience.[37] On this note, a recurrent motif in Johnson's novel about Olof is searching for the words and not finding them. The boy dreams about saying the right thing, but knows that he has to wait—he still does not have the words. Passages such as "Perhaps there were no words yet for what he was feeling" are repeated throughout the novel.[38] While waiting for the right words to appear, Olof chooses silence.

In the fourth part of the novel, there are sections where different literary styles are used—such as Homer's, reminiscent in many ways of James Joyce's *Ulysses*—and it is obvious that they all come up short. One cannot write about the life of Olof in the style of others, seems to be the implicit conclusion—a new form is needed in order to tell this new story. But in using the form this way, the novel tells the story of an author trying to find his own voice, and on the way to finding it, using the voices of others who came before him. It is very much a portrait of the artist as he is born. Lo-Johansson's Mikael is also a writer waiting to be born. He ponders over the sound and connotations of words, and plays with language. Meanwhile, he dreams of being able to tell the story of the rural laborers, but he is unable to write—up until the very end of the book where it all comes to him, and he receives the outline of the poem that is cited in the beginning of the novel as if in a vision.

The acts of reading and telling stories are highly symbolic acts, as they point forward to the future artist who, as the reader can easily think, wrote these novels. Thus, the literary education of these children is a theme that foreshadows the fact that soon their story will be told and fill a gap within national self-understanding.

Waiting for the New

In its wake, the twentieth century saw many technical and ideological innovations. The children of these novels, are, however, still left on the margin, in the backwater, experiencing modernity in spurts and from a distance; the *Folkhem* has yet to arrive. Mikael's parents win a lamp in a lottery, but when they go to town to buy a light bulb for it they are told that they need electricity for it to work. Johnson's Olof experiences electricity at the lumber mill where he works, and reflects on the fact that the outbuildings—such as the pigsty—have electricity, but the barracks where the laborers stay do not. While Mia hears the word "strike" and later gets to experience what it means, the grown narrator adds that telephones and trams are in Stockholm but nowhere near the young protagonist. The strike in Lo-Johansson's *Breaking Free* happens at a neighboring estate, only heard of by the novel's characters, who in turn are weary of the ideology of the political agitators. Change is both wanted and not wanted, in an ambivalence that can be interpreted as a way of illustrating the novels roles as stepping stones, marking the threshold between the old and the new.[39] Progress is still not for everyone. It is obvious that these children will become more radical and political than their parents, the novels mirroring on a microlevel what was happening at the time on the macrolevel in Swedish society.

Also on the theme of modernity, however, there is ambiguity. The bleak outlook of Harry Martinson's novel, for example, is rather that modern times are as bad as the old. "Yes, those were the olden days. The good old days, when only the *First* World War raged," his narrator muses ironically.[40] An agricultural student in *Flowering Nettle* who practices modern farming is cold hearted bordering on sadistic, and clearly echoes the agricultural student of Nexø's *Pelle the Conqueror*.[41] Modernity does not necessarily equal progress.[42]

Conclusion

The childhood narratives discussed here were all written just a few years after the metaphor of the *Folkhem* gained footing in the 1930s, and as they all are set in the years shortly after 1900, they depict the world of the child—the weakest and most dependent member of a home as well as of a nation—before the advent of the *Folkhem*. As such, they tell the before story in the greater national narrative of Swedish twentieth-century history.[43]

In these novels, the child figure is used to represent change, alienation, nature, futurity, innocence, and vulnerability. It is given and declined agency. It is my conviction that these novels have been important to the telling of the advent of the *Folkhem* in a national setting. Conversely, the metaphor of the *Folkhem* has made these stories on working class childhood central in the Swedish canon, as it has given them symbolical importance as well as the status of testimonials.

The novels discussed in this chapter all tell stories about past society's failure to care for their own and the failure of adults overall to be just that, while they also tell stories of individuals fending for themselves, about small people making do. Their children have become symbols and signs, actors in a strong-lived national narrative of change and futurity, but they also tell individual stories of childhood, of innocence and vulnerability, of experience and determination, and as such they are keys to understanding how children and childhood were constructed at the beginning of the twentieth century in Sweden, and the imagery that surrounded the idea of the working-class child. As I have shown, this construction is paradoxical in a number of ways. They depict children as innocent victims as well as mature and resourceful agents. Even the novels themselves are paradoxes, simultaneously praising collectivism and individual strength. Their children are representatives of an experience shared by many while they are utterly alone, figuratively and often literally. What has granted them their place in the making of the grand national *Folkhem* narrative of progress, is, however, what they signify. These children are signs of futurity, arrows, pointing toward a future that promised to be different, for everyone.

Notes

1 Among the most recent examples is Mischliwietz 2014, where she discusses the importance of the novels at 29. See also Furuland and Svedjedal 2006: 15.
2 In the decades prior to this, prominent authors such as Martin Andersen Nexø, August Strindberg, Selma Lagerlöf, and Bertil Malmberg had published acclaimed novels where children were the main protagonists.
3 The research on these novels is vast and cannot be presented in full here. The work that has been most important to this chapter is, however, the recent work by the German scholar, Sandra Mischliwietz, who studies the novels from a Marxist point of view, arguing that the children of these titles represent and negotiate the concept of the working class and are to be read as stories of the collective rather than as Bildungsromane. In choosing her argument, her thesis gives further weight to mine—it becomes part of the reception that reads these novels as part of a larger, national political narrative. Mischliwietz reads the novels as being written as part of a political strategy on the authors' part where the children protagonists are used as political devices, whereas I suggest that this point of view rather belongs to their reception history.
4 In a presentation of the publications of 1933, literature professor, Ivar Harrie, wrote that the discovery of the class of the farm tenants was the biggest and most surprising literary event of the year. In addition to Ivar Lo-Johansson, Jan Fridegård and Moa Martinson had published on the subject. Furuland 2002: 65.
5 Examples of the former are Lindberger 1986, Espmark 2005, and Söderblom 1994, while Mischliwietz stands for the latter ideal.

6 Cf. Edelman 2004; Nykvist 2013; Kelen and Sundmark 2013.
7 Cf. Sandin 1995.
8 Myrdal and Myrdal 1934.
9 Cf. Brembeck et al. 2004.
10 Quoted in Tilton 1988: 411–12.
11 Cf. Tsarouhas 2008: 38ff.
12 A well-known photograph of Ivar Lo-Johansson shows him standing in front of what is called the last tenant farmer's move in 1945, promoting the political role played by his authorship in modern Swedish history.
13 Lyotard 1979, *passim.*
14 Abbott 2002: 43.
15 Anker Gemzøe makes a similar point, suggesting that in the working-class childhood narratives, personal and historical change is mirrored, thus making for powerful stories. Gemzøe 2011: 163.
16 Johnson 1970: 109.
17 Johnson 1970: 109.
18 Lo-Johansson 1990: 24.
19 Cf. Berggren and Trägårdh 2009, *passim*; Trägårdh 1997: 253ff; Ohlander 1988: 226ff; Tsarouhas: 37.
20 Cf. Mischliwietz 2014: 488ff.
21 Cf. Holmgren 1988: 11. On Lo-Johansson as a writer of the collective, cf. Nilsson 2003: 260–7.
22 Johnson 1970: 39.
23 Mischliwietz regards the figure of the child in these novels as a product of a textual strategy on the authors' part, and reads them more or less allegorically, as signs representing the working class and its situation, a reading that I find somewhat reductive.
24 M. Martinson 1988: ix.
25 Genette: 189ff; Rimmon-Kenan 1983: 72ff.
26 M. Martinson 1988: 270.
27 Mischliwietz 2014: 530 discusses this from a Foucauldian perspective; *passim.*
28 H. Martinson 1936: 76.
29 Lo-Johansson1990: 35.
30 Lo-Johansson 1990: 5.
31 M. Martinson 1988: 30–1.
32 H. Martinson 1936: 144–5.
33 Cf. Lindensjö 1988: 307ff; Key 1900/1909.
34 Husén 2002.
35 Cf. Mischliwietz 2014: 288.
36 The intertextual importance of Gorky in relation to these novels has been pointed out by many scholars, for example Witt-Brattström 1988: 93, 133; Espmark 2005: 76.
37 M. Martinson 1988: 179.
38 Johnson 1970: 18. Translation modified.
39 Mischliwietz's use of Foucault's idea of the Panopticon and the internalized power structures that hinder the proletariat from taking action and even realizing their level of suppression is also a valid way of understanding these texts. See Mischliwietz 2014: 248–51.
40 H. Martinson 1935: 169. My translation.
41 Andersen Nexø 2012.
42 The young man in question clearly echoes the agricultural student of Martin Andersen Nexø's *Pelle the Conqueror*. Nexø has, as Per Olof Mattsson and others have shown, been a great influence on the novels studies in this article. Cf. Mattson 2011; 2014.

43 Interestingly enough, in the era following what is widely considered the breakdown of the people's home—the Social Democratic lease on power gone (between 1932 and 2006 they were in power for all but nine years), the income gaps of society widening, make for the common opinion that the people's home is a thing of the past—saw a surge in childhood narratives with remarkably strong intertextual ties to these early novels, furthering the bond between literary depictions of childhood and the grand narrative of the welfare state. Cf. Andersson 1999; Flygt 2001; Alakoski 2006; Linderborg 2007; Hetekivi Olsson 2012.

Select Bibliography

A number of important works in English about childhood in the Nordic countries, childhood studies, and the Nordic "welfare" model are listed below:

Appel, Charlotte. "Literacy in Seventeenth Century Denmark." In *Literacy in Medieval and Early Modern Scandinavian Culture*, edited by Pernille Hermann, 323–45. Odense: University Press of Southern Denmark, 2005.

Baldwin, Peter. "The Scandinavian Origins of the Social Interpretation of the Welfare State." *Comparative Studies in Society and History* 31, no. 1 (1989): 3–24.

Beyme, Klaus von. "The Significance of the Nordic Model." In *The Source of Liberty. The Nordic Contribution to Europe*, edited by Svenolof Karlsson, 188–210. Stockholm: The Nordic Council, 1992.

Booth, Michael. *The Almost Nearly Perfect People: The Truth About the Nordic Miracle*. London: Jonathan Cape, 2014.

Brembeck, Helene, Barbro Johansson, and Jan Kampmann, eds. *Beyond the Competent Child: Exploring Contemporary Childhoods in the Nordic Welfare Societies*. Fredriksberg: Roskilde University Press, 2004.

Brandal, Nik, Øivind Bratberg, and Dag Einar Thorsen. *The Nordic Model of Social Democracy*. Basingstoke: Palgrave Macmillan, 2013.

Christiansen, Niels Finn, Klaus Petersen, Nils Edling, and Per Haave, eds. *The Nordic Model of Welfare: A Historical Reappraisal*. Copenhagen: Museum Tuscalanum Press, University of Copenhagen, 2006.

Christensen, Nina. "Contemporary Picturebooks in the Nordic Countries. Concepts of Literature and Childhood." In *Looking out and Looking in: National Identity in Picturebooks of the New Millennium*, edited by Åse Marie Ommundsen, 182–94. Oslo: Novus, 2013.

Christensen, Nina. "Lust for Reading and Thirst for Knowledge. Fictive Letters in a Danish Children's Magazine of 1770." *The Lion and the Unicorn* 33, no. 2 (2009): 289–301.

de Coninck-Smith, Ning, Ellen Schrumpf, and Bengt Sandin, eds. *Industrious Children. Work and Childhood in the Nordic Countries 1850–1990*. Odense: Odense University Press, 1997.

Einarsdottir, Johanna and Judtih Wagner. *Nordic Childhoods and Early Education. Philosophy, Research, Policy and Practice in Denmark, Finland, Iceland, Norway and Sweden*. Greenwich, Connecticut: Information Age Publishing, 2006.

Esping-Andersen, Gösta. *Politics against Markets: The Social Democratic Road to Power*. Princeton, CT: Princeton University Press, 1985.

Esping-Andersen, Gösta. *The Three Worlds of Welfare Capitalism*. Cambridge: Polity Press, 1990.

Goga, Nina. "Children and Childhood in Scandinavian Children's Literature over the Last Fifty Years." In *Bologna: Fifty Years of Children's Books from around the World*, edited by Giorgia Grilli, 235–52. Bologna: Bologna University Press, 2013.

Greve, Bent, "What Characterize the Nordic Welfare State Model." *Journal of Social Sciences* 3, no 2 (2007), 43–51.

Hagtvet, Bernt and Erik Rudeng. "Scandinavia: Achievements, Dilemmas, Challenges." In *Norden – the Passion for Equality*, edited by Stephen R. Graubard, 227–56. Oslo: Norwegian University Press, 1986.

Hilson, Mary. *The Nordic Model. Scandinavia Since 1945*. London: Reaktion Books, 2008.

Ihalainen, Pasi, Michael Bregnsbo, Karin Sennenfelt, and Patrik Winton, eds. *Scandinavia in the Age of Revolution: Nordic Political Cultures, 1740–1820*. Farnham/Burlington: Ashgate, 2011.

Kvist, Jon, Johan Fritzell, Bjørn Hvinden, and Olli Kangas, eds. *Changing Social Equality. The Nordic Welfare Model in the 21st Century*. Bristol: Policy Press, 2013.

Lauwerys, Joseph Albert. *Scandinavian Democracy: Development of democratic thought and institutions in Denmark, Norway and Sweden*. Copenhagen: The Danish Institute and others,1958.

Meek, Margaret. *Children's Literature and National Identity*. Stoke on Trent: Trentham Books, 2001.

Misgeld, Klaus, ed. *Creating Social Democracy: A Century of the Social Democratic Labor Party in Sweden*. University Park, PA: Pennsylvania State University Press, 1988.

Mjøset, Lars. "The Nordic Model Never Existed, But Does It Have a Future." *Scandinavian Studies* 64, no. 4 (1992): 652–71.

O'Malley, Andrew. *The Making of the Modern Child: Children's Literature and Childhood in the Late Eighteenth Century*. New York: Routledge, 2003.

Ozment, Steven. *When Fathers Ruled. Family Life in Reformation Europe*. Cambridge, MA: Harvard University Press, 1983.

Qvortrup, Jens. *Childhood Matters: Social Theory, Practice and Policies*. Aldershot: Avebury, 1994.

Sandin, Bengt. "Children and the Swedish Welfare State: From Different to Similar." In *Reinventing Childhood after World War II*, edited by Paula Fass, and Michael Grossberg, 110–38. Grossberg, PA: University of Pennsylvania, 2012.

Sandin, Bengt. "Split Visions, Changing Childhoods and the Welfare State in Sweden. Reflections on the Century of the Child." *Working Papers on Childhood and the Study of Children* 4 (1995): 1–17.

Sommer Dion, Ingrid Pramling Samuelsson, and Karsten Hundeide. *Child Perspectives and Children's Perspectives in Theory and Practice*. Dordrecht: Springer, 2009.

Sørensen, Øystein and Bo Stråth. *The Cultural Construction of Norden*. Oslo: Scandinavian University Press, 1997.

References

År 1724 och 1807 skolordningar. In Sveriges allmänna läroverksstadgar 1561–1905. 7, 1820 års skolordning, edited by B. Rudolf Hall. Lund: Fören. för svensk undervisningshistoria, 1923.

Åsa, Linderborg. Mig äger ingen. Stockholm: Atlas, 2007.

Aavitsland, Kristin. "Remembering Death in Denmark–Norway During the Period of Lutheran Orthodoxy." In Preparing for Death, Remembering the Dead, edited by Tarald Rasmussen and Jon Ø. Flæten, 241–64. Göttingen: Vandenhoeck und Ruprecht, 2015.

Abbott, H. Porter. The Cambridge Introduction to Narrative. Cambridge: Cambridge University Press, 2002.

Ärkebiskopens skrivelse med anledning av konsistoriets inlaga till Kongl. Majt (Lindblom, 16 October 1817). In Acta till Stockholms större latinläroverks historia 1419–1840, edited by Rudolf B. Hall. Stockholm: Fören. för svensk undervisningshistoria, 1939.

Agrell, Jan. "Den pedagogiska debatten i Sverige 1807–1820." Pedagogisk Tidskrift 96 (1960): 11–24.

Ahnlund, Nils and Simon Skoglund. Ladugårdslandet: Till Hedvig Eleonora kyrkas 200-årsminne 1737–1937. Stockholm: Svenska Kyrkans Diakonistyrelses Bokförlag, 1937.

Ahonen, Sirkka. "Millä opeilla opettajia koulutettiin?" In Valistus ja koulunpenkki: Kasvatus ja koulutus Suomessa 1860-luvulta 1960-luvulle, edited by Anja Heikkinen and Pirkko Leino-Kaukiainen, 239–52. Helsinki: Finnish Literature Society, 2011.

Alakoski, Susanna. Svinalängorna. Stockholm: Bonnier, 2006.

Allchin, M. N. F. S. Grundtvig: An Introduction to His Life and Work. Aarhus: Aarhus University Press, 1997/2016.

Alnæs, Karsten. 1814. Miraklenes år. Oslo: Schibsted Forlag, 2013.

Alston, Philippe. "Does the Past Matter. On the Origin of Human Rights. Book Review." Harvard Law Journal 126 (2013): 2043–81.

Alþingistíðindi 1962–1966. Reykjavík, 1963–1967.

Amundsen, Arne Bugge. Dåp og tradisjon. Dåpstro og dåpspraksis i noen Østfolddistrikter på 1700- og 1800-tallet. Oslo, Bergen, and Tromsø: Universitetsforlaget, 1983.

Amundsen, Arne Bugge. "Peder Hansen (1746–1810)." In Folkloristiske klassikere 1800–1930, edited by Anne Eriksen and Arne Bugge Amundsen, 9–10. Norsk Folkeminnelags Skrifter. Vol. 147. Oslo: Norsk Folkeminnelag/Aschehoug, 1999.

Andersen, Hans Christian. *Tales of Hans Christian Andersen*. Translated by Naomi Lewis. London: Walker Books, 2004.

Andersen, Hans Christian. "The Ugly Duckling." In *The Annotated Hans Christian Andersen*, edited by Maria Tatar, 98–118. New York: W. W. Norton, 2008.

Andersen, Hans Christian. "The Little Mermaid." In *The Annotated Hans Christian Andersen*, edited by Maria Tatar, 119–55. New York: W. W. Norton, 2008.

Andersen, Hans Christian. "The Little Match Girl." In *The Annotated Hans Christian Andersen*, edited by Maria Tatar, 214–22. New York: W. W. Norton, 2008.

Andersen Nexø, Martin. *Pelle Erobreren*. Copenhagen: Gyldendal, 2012.

Anderson, Christiane D. "Religiöse Bilder Cranachs Im Dienst Der Reformation." In *Humanismus Und Reformation Als Kulturelle Kräfte in Der Deutschen Geschichte*, edited by Lewis W. Spitz, 43–79. Berlin and New York: Walter de Gruyter, 1981.

Andersson, Lena. *Var det bra så?* Stockholm: Natur & Kultur, 1999.

Andresen, Astri. Ólöf Garðarsdóttir, Monika Janfelt, Cecilia Lindgren, Pirjo Markkola, and Ingrid Söderlind. *Barnen och välfärdspolitiken. Nordiska barndomar 1900–2000*. Stockholm: Dialogos Forlag, 2011.

"Anordning for Almueskolevæsenet paa Landet i Danmark af 29. Juli 1814." In *Skolelovene af 1814 og deres Tilblivelse, aktmæssigt fremstillet*, edited by Joakim Larsen. Copenhagen: Schultz Forlag, 1914.

Appel, Charlotte. *Læsning og bogmarked i 1600-tallets Danmark*. 2 vols. Odense: University Press of Southern Denmark, 2001.

Appel, Charlotte. "Literacy in Seventeenth Century Denmark." In *Literacy in Medieval and Early Modern Scandinavian Culture*, edited by Pernille Hermann, 323–45. Odense: University Press of Southern Denmark, 2005.

Appel, Charlotte, and Morten Fink-Jensen. *Da læreren holdt skole. Tiden før 1780*. Dansk Skolehistorie. Vol. 1. Aarhus: Aarhus University Press, 2013.

Appel, Hans-Henrik. *Tinget, magten og æren. Studier i sociale processer og magtrelationer i et jysk bondesamfund i 1600-tallet*. Odense: Odense Universitetsforlag, 1999.

Arden, Everett G. *Four Northern Lights: Men Who Shaped Scandinavian Churches*. Minneapolis: Augsburg, 1964.

Ariès, Philippe. *Centuries of Childhood. A Social History of Family Life*. New York: Alfred A. Knopf, 1962. French original: *L'Enfant et la vie familiale sous l'Ancien Régime* (Plon, 1960).

Ariès, Philippe. *Centuries of Childhood*. Harmondsworth: Penguin Books, 1973.

Ariès, Philippe. *Barndommens historie*. Oslo: Gyldendal, 1980.

Ariès, Philippe. *The Hour of Our Death*. Oxford: Oxford University Press, 1991.

Aronsson, Peter. "Mentalitet, norm, verklighet – Hustavlan i lokalsamhället." In *Hilding Pleijel Symposium. 19 oktober 1893 – 19 oktober 1993. Ett hundraårsjubileum*, edited by Ingemar Brohed, 51–71. Bibliotheca Historico-Ecclesiastica Lundensis 34. Lund: Lund University Press, 1993.

Asplund-Carlsson, Maj. "Om barnperspektivet i barndomslitteraturen." *Pedagogisk forskning i Sverige* 1–2 (2003): 6–11.

Aune, Hermann. *Skikk og tru. Folkeminne frå Gauldal*. Norsk Folkeminnelags Skrifter. Vol. 42. Oslo: Norsk Folkeminnelag, 1939.

Aurom, Magne. *Liv og lagnad. Folkeminne frå Sør-Odal*. Norsk Folkeminnelags Skrifter. Vol. 48. Oslo: Norsk Folkeminnelag, 1942.

Avis for Børn. Copenhagen: Avise-Contoiret, 1779–1782.

Bachelard, Gaston. *The Right to Dream*. Dallas, TX: Dallas Institute of Humanities and Culture, 1989.

Bache-Wiig, Harald. *Norsk barnelitteratur – Lek på alvor: Glimt gjennom hundre år*. Oslo: Cappelen Akademisk Forlag, 1996.

Bache-Wiig, Harald. *Norsk barndom i to etapper*. Bergen-Sandviken: Fagbokforlaget, 1999.

Bache-Wiig, Harald. "Avis for Børn (1779–1782): Lesestykker om 'Ungdommens Tilbøielighed til Dyden eller Lasten' – et monotont repertoar." In *Kritikk før 1814. 1700-tallets politiske og litterære offentlighet*, edited by Eivind Tjønneland, 451–64. Oslo: Dreyers Forlag, 2014.

Bak, Krzysztof. "Genreekvilibristen Astrid Lindgren." *Studia Litteraria Universitatis Iagellonicae Cracoviensis* 6 (2011): 7–28.

Balle, N. E. *Doctor Morten Luthers Lille Catechismus paa nye udgivet og forsynet med Anmærkninger til Veiledelse for Skoleholdere i deres Underviisning samt til Øvelse i Boglæsning for Børn og til Opbyggelse for de ældre, som ville korteligen igientage deres Christelige Børne-Lærdom*. Copenhagen: Thiele, 1786.

Balle, N. E. *Lærebog i den evangelisk-christelige Religion indrettet til Brug i de danske Skoler*. Copenhagen: Johan Frederik Schultz, 1791.

Balto, Asta. *Samisk barneoppdragelse i endring*. Oslo: Ad notam Gyldendal, 1997.

Balto, Asta. "Sami Teachers Transforming Traditional Culture to the Next Generations: Action Research about Decolonization in Sápmi in Sweden." Kautokeino: Sámi allaskuvla, 2008.

Bang, Anton Christian. *Norske Hexeformularer og magiske Opskrifter*. Videnskabs-selskabets Skrifter II. Historisk-Filos. Vol. 1. Kristiania: A. W. Brøggers Bogtrykkeri, 1901–1902.

Barker, Emma. "Imagining Childhood in Eighteenth-Century France: Greuze's Little Girl with a Dog." *The Art Bulletin* 91, no. 4 (2009): 426–45.

Barnafræðsluskýrslur árin 1920–1966. Statistics of Iceland, Aukaflokkur 1. Reykjavík: Statistics Iceland, 1967.

"Barna- og unglingavinna við Reykjavíkurhöfn eykst enn." *Þjóðviljinn* 18. July 1965: 1. Online at http://timarit.is/files/14291085.pdf#navpanes=1&view=FitH.

"Barnavinnan við höfnina til umræðu í borgarstjórn: Starfskilyrði barnaverndarnefndar verða að batna." *Þjóðviljinn* 23. September 1965: 2. Online at http://timarit.is/files/14293315.pdf#navpanes=1&view=FitH.

Barneombudene i Norden. "Retten til delaktighet og innflytelse for samiske barn og ungdom." Stockholm: Et samarbeid mellom barnombudsmannen i Finland, Barneombudet i Norge og Barneombudsmannen i Sverige, 2008.

Barton, Hildor Arnold. "Popular Education in Sweden: Theory and Practice." In *Facets of Education in the Eighteenth Century. Studies on Voltaire and the Eighteenth Century*, edited by James A. Leith, 523–41. Oxford: The Voltaire Foundation at the Taylor Institution, 1977.

Bauman, Zygmunt. *Legislators and Interpreters: On Modernity, Post-Modernity and Intellectuals*. Cambridge: Polity Press, 1989.

Bayer, Oswald. "Nature and Institution: Luther's Doctrine of the Three Orders." *Lutheran Quarterly* 12 (1998): 125–59.

Beckett, Sandra. *Transcending Boundaries: Writing for a Dual Audience of Children and Adults*. New York: Garland, 1999.

Behrendt, Walther. *Lehr-, Wehr- und Nährstand. Haustafellitteratur und Dreiständelehre im 16. Jahrhundert*. PhD diss., Freie Universität Berlin, 2009.

Benjamin, Walter. *The Work of Art in the Age of Its Technological Reproducibility, and Other Writings on Media*, edited by Michael W. Jennings, Brigid Doherty, and Thomas Y. Levin. Cambridge, MA: Harvard University Press, 2008.

Bentzon, Svend. *Uægte Børn. Deres Ret I Nutid Og Fremtid*. Copenhagen and Kristiania: Gyldendalske Boghandel, Nordisk Forlag, 1906.

Berg, Mads. *Skolens Sangbok*. Kristiania: H. Aschehoug & Co. (W. Nygaard), 1914.

Berg, Mads. *Skolens Sangbok*. Oslo: H. Aschehoug & Co. (W. Nygaard), 1949.

Berg, Mads. *Skolens Sangbok*. 25th revised edition by Åse and Arnfinn Klakegg. Oslo: H. Aschehoug & Co (W. Nygaard), 1964.

Berger, Peter and Thomas Luckmann. *The Social Construction of Reality. A Treatise in the Sociology of Knowledge*. Harmondsworth: Penguin books, 1991.

Berggren Henrik and Lars Trägårdh. *Är svensken människa? Gemenskap och oberoende i det moderna Sverige*. Stockholm: Norstedt, 2009.

Bergman, Helena. *Att fostra till föräldraskap: Barnavårdsmän, genuspolitik och välfärdsstat 1900–1950*. Stockholm: Acta Universitatis Stockholmiensis, 2003.

Bergstrøm, Grete Gunn. "Tradisjonell kunnskap og samisk modernitet. En studie av vilkår for tilegnelse av tradisjonell kunnskap i en moderne samisk samfunnskontekst." Master thesis, University of Tromsø, 2001.

Bergstøl, Tore. *Atterljom. Folkeminne fraa smaadalane kring Lindesnes II*. Norsk Folkeminnelags Skrifter. Vol. 22. Oslo: Norsk Folkeminnelag, 1956.

Bernharðsson, Eggert Þór. *Saga Reykjavíkur. Vol 2. Borgin 1940–1990*. Reykjavík: Iðunn, 1998.

Berättelse om fattigvården i Stockholm från den första april 1810 till samma tid 1811. Stockholm, 1811.

Beskow, Elsa. *Duktiga Annika: bilderbok*. Stockholm: Bonnier, 1941.

Betänkande om inrättningen af Stockholms fattigvård, Församlingsvis. Stockholm, 1812.Bettelheim, Bruno. *The Uses of Enchantment*. New York: Random House, 1976.

Birch, Carl Christian. *Tvende Taler holdne i Anledning af Skolevæsenets forbedrede Indretning i Brahetrolleborg Sogn*, Tale 2. Ved Indvidelsen af Haagerup og Gierup Skoler holden paa begge Steder den 18.de December 1783.

Birch, Carl Christian. *Forskrifter Med Anviisning til den rette Brug af dem. Udarbeidet til Skolernes Nytte i Brahetrolleborg Sogn*. Brahetrolleborg godsarkiv, Rigsarkivet, Odense. 1784.

Birkeland, Tone, Gunvor Risa, and Karin Beate Vold. *Norsk barnelitteraturhistorie*. Oslo: Samlaget, 1997.

Bjerregaard, Peter M. D., and T. Kue Young. *Health Transitions in Arctic Populations*. Toronto: University of Toronto Press, 2008.

Bjørklund, Ivar. *Fjordfolket i Kvænangen: fra samisk samfunn til norsk utkant 1550–1980*. Tromsø: Universitetsforlaget, 1985.

Blehr, Otto. *Folketro fra Sørkedalen*. Norsk Folkeminnelags skrifter. Vol. 96. Oslo: Universitetsforlaget, 1966.

Bly, Robert. *The Sibling Society*. Reading, MA: Addison-Wesley, 1996.

Boli, John. *New Citizens for a New Society: The Institutional Origins of Mass Schooling*. Oxford: Pergamon, 1989.

Booth, Michael. *The Almost Nearly Perfect People: The Truth About the Nordic Miracle*. London: Jonathan Cape, 2014.

Borchgrevink, Louise Storm. *Frå ei anna tid. Folkeminne frå Nordfjord.* Norsk Folkeminnelags Skrifter. Vol. 78. Oslo: Norsk Folkeminnelag, 1956.

Borge, Bård H. *I rettsoppgjørets lange skygger. Andre generasjons problemer i lys av moderne transisjonsteori.* PhD diss., University of Bergen, 2012.

Borge, Bård H. "Svar til Knut Engelskjøn om NS-barn." *Historisk tidsskrift* 3 (2014): 475–86.

Bradbury, Bettina. "Women's History and Working-Class History." *Labour / Le Travail* 19 (Spring 1987): 23–43.

Brecht, Martin, Klaus Deppermann, Ulrich Gäbler, and Hartmut Lehmann, eds. *Der Pietismus im achtzehnten Jahrhundert. Geschichte des Pietismus.* Vol. 2. Göttingen: Vandenhoeck und Ruprecht, 1995.

Bregnsbo, Michael, *Samfundsorden og statsmagt set fra prædikestolen. Udviklingen i præsterne syn på samfundsorden og statsmagt i Danmark 1750–1848, belyst ved trykte prædikener.* Copenhagen: Museum Tusculanum, 1997.

Bregnsbo, Michael, and Pasi Ihalainen. "Gradual Reconsiderations of Lutheran Conceptions of Politics." In *Scandinavia in the Age of Revolution. Nordic Political Cultures, 1740–1820,* edited by Pasi Ihalainen et al., 107–19. Farnham and Burlington: Ashgate, 2011.

Brembeck, Helene, Barbro Johansson, and Jan Kampmann, eds. *Beyond the Competent Child: Exploring Contemporary Childhoods in the Nordic Welfare Societies.* Fredriksberg: Roskilde University Press, 2004.

Broch, Johan Jørgen. *Politiske Aphorismer eller Bemærkninger over Statsforfatninger i Almindelighed, over den norske Statsforfatning i Særdeleshed, og over de til Afgjørelse paa førstkommende ordentlige Storthing fremsatte Constitutionsforslage.* Christiansand, 1823.

Brunner, Otto. *Neue Wege der Verfassungs- und Sozialgeschichte.* Göttingen: Vandenhoeck und Ruprecht, 1968.

Brustad, M., K. L. Hansen, A. R. Broderstad, S. Hansen, and M. Melhus. "A population-based study on health and living conditions in areas with mixed Sami and Norwegian settlements – the SAMINOR 2 questionnaire study." *Int J Circumpolar Health* 73 (2014): 23147.

Bugenhagen, Johannes. *Der XXIX. Psalm ausgelegt. Darinnen auch von der Kinder Tauffe. Item von den vngeborn Kindern vnd von den Kindern die man nicht teuffen kann.* Wittenberg: Joseph Klug, 1542.

Bugge, K. E. "Grundtvig's Educational Ideas." In *N. F. S. Grundtvig: Tradition and Renewal: Grundtvig's Vision of Man and People, Education and the Church, in Relation to World Issues Today,* edited by Christian Thodberg and Anders Pontoppidan Thyssen. Copenhagen: The Danish Institute, 1983.

Bugge, Kristian. *Folkeminneoptegnelser. Et utvalg.* Norsk Folkeminnelags Skrifter. Vol. 31. Oslo: Norsk Folkeminnelag, 1934.

Bull, Edvard. "Industrial Boy Labour in Norway." In *Our Common History. The Transformation of Europe,* edited by Paul Thompson. Atlantic Highlands: Humanities Press, 1982.

Bø, Olav. "Øskjer i kyrkjemuren." *Norveg* 7 (1960): 99–152.

Bø, Olav. *Trollmakter og godvette. Overnaturlege vesen i norsk folketru.* Oslo: Samlaget, 1987.

Bøggild Johannsen, Birgitte, and Hugo Johannsen. "Re-forming the Confessional Space: Early Lutheran Churches in Denmark, c. 1536–1660." In *Lutheran Churches in Early Modern Europe,* edited by Andrew Spicer, 241–276. Farnham: Ashgate, 2011.

Bøyum, Sjur. Balestrand prestegjeld 1929–30. Norsk Folkeminnesamling (NFS), Institutt for kulturstudier og orientalske språk (IKOS), University of Oslo.

Carlgren, Ingrid, Kirsti Klette, Sigurjón Mýrdal, Karsten Schnack, and Hannu Simola. "Changes in Nordic Teaching Practices: From Individualised Teaching to the Teaching of Individuals." *Scandinavian Journal of Educational Research* 50, no. 3 (July 2006): 301–26.

Castberg, Frede. *The Norwegian Way of Life*. London: Heinemann, 1954.

Christensen, Nina. "Om barnet, kunstneren og dyret. Med utgangspunkt i H. V. Kaalund og J. Th. Lundbyes *Fabler for børn*." In *På opdagelse i børnelitteraturen*, edited by Christensen and Skyggebjerg, 154–170. Copenhagen: Høst & Søn, 2006.

Christensen, Nina. "Lust for Reading and Thirst for Knowledge. Fictive Letters in a Danish Children's Magazine of 1770." *The Lion and the Unicorn* 33, no. 2 (2009): 289–301.

Christensen, Nina. *Videbegær. Oplysning, børnelitteratur, dannelse*. Aarhus: Aarhus Universitetsforlag, 2012.

Christensen, Nina. "Contemporary Picturebooks in the Nordic Countries. Concepts of Literature and Childhood." In *Looking out and Looking in: National Identity in Picturebooks of the New Millennium*, edited by Åse Marie Ommundsen, 182–94. Oslo: Novus, 2013.

Christiansen, Reidar Th. *Norske folkeminne. En veiledning for samlere og interesserte*. Norsk Folkeminnelags Skrifter. Vol. 12. Oslo: Norsk Folkeminnelag, 1925.

Christoffersen, Svein Aage, ed. *Hans Nielsen Hauge og det moderne Norge*. Oslo: Norges Forskningsråd, 1996.

Comer Kidd, David, and Emaneuele Castano. "Reading Literary Fiction Improves Theory of Mind." *Science* 342 (2013): 377–80.

Cramer, Johann Andreas. *Kort Underviisning i* Christendommen, *oversat efter den for Skolerne i Hertugdømmerne anordnede Forklaring til rigtig at forstaae Luthers lille Catechismus*. Copanhagen,1785.

Cross, Gary. "Play, Games, and Toys." In The Routledge *History of Childhood in the Western World*, edited by Paula S. Fass, 267–82. London: Routledge, 2013.

Cunningham, Hugh. "The Employment and Unemployment of Children in England c. 1680–1851." *Past & Present* 126 (1990): 115–50.

Cunningham, Hugh. "The Rights of the Child from the Mid-Eighteenth to the Early Twentieth Century." *Aspects of Education. Journal of the Institute of Education* (1994): 2–16.

Cunningham, Hugh. *Children and Childhood in Western Societies since 1500*. London: Longman, 1995.

Cunningham, Hugh, and Harald Thuen. *Barn og barndom: fra middelalder til moderne tid*. Oslo: Ad Notam Gyldendal, 1996.

Czaika, Otfried. "Dying Unprepared in Early Modern Swedish Funeral Sermons." In *Preparing for Death*, edited by Anu Lahtinen and Mia Korpiola. Leiden: Brill (forthcoming).

"Dagsbrún mótmælir barnavinnu við Reykjavíkurhöfn." *Tíminn* 21 July 1965: 16. Online at http://timarit.is/files/12014287.pdf#navpanes=1&view=FitH.

Dahl, H. *Språkpolitikk og skolestell i Finnmark 1814–1905*. Oslo: Universitetsforlaget, 1957.

Dankertsen, Astri. *Samisk artikulasjon: melankoli, tap og forsoning i en (nord)norsk hverdag*. PhD diss., University of Nordland, 2014.

Danske Lov. Secher, V. A., ed. *Kong Christian den Femtis Danske Lov* [1683]. Copenhagen: G. E. C. Gads Forlag, 1929.

Dass, Petter. "Katekismesangene." In *Samlede Verker*, vol. 2, edited by Kjell Heggelund and Sverre Inge Apenes. Oslo: Gyldendal, 1997.

Dawson, Janis. "The Origin of the Nineteenth Century Juvenile Periodicals. The Young Gentleman's and Lady's Magazine (1799–1800)." *Victorian Periodicals Review* 29, no. 3 (1996): 217–41.

de Certeau, Michel. *The Practice of Everyday Life*. 3rd edition. Berkeley: University of California Press, 2011.

de Coninck-Smith, Ning, Bengt Sandin, and Ellen Schrumpf, eds. *Industrious Children. Work and Childhood in the* Nordic Countries *1850–1990*. Odense: Odense University Press, 1997.

de Coninck-Smith, Ning. "The Struggle for the Child's Time – at All Times. School and Children's Work in Town and Country in Denmark 1900 to the 1960s." In *Industrious Children. Work and Childhood in the Nordic Countries 1850–1990*, edited by Ning de Coninck-Smith, Bengt Sandin, and Ellen Schrumpf, 129–59. Odense: Odense University Press, 1997.

Draper, Sharon. *Out of My Mind*. New York: Atheneum, 2012.

Edelman, Lee. *No Future. Queer Theory and the Death Drive*. Durham: Duke University Press, 2004.

Edvardsen, Edmund. *Den gjenstridige allmue. Skole og levebrød i et nordnosk kystsamfunn c. 1850–1900*. Oslo: Solum forlag, 1989.

Eide, Gjertrud. "Ære, pryd og ihukommelse: en empirisk studie av epitafier fra Vestlandet fra reformasjonen til sent 1600-tall." Master thesis, University of Bergen, 2006.

Eide, Brit and Nina Winger. *Kompetente barn og kvalifiserte pedagoger i den nye småskolen*. Oslo: Cappelen Akademisk, 1996.

Einarsdottir, Johanna, and Judith Wagner. *Nordic Childhoods and Early Education. Philosophy, Research, Policy and Practice in Denmark, Finland, Iceland, Norway and Sweden*. Greenwich, CT: Information Age Publishing, 2006.

Eliot, George. "The Natural History of German Life." In *Selected Critical Writings*, edited by Rosemary Ashton, 260–95. Oxford: Oxford University Press, 1992.

Ellingsen, Terje, ed. *Kirkeordinansen av 1537: Reformasjonens kirkelov*. Oslo: Verbum, 1990.

"En Klokkering for De Underjordiske." *Historisk Tidsskrift* (1877): 553–55.

Ericsson, Kjersti, and Eva Simonsen, eds. *Children of World War II. The Hidden Enemy Legacy*. Oxford and New York: Berg, 2005.

Eriksen, Anne. *Historie, minne og myte*. Oslo: Pax forlag, 1999.

Eriksen, Astrid M., Ketil Lenert Hansen, Cecilie Javo, and Berit Schei. "Emotional, physical and sexual violence among Sami and non-Sami populations in Norway: The SAMINOR 2 questionnaire study." *Scand J Public Health* 43, no. 6 (2015): 588–96.

Eriksen, K. E. and E. Niemi. *Den finske fare. Sikkerhetsproblemer og minoritetspolitikk i nord 1860–1940*. Oslo, Bergen, and Tromsø: Universitetsforlaget, 1981.

Esping-Andersen, Gösta. *The Three Worlds of Welfare Capitalism*. Cambridge: Polity Press, 1990.

Espmark, Kjell. *Harry Martinson. Mästaren*. Stockholm: Norstedt, 2005.

Evangelical Lutheran Worship. Minneapolis: Augsburg Fortress, 2006.

Fass, Paula S., ed. *Encyclopedia of Children and Childhood in History and Society.* Vol. 1–3. New York: MacMillan Reference, 2004.

Fass, Paula S. "A Historical Context for the United Nations Convention on the Rights of the Child." *Annals of the American Academy of Political and Social Science* 633 (2011): 17–29.

Fauskanger, Unn. "Skolen som en del av barns oppvekst." In *Skolen 1739–1989*, edited by Hans-Jørgen Dokka, Knut Jordheim, and Jenny Lippestad, 166–72. Oslo: NKS-forlaget, 1989.

Faye Jacobsen, Anette. "Kontrol og demokrati. Bidrag til dansk børneforsorgs historie ca. 1930 til 1960." *Historisk Tidsskrift* 89 (1989): 255–89.

Faye Jacobsen, Anette. *Husbondret. Rettighedskulturer i Danmark, 1750–1920.* Copenhagen: Museum Tusculanum, 2008. Online at http://www.werkshop.dk/ producenter/30-temp-hist/422-temp-nr-10---2015/" \t "_blank.

Faye Jacobsen, Anette. "Citizenship and National Identity: Faith as an Innovative Force in Elementary-School Teaching from 1850 to 1920." In *Education, State and Citizenship*, edited by Mette Buchardt, Pirjo Markkola, and Heli Valtonen, 56–80. NordWel Studies in Historical Welfare State Research 4. Helsinki: Nordic Centre of Excellence NordWel, 2013.

Faye Jacobsen, Anette. "Stat og civilsamfund i nye relationer. FN's Børnekonventions historie i Danmark." *Temp – tidsskrift for historie* 10 (2015): 60–91.

Fjellstad, Lars M. *Gammalt frå Elvrom.* Norsk Folkeminnelags Skrifter. Vol. 57. Oslo: Norsk Folkeminnelag, 1945.

Flekkøy, Målfrid Grude. *A Voice for Children. Speaking out as Their Ombudsman.* London: Jessica Kingsley Publishers, 1991.

Florin, Christina. "Från folkskola till grundskola 1842–1962." Online at www. lararnashistoria.se/sites/www.lararnashistoria.se/files/artiklar/Fr%C3%A5n%20 folkskola%20till%20grundskola_0.pdf.

Flygt, Torbjörn. *Underdog.* Stockholm: Bonnier, 2001.

Folklife archives, University of Tampere.

Folklore archives, Finnish Literature Society.

Fonk, Terje. "La de små barn komme til meg – Lucas Cranachs maleri i Larvik kirke." In *Gloria mundi. Kirkekunsten i Vestfold*, edited by Tone Lyngstad Nyaas, 23–30. Tønsberg: Orfeus/Haugar museum, 2011.

Formulär Till målsmansförbindelse i avseende på riktig hemfostran och de växandes ordentliga skolgång. In *Acta till Stockholms folkundervisnings historia: 1533–1847*, edited by B. Rudolf Hall. Stockholm: Fören. för svensk undervisningshistoria, 1940.

Forsøksrådet for skoleverket. *Læreplan for forsøk med 9-årig skole.* 2nd edition. Oslo: H. Aschehoug & Co (W. Nygaard), 1964.

"Fortællinger om Indtagelse i Berg." *Historisk Tidsskrift.* Anden Række, tredie Bind. Kristiania (1882): 141–44.

Foucault, Michel. "The Subject and Power." *Critical Inquiry* 8 (1982): 777–95.

Fredriksen, Lill Tove. "Fornorskningen var et sjeleran." *Nordlys*, 26 April 2016. Online at http://nordnorskdebatt.no/article/fornorskningspolitikken-et. Tromsø: Amedia 2016.

Fryxell, Olof. *Snöfästningen: Berättelse för Landt-Gåßar.* Stockholm: Hörberg, 1830.

Furre, Berge. *Vårt hundreår. Norsk historie 1905–1990.* Oslo: Samlaget, 1991.

Furuland, Lars. "Att erövra ett språk. Ivar Lo-Johansson (1901–1990). In *Svenska 1900-talsklassiker vol. 2 – Från Agnes von Krusenstjerna till Elin Wägner.* Lund: Bibliotekstjänst 2002, 60–81.

Furuland, Lars, and John Svedjedal. *Svensk arbetarlitteratur.* Stockholm: Atlas, 2006.

Fyhn, Anne. "Sami Culture and Values: A Study of the National Mathematics Exam for the Compulsory School in Norway." *A Quarterly Review of Education* 44, no. 3 (2013): 349–67.

Fällström, Anne-Marie. "Pauperismen och samhällsutvecklingen: sociala problem i Göteborg före, under och efter kontinentalblockadens tid." PhD diss., University of Gothenburg, 1974.

Garðarsdóttir, Ólöf. "Working Children in Urban Iceland 1930–1990. Ideology of Work, Work-Schools and Gender Relations in Modern Iceland." In *Industrious Children. Work and Childhood in the Nordic Countries 1850–1990,* edited by Ning de Coninck-Smith, Bengt Sandin, and Ellen Schrumpf, 160–85. Odense: Odense University Press, 1997.

Garðarsdóttir, Ólöf. "Hugleiðingar um kynbundinn mun í fræðslu barna og unglinga." In *Kvennaslóðir. Rit til heiðurs Sigríði Th. Erlendsdóttur sagnfræðingi,* edited by Anna Agnarsdóttir et al., 424–25. Reykjavík: Kvennasögusafn Íslands, 2001.

Garðarsdóttir, Ólöf. "Working and Going to School. Childhood Experiences in Post-War Reykjavík." *Barn* 27, no. 3–4 (2009): 173–85.

Garðarsdóttir, Ólöf and Loftur Guttormsson. "Changes in Schooling Arrangements and in the Demographic and Social Profile of Teachers in Iceland 1930–1960." *Nordic Journal of Educational History* 1, no. 1–2 (2014): 7–20.

Gaski, Harald. *Sami Culture in a New Era: The Norwegian Sami Experience.* Karasjok: Davvi Girji, 1997.

Gebhard, Hannes. *Työväenperheitten asunto- ja maataloudellisia oloja. Tilastollinen tutkimus yhteiskuntataloudellisista oloista Suomen maalaiskunnissa v. 1901.* Tilattoman Väestön Alakomitea. Helsinki, 1916.

Gemzøe, Anker. "Barnet i nordisk arbejderlitteratur. Nu og før." In *Från Nexø till Alakoski. Aspekter på nordisk arbetarlitteratur,* edited by Bibi Jonsson et al., 163–75. Lund: Absalon, 2011.

Genette, Gérard. *Narrative Discourse.* Ithaca: Cornell University Press, 1980.

Gilgren, Peter. *Gåva och själ. Epitafiemaleriet under stormaktstiden.* Uppsala: Acta Universitatis Upsaliensis, 1995.

Gjerløff, Anne Katrine, and Anette Faye Jacobsen. *Da skolen blev sat i system 1850–1920.* Dansk skolehistorie. Vol. 3. Aarhus: Aarhus Universitetsforlag, 2014.

Goga, Nina. "Children and Childhood in Scandinavian Children's Literature over the Last Fifty Years." In *Bologna: Fifty Years of Children's Books from around the World,* edited by Giorgia Grilli. Bologna: Bologna University Press, 2013.

Grankvist, Rolf. *Utsyn over norsk skole: Norsk utdanning gjennom 1000 år.* Trondheim: Tapir forlag, 2000.

Green, Todd. "The Partnering of Church and School in Nineteenth-Century Sweden." *Journal of Church and State* 50, no. 2 (Spring 2008): 331–49.

Grell, Ole Peter, Thorkild Lyby, and Martin Schwarz Lausten. *The Scandinavian Reformation: From Evangelical Movement to Institutionalization of Reform.* Cambridge: Cambridge University Press, 1995.

Grenby, M. O. *The Child Reader 1700–1840.* Cambridge: Cambridge University Press, 2011.

Grimstad, Edvard. *Etter gamalt. Folkeminne frå Gudbrandsdalen.* Norsk Folkeminnelags Skrifter. Vol. 58. Oslo: Norsk Folkeminnelag, 1945.

Grinde, Turid Vogt. *Barn og barnevern i Norden. Samfunnets respektive familiens ansvar for barna.* Oslo: Tano og Nordisk Ministerråd, 1989.

Grum-Schwensen, Ane. "Andersen og Astrid." *Fynske minder* (2007): 101–17.

Grundtvig, N. F. S. *Selected Writings*. Edited and introduced by J. Knudsen. Philadelphia: Fortress Press, 1976.

Grundtvig, N. F. S. *What Constitutes Authentic Christianity?* Translated and edited by Ernest D. Nielsen. Philadelphia: Fortress Press, 1985.

Grundtvig, N. F. S. *The School for Life: N.F.S. Grundtvig on Education for the People*. Edited by Edward Broadbridge, Clay Warren and Uffe Jonas. Translated and edited by Edward Broadbridge. Aarhus: Aarhus University Press, 2011.

Grundtvig, N. F. S. *Living Wellsprings: The Hymns, Songs, and Poems of N. F. S. Grundtvig*. Edited and translated by Edward Broadbridge, and introduced by Uffe Jonas. Aarhus: Aarhus University Press, 2015.

Grøgaard, Hans Jacob. *Lommebog for Gode Børn*. Bergen, 1829.

Grøgaard, Hans Jacob. *Læsebog for Børn, en Forberedelse til religionsunderviis-ningen, især i Norges Omgangsskoledistrikter*. 11th edition. Christiania, 1843.

Guddal, Peder Martin. "Minneoppgaven 1964/65, Sogn og Fjordane." Norsk Folkeminnesamling (NFS), Institutt for kulturstudier og orientalske språk (IKOS), University of Oslo.

Gunnlaugsson, Gísli Ágúst. *Family and Household in Iceland 1801–1930. Studies in the Relationship between Demographic and Socio-Economic Development, Social Legislation and Family and Household Structures*. Uppsala: Studia historica upsaliencia, 1988.

Gustavson, Harald. *Nordens historia. En europeisk region under 1200 år*. Lund: Studentlitteratur, 2007.

Guttormsen, Loftur. "Læsefærdighed og folkeuddannelse 1540–1800." In *Ur nordisk kulturhistoria. Läskunnighet och folkbildning före folkskoleväsendet*, 123–165. Jyväskylä: University of Jyväskylä, 1981.

Guttormsson, Loftur. "Farskólahald í sextíu ár (1890–1950). Nokkrir megindrættir." *Uppeldi og menntun* 1 (1992): 207–222.

Guttormsson, Loftur. "Heimili og Skóli." In *Almenningsfræðsla á Íslandi*. Vol 1: *Skólahald í bæ og sveit 1880–1945*, edited by Loftur Guttormsson, 284–98. Reykjavík: Háskólaútgáfan, 2008.

Haapala, Pertti. *Tehtaan valossa. Teollistuminen ja työväestön muodostuminen Tampereella 1820–1920*. Helsinki: Finnish Historical Society, 1986.

Haapala, Pertti. "Nuoriso numeroina." In *Nuoruuden vuosisata. Suomalaisen nuorison historia*, edited by S. Aapola, and M. Kaarninen, 67–85. Helsinki: SKS, 2003.

Haarberg, Jon. "'Jeg fant dem der jeg minst ventet det'. Petter Dass' Catechismus-Sange i Drammen." *Bøygen* 1 (2003): 22–28.

Haarberg, Jon. "Petter Dass fra litteraturhistorie til bokhistorien: Katekismesangene (1715) som barnelærdom, folkelesning og nasjonallitteratur." *Nordisk Tidskrift för Bok- och Bibliotekshistoria* (2006): 41–61.

Haarberg, Jon. "Singing the Catechism in Denmark-Norway 1569–1756." In *Religious Reading in the Lutheran North. Studies in Early Modern Scandinavian Book Culture*, edited by Charlotte Appel and Morten Fink-Jensen. Cambridge: Cambridge Scholars Publishing, 2011.

Haarberg, Jon. *Peter Dass. Katekismesanger*. Historisk-kritisk utgave by Jon Haarberg. Oslo: Det norske språk- og litteraturselskap, 2013. Online at http://www.bokselskap.no/wp-content/themes/bokselskap/tekster/pdf/katekismesanger.pdf.

Hagberg, Louise. "Seder och tro vid märkestillfällena i barnets liv." In *Nordisk kultur XX. Livets högtider*, edited by K. Robert V. Wikman, 16–36. Stockholm: Bonnier, 1949.

Hagemann, Sonja. *Jørgen Moe: Barnas dikter.* Oslo: Aschehoug, 1963.

Hagemann, Sonja. *Barnelitteratur i Norge 1850–1914.* Oslo: Aschehoug, 1970.

Hammarberg, Thomas. "Alla barns rättigheter." In *Barnets rättigheter – och samhällets skyldigheter: lagar och regler,* edited by Annika Rembe. Stockholm: Wahlström & Widstrand, 1991.

Handlingar rörande den nya organisationen av Stockholms stads undervisningsverk (1819). In *Acta till Stockholms större latinläroverks historia 1419–1840,* edited by B. Rudolf Hall. Stockholm: Fören. för svensk undervisningshistoria, 1939.

Hansen, Ketil Lenert. *Ethnic Discrimination and Bullying in relation to self-reported Physical and Mental Health in Sami Settlement Areas in Norway: the Saminor Study.* PhD diss., University of Tromsø, 2011.

Hansen, Ketil Lenert, Marita Melhus, Asle Høgmo, and Eiliv Lund. "Ethnic discrimination and bullying in the Sami and non-Sami populations in Norway: The SAMINOR study." *Int J Circumpolar Health* 67, no. 1 (2008): 97–113.

Hansen, Lars Ivar, and Bjørnar Olsen. *Samernas historia fram till 1750.* Stockholm: Liber, 2006.

Hansen, Miriam Bratu. "Benjamin's Aura." *Critical Inquiry* 34 (2008): 336–75.

Hansen, Peder. "Levninger af overtroe, der endnu finder sted hos mange af landalmuen i Christiansands stift (1803)." In *Folkloristiske klassikere 1800–1930,* edited by Anne Eriksen and Arne Bugge Amundsen, 11–15. Norsk Folkeminnelags Skrifter. Vol. 147. Oslo: Norsk Folkeminnelag/Aschehoug, 1999.

Hanska, Jussi, and Anu Lahtinen. "Keskiajalta 1500-luvun lopulle." In *Huoneentaulun maailma. Kasvatus ja koulutus Suomessa keskiajalta 1860-luvulle,* edited by Jussi Hanska and Kirsi Vainio-Korhonen, 17–111. Helsinki: Finnish Literature Society, 2010.

Hartwell, R. M. *The Industrial Revolution and Economic Growth.* London: Methuen, 1971.

Hassler, Sven. *The Health Condition in the Sami Population of Sweden, 1961–2002: Causes of Death and Incidences of Cancer and Cardiovascular Diseases.* PhD diss., Umeå University, 2005.

Hatje, Ann-Katrin. "Folkbarnträdgården i Norden under 1880–1930-tallet." *Filantropi: mellem almisse og velfærdsstat. Den jyske historiker* 67 (July 1994): 81–103.

Hawes, Joseph M. *The Children's Rights Movement. A History of Advocacy and Protection.* Boston: Twayne Publishers, 1991.

Heal, Bridget. *The Cult of the Virgin Mary in Early Modern Germany: Protestant and Catholic Piety, 1500–1648.* Cambridge: Cambridge University Press, 2007.

Hedenborg, Susanna. *Det gåtfulla folket: barns villkor och uppfattningar av barnet i 1700-talets Stockholm.* Stockholm: Almqvist & Wiksell International, 1997.

Heikkinen, Anja and Pirkko Leino-Kaukiainen. "Johdanto. Koko kansa koulun penkille." In *Valistus ja koulunpenkki: Kasvatus ja koulutus Suomessa 1860-luvulta 1960-luvulle,* edited by Anja Heikkinen and Pirkko Leino-Kaukiainen, 11–15. Helsinki: Finnish Literature Society, 2011.

Helsingfors dagblad (newspaper), 1861–1889.

Helsingfors tidningar (newspaper), 1821–1866.

Hermundstad, Knut. *Gamletidi talar. Gamal Valdreskultur I.* Norsk Folkeminnelags Skrifter. Vol. 36. Oslo: Norsk Folkeminnelag, 1936.

Hermundstad, Knut. *Ættararv. Gamal Valdres-kultur IV.* Norsk Folkeminnelags Skrifter. Vol. 65. Oslo: Norsk Folkeminnelag, 1950.

Henningsen, Lars. "Landsbylærer i Asserballeskov og Bovrup 1750–1785, af Johannes Pades erindringer", *Sønderjyske Årbøger,* 2000, 77–148.

Hetekivi Olsson, Eija. *Ingenbarnsland [No child's land]*. Stockholm: Norstedt, 2012.

Higonnet, Anne. *Pictures of Innocence. The History and Crisis of Ideal Childhood.* London: Thames and Hudson, 1998.

Higonnet, Anne. "Picturing Childhood in the Modern West." In *The Routledge History of Childhood in the Western World*, edited by Paula S. Fass, 296–312. London and New York: Routledge, 2013.

Hirdman, Yvonne. *Den socialistiska hemmafrun och andra kvinnohistorier.* Stockholm: Carlssons, 1992.

Hjelt, Vera. *Tutkimus ammattityöläisten toimeentuloehdoista Suomessa 1908– 1909. Työtilastollisia tutkimuksia – Arbetsstatistik XII.* Helsinki, 1912.

"Hjertespråket – Forslag til lovverk, tiltak og ordninger for samisk språk." In *NOU 2016:18*. Oslo: Kommunal- og moderniseringsdepartementet, 2016.

Hodne, Bjarne. *Å leve med døden. Folkelige forestillinger om døden og de døde.* Oslo: Aschehoug, 1980.

Hodne, Ørnulf. "Fadderskapet og dets funksjoner i norsk folketradisjon." *Heimen* 1 (1979): 3–22.

Hodne, Ørnulf. "Spedbarnet i norsk folkekultur." In *Barn av sin tid. Fra norske barns historie*, edited by Bjarne Hodne og Sølvi Sogner. Oslo, Bergen, Stavanger, and Tromsø: Universitetsforlaget, 1984.

Hodne, Ørnulf. *Vetter og skrømt i norsk folketro.* Oslo: Cappelen, 1995.

Hodne, Ørnulf. *Norsk folketro.* Oslo: Cappelen, 1999.

Hodne, Ørnulf. *Mystiske steder i Norge.* Oslo: Cappelen, 2000.

Hoëm, Anton. *Fra noaidiens verden til forskerens: misjon, kunnskap og modernisering i sameland 1715–2007.* Oslo: Novus forlag, 2007.

Hoffmann, Stefan-Ludwig, ed. *Human Rights in the Twentieth Century.* New York: Cambridge University Press, 2011.

Holck, Per. *Norsk folkemedisin. Kloke koner, urtekurer og magi.* Cappelen: Oslo, 1996.

Holmgren, Ola. *Ivar Lo-Johansson. Frihetens väg.* Stockholm: Natur & Kultur, 1998.

Holst, Elling and Eivind Nielsen. *Norsk Billedbog for Børn.* Christiania: Alb. Cammermeyers forlag, 1888.

Holstad, Birgit. "Elias Fiigenschoug som portrettmaler: en studie av utvalgte epitafier." Master thesis, University of Bergen, 2008.

Honnens de Lichtenberg, Hanne. *Tro, håb og forfængelighed: kunstneriske udtryksformer i 1500-tallets Danmark.* Copenhagen: Museum Tusculanum Press, 1989.

Hope, Nicholas. *German and Scandinavian Protestantism 1700–1918.* Oxford: Oxford University Press, 1995.

Hoprekstad, Eldrid Valebjørg. Vik i Sogn 1954. Norsk Folkeminnesamling (NFS), Institutt for kulturstudier og orientalske språk (IKOS), University of Oslo.

Horrell, Sara and Jane Humphries. "'The Exploitation of Little Children': Child Labor and the Family Economy in the Industrial Revolution." *Explorations in Economic History* 32 (1995): 485–516.

Horstbøll, Henrik. "Bolle Willum Luxdorphs samling af trykkefrihedens skrifter 1770–1772." In *Fund Og Forskning I Det Kongelige Biblioteks Samlinger*, 371– 414. Copenhagen: The Royal Library, 2005.

Hufvudstadsbladet (newspaper), 1864–.

Hult, Ruth. *Østfoldminne.* Norsk Folkeminnelags Skrifter. Vol. 39. Oslo: Norsk Folkeminnelag, 1937.

Humphries, Stephen. *Hooligans or Rebels? An Oral History of Working-Class Childhood and Youth 1889–1939*. Oxford: Basil Blackwell, 1981.

Hunt, Lynn. "The Paradoxical Origins of Human Rights." In *Human Rights and Revolutions*, edited by Jeffrey Wasserstein, Lynn Hunt, and Marilyn B. Young. Lanham, MD: Rowman & Littlefield, 2000.

Hunt, Lynn. *Inventing Human Rights: A History*. New York: Norton & Co., 2007.

Hurtigkarl, Frederik Theodor. *Den Danske og Norske Rets første Grunde. Første Deel*. Copenhagen, 1813.

Husén, Torsten. "Begåvningsreserven då och nu." *Pedagogisk forskning i Sverige* 3 (2002): 164–67.

Hveding, Johan. *Folketru og folkeliv på Hålogaland*. Norsk Folkeminnelags Skrifter. Vol. 33. Oslo: Norsk Folkeminnelag, 1935.

Hübner, Johann. *To gange To og Halvtredsindstyve udvalgte Bibliske Historier af det Gamle og Nye Testamente, Ungdommen til Beste*. Copenhagen, 1728.

Hyltenstam, Kenneth. "Kvenskans status: Rapport for Kommunal- og regionaldepartementet og Kultur-og kirkedepartementet i Norge." Oslo, 2003.

Hyltze, Anna. *Hjortbergstavlan. Kring ett familjeporträtt i Släps kyrka*. Gothenburg: University of Gothenburg, 1995.

Hyvinkää City Museum Archives.

Hyvinkään Sanomat (newspaper).

Hyyrö, Tuula. "Alkuopetus kiertokoulutusta alakansakouluun." In *Valistus ja koulunpenkki. Kasvatus ja koulutus Suomessa 1860-luvulta 1960-luvulle*, edited by A. Heikkinen, and P. Leino-Kaukiainen, 327–51. Helsinki: Finnish Literature Society, 2011.

Høgmo, Asle. *Norske idealer og samisk virkelighet: om skoleutvikling i det samiske området*. Oslo: Gyldendal, 1989.

Højberg Christensen, Axel Christian, Knud Grue-Sørensen, and Axel Skalts, eds. *Leksikon for opdragere. Pædagogisk-psykologisk-social håndbog*. Vol. I–II. Copenhagen: J. H. Schultz Forlag, 1953.

Højskolesangbogen. 18th edition. Copanhagen: Foreningen for Folkehøjskoler, 2006.

Hoëm, Anton. *Fra noaidiens verden til forskerens: misjon, kunnskap og modernisering i sameland 1715-2007*. Oslo: Novus forlag, 2007.

Ihalainen, Pasi, Michael Bregnsbo, Karin Sennenfelt, and Patrik Winton, eds. *Scandinavia in the Age of Revolution: Nordic Political Cultures, 1740–1820*. Farnham and Burlington: Ashgate, 2011.

International Labor Office. *Indigenous and Tribal Peoples' Rights in Practice: A Guide to ILO Convention No. 169*. Geneva: ILO Publications, 2009.

Isling, Åke. *Kampen för och mot en demokratisk skola. 1. Samhällsstruktur och skolorganisation*. Stockholm: Sober, 1980.

Jalava, Marja. "Kansanopetuksen suuri murros ja 1860-luvun väittely." In *Valistus ja koulunpenkki: Kasvatus ja koulutus Suomessa 1860-luvulta 1960-luvulle*, edited by Anja Heikkinen and Pirkko Leino-Kaukiainen, 74–79. Helsinki: Finnish Literature Society, 2011.

James, Alison and Alan Prout, eds. *Constructing and Reconstructing Childhood: Contemporary Issues in the Sociological Study of Childhood*. London and Bristol: Falmer Press, 1990.

James, Allison, Chris Jenks, and Alan Prout, eds. *Theorizing Childhood*. Oxford: Polity Press, 1998.

James, Allison, Chris Jenks, and Alan Prout, eds. *Den teoretiske barndom*. Oslo: Gyldendal, 1999.

Javo, Cecilie. *Kulturens betydning for oppdragelse og atferdsproblemer: transkulturell forståelse, veiledning og behandling*. Oslo: Universitetsforlaget, 2010.

Javo, Cecilie, John Andreas Rønning, and Sonja Heyerdahl. "Child-rearing in an indigenous Sami population in Norway: a cross-cultural comparison of parental attitudes and expectations." *Scand J Psychol* 45, no. 1 (2004): 67–78.

Jensen, Eivind Bråstad. *Fra fornorskningspolitikk mot kulturelt mangfold*. Stonglandseidet: Nordkalott-forlaget, 1991.

Jensen, Eivind Bråstad. *Skoleverket og de tre stammers møte*. Tromsø: Eureka, 2005.

Jensen, Eivind Bråstad. *Tromsøseminarister i møte med en flerkulturell landsdel*. Stonglandseidet: Nordkalottforlaget, 2015.

Jernsletten, Nils. "Sami Language Communities and the Conflict between Sami and Norwegian." In *Language Conflict and Language Planning. Trends in Linguistics*, edited by Ernst H. Jahr, 115–132. Berlin and New York: Mouton de Gruyter, 1993.

Johansson, Egil. "Den kyrkliga lästraditionen i Sverige – en konturteckning." In *Ur nordisk kulturhistoria. Läskunnighet och folkbildning före folkskoleväsendet*, 193–212. Jyväskylä: University of Jyväskylä, 1981,

Johansson, Egil. "Staten och skolan vid 1800-talets mitt." In *Utbildningshistoria*, edited by E. Johansson, and S. Nordström. Uppsala: Föreningen för svensk undervisningehistoria, 1992.

Johnsen, Berit. *Et historisk perspektiv på en skole for alle. Rekonstruksjon av sentrale tanker og tradisjoner med basis i Erik Pontoppidans og Ole Vigs pedagogiske tekster*. PhD diss., University of Oslo, 1998.

Johnson, Eyvind. *Nu var det 1914*. Stockholm: Bonnier, 1935.

Johnson, Eyvind. *1914*. Translated by Mary Sandbach. London: Adam Books, 1970.

Jónasson, Jón Torfi. "Grunnskóli verður til." In *Almenningsfræðsla á Íslandi*. Vol. 2: *Skóli fyrir alla 1946–2008*, edited by Loftur Guttormsson, 102–17. Reykjavík: Háskólaútgáfan, 2008.

Jónsson, Guðmundur and Magnús S. Magnússon, eds. *Hagskinna. Icelandic Historical Statistics*. Reykjavík: Statistics Iceland, 1997.

Jónsson, Jónas B. "Tómstundir og tómstundaiðja íslenzkra ungmenna. Erindi flutt á 18. norræna kennaraþinginu í Khöfn 1961." *Menntamál* 34, no. 3 (1961): 237–44.

Jordheim, Knut. "Skolens rolle." In *Barn av sin tid*, edited by Bjarne Hodne and Sølvi Sogner, 89–101. Oslo: Universitetsforlaget, 1985.

Joutsivuo, Timo. "Papeiksi ja virkamiehiksi." In *Huoneentaulun maailma. Kasvatus ja koulutus Suomessa keskiajalta 1860-luvulle*, edited by Jussi Hanska and Kirsi Vainio-Korhonen, 112–83. Helsinki: Finnish Literature Society, 2010.

Junilla, Marianne and Seija Jalagin. "Encapsulated Experiences. Children in the Finnish Civil War." (Working paper).

Junnila, Olavi. *Hyvinkään seudun historia*. Hyvinkää: Hyvinkään kaupunki, 1988.

Junnila, Olavi. *Hyvinkään seurakunta 1917–1992*. Hyvinkää: Hyvinkään seurakunta, 1992.

Juul, Jesper. *Her er jeg! Hvem er du? Om nærvær, respekt og grenser mellom voksne og barn*. Oslo: Pedagogisk forum, (1998).

Jørgensen, Alfred Th. *Filantropiens Førere og Former i det Nittende Aarhundrede*. Copenhagen: Gyldendal, 1921.

Kaiser, Birgit. . . .ind i de voksnes rækker. En bog om konfirmationen. Copenhagen: Gad, 1992.

Kaldal, Ingar. Historisk forståing og forteljing. Oslo: Samlaget, 2003.

Kallenautio, Jorma. Lopen historia kunnallisen itsehallinnon aikana I. Loppi: Lopen kunta, seurakunta ja manttaalikunta, 1976.

Kanerva, Unto. Pumpulilaisia ja pruukilaisia. Tehdastyöväen työ- ja kotioloja Tampereella viime vuosisadalla. Helsinki: Tammi, 1946.

Karlsen Seim, Turid. "Hustavlen 1 Pet. 3.1–7 og dens tradisjonshistoriske sammenheng." Norsk teologisk Tidsskrift (1990): 101–114.

Karlsen Seim, Turid. "Interfacing House and Church: Converting Household Codes to Church Order." In Text, Image and Christians in the Græco-Roman World, edited by E. Alio Cisse Niang and Carolyn Osiek. Eugene, OR: Wipf & Stock Pub, 2012.

Kelen, Christopher (Kit) and Björn Sundmark, eds. The Nation in Children's Literature. London: Routledge, 2013.

Kennedy, David. The Well of Being: Childhood, Subjectivity, and Education. Albany: State University of New York Press, 2012.

Kent, Neil. The Sámi peoples of the North: a social and cultural history. London: Hurst, 2014.

Keskitalo, Oiva. Hausjärven historia. Hausjärvi: Hausjärven kunta ja Hausjärven seurakunta, 1964.

Kessler-Harris, Alice. Out to Work. A History of Wage-Earning Women in the United States. Oxford: Oxford University Press, 1983.

Key, Ellen. Barnets århundrade. Stockholm: Bonnier, 1900.

Key, Ellen. The Century of the Child. New York: G. P. Putnam's Sons, 1909.

Kibish, Christine Ozarowska. "Lucas Cranach's Christ Blessing the Children. A Problem of Lutheran Iconography." The Art Bulletin 37, no. 3 (1955): 196–203.

Kivi, Aleksis. Seven Brothers. Original in Finnish Seitsemän Veljestä (1870). Translated by Richard A. Impola. Beaverton, Ontario: Aspasia Books, Inc., 2005.

Kjartansson, Helgi Skúli. "Bókvitið í askana." In Almenningsfræðsla á Íslandi. Vol. 2: Skóli fyrir alla 1946–2008, edited by Loftur Guttormsson, 85–98. Reykjavík: Háskólaútgáfan, 2008a.

Kjartansson, Helgi Skúli. "Fræðslulögin í framkvæmd." In Almenningsfræðsla á Íslandi. Vol. 2: Skóli fyrir alla 1946-2008, edited by Loftur Guttormsson, 44–63. Reykjavík: Háskólaútgáfan, 2008b.

Kjørholt, Anne Trine. Barn som samfunnsborgere – til barnets beste? Oslo: Universitetsforlaget, 2010.

Klingberg, Göte. Den tidiga barnboken i Sverige: litterära strömningar, marknad, bildproduktion. Stockholm: Natur & kultur, 1998.

Koch, Hal. Grundtvig. Translated by Llewellyn Johns. Yellow Springs, OH: Antioch Press, 1952.

Kommissionen angaaende Statstilsyn med Børneopdragelsen. Betænkning. Copenhagen, 1895.

Kongl. Maj:ts Committerades betänkande om möjeligheten utaf Tiggeriets utrotande uti Götheborg genom förbättrade Arbetshus- och Fattigförsörjnings-Anstalter. Stockholm: Kongl. tryckeriet, 1797.

Kongl. Maj:ts Nådiga Kungörelse, Angående Den allmänna skyldigheten at bidraga til de Fattiges wård och försörjande. Gifwen Stockholms Slott den 14 Februarii 1811. Stockholm: Kongl. Tryckeriet, 1811.

Konsistorii Protokoll 7 och13 June 1808. In *Acta Till Stockholms Folkundervisnings Historia: 1533–1847,* edited by B. Rudolf Hall. Stockholm: Fören. för svensk undervisningshistoria, 1940.

Korsgaard, Ove. N. F. S. *Grundtvig – as a Political Thinker.* Translated by Edward Broadbridge. Copenhagen: Djof Publishing, 2014.

Kotivuori, Yrjö. *Ylioppilasmatrikkeli 1640–1852: Jakob Mudelius.* Verkkojulkaisu 2005. Online at www.helsinki.fi/ylioppilasmatrikkeli/henkilo.php?id=7515.

Krefting, Ellen, Aina Nøding, and Mona Ringvej. *En pokkers skrivesyge. 1700-tallets dansk-norske tidsskrifter mellom sensur og ytringsfrihet.* Oslo: Scandinavian Academic Press, 2014.

Kristelig Forening til Børns Redning. Jubilæumsskrift i Anledning af Foreningens 25-Aars Jubilæum. Copenhagen, 1923.

Kristensen, Evald Tang. *Sagn og overtro fra Jylland, samlede af Folkemunde. Sjette Samling.* Copenhagen, 1883.

Kristensen, Evald Tang. *Sagn og overtro fra Jylland, samlede af folkemunde. Anden samlings første afdeling.* Kolding, 1886.

Kristjansson, Baldur. "The Making of Nordic Childhood." In *Nordic Childhoods and Early Education: Philosophy, Research, Policy, and Practice in Denmark, Finland, Iceland, Norway, and Sweden,* edited by Johanna Einarsdottir and Judith T. Wagner, 13–42. Greenwich, CT: Information Age Publishing, 2006.

Kuparinen, Riitta. "Seitsemän veljeksen rippikoulu." Master thesis, University of Helsinki, 2012.

Kuusanmäki, Lauri. *Elämänmenoa entisaikaan.* Helsinki: WSOY, 1954.

Kuznets, Lois Rostow. *When Toys Come Alive: Narratives of Animation, Metamorphosis, and Development.* New Haven: Yale University Press, 1994.

Kåreland, Lena. "'Det är precis som om du var min mamma'. Det kompetenta barnet – ett tema i barnlitteraturen." In *Nedslag i børnelitteraturforskningen* 7, 163–186. Frederiksberg: Roskilde Universitetsforlag, 2006.

Lahtinen, Anu. "Piika: nuori, naimaton palvelusnainen 1300–1600." In *Työteliäs ja uskollinen: Naiset piikoina ja palvelijoina keskiajalta nykyaikaan,* edited by Marjatta Rahikainen and Kirsi Vainio-Korhonen, 32–49. Helsinki: Finnish Literature Society, 2006.

Lahtinen, Anu. "Mägde und weibliches Gesinde 1300–1600." In *Arbeitsam und gefügig: Zur Geschichte der Frauenarbeit in Finnland,* edited by Marjatta Rahikainen and Kirsi Vainio-Korhonen, 23–39. Berlin: Berliner Wissenschaftsverlag, 2007.

Laine, Esko M. and Tuija Laine. "Kirkollinen kansanopetus." In *Huoneentaulun maailma. Kasvatus ja koulutus Suomessa keskiajalta 1860-luvulle,* edited by Jussi Hanska and Kirsi Vainio-Korhonen, 258–306. Helsinki: Finnish Literature Society, 2010.

Laine, Leena and Pirjo Markkola, eds. *Tuntematon työläisnainen.* Tampere: Vastapaino, 1989.

Landstad, Magnus B. *Fra Telemarken. Skik og Sagn. Efterladte Optegnelser.* Norsk Folkeminnelags Skrifter. Vol. 15. Oslo: Norsk Folkeminnelag, 1927.

Landstad, Magnus B. *Skrifter 1. Sagn. Med innledning og kommentarer av Ørnulf Hodne,* edited by Herleik Baklid. Oslo: Novus, 2012.

Langset, Edvard. *Segner, gåter, folketru på Nordmør.* Norsk Folkeminnelags Skrifter. Vol. 61. Oslo: Norsk Folkeminnelag, 1948.

Larsen, Christian, Erik Nørr, and Pernille Sonne. *Da skolen tog form: 1780–1850.* Dansk skolehistorie. Vol. 2. Aarhus: Aarhus Universitetsforlag, 2013.

Lee, Nick. *Childhood and Society: Growing up in an Age of Uncertainty.* Buckingham: Open University Press, 2001.

Lehto, Katri. *Maria Heikintytär Kytäjältä: Ihmisiä ja kohtaloita 1700-luvun Suomessa.* Helsinki: Otava, 1989.

Lehto, Katri. "Linder, Marie (1840–1870)." In *Kansallisbiografia*, edited by Matti Klinge et al. Helsinki: Finnish Literature Society, 2000. Online at www.kansallisbiografia.fi.

Lehto, Katri. "Rahkonen, Aleksanteri (1841–1877)." In *Kansallisbiografia*, edited by Matti Klinge et al. Helsinki: Finnish Literature Society, 2000. Online at www.kansallisbiografia.fi.

Lehto, Katri. "Kytäjän ensimmäinen kansakoulu ja sen opettaja Aleksanteri Rahkonen." In *Mennyttä aikaa muistellen: Kytäjä ennen ja nyt*, edited by Raimo Pajamo, 9–15. Hyvinkää: Kytäjän kyläyhdistys, 2010.

Leinberg, K. G. *Handlingar rörande finska kyrkan och presterskapet: 1535–1627.* Jyväskylä: Jyväskylä Boktryckeri, 1892.

Leino-Kaukiainen, Pirkko and Anja Heikkinen. "Yhteiskunta ja koulutus." In *Valistus ja koulunpenkki. Kasvatus ja koulutus Suomessa 1860-luvulta 1960-luvulle*, edited by A. Heikkinen and P. Leino-Kaukiainen, 16–33. Helsinki: Finnish Literature Society, 2011.

Lewis, C. S. "Sometimes Fairy Stories May Say Best What's to Be Said." In *Of Other Worlds: Essays and Stories*, edited by C. S. Lewis, 35–38. New York: Harcourt, 1994.

Lilius, A. *Tilattoman väen oloista Kuopion läänissä.* Tutkimuksia taloudellisista oloista Suomen maaseudulla. Vol. 3. Helsinki, 1889.

Lindberger, Örjan. *Människan i tiden. Eyvind Johnsons liv och författarskap 1938–1976 – Norrbottningen som blev europé. Eyvind Johnsons liv och författarskap till och med Romanen om Olof.* Stockholm: Bonnier, 1986.

Lindén, Astrid. "Sex meter tarmar och samma rättigheter." *Författarbloggen.* Nerikes Allehanda, 2013.

Lindensjö, Bo. "From Liberal Common School to State Primary School. A Main Line in Social Democratic Educational Policy." In *Creating Social Democracy: A Century of the Social Democratic Labor Party in Sweden*, edited by Klaus Misgeld et al., 307–37. University Park, PA: Penn. State University Press, 1988.

Lindgren, Astrid and Ingrid Vang Nyman. *Pippi Långstrump.* Stockholm: Rabén & Sjögren, 1944.

Lindgren, Astrid. *Aldrig Våld!.* Lidingö: Salikon, 1978/2011.

Lindgren, Astrid. *Pippi in the South Seas.* Translated by Marianne Turner. Oxford and New York: Oxford University Press, 2012.

Lindmark, Daniel. "New Wine into Old Bottles. Luther's Table of Duties as a Vehicle of Changing Civic Virtues in 18th- and 19th-Century Sweden." In *Schooling and the Making of Citizens in the Long Nineteenth Century: Comparative Visions*, edited by Daniel Tröhler et al. London and New York: Routledge, 2011.

Linge, Karl. *Stockholms folkskolors organisation och förvaltning åren 1842–1861: studier i den svenska folkskolans historia.* Stockholm: Norstedt, 1914.

Lohse, Bernhard. *Luthers Theologie in ihrer historischen Entwicklung.* Göttingen: Vandenhoeck und Ruprecht, 1995.

Lo-Johansson, Ivar. *God-natt, Jord.* Stockholm: Bonnier, 1933.

Lo-Johansson, Ivar. *Breaking Free.* Translated by Rochelle Wright. Lincoln: University of Nebraska, 1990.

Lord, Cynthia. *Rules.* New York: Scholastic, 2008.

Lorås, Jostein. "Muntlige kilder – faktuelle eller narrative lesemåter?" *Historisk tidsskrift* 3 (2007): 433–47.

"Lov om Behandling af forbryderske og forsømte Børn og unge Personer." *Lovtidende for 1905* no. 29. 1905.

Lund, Eiliv, Marita Melhus, Ketil Lenert Hansen, Tove Nystad, Ann Ragnhild Broderstad, Randi Selmer, and Per G. Lund-Larsen. "Population based study of health and living conditions in areas with both Sami and Norwegian populations – the SAMINOR study." *Int J Circumpolar Health* 66, no. 2 (2007): 113–28.

Lund, Ragnhild Elisabeth. "'I sangen møtes vi på felles grunn' – om sang og sangbøker i norsk skole." *Acta Didactica* 4, no. 1 (2010): 1-21. Online at www.journals.uio.no/index.php/adno/index.

Lund, Svein, Elfrid Boine, and Siri Broch Johansen, eds. *Sámi skuvlahistorjá: artihkkalat ja muitalusat Sámi skuvlaeallimis.* Vol. 1. Karasjok: Davvi Girji, 2005.

Lunde, Peter. *Kynnehuset. Vestegdske folkeminne.* Norsk Folkeminnelags Skrifter. Vol. 6. Oslo: Norsk Folkeminnelag, 1924.

Lunde, Peter. *Folkeminne frå Søgne.* Norsk Folkeminnelags Skrifter. Vol. 103. Oslo: Universitetsforlaget, 1969.

Lundgreen-Nielsen, Flemming. "Grundtvig and Romanticism." In *Kierkegaard and His Contemporaries: The Culture of Golden Age Denmark*, edited by Jon Stewart. Berlin: Walter de Gruyter, 2003.

Lundqvist, Ulla. "Always on the Child's Side." *Barnboken: Astrid Lindgren Centennial Conference* 1–2 (2007): 6–14.

Luther, Martin. *Das Taufbüchlein.* Wittenberg, 1523.

Luther, Martin. *An die Ratsherren aller Städte deutschen Landes, daß sie christliche Schulen aufrichten und halten sollen (1524).* In *D. Martin Luthers Werke. Kritische Gesamtausgabe*, edited by Paul Pietsch, 9–53. Weimar: Hermann Böhlaus Nachfolger, 1899.

Luther, Martin. *Vom ehelichen Leben.* In *D. Martin Luthers Werke. Kritische Gesamtausgabe*, vol. 10/2, edited by Karl Drescher, 267–304. Weimar: Hermann Böhlaus Nachfolger, 1907.

Luther, Martin. *Der Grosse Katechismus, 1529.* In *D. Martin Luthers Werke. Kritische Gesamtausgabe*, vol. 30/1, edited by Karl Drescher, 123–238. Weimar: Hermann Böhlaus Nachfolger, 1910.

Luther, Martin. "Open Letter to the Christian Nobility of the German Nation Concerning the Reform of the Christian Estate [1520]." In M. Luther, *Three Treatises*, 7–113. Philadelphia: Fortress Press, 1960.

Lyotard, Jean-François. *La condition postmoderne. Rapport sur le savoir.* Paris: Éditions de minuit, 1979.

Lüthi, Max. *The European Folktale: Form and Nature.* Bloomington: Indiana University Press, 1986.

Lög um fræðslu barna nr. 94/1936.

Lög um fræðslu barna nr. 34/1946.

Løkke, Anne. *Vildfarende Børn – om forsømte og kriminelle børn mellem filantropi og stat 1880–1920.* Holte: Forlaget SocPol, 1990.

MacLean, Robert. "Hans Christian Andersen's 'The Steadfast Tin Soldier': Variations upon Silence and Love." *Ritsumeikan Bungaku* no. 586 (2004): 25–42.

Markkola, Pirjo. *Työläiskodin synty. Tamperelaiset työläisperheet ja yhteiskunnallinen kysymys 1870-luvulta 1910-luvulle.* Helsinki: Finnish Historical Society, 1994.

Markkola, Pirjo. "'God Wouldn't Send a Child into the World without a Crust of Bread'. Child Labour as Part of Working-Class Family Economy in Finland 1890–1920." In *Industrious Children. Work and Childhood in the Nordic Countries 1850–1990*, edited by N. de Coninck-Smith, B. Sandin, and E. Schrumpf, 79–105. Odense: Odense University Press, 1997.

Markkola, Pirjo. "Moninainen maalaisnuoriso." In *Nuoruuden vuosisata. Suomalaisen nuorison historia*, edited by S. Aapola and M. Kaarninen, 129–59. Helsinki: Finnish Literature Society, 2003.

Markkola, Pirjo, and Ann-Catrin Östman. "Torparfrågan tillspetsas. Frigörelse, oberoende och arbete – 1918 års torparlagstiftning ur mansperspektiv." *Historisk tidskrift för Finland* 1 (2012): 17–41.

Markussen, Ingrid. *Visdommens lænker : studier i enevældens skolereformer fra Reventlow til skolelov*. Odense: Landbohistorisk Selskab, 1988.

Markussen, Ingrid. *Til Skaberens Ære, Statens Tjeneste og Vor Egen Nytte. Pietistiske og kameralistiske ideer bag fremkomsten af en offentlig skole i land-distrikterne i Danmark i 1700-tallet*. Odense: Odense Universitetsforlag, 1995.

Markussen, Ingrid. "Hustavlen og Aristoteles – en disciplinerende affære." *ARR. Idehistorisk tidsskrift* 4 (2013): 37–51.

Markussen, Ingrid. *"Sagens rette Beskaffenhed." Johan Ludvig Reventlows skolere-former 1783 set i lyset af en forældreklage*. Forthcoming.

Marshall, Peter. *Beliefs and the Dead in Reformation England*. Oxford: Oxford University Press, 2002.

Marshall, Thomas Humphrey, and Tom Bottomore. *Citizenship and Social Class*. London: Pluto Press, 1992.

Martikainen, Eeva. "Baptism." In *Engaging Luther. A (New) Theological Assessment*, edited by Olla-Pekka Vainio, 95–107. Eugene, OR: Cascade Books, 2010.

Martin, Andrew J., Brad Papworth, Paul Ginns, and Gregory Arief D. Liem. "Boarding School, Academic Motivation and Engagement, and Psychological Well-Being." *American Educational Research Journal* 51, no. 5 (2014): 1007–49.

Martinson, Harry. *Nässlorna blomma*. Stockholm: Bonnier, 1935.

Martinson, Harry. *Flowering Nettle*. Translated by Naomi Walford. London: Cresset Press, 1936.

Martinson, Moa. *Mor gifter sig*. Stockholm: Bonnier, 1936.

Martinson, Moa. *My Mother Gets Married*. Translated by Margaret S. Lacy. New York: Feminist Press, 1988.

Mason, Mary Ann. *From Father's Property to Children's Rights: A History of Child Custody in America*. New York: Columbia University Press, 1994.

Mattsson, Per Olof. "Eyvind Johnsons brottning med Martin Andersen Nexø." In *Från Nexø till Alakoski. Aspekter på nordisk arbetarlitteratur*, edited by Bibi Jonsson et al., 115–29. Lund: Absalon, 2011.

Mattsson, Per Olof. "Vem sökte upp vem? Ivar Lo-Johanssons relation till Martin Andersen Nexø." In *Från Bruket till Yarden. Nordiska perspektiv på arbetarlit-teratur*, edited by Bibi Jonsson et al., 69–81. Lund: Absalon, 2014.

Mauland, Torkell. *Folkeminne fraa Rogaland. Fyrste bandet*. Norsk Folkeminnelags Skrifter. Vol. 17. Oslo: Norsk Folkeminnelag, 1928.

Mauland, Torkell. *Folkeminne fraa Rogaland. Andre bandet*. Norsk Folkeminnelags Skrifter. Vol. 26. Oslo: Norsk Folkeminnelag, 1931.

Maurer, Wilhelm. *Luthers Lehre von den drei Hierarchien und ihr mittelalterlicher Hintergrund*. Bayerische Akademie der Wissenschaften, philologische-historische

Klasse, Sitzungsbereich, Vol. 4. Munich: Verlag der Bayerischen Akademie der Wissenschaften, 1970.

McClennen, Sophia A., and Alexandra S. Moore, eds. *The Routledge Companion to Literature and Human Rights*. Abingdon, Oxon: Routledge, 2015.

Meek, Margaret. *Children's Literature and National Identity*. Stoke-on-Trent: Trentham Books, 2001.

Melbøe, Line, Bjørn-Eirik Johansen, Gunn Elin Fredreheim, and Ketil Lenert Hansen. "Situasjonen til samer med funksjonsnedsettelse." Stockholm: Nordens Välfärdscenter, 2016.

Melbøe, Line, Ketil Lenert Hansen, Bjørn-Eirik Johansen, Gunn Elin Fedreheim, Tone Dinesen, Gunn-Tove Minde, and Marit Rustad. "Ethical and methodological issues in research with Sami experiencing disability." *Int J Circumpolar Health* 75 (2016): 31656.

Melton, James Van Horn. *Absolutism and the Eighteenth-Century Origins of Compulsory Schooling in Prussia and Austria*. Cambridge: Cambridge University Press, 1988.

Meløy, Lydolf Lind. *Internatliv i Finnmark: skolepolitikk 1900–1940*. Oslo: Samlaget, 1980.

Merleau-Ponty, Maurice. *Phenomenology of Perception*. London and New York: Routledge, 2012.

Miettinen, Tiina. *Ihanteista irrallaan: Hämeen maaseudun nainen osana perhettä ja asiakirjoja 1600-luvun alusta 1800-luvun alkuun*. Tampere: Tampereen yliopisto, 2012.

Miller, Pavla. *Transformations of Patriarchy in the West, 1500–1800*. Bloomington and Indianapolis: Indiana University Press, 1998.

Minde, Henry. "Assimilation of the Sami: Implementation and Consequences." *Acta Borealia* 2 (2003): 121–46.

Minde, Henry. *Assimilation of the Sami: implementation and consequences*. Kautokeino: Resource Centre for the Rights of Indigenous Peoples, 2005.

Mischliwietz, Sandra. "Att uppfinna ord – Kindheit als Strategie der Weltaneignung in der Schwedischen Arbeiterliteratur der 1930er Jahre." Münster: Monstenstein und Vannerdat, 2014.

Moe, Birgitte Furberg. "Barndomshistorier i tre århundrer: en bokhistorisk analyse av I brønnen og i tjernet." Master thesis, University of Oslo, 2009.

Moe, Jørgen. *I Brønden og i Kjærnet: Smaahistorier for Børn*. Christiania: Feilberg & Landmark, 1851.

Moe, Jørgen. *In the Pond and on the Hill. Stories for Boys and Girls*. Translated by Jessie Young. London: Suttaby & Co., 1883.

Moe, Moltke. *Folkeminne frå Bøherad. Etter uppskrifter av Moltke Moe*. Norsk Folkeminnelags Skrifter. Vol. 9. Oslo: Norsk Folkeminnelag, 1925.

Moeller, Bernd, ed. *Die frühe Reformation in Deutschland als Umbruch*. Schriften des Vereins für Reformationsgeschichte 199. Gütersloh: Gütersloher Verlagshaus, 1998.

Morsink, Johannes. "World War Two and the Universal Declaration. (1948 UN Universal Declaration of Human Rights)." *Human Rights Quarterly* 15, no. 2 (1993): 357–405.

Myhre, Reidar. *Idé og virkelighet. Den norske skoles utvikling*. Oslo: Ad Notam Gyldendal, 1992.

Myrdal, Alva and Gunnar Myrdal. *Kris i befolkningsfrågan*. Stockholm: Bonnier, 1934.

Müller, Joseph. *Fattigvården i Stockholm från äldre till nyare tid: jämte beskrifning af Stockholms stads arbetsinrättningar med anledning af den nya arbetsinrättningens fullbordan: en historisk öfversikt.* Stockholm: Kungl. Hofboktryckeriet, Iduns Tryckeri Aktiebolag 1906.

Müller, Poul. "Af en skoledrengs taske." *Af landsbyskolens saga.* Danmarks Lærerforening. 1964.

Mørch, Andreas. *Frå gamle dagar. Folkeminne frå Sigdal og Eggedal.* Norsk Folkeminnelags Skrifter. Vol. 27. Oslo: Norsk Folkeminnelag, 1932.

National Archives of Finland, the: Hausjärvi Parish Archives, Linder Family Records, Loppi Parish Archives, Nurmijärvi Parish Archives.

Nergård, Jens-Ivar. "Virksomhet, konvensjonalitet og menneske: en sosialfilosofisk studie av avvik." Tromsø: PhD thesis, University of Tromsø 1979.

Nergård, Jens-Ivar and Hans Ragnar Mathiesen. *Det skjulte Nord-Norge.* Oslo: Ad Notam Gyldendal, 1994.

Nergård, Jens-Ivar and Jan Eriksen. *Den levende erfaring: en studie i samisk kunnskapstradisjon.* Oslo: Cappelen akademisk, 2006.

Nielsen, Beth Grothe. *"Letfærdige Qvindfolk."* Fosterdrab og fødsel i dølgsmål i retshistorisk belysning. Hæfte 1, Stencilserie Nr. 11. Copenhagen: Kriminalistisk Institut, Københavns Universitet, 1980.

Nielsen, Ernest D. "N. F. S. Grundtvig on Luther." In *Interpreters of Luther,* edited by Jaroslav Pelikan. Philadelphia: Fortress Press, 1968.

Nikolajeva, Maria. *Power, Voice and Subjectivity in Literature for Young Readers.* New York: Routledge, 2010.

Nilsson, Magnus. *Den moderne Ivar Lo-Johansson. Modernisering, modernitet och modernism i statarromanerna.* Hedemora: Gidlunds, 2003.

Nissen, Gunnhild. *Bønder, skole og demokrati: En undersøgelse i fire provstier af forhldet mellem den offentlige skole og befolkningen på landet i tiden ca. 1880–1910.* Copenhagen: Institut for dansk skolehistorie, 1973.

Nordbø, Olav. *Før i tida. Gamalt frå Bøherad.* Norsk Folkeminnelags Skrifter. Vol. 85. Oslo: Universitetsforlaget, 1960.

Norske lov. *Kong Christian Den Femtes Norske Lov 15de April 1687.* Oslo: Universitetsforlaget, 1982. Online at www.hf.uio.no/iakh/forskning/prosjekter/tingbok/kilder/chr5web/chr5register.html.

Noss, Aagot. *Høgtider og samkomer.* Norsk Folkeminnelags Skrifter. Vol. 90. Oslo: Universitetsforlaget, 1963.

Nurmi, Veli. "Wallin, Olai (1832–1896)." In *Kansallisbiografia,* edited by Matti Klinge et al. Helsinki: Finnish Literature Society, 2007. Online at www.kansallisbiografia.fi.

Nykvist, Karin. "Through the Eyes of a Child: Childhood and Mass Dictatorship in Modern European Literature." In *Imagining Mass Dictatorships. The Individual and the Masses in Literature and Cinema,* edited by Michael Schoenhals et al., 94–120. London: Palgrave MacMillan, 2013.

Nystad, Inger Marie K. *Mannen mellom myte og modernitet.* Nesbru: Vett og viten, 2003.

Nyström, Per. *Stadsindustriens arbetare före 1800-talet: bidrag till kännedom om den svenska manufakturindustrien och dess sociala förhållanden.* Stockholm: Tiden, 1955.

Nøkleby, Berit, and Guri Hjeltnes. *Barn under krigen.* Oslo: Aschehoug, 2000.

Nørregaard, Lauritz. *Natur-Rettens første Grunde.* Copenhagen, 1784.

Österlund, Mia. "Flickan ritar sig fri: det naiva barnperspektivet i den postmoderna bilderboken." *Tidskrift för litteraturvetenskap* 1 (2009): 19–33.

Oftestad, Bernt T., Jan Schumacher, and Tarald Rasmussen. *Norsk kirkehistorie.* Oslo: Universitetsforlaget, 1993.

Ohlander, Ann-Sofie. "The Invisible Child? The Struggle over Social Democratic Family Policy." In *Creating Social Democracy: A Century of the Social Democratic Labor Party in Sweden,* edited by Klaus Misgeld et al., 213–36. University Park, PA: Pennsylvania State University Press, 1988.

Ojala, Jari, Jari Eloranta and Jukka Jalava, eds. *The Road to Prosperity. An Economic History of Finland.* Helsinki: Finnish Literature Society, 2006.

Ólafsson, Stefán. "Vinnan og menningin. Um áhrif lífsskoðunar á vinnuna." *Skírnir* 164 (1996): 99–124.

Olsen, Kåre. *Krigens barn. De norske krigsbarn og deres mødre.* Oslo: Aschehoug, 1998.

Olsen, Ole Tobias. *Norske folkeeventyr og sagn. Samlet i Nordland.* Kristiania: Cappelen, 1912.

Olsson, Lars. *Då barn var lönsamma. Om arbetsdelning, barnarbete och teknologiska förändringar i några svenska industrier under 1800- och början av 1900-talet.* Stockholm: Tidens förlag, 1980.

O'Malley, Andrew. *The Making of the Modern Child: Children's Literature and Childhood in the Late Eighteenth Century.* New York: Routledge, 2003.

Ommundsen, Åse Marie. *Djevelfrø og englebarn: synet på barn i kristne barneblader i perioden 1875 til 1910.* Oslo: University of Oslo, 1998.

Ommundsen, Åse Marie. "Barnebokas begynnelse. Kulturkamp, identitet og nasjonsbygging i 1800-tallets Norge." In *På terskelen. Bidrag om nordisk barne- og ungdomslitteratur,* edited by Harald Bache-Wiig, 27–38. Oslo: Novus, 2006.

Ommundsen, Åse Marie. *Litterære grenseoverskridelser. Når grensene mellom barne- og voksenlitteraturen viskes ut.* Oslo: Universitetet i Oslo, 2010.

Ommundsen, Åse Marie. "Avkolonisert barndom, koloniserende teori? – Internasjonal barnelitterær teori i konflikt med kunstnerisk praksis i samtidens norske barnelitteratur." *Edda* 112, no. 2 (2012): 104–15.

Ommundsen, Åse Marie. *Looking out and Looking in: National Identity in Picturebooks of the New Millennium.* Oslo: Novus Press, 2013a.

Ommundsen, Åse Marie. "Tales of the King: Building National Identity in Contemporary Norwegian Picturebooks About the King." In *Looking out and Looking in: National Identity in Picturebooks of the New Millennium,* edited by Åse Marie Ommundsen. Oslo: Novus Press, 2013b.

Ommundsen, Åse Marie. "Who Are These Picturebooks For? Controversial Picturebooks and the Question of Audience." In *Challenging and Controversial Picturebooks,* edited by Janet Evans. London and New York: Routledge, 2015.

Opedal, Halldor O. *Makter og menneske. Folkeminne ifrå Hardanger II.* Norsk Folkeminnelags Skrifter. Vol. 32. Oslo: Norsk Folkeminnelag, 1934.

Opedal, Halldor O. *Makter og menneske. Folkeminne ifrå Hardanger III.* Norsk Folkeminnelags Skrifter. Vol. 38. Oslo: Norsk Folkeminnelag, 1937.

Orlov, Janina. "'Var glad som sparven kvittrar' – barnlitteraturen." In *Finlands svenska litteraturhistoria,* edited by Johan Wrede. Stockholm: Atlantis, 1999.

O'Sullivan, Emer. "Internationalism, the Universal Child and the World of Children's Literature." In *International Companion Encyclopedia of Children's Literature,* edited by Peter Hunt. London: Routledge, 2004.

Ot.prp. nr. 33 (1986–87): *Om lov om Sametinget og andre samiske rettsforhold. (Sameloven)*. Oslo: Justis- og politidepartementet, 1987.

Ozment, Steven. *When Fathers Ruled. Family Life in Reformation Europe.* Cambridge, MA: Harvard University Press, 1983.

Ozment, Steven. *The Serpent and the Lamb. Cranach, Luther, and the Making of the Reformation.* New Haven and London: Yale University Press, 2011.

Palacio, R. J. *Wonder.* New York: Knopf, 2012.

Palander, Seppo. *Hausjärven suutarit: sosiaalinen sukututkimus Hausjärvellä 1771– 1894 toimineista suutareista.* Helsinki: Seppo Palander, 1998.

Palladius, Peder. "Visitasbog." In *Peder Palladius' Danske Skrifter*, vol. 5, edited by Lis Jacobsen, 1–240. Copenhagen: Universitets-Jubilæets danske Samfund, 1925–1926.

Palmenfelt, Ulf. "Barndom som kultur." In *Barndomens kulturalisering. Kulturforskning i Norden 1*, edited by Ulf Palmenfelt, 7–15. Åbo: NNF, 1999.

Parr, Joy. *Labouring Children. British Immigrant Apprentices to Canada, 1869– 1924.* Toronto: University of Toronto Press, 1980.

Pelikan, Jaroslav and Helmut T. Lehmann, eds. *Luthers' Works.* 55 vols. Philadelphia: Muehlenberg and Fortress; and St. Louis: Concordia, 1955–1986.

Petersson, Annie, ed. *Nu ska vi sjunga.* Stockholm: Almquist & Wiksells Förlag, 1943.

Pettersen, Torunn. "Sámi ethnicity as variable. Premises and implications for population-based studies on health and living conditions in Norway." PhD thesis. The Arctic University of Norway (Tromsø) 2015.

Pettersen, Torunn, and Magritt Brustad. "Same Sámi? A comparison of self-reported Sámi ethnicity measures in 1970 and 2003 in selected rural areas in northern Norway." *Ethnic and Racial Studies* 38, no 12. (2015): 2071–89.

Pinchbeck, Ivy and Margaret Hewitt. *Children in English Society.* Vol. 2. London: Routledge & Kegan Paul, 1973.

Pinker, Steven. *The Better Angels of Our Nature: Why Violence Has Declined.* New York: Penguin, 2011.

Pleijel, Hilding. *Från Hustavlans tid. Kyrkohistoriska folklivsstudier.* Stockholm: Svenska kyrkans diakonistyrelses bokförlag, 1951.

Pleijel, Hilding. *Hustavlans värld. Kyrkligt folkliv i äldre tiders Sverige.* Stockholm: Verbum, 1970.

Pontoppidan, Erik. *Sandhed til Gudfrygtighed, udi Een eenfoldig og efter Muelighed kort, dog Tilstrekkelig Forklaring over Sal. Doct. Mort. Luthers Liden Catechismo, Indholdende Alt det, som den, der vil blive salig, har behov at vide og giøre, paa Kongel. allernaadigste befaling. Til almindelig Brug.* Copenhagen, 1737.

Pontoppidan Erik. *Kort og eenfoldig Underviisning for Skoleholderne. Om den Maade paa hvilken, de best kunde lere at lese i Bøger, Saa og med Barnagtige Ord begynde at tae med dem om GUD og hans Villie til vor Salighed.* Bergen, 1748; Copenhagen, 1763.

Pontoppidan, Erik. *Opvækkelige Hyrde-Breve 1749–52.* Bergen, 1753.

Pontoppidan, Erik. *Explanation of Luther's Small Catechism.* Based on Dr. Erick Pontoppidan by Rev. H. U. Sverdrup. Minneapolis, 1900.

Pontoppidan, Erik. *FEJEKOST til at udfeje den gamle surdejg eller de i de danske lande tiloversblevne og her for dagen bragte levninger af saavel hedenskab som papisme. 1736.* Translated by Jørgen Olrik. Folkeminder nr. 27. Copenhagen: Det Schønbergske Forlag, 1923.

Pontoppidan, Erik. *Collegium Pastorale Practicum, Indeholdende en fornøden Underviisning, Advarsel, Raadførelse og Opmuntring for dennem, som enten berede sig til at tiene Gud og Næsten i det hellige Præste-Embede, eller og leve allerede deri, og yndske at udrette med Frugt og Opbyggelse.* Copenhagen, 1757; Christiansand: Steen, 1850; Oslo: Luther Forlag i samarbeid med DELK, 1986.

Private archives of the descendants of Pelet and Ida Sykäri, Estate of Sykäri.

Private archives of the Manor of Kytäjä.

Pullman, Philip. *Fairy Tales from the Brothers Grimm: A New English Version.* New York: Viking, 2012.

Puntila, L. A. "Yliopistonkäynti Hämeen läänin pitäjistä vv. 1800–49." In *Hämeenmaa IV. Hämeen elämää ja oloja,* edited by S. Mattsson, Elis Nieminen, Aukusti Salo, Felix Seppälä, Väinö Uusoksa, and Antti Valve, 93–140. Hämeenlinna: Hämeenlinnan heimoliitto, 1934.

Qvarsell, Birgitta. "Barns perspektiv och mänskliga rättigheter. Godhetsmaximering eller kunskapsbildning?" *Pedagogisk Forskning i Sverige* 1–2 (2003): 101–13.

Qvist, Gunnar. "Kvinnofrågan i Sverige 1809–1846: studier rörande kvinnans näringsfrihet inom de borgerliga yrkena." PhD. diss, University of Gothenburg, 1960.

Qvortrup, Jens. *Childhood Matters: Social Theory, Practice and Policies.* Aldershot: Avebury, 1994.

Rahikainen, Marjatta. "Rahvaan lapset." In *Huoneentaulun maailma. Kasvatus ja koulutus Suomessa keskiajalta 1860-luvulle,* edited by Jussi Hanska and Kirsi Vainio-Korhonen, 340–60. Helsinki: Finnish Literature Society, 2010.

Rapport till uppfostringskommittén 1813. In *Acta till Stockholms större latinläroverks historia 1419–1840,* edited by B. Rudolf Hall. Stockholm: Fören. för svensk undervisningshistoria, 1939.

Rasmussen Søkilde, Niels. "De Reventlowske Skoler for 100 Aar siden som de første filantropiske Folkeskoler i Danmark med Seminariet og Opdragelsesanstalten Bernstorfsminde." 1883.

Reeh, Niels. "Religion and the State of Denmark – State Religious Politics in the Elementary School System from 1721 to 1975: An Alternative Approach to Secularization." PhD diss., University of Copenhagen, 2006.

Reiersen, John. *Skolen i Finnmarken.* Hammerfest: Hagen, 1915.

Rektors reformkrav och redogörelse 1813. In *Acta till Stockholms större latinläroverks historia 1419–1840,* edited by B. Rudolf Hall. Stockholm: Fören. för svensk undervisningshistoria, 1939.

Rendahl, Viking. "Grunddragen av skolväsendets organisation i Stockholm under 1800-talet." In *Årsberättelse / Stockholms stads arkivnämnd och stadsarkiv,* 18–72. Stockholm: Stockhoms Stadsarkiv, 1974.

Retssagen mod Skoleholder Pade. Brahetrolleborg godsarkiv, Rigsarkivet, Odense.

Rhedin, Ulla. "Det konsekventa barnperspektivet i barnlitteraturen." In *Barndomens kulturalisering. Kulturforskning i Norden 1,* edited by Ulf Palmenfelt, 93–108. Åbo: NNF, 1999.

Rhedin, Ulla. "Kaos och ordning: att berätta ur barnets perspektiv och våga möta barndomens mörker." In *En fanfar för bilderboken!,* edited by Ulla Rhedin, Lena Eriksson, and Oscar K., 11–14. Stockholm: Alfabeta, 2013.

Richardson, Gunnar, ed. *Ett folk börjar skolan. Folkskolan 150 år. 1842–1992.* Stockholm: Allmänna Förlaget, 1992.

Riedel, Manfred. "Bürger, Staatsbürger, Bürgertum." In *Geschichtliche Grundbegriffe. Historisches Lexikon zur politisch-sozialen Sprache in Deutschland*, edited by Otto Brunner, Werner Conze, and Reinhart Koselleck. Stuttgart: Klett-Cotta, 1972.

Rimmon-Kenan, Shlomith. *Narrative Fiction: Contemporary Poetics*. London and New York: Routledge, 1983.

Ringvej, Mona. *Marcus Thrane. Forbrytelse og straff*. Oslo: Pax, 2014.

Roberts, Elizabeth. *A Woman's Place: An Oral History of Working-Class Women 1890–1940*. Oxford: Blackwell, 1984.

Roos, Merethe. *Enlightened Preaching. Balthasar Münter's Authorship 1772–1793*. Leiden: Brill, 2013.

Rosén, Ragnar, ed. *Liber Scholae Helsingforsensis 1691–1865*. Helsinki: Suomen sukututkimusseura, 1936.

Rosenblatt, Roger. "Journalist, Author Roger Rosenblatt Outlines His 4 Reasons to Write," Interview by Jeffrey Brown at PBS NEWSHOUR (2011). Online at www. pbs.org/newshour/bb/entertainment-jan-june11-rosenblatt_01-31/.

Rudberg, Monica. *Dydige, sterke, lykkelige barn: ideer om oppdragelse i borgelig tradisjon*. Oslo: Universitetsforlaget, 1983.

Rudd, David. *Reading the Child in Children's Literature: An Heretical Approach*. Basingstoke: Palgrave Macmillan, 2013.

Rust, Val D. *The Democratic Tradition and the Evolution of Schooling in Norway*. New York: Praeger, 1989.

Rönbeck, Carl Sonnberg, ed. *Kongl. commiténs till öfwerseende och förbättring af fattigwården i Stockholm underdåniga skrifwelse till kongl. maj:t i anledning af hosgående plan. Med kongl. maj:ts allernådigste tillstånd från trycket utgifwen af S. Rönbeck*. Stockholm: Carl Delén, 1807.

Rørvik, Thor Inge. "The Generation of 1814. Aspects of an Extinct Paradigm of Breeding." In *Scandinavian Studies in Rhetoric. Rhetorica Scandinavica 1977–2010*, edited by Jens E. Kjeldsen, and Jan Grue, 330–49. Ödåkra: Retorikförlaget, 2011.

Røstad, Anton. *Frå gamal tid. Folkeminne frå Verdal*. Norsk Folkeminnelags Skrifter. Vol. 25. Oslo: Norsk Folkeminnelag, 1931.

Saguisag, Lara and Matthew B. Prickett. "Introduction: Children's Rights and Children's Literature." *The Lion and the Unicorn* 40, no. 2 (2016): v–xii.

Sámi logut muitalit 8: čielggaduvvon sámi statistihkka 2015. Kautokeino: Sámi allaskuvla, 2015.

Sámi logut muitalit 9: čielggaduvvon sámi statistihkka 2016. Kautokeino: Sámi allaskuvla, 2016.

Samuelsen, Jakob Andr. *Vesterålen*. Norsk Folkeminnesamling (NFS), Institutt for kulturstudier og orientalske språk (IKOS), University of Oslo. 1935.

Samuelsen, Jakob Andr. *Folkeminne frå Modum*. Norsk Folkeminnelags Skrifter. Vol. 97. Oslo: Universitetsforlaget, 1966.

Sandin, Bengt. *Hemmet, gatan, fabriken eller skolan: folkundervisning och barnupp-fostran i svenska städer 1600–1850*. PhD diss. Lund: Arkiv Förlag, 1986.

Sandin, Bengt. "Education, Culture and Surveillance of the Population in Stockholm 1600–1840. Continuity and Change of Culture and Social Structure in an Early Modern Society." *Continuity and Change* 1 (1988): 357–390.

Sandin, Bengt. "Split Visions, Changing Childhoods and the Welfare State in Sweden. Reflections on the Century of the Child." *Working Papers on Childhood and the Study of Children* 4 (1995): 1–17.

Sandin, Bengt. "Children and the Swedish Welfare State: From Different to Similar." In *Reinventing Childhood after World War II*, edited by Paula S. Fass and Michael Grossberg. Philadelphia: University of Pennsylvania, 2012.

Sandin, Bengt. "Infanticide, Abortion, Children, and Childhood in Sweden, 1000–1980." In *The Routledge History of Childhood in the Western World*, edited by Paula S. Fass, 360–79. Abingdon, Oxon: Routledge, 2013.

Sandin, Bengt. "Education." In *A Cultural History of Childhood and Family in the Age of Empire*, edited by Colin Heywood. Oxford: Berg, 2014.

Sandin, Bengt and Maria Sundkvist. *Barn, barndom och samhälle: svensk utbildningshistoria*. Malmö: Gleerups, 2014.

Sárgon, Sollaug. "Konsekvenser av statens fornorskningspolitikk: med fokus på tapt skolegang under andre verdenskrig". Master thesis, University of Tromsø, 2007.

Schorn-Schütte, Luise. "Die Drei-Stände-Lehre im reformatorischen Umbruch." In *Die frühe Reformation als Umbruch*, edited by Bernd Moeller, 435–461. Gütersloh: Gütersloher Verlagshaus, 1998.

Schrumpf, Ellen. *Barnearbeid – plikt eller privilegium? Barnearbeid og oppvekst i to norske industrisamfunn i perioden 1850–1910*. PhD diss., Høgskolen i Telemark, 1997.

Schrumpf, Ellen. *Barndomshistorie*. Oslo: Samlaget, 2007.

Schrumpf, Ellen. "En tredje vending i barndomshistorien? Fra struktur til kultur og materialitet." *Historisk tidsskrift* 2 (2012): 251–81.

Schwartz Lausten, Martin. *Oplysning i kirke og synagoge. Forholdet mellem kristne og jøder i den danske Oplysningstid (1760–1814)*. Copenhagen: Akademisk Forlag, 2002.

Schön, Ebbe. *Svensk folktro A-Ö. Hur vi tänkt, trott och trollat*. Stockholm: Prisma, 1998.

Sennett, Richard. *The Fall of Public Man*. New York: Penguin, 2002.

Seppälä, Felix. "Kievareita ja kyydintekoa vuosisata sitten." In *Hämeenmaa 10*, edited by Y. S. Koskimies, 198–204. Hämeenlinna: Hämeen heimoliitto, 1959.

Shanahan, Suzanne. "Lost and Found: The Sociological Ambivalence toward Childhood." *Annual Review of Sociology* 33 (2007): 407–28.

Sidén, Karin. *Den ideala barndomen. Studier i det stormaktstida barnporträttets ikonografi och function*. Stockholm: Raster förlag, 2001.

Sigurðsson, Páll. "Danske og Norske Lov i Island og de islandske kodifikationsplaner." In *Danske og Norske Lov i 300 år*, edited by Ditlev Tamm, 347–66. Copenhagen: Jurist- og Økonomforbundets Forlag, 1983.

Silverstolpe, Gustaf Abraham. *Försök till en framställning af allmänna läro-verkets närvarande tillstånd i Sverige, af Gustaf Abraham Silverstolpe .. jemte utlåtanden deröfver af Carl Ulric Broocman .. Johan Åström .. och Carl von Rosenstein .. samt rektor Silverstolpes: derå gifna förklaringar: till hans kongl. höghet kronprinsen i underdånighet aflemnade, samt på dess befallning och bekostnad utgifne af kongl. uppfostrings-comitén*. Stockholm: Kongl. tryckeriet, 1813.

Sjöberg, Mats. *Att säkra familjens skördar. Barndom, skola och arbete i agrar miljö: Bolstad pastorat 1860–1930*. PhD diss., Linköping university, 1996.

Sjöberg, Mats. "Working Rural Children. Herding, Child Labour and Childhood in the Swedish Rural Environment 1850–1950." In *Industrious Children: Work and Childhood in the Nordic Countries 1850–1990*, edited by Ning de Coninck-Smith, Bengt Sandin, and Ellen Schrumpf, 106–28. Odense: Odense University Press, 1997.

Sjöstrand, Wilhelm. *Pedagogikens historia.* 3:2, *Utvecklingen i Sverige under tiden 1809–1920.* Lund: Gleerup, 1965.

Skar, Johannes. *Gamalt or Sætesdal. Samla utgåve.* Vol. I–II. Oslo: Samlaget, 1961.

Skjelbred, Ann Helene Bolstad. *Uren og hedning. Barselkvinnen i norsk folketradisjon.* Oslo, Bergen, and Tromsø: Universitetsforlaget, 1972.

Skrindsrud, Johan. *På heimleg grunn. Folkeminne frå Etnedal.* Norsk Folkeminnelags Skrifter. Vol. 77. Oslo: Norsk Folkeminnelag, 1956.

Skrivelse från konsistoriet till Kungl. Majt, 9 September 1817. In *Acta till Stockholms större latinläroverks historia 1419–1840,* edited by B. Rudolf Hall. Stockholm: Fören. för svensk undervisningshistoria, 1939.

Skutnabb-Kangas, Tove. *Tvåspråkighet.* Lund: Liber, 1981.

Skýrsla um Barnaskóla Reykjavíkur skólaárið 1923–1924. Reykjavík, 1925.

Slaastad, Tove Irene. "Samisk statistikk 2016 = Sámi statistihkka 2016." In *Sámi statistihkka 2016.* Oslo: Statistisk sentralbyrå, 2016.

Sleman, Folke. *Kungl. Direktionen över Stockholms stads undervisningsverk.* In *Årsberättelse / Stockholms stads arkivnämnd och stadsarkiv, 1948* (1949): 17–40.

Sletvold, Sverre. *Norske lesebøker 1777–1969.* Trondheim, Oslo, Bergen, and Tromsø: Universitetsforlaget, 1971.

Snellman, G. R. *Undersökning af folkskolebarnens i Helsingfors, Åbo, Tammerfors och Viborg arbete utom skolan. Arbetsstatistik V.* Helsinki: Kejserliga Senatens Tryckeri, 1908.

Solheim, Svale. *Karmøy 1930–32.* Norsk Folkeminnesamling (NFS), Institutt for kulturstudier og orientalske språk (IKOS), University of Oslo.

Sommer, Dion. *Barndomspsykologi: udvikling i en forandret verden.* Copenhagen: Hans Reitzel, 1996.

Sommer, Dion, Ingrid Pramling Samuelsson, and Karsten Hundeide. *Child Perspectives and Children's Perspectives in Theory and Practice.* Dordrecht: Springer, 2009.

Spink, Reginald. *Hans Christian Andersen: The Man and His Work.* 3rd edition. Copenhagen: Høst, 1981.

Stang Dahl, Tove. *Barnevern og samfunnsvern. Om stat, vitenskap og profesjoner under barnevernets oppkomst i Norge.* Oslo: Pax Forlag, 1978/1992.

Stenbæk, Jørgen. "Ecclesia particularis – republica christiana. Dansk kirkeretstænkning i 1600-tallet og dens europæiske forudsætninger." In *Kirkehistoriske Samlinger* (1975): 34–60.

Stenbæk, Jørgen. "To eller tre regimenter i den lutherske kaldsetik? Udvikling og aktualitet i luthersk socialetik." *Religionsvidenskabeligt Tidsskrift* 17 (1990): 61–85.

Storaker, Johan Th. *Menneskelivet i den norske folketro. (Storakers samlinger VI)* ved Nils Lid. Norsk Folkeminnelags skrifter. Vol. 34. Oslo: Norsk Folkeminnelag, 1935.

Strindberg, August. "H. C. Andersen. Till Andersen-jubileet 2 April 1905." In *Samlade skrifter av August Strindberg,* edited by John Landquist, 443–45. Stockholm: Bonnier, 1920.

Strohl, Jane E. "The Child in Luther's Theology: 'For What Purpose Do We Older Folks Exist, Other Than to Care for … the Young?'" In *The Child in Christian Thought,* edited by Marcia J. Bunge, 134–59. Cambridge: Eerdmans, 2001.

Strompdal, Knut. *Gamalt frå Helgeland.* Norsk Folkeminnelags skrifter. Vol. 19. Oslo: Norsk Folkeminnelag, 1929.

Strompdal, Knut. *Gamalt frå Helgeland III.* Norsk Folkeminnelags skrifter. Vol. 44. Oslo: Norsk Folkeminnelag, 1939.

Stubhaug, Arild. *Called Too Soon by Flames Afar. Niels Henrik Abel and His Times.* Berlin, Heidelberg, and New York: Springer-Verlag, 2000.

Sundt, Eilert. *Harham – et eksempel fra fiskeridistriktene.* Bergen, Oslo, and Tromsø: Universitetsforlaget, 1971.

Suomen Asetuskokoelma 18/1889.

Suometar. 1847–1866.

Svensen, Åsfrid. *Å bygge en verden av ord: lyst og læring i barne- og ungdomslitteratur.* Bergen: Fagbokforlaget, 2001.

Svensson, Sonja. "'En barntidning utan ZT är som en kyrka utan prest!': Zacharias Topelius och nordiska barntidningar." In *Taru ja totuus*, edited by Elina Pöykkö and Märtha Norrback, 126–65. Helsinki: Topelius-seura, 2008.

Söderblom, Staffan. *Harry Martinson.* Stockholm: Natur & Kultur, 1994.

Söderlind, Ingrid, and Kristina Engwall. *Barndom och arbete.* Umeå: Boréa, 2008.

Sørensen, Øystein, and Bo Stråth. *The Cultural Construction of Norden.* Oslo: Scandinavian University Press, 1997.

Talleraashaugen, Ola. *Lesja 1928–30.* Norsk Folkeminnesamling (NFS), Institutt for kulturstudier og orientalske språk (IKOS), University of Oslo.

Tamm, Ditlev, ed. *Danske og Norske Lov i 300 år.* Copenhagen: Jurist- og Økonomforbundets Forlag, 1983.

Taussi- Sjöberg, Marja and Tinne Vammen. *På trösklen till välfärden. Välgörenhetsformer och arenor i Norden 1800–1930.* Stockholm: Carlsons Bokförlag, 1995.

Teilhaug, Alfred Oftedal. "From Descriptive to Theory-Oriented Research: Norwegian Historical-Educational Research in a Historical Perspective." In *Knowledge, Politics and the History of Education*, edited by Jesper Eckhardt Larsen, 195–224. Berlin: Lit Verlag, 2012.

"'Þeir reyna að sýna kraftana, þegar við horfum á þá!' Unglingsstúlkur og piltar í uppskipunarvinnu við höfnina." *Morgunblaðið* 17. July 1965: 3. Online at http://timarit.is/files/16100262.pdf#navpanes=1&view=FitH.

Therborn, Göran. "The Politics of Childhood: The Rights of Children in Modern Times." In *Families of Nations. Patterns of Public Policy in Western Democracies*, edited by Francis G. Castles, 241–91. Aldershot: Dartmouth, 1993.

Thodberg, Christian. "Grundtvig the Hymnwriter." In *N. F. S. Grundtvig: Tradition and Renewal: Grundtvig's Vision of Man and People, Education and the Church, in Relation to World Issues Today*, edited by Christian Thodberg and Anders Pontoppidan Thyssen. Copenhagen: The Danish Institute, 1953.

Thodberg, Christian. "The Importance of Baptism in Grundtvig's View of Christianity." In *Heritage and Prophecy: Grundtvig and the English-Speaking World*, edited by A. M. Allchin, D. Jasper, J. H. Schjørring, and K. Stevenson. Norwich: Canterbury Press, 1994.

Thompson, E. P. *The Making of the English Working-Class.* London: Victor Gollancz, 1963.

Thuen, Harald. *Om barnet. Oppdragelse, opplæring og omsorg gjennom historien.* Oslo: Abstrakt forlag, 2011.

Thuen, Trond. *Quest for equity: Norway and the Saami challenge.* St. John's, Nfld: ISER, 1995.

Thaarup, Frederik. *Den virksomme Emmanuel Balling.* Copenhagen: Sebastian Popp, 1795.

Tiensuu, Kyllikki. "Bergh, Johan Fredrik (1795–1866)." In *Kansallisbiografia*, edited by Matti Klinge et al. Helsinki: Finnish Literature Society, 2007. Online at www.kansallisbiografia.fi.

Tilly, Louise and Joan Scott. *Women, Work and Family*. New York: Holt, Rinehart and Winston, 1978.

Tilråding V om opplæring for born som treng serskoler. Samordningsnemnda for skoleverket. Oslo: Kirke- og undervisningsdepartementet, 1948.

Tilton, Tim. "The Role of Ideology in Social Democratic Politics." In *Creating Social Democracy: A Century of the Social Democratic Labor Party in Sweden*, edited by Klaus Misgeld et al., 409–27. University Park, PA: Penn. State University Press, 1988.

Tjelle, Ingjerd. *Bortsendt og internert: møter med internatbarn*. Tromsø: Polar forlag, 2000.

Todal, Jon. "Minorities with a Minority: Language and the School in the Sámi Areas of Norway." *Language, Culture, and Curriculum* 11, no. 3 (1998): 354–66.

Todres, Jonathan and Sarah Higinbotham. "A Person's a Person: Children's Rights in Children's Literature." *Columbia Human Rights Law Review* 1 (2013): 1–56.

Tommila, Päiviö. *Nurmijärven pitäjän historia I. Asutus ja väestö*. Nurmijärvi: Nurmijärven kunta, 1958/2003.

Tommila, Päiviö. *Nurmijärven pitäjän historia II*. Nurmijärvi: Nurmijärven kunta, 1959.

Topelius, Zacharias. *Läsning för barn. 1, Lekar*. Stockholm: Bonnier, 1865/1883.

Topelius, Zacharias. *Läsning för barn. 3, Visor och sagor*. Stockholm: Bonnier, 1867/1883.

Tradisjonsinnsamling på 1800-talet. Stipendmeldingar frå P. Chr. Asbjørnsen, J. Moe, L. Lindeman, S. Bugge, M. Moe. Norsk Folkeminnelags Skrifter. Vol. 92. Oslo: Universitetsforlaget, 1964.

Treschow, Niels. *Lovgivnings-Principier, eller Om Staten i Forhold til Religion, Sæder og Cultur*. Christiania: Grøndahl, 1920.

Troels-Lund, Troels Frederik. *Dagligt liv i Norden i det sekstende aarhundrede. Femte udgave ved Knud Fabricius*. Vol. II: Bønder- og købstadboliger. Copenhagen: Gyldendal, 1929–1931.

Troels-Lund, Troels Frederik. *Dagligt liv i Norden i det sekstende aarhundrede. Femte udgave ved Knud Fabricius*. Vol. IV: Klædedragt. Copenhagen: Gyldendal, 1929–1931.

Troels-Lund, Troels Frederik. *Dagligt liv i Norden i det sekstende aarhundrede. Femte udgave ved Knud Fabricius*. Vol. VIII: Fødsel og daab. Copenhagen: Gyldendal, 1929–1931.

Trägårdh, Lars. "Statist Individualim: On the Culturality of the Nordic Welfare State." In *The Cultural Construction of Norden*, edited by Øystein Sørensen, and Bo Stråth, 253–85. Oslo: Scandinavian University Press, 1997.

Tsarouhas, Dimitris. *Social Democracy in Sweden. The Threat from a Globalized World*. London and New York: Tauris, 2008.

Tufte, Birgitte, Jan Kampmann, and Monica Hassel. *Børnekultur. Et begreb i bevegelse*. Copenhagen: Akademisk Forlag, 2003.

Tuhkanen, Tuija. *In memoriam sui et suorum posuit. Lahjoittajien muistokuvat Suomen kirkoissa 1400-luvulta 1700-luvun lopulle*. Åbo: Åbo Akademi University Press, 2005.

Turi, Johan, and Harald O. Lindbach. *Min bok om samene*. Karasjok: ČálliidLágádus, 2011.

Tutkimuksia taloudellisista oloista Suomen maaseudulla. 5 vols, 1885–1893.

Tveit, Knut. "Tradisjonar i norsk skolehistorisk forskning." *Norsk Pedagogisk Tidsskrift* (1983): 337–44.

Työtilastollisia tutkimuksia – Arbetsstatistiska Undersökningar. 16 vols, 1903–1914.

Tønnessen, Liv Kari Bondevik. *Norsk utdanningshistorie: en innføring med fokus på grunnskolens utvikling*. Bergen: Fagbokforlaget, 2011.

Underdånigt betänkande med dertill hörande handlingar angående fattigvården i Stockholms stad. Stockholm: N&S, 1839.

Ungberg, Carl Fredric. *Projekt till förändrad organisation af polisvården inom hufvudstaden äfvensom till instruktion för de till den nya polis-styrelsen föreslagne tjenstemän och betjente*. Stockholm: P. A. Nordstedt & Söner, Kongl. boktryckare, 1840.

"Unglingavinnan við höfnina." *Þjóðviljinn* 23. May 1965: 1 and 12. Online at http://timarit.is/files/14289234.pdf#navpanes=1&view=FitH, and http://timarit.is/files/14289273.pdf#navpanes=1&view=FitH.

"Unglingsstúlkur komnar í uppskipun." *Tíminn* 16. July 1965: 16. Online at http://timarit.is/files/12014063.pdf#navpanes=1&view=FitH.

Uppfostringskommitténs organisations och gymnasieförslag, 17 April 1817. In *Acta till Stockholms större latinläroverks historia 1419–1840*, edited by B. Rudolf Hall. Stockholm: Fören. för svensk undervisningshistoria, 1939.

Uppfostringskommitténs svar, 14 November 1818. In *Acta till Stockholms större latinläroverks historia 1419–1840*, edited by B. Rudolf Hall. Stockholm: Fören. för svensk undervisningshistoria, 1939.

Uppgifter om skolan 1649–1793 (Klara School). In *Acta till Stockholms folkundervisnings historia: 1533–1847*, edited by B. Rudolf Hall. Stockholm: Fören. för svensk undervisningshistoria, 1940.

Valen, Henry and Daniel Katz. *Political Parties in Norway*. Oslo: Universitetsforlaget, 1964.

Vammen, Tinne. "Inden- og udenfor visse grænser. Hovedstadens børnhavesag 1880–1940 i europæiske perspektiv." In *Den privat-offentliga gränsen. Det sociala arbetets strategier och aktörer i Norden 1860–1940*, edited by Monika Janfelt, 79–133. Copenhagen: Nordiske Ministerråd, 1999.

Vilkuna, Kustaa H. J. "Lapsuuden ja puolikasvuisuuden kynnyksillä." In *Toivon historia. Toivo Nygårdille omistettu juhlakirja*, edited by Kalevi Ahonen, Petri Karonen, Ilkka Nummela, Jari Ojala, and Kustaa H. J. Vilkuna, 23–34. Jyväskylä: Jyväskylän yliopiston historian ja etnologian laitos, 2003.

Von Rochow, Friedrich Eberhart. *Der Kinderfreund. Ein Lesebuch zum Gebrauch im Landschulen*. 1777.

Von Schulzenheim, David. *Tal, om den offenteliga vården, i hänseende til folkets seder och helsa, samt de fattigas lifbergning, hållet för k:gl. svenska vetenskaps-academien vid præsidii nedläggande, andra gången, den 30 januarii, år 1799. Af David Schulz von Schulzenheim*. Stockholm: Joh. P. Lindh, 1801.

Von Zweigbergk, Eva. *Barnboken i Sverige 1750–1950*. Stockholm: Rabén & Sjögren, 1965.

Wagner, Wolfgang. "Danske Lov og dansk lovgiving i europæisk ramme." In *Danske og Norske Lov i 300 år*, edited by Ditlev Tamm, 207–54. Copenhagen: Jurist- og Økonomforbundets Forlag, 1983.

Weinreich, Torben. *Historien om børnelitteratur: dansk børnelitteratur gennem 400 år*. Vejle: Branner og Korch, 2004.

Weiser-Aall, Lily. *Svangerskap og fødsel i nyere norsk tradisjon. En kildekritisk studie*. Oslo: Norsk folkemuseum, 1968.

Weiss. C. F. *Børnevennen. En Læsebog til brug i Landsbyeskoler*. 1784.

White, Hayden. "Historisk innplotting og sannhetsproblemet." In *Historie og fortelling. Utvalgte essay*, 124–44. Oslo: Pax forlag, 2003.

Widhe, Olle. *Dö din hund!: krig, lek och läsning i svensk barnboksutgivning under 200 år*. Lund: Ellerström, 2015.

Widholm, Annika. "Barnlitteraturens betydelse för ungas rättigheter." In *Barnlitteraturens värden och värderingar*, edited by Sara Kärrholm, and Paul Tenngart, 39–50. Lund: Studentlitteratur, 2012.

Wigström, Eva. *Svenska sagor och sägner. II. Folktro och sägner från skilda landskap*. Published by Aina Stenklo. Uppsala and Copenhagen: Gustav Adolfs Akademien, 1952.

Wikander, Ulla. *Kvinnors och mäns arbeten: Gustavsberg 1880–1980: genusarbetsdelning och arbetets degradering vid en porslinsfabrik*. Lund: Arkiv, 1988.

Wille, Hans Jacob. *Beskrivelse over Sillejords Præstegield i Øvre-Tellemarken i Norge*. Copenhagen, 1786.

Wilson, Jean. "Holy Innocents: Some Aspects of the Iconography of Children on English Renaissance Tombs." *Church Monuments* 5 (1990): 57–63.

Wingender, Nete Balslev. *"Drivhuset for den sygnende Plante!" Børn og opdragelse i åndssvageanstalten Gl. Bakkehus. 1855–1902*. Copenhagen: Dansk Psykologisk Forlag, 1992.

Witt-Brattström, Ebba. *Moa Martinson. Skrift och drift i trettiotalet*. Stockholm: Norstedt, 1988.

Woolf, Virginia. "On Being Ill." In *Collected Essays*. New York: Harcourt, 1967.

Wullschlager, Jackie. *Hans Christian Andersen: The Life of a Storyteller*. New York: Knopf, 2000.

Wynn-Jones, Tim. Online at www.azquotes.com/quote/618690.

Zwilgmeyer, Dikken, and G. Munthe. *Vi børn*. Bergen: Fr. Nygaards forlag, 1890.

Ärkebiskopens skrivelse med anledning av konsistoriets inlaga till Kongl. Majt (Lindblom, 16 October 1817). In *Acta till Stockholms större latinläroverks historia 1419–1840*, edited by Rudolf B. Hall. Stockholm: Fören. för svensk undervisningshistoria, 1939.

Index

Aakjær, Jeppe 230, 233
Aasen, Ivar 223, 227, 231
abandonment 25, 27, 138, 146, 153, 189, 201
ability, abilities: 7, 13, 21, 44, 79, 83, 97, 124, 155, 255, 262, 266, 268, 278; of children 35, 53, 128, 140, 168, 195, 212, 216, 242, 246–7, 249
abortion 31
absence, of parents 71–3
absolutist state 96, 148, 152–4, 161, 245
abuse, abuses 29, 101–2, 198, 269, 281
accident, accidents 182–3, 208
accountable 101
activities: physical 118; educational 140; of leisure 7, 175, 184, 290, 294–5
adolescent, adolescents 95, 100, 156, 175, 201, 241; see also teenagers ; youths
adorable 72
adultism 72, 75
affection 248
afflict, afflicted 23, 25, 27, 142
afterlife 72, 159, 247–8, 259
age: limit 78; of children 32, 47, 63, 86, 112, 167, 170–1, 184, 198, 202, 287
agency, of children 4, 11, 164, 172, 213
agent, agents 9, 13, 72, 101–2, 206, 217, 258, 286
aggression, aggressive 26, 43, 224–5, 234–5
allegory 65, 258
allmän folkskola 152; see also elementary education; folkeskole
alphabet 56, 76, 84, 87, 159
ambition, ambitions 74, 82, 101, 118, 133–4, 136, 138, 144, 163

ambulatory schools 77, 83, 88, 161, 167, 177–9, 181–2, 185–7
amputation 259
amulet 21
amuse 140
Anabaptists 60
Andersen, Hans Christian 163, 233, 254–63, 267, 270–3, 276, 281
anecdote 268–9
anger, angry 26, 154, 296, 298
animal, animals 11, 18–20, 32, 114, 167–9, 177, 180, 228, 232–3, 283–5, 297, 300
animal husbandry 167–8, 193
anthropology 61
apostle, apostles 51, 122, 124, 158
apotropaic 17, 19
apprentice, apprenticeship 55, 87, 136–7, 171
arithmetic 87, 97, 132, 143, 150, 153, 228
Asbjørnsen, Peter Christian 17, 36, 273, 288
attitude, attitudes: of children 207, 267; to children 6, 58, 66, 101, 103, 176, 181, 213, 266, 280; to death 213; towards Sami 191–2; to schooling 152, 154, to superstitions 36–8
authoritarian, authoritative 58, 144, 283, 300
authority, authorities: civil 1, 10, 33, 79–80, 142–4, 152, 154–5, 171, 176, 182, 188–9, 195, 197, 199, 202, 223, 226, 229, 267; religious 8, 40, 50, 52, 54, 59, 62, 65; parental 46, 51, 93; poor-relief authorities 132–9, 143–4; school authorities 176, 180 182–3

autonomy, autonomous 5, 74, 94, 97, 193, 250, 266, 285, 289–90, 299–301

baby, babies 1, 27–8, 66, 68–70, 115, 165–6, 172, 220, 254
ball 278
baptism 23, 26–31, 30–1, 33, 40–1, 60–1, 65, 69–70, 74, 95, 123–5, 130
bathed, bathing 115, 211
bear, bears 18, 20, 35, 59–60, 148, 210, 249, 300; *see also* animal, animals
beat, beaten, beating 26, 80, 94, 135, 215, 228, 260
beautiful 19–21, 29, 208, 213, 224, 226, 232, 235, 252, 255, 257–9, 263, 289, 299
beauty 116, 126, 208, 254–6, 258–9, 261, 263, 275
beggars, children as 86, 133, 137, 169, 172–3
behave, behaving 29, 51, 64, 228, 245, 262, 266, 273, 278, 297–9
behavior 17, 19, 32, 139–40, 215, 218, 242, 247, 249, 253, 259, 298
belief, beliefs 5–6, 8–9, 13, 17–18, 19–23, 25, 27–9, 31–3, 35–9, 79, 101, 113, 115, 120, 127–8, 154, 206, 229, 234, 248, 277
beloved 86, 159, 213, 216, 229, 289
Berg, Mads 221–2, 225, 232–3, 235
Bergh, Johan Fredrik 83–4
Beskow, Elsa 284, 286, 297–300
bestiality 81
bestow, bestowal 26–7
betrothed 47
Bible 10, 47, 49, 56, 74, 83, 117, 122, 188, 249
biblical 8, 41–2, 44–6, 49, 54, 60–1, 74, 116, 120, 123, 127, 150, 152–3, 158, 260
Birch, Carl Christian 50–2, 56–7
bird, birds 11, 18, 114–15, 118–19, 123–4, 257, 259
birth, births 17–18, 20–1, 23, 27, 29, 31, 50, 69–70, 76, 80, 94, 112, 124, 131, 142, 144, 147, 166, 190
birthday 271, 273, 289
Bjørnson, Bjørnstjerne 224, 226, 231, 236, 283–4
Blix, Elias 232, 234

body, bodies 2, 18–19, 26, 74, 93, 114–16, 132, 135, 142, 195, 208, 214, 249, 261
book, books for children 2, 4, 45, 48–9, 52, 54–5, 79, 84, 86, 158–60, 167, 173, 245, 249, 257–8, 266–71, 278–80, 283, 286–301
born 18–23, 25, 27, 29, 50, 54, 62, 80, 94–5, 105, 126, 164, 168–9, 171, 200, 204, 230, 250, 267, 285
boy, boys 2–3, 9–10, 13, 30, 32, 40, 45, 54, 64–5, 80–3, 86, 88, 111, 114, 117–18, 126, 133–4, 139–41, 157, 167–8, 171, 183–5, 194, 205, 209, 211, 213, 217, 224, 234, 242, 244–5, 247–8, 251–2, 270, 272–3, 275–6, 279, 281, 286, 290, 292, 294–6
brave 211, 231, 290, 297
brother, brothers 21, 66, 68, 77, 84–5, 87, 89, 95, 125, 170, 209–10, 212, 216, 219, 227, 245, 247, 254, 256–7, 260, 274, 287–9; *see also* sibling, siblings
Bugenhagen, Johann 70, 75
bullying, bullied 200, 202, 296
burial, buried 17, 26, 29, 31, 37, 215
Børnevennen 48–9, 52, 54

candy 269
care 18, 24, 38, 93, 116, 120, 132, 134–5, 139, 151, 166, 307, 315
caregivers 243
careless, carelessly 28, 35, 101, 138, 278
caretakers 250
caring 36, 96, 100, 127, 166, 250
catechetical 78–9, 84–5, 138
Catechism 4, 8, 40–1, 43–6, 48–50, 52, 54–6, 61, 65, 72, 74, 79, 83, 98, 111, 122–4, 133, 152, 154, 161, 167, 173, 244
changeling, changelings 23, 25–6, 29, 35
character, characters 22, 48, 132, 137, 141, 144, 157, 242, 245, 255–8, 260, 262–3, 271–2, 274–6, 284, 287–8, 295–7, 299
charity 112, 118, 142
charms 72
chastity 60, 86
cheeks 63, 115, 129, 227, 234, 259
cheerful 20, 23, 65, 111–12, 126, 130, 227, 259

child, children: as equal to adults 13, 112–13, 128, 242; destiny of 17, 20–3, 38; everyday experiences of 9, 80, 88, 185, 199–200, 207, 230, 271–2, 276; formation of 6, 9–11, 123–4, 157, 189, 192; own perspective 164, 271
childbearing 58
childbed 34
childcare 18, 36
childcentered 222
childhood 2–9, 11–14, 21, 40, 52, 59–62, 64–5, 72, 75–6, 78, 84, 87–8, 91, 93, 101, 103–5, 111–13, 115, 118, 122–3, 125–9, 131–2, 135–6, 140, 144, 150–1, 155, 163–5, 167–70, 172, 175, 200–2, 205–7, 210, 213, 217, 220–1, 242–3, 248, 266–7, 269–73, 276–8, 280–1, 283–8, 290–1, 296–7, 299–300
childish, childishness 63–4, 72, 233, 235
childlike, childlikeness 112, 118
childminders 87
choir 123, 220, 226
chores 167, 250
Christ 10, 60, 65, 70, 116, 121–2, 124, 126–7, 130
christened, christening 17, 26–9, 31, 33, 79, 95, 102
Christensen, Nina 105, 242–3, 251, 300–1
Christian: beliefs 79, 128, 310; church 40; communities 42; education 27, 40, 43, 47–50, 79, 97, 120–1; ideas 11, 85, 128; faith 27, 43, 69, 122; life 41, 60, 123, 125–6, 154; message 41, 43, 54, 98, 188; understanding 115–16; vocation 61; virtues 63–5
Christianity 33, 49, 69, 99, 112–13, 115–16, 120–5, 129–30, 136, 139, 225
Christmas 17, 22, 27, 30, 38, 115, 130, 159, 215, 223, 225–6, 229–30, 232, 278
church: attendance by children 46, 63, 83; church bells 32, 77; Catholic 79; Lutheran 6, 8–9, 11, 42, 48, 52, 55, 70, 74, 76, 83, 103–4, 132, 167, 244; church law 79, 153 275; parochial 58–63, 65, 69, 71, 77, 88, 95
civic 1, 8, 119, 135–6, 143, 152, 155–6
civilization 188, 195

civilized, civilizing 192, 259
class, classes: social 2, 5–6, 9–11, 13, 35, 65, 80, 97–101, 119, 131–45, 154–6, 159–60, 167, 241, 269, 272, 275, 280, 285–7, 289, 294–6, 299, 305, 308–10, 312; school classes 50, 86, 149, 170; working-class 9, 133, 139, 163–70, 172–3, 236, 296, 303, 315
classical languages 118, 149–50, 157, 160
classroom 52, 222, 224, 227, 229
clergy 41–2, 46–7, 49, 51, 55, 81, 83–4, 88, 119, 132, 139–40
clergymen 41, 43–4, 46–7, 54, 56, 58, 73–4, 82, 195, 252
closeness 11, 193, 266
clothes, of children 1, 24, 29, 33–35, 142; *see also* dress, dresses of children
clothing 64, 144, 161, 294
code, codes, *see* laws; Household Code
coercion 121
coffin 21, 34, 66–8, 248
cognitive 261–2
college 2, 85, 188, 194, 202
comfort 122, 125–6, 243, 247–8, 260–1
comforting 247–9
commandment, commandments 40, 43, 45–6, 49, 56, 63–4, 154
commemorative 58–9, 62–3, 66–9, 71–4
committee, committees 134, 137–40, 141–3, 201
communion 114, 122–3
compassion 26, 32, 217, 231, 260, 262–3, 269
compassionate 116, 262
competence, competencies 8, 11, 101, 152, 202, 286–7, 293, 296, 299
competent 11–13, 101, 135–6, 139, 156, 217, 243–4, 250, 283, 285–7, 289–93, 295–7, 299–301
competition 172, 205, 207, 218, 220, 236
comrades, comradeship 209, 275
conception, conceptions: of children 4–5, 7–9, 11, 13, 59, 64, 72, 91, 111–16, 127–8, 147–8, 150, 160, 220–1, 223–7, 234–7, 244, 250, 283, 287; of childhood 283; of family 243

concern 7–8, 20, 35, 101, 120, 138–9, 173, 186
confession 32, 123, 247
confidence 10, 69, 104, 141, 247
confirmation 10, 45, 47, 49, 55, 78, 83, 87, 96, 126, 152, 167, 195
conflict, conflicts 9, 18, 27, 42, 48, 83, 101, 115, 131–2, 134, 144–5, 182, 201, 210, 275, 287
congregation, congregations 65, 78, 99, 122–3, 140
consciousness 200, 218, 261
Consistory 132, 137, 141–2
constitution 57, 106, 148, 156, 160, 121, 220–2, 234, 236
convention 63, 101, 203, 265, 301
corporal 51, 268–9, 285
council, councils 104, 137, 139, 143, 175, 182, 200, 222, 232, 285
countryside 48–9, 79, 82, 87, 100, 161, 166–7, 169, 176, 178, 184, 275, 283
courage, courageous 35 116, 211–13, 224, 290, 292, 298
cousin 211, 213, 224
cradle, cradles 17, 22–5, 35, 66–9, 75, 115, 234
craft, crafts 135, 143, 167, 221
Cramer, Johan Andreas 49–50, 52, 56
Cranach (the Elder), Lucas 59–61
creation 11, 113, 115–16, 125, 127, 133, 144–5, 158, 222, 270, 293
creative, creativity 12–13, 112–13, 116–19, 127, 242
creed 40, 122
cross 24–5, 33, 70, 124–5, 190, 211, 225, 231, 281, 293
crying 21, 29–31, 167, 172, 248, 268, 289, 296; *see also* tears
cult 258, 261
cultural 1, 3, 5, 7, 33, 36, 55, 60, 63, 69, 120, 127, 157, 190–3, 195, 197, 199, 201–2, 205–6, 217, 220, 227, 232–4, 237, 243, 254, 267, 287, 293
culture, cultures 4, 7, 10, 12–14, 17–18, 36, 44, 58–9, 60–3, 65, 67, 69, 71, 73, 75, 119, 145, 155, 163, 188, 191–3, 195, 197–8, 200–3, 206, 227, 241, 244, 259, 279, 285, 293
curious, curiosity 248, 259, 261, 300
curriculum, curricula 2, 45, 76, 82, 87, 95, 97, 99, 135–6, 149, 157–8, 160, 162, 194, 196, 222–3, 232

custom, customs 21, 23, 26–9, 139; *see also* habit, habit, habits; traditions

dance, dancing 11, 46, 211, 220, 228, 254, 259, 261
Dass, Petter 44–5, 56, 74, 111
daughter, daughters 19, 63, 66–8, 83, 87, 114–15, 165, 168–71, 173, 215, 227, 248, 251, 261, 296
dead 19, 26–7, 66, 68–70, 157, 212, 214–16, 242–3, 246, 248–50, 272–3
dear 49, 52, 70, 124–5, 252, 274, 277
death 19, 21, 27, 33, 43, 49, 52, 66, 69, 71, 75, 94, 118–19, 123, 125–7, 166, 169, 171, 190, 206, 208, 212–15, 225, 241–3, 245–8, 249–53, 259–60, 281, 290
deathbed 247–9, 259
deceased 26, 42, 68–9, 71, 246, 248
decorum 157
defective 35
defects of children, *see* deformed children
deformed children 18, 25–6, 35
delicate 11, 115
delight, delights 65, 70, 115
delightful 269
delinquent children 100
dependent, dependents 11, 62–3, 85, 88, 96, 243, 270, 285, 299
depression 20, 125
desirable 138, 263
desire, desires 21, 25, 27, 64, 117–18, 126, 143, 248, 252, 262, 269
development 5–6, 12, 20, 48, 55, 65, 70, 85, 87, 91–2, 98, 100–1, 103, 105, 109, 112, 114–17, 119, 134, 136, 147, 166, 176, 182, 186, 188–9, 192, 196, 225, 232, 234, 265, 267, 270, 279–80, 285, 289–90
devices: apotropaic 17, 19, 23–24 ; literary 210, 257
devil 28, 125, 287
devotion, to children 243
diapers 61
didactic 59, 64, 242, 278, 283, 294
didacticism 288
dignity 4, 265, 269
diligence 159
disability, dissabilities 2, 13, 55, 200, 263
discipline 4, 61, 64–5, 73, 84, 98, 149, 155, 195, 268, 290

disciplined, disciplining 44–5, 78, 84, 280, 291
discrimination 200, 265
diseases 142, 214
disobedient, disobedience 209, 242, 259
distinctive 3–4, 114
diversity 3, 7, 11–13, 128, 231, 241, 251 , 281
divine 60, 62, 79, 121
docile 155, 158–9, 259
docility 156
doctor 213, 246–7, 249, 252
doctrine, doctrines 42–4, 49–50, 52, 54, 70, 79, 83, 95, 161, 252
doll 233, 271–4, 288–93
domestic 8, 80, 139, 165–7, 173, 185, 228, 233
drama, dramas 38, 211, 242, 245–7, 262, 276
dramatic 11, 27, 205, 207, 214, 227, 248
dream, dreams 27, 35, 171, 230, 279, 290, 293
dress, dresses of children 64, 72, 229, 293–4; *see also* cloths, clothing
drowning 223, 289, 296
dumb children 26, 142
duty, duties: to children 8–10, 28, 54, 62, 85, 95–6, 117, 134, 137, 143, 153; Christian 100; of children 8, 54, 92, 94, 103, 135, 155, 158, 178, 206, 217, 266, 290; *see also* obligations, to children
dutiful 291, 297
dwarves 225, 230; *see also* gnomes
dying children 19, 125, 213, 241–3, 245–7, 249–50, 253
Dürchs, Jonas 68

Easter 17, 22
eating 60, 140, 200, 227
ecclesiastical 9, 44, 50, 52, 54–5, 71, 74, 132, 161
Eckersberg, Christoffer Wilhelm 71–2
economy 136, 169, 171–3, 175–6, 180
educate, educating 8, 43, 77–8, 85, 96, 99, 117, 119, 122, 131, 153, 159
educated 62, 64, 119, 135, 148, 160, 197–8
education 2, 5–11, 13, 37, 58, 65, 72, 76–9, 92, 104, 111–20, 122–3, 127–8, 131–4, 136–9, 143–5, 163–5, 176, 181, 188–9, 192–5, 200, 206,

216, 232, 235, 244, 246, 286–7, 303–4, 308, 311–14; Christian/ religious 27, 40–2, 44, 47–50, 52, 55, 62, 92–9, 99, 220; elementary/ primary 80–2, 84–8, 96, 99, 111, 117, 134, 144, 147–8, 152–4, 156, 158, 160–1, 166–7, 172–3; higher 77, 139–42, 144, 147; 312; moral 99, 101, 144, 259; secondary 134, 147
educator, educators 175, 180, 183, 277
egalitarian 131, 145, 148, 153–4, 223
elite, elites 9, 85, 97, 132, 148, 157, 197
embrace 124, 136, 255, 260
embryo 88
emotions 157, 213, 217, 259, 271
empathetic 261–2
empathy 212, 216–17, 255, 260–2, 279–80
Enlightenment 5, 10, 32, 35–6, 40, 42, 47–9, 52, 54, 59, 72, 81, 85, 88, 97, 112, 127–8, 150, 225, 244
entertain, entertaining 79, 249, 260, 283
entertainment 71, 259, 262, 264
epitaph 42, 246, 252
ethical 36, 55, 276
ethics 45, 49, 255
ethnic 7, 13, 191–2, 202
Eucharist 95; *see also* liturgy
Evangelical 62, 64–5, 74–5, 95, 97, 130, 220
evil 21–4, 35, 38, 100, 121, 158, 162, 210, 215, 259–60, 263, 289
evildoers 260
exercises 157–9
expectation, expectations 96, 151, 171, 235, 242, 249
exposed 29, 32–3, 64, 101, 200, 202, 207, 213–14, 269
exposure 208, 241

fables 245, 259
factory, factories 135, 138, 142, 163–4, 166, 169–73, 182, 270
failure, failures 17, 29, 33, 80, 138, 198
fairy tale 2, 6, 163, 169, 239, 254–61, 263, 270–2, 287, 297, 313
faith 27–8, 40–1, 43, 46, 58–9, 61, 64–5, 69–70, 75, 85, 111, 113, 117, 120–4, 129, 225, 234, 248, 263, 277
family 6, 8, 10, 13, 20–1, 23, 26, 29, 41–2, 46, 55, 58–74, 77, 80–2, 86, 93–4, 96, 98, 101–2, 135–7, 149, 153, 161, 163–6, 168–73, 176, 190,

198–9, 202, 206–8, 212–17, 223, 227, 230, 234, 237, 242–3, 247–50, 270, 283, 285, 289–90, 297

famine 80, 169

fantasy, fantasies 246, 260, 272, 279, 298

farming 165–168, 175, 177, 190–2, 198, 284

farms 29, 78, 80–2, 165, 177–8, 184, 290

fate 26, 70, 163, 262

father, fathers 23, 32, 37, 40–1, 43, 45–6, 48–9, 50–1, 53–4, 58, 61–3, 68, 95, 112, 124, 126, 157, 159–60, 165, 169–71, 173, 210, 212, 216, 221, 227–8, 230, 233–4, 246–7, 252, 260, 274–5, 278, 289–90, 293–4

fatherless 94–5

fear 20–1, 23, 26–8, 33, 36, 65, 81, 102, 125, 192, 207–8, 211, 214–17, 245, 247, 252, 260

feed, feeding 158, 180, 212, 227, 298

feeling, feelings 121, 208, 215–16, 223–4, 227, 232, 235, 248, 255, 260, 262, 266, 268, 270, 272, 277, 280, 288–9

female, females 80, 93–4, 103–4, 113, 135, 139, 169, 172, 181, 183, 185, 233

fetus, fetuses 19, 31, 34–5, 70, 155

fiction, fictional 77, 84, 207, 210, 242, 244–5, 251, 256–8, 262, 272; *see also* reality, realities

fight 35, 209–10, 275, 295–6

fishery, fisheries 5, 177–8

fishing 17–18, 168, 175, 181, 183, 186, 190, 213

folk beliefs 6, 8–9, 17–18, 27, 32, 35–8

folkeskole 160, 162, 292; *see also* *allmän folkskolai;* elementary education

folklore 17, 19, 22, 35, 119, 174, 267, 283, 298

food 26, 81, 144, 161, 168–9, 173, 199–200, 211–12, 227

foolish, foolishness 33, 48, 249

forestry 167

forests 5, 84, 88, 114–15, 223

forgiveness 32, 121–2, 247, 289, 296

formative 144, 151

foundation, foundations 50, 52, 59, 79, 92, 122, 127, 135, 138, 157, 196, 201, 266

foundlings 94

fragile 151

freedom 112, 118, 120–1, 127, 136, 143, 152, 171, 193–4, 221–2, 224–5, 229, 234–5, 241, 269

friend, friends 48, 56, 59, 85, 117, 125, 159, 184, 210, 216, 244, 247–51, 289–91, 295–8

friendship 232, 247, 275

frightening 18, 25, 17–19, 26, 29, 38, 81, 84, 134, 193, 212–13, 296, 298

Fröbel, Friedrich 65, 75

Fryxell, Olof 275, 277

funeral 289, 293

funny 295

Gaarder, Jostein 283, 301

game, games 193, 258, 262, 273, 275, 277, 279, 300

garments, of children 28–9; *see also* cloths; dress, dresses of children

gender, genders 1–2, 4–5, 9–11, 13, 30, 64–5, 67, 81, 96–7, 99, 131, 135, 144, 164, 167, 234–5, 250–1, 278, 285–7, 291, 297–8; *see also* boys; female, females; girl, girls; male, males

generation, generations 29, 64, 82, 84–5, 91, 99, 101, 123, 151, 153–4, 157, 191–2, 199, 194, 202, 220, 225, 229, 293

genre, genres 2, 6, 58, 69, 71–3, 206, 245–6, 250, 258, 260, 287, 263

gentle, gently 115, 124, 214

gesture, gestures 69, 295

ghost, ghosts 26, 29–30, 33–4, 37

girl, girls 2–3, 9–10, 13, 19–21, 23, 26–7, 29–30, 40, 45, 47–8, 54, 64–7, 72, 78, 80–3, 86, 102, 111, 114, 117, 132–5, 137, 139–41, 159, 165, 167–9, 173, 181, 183–5, 194, 205, 210, 213, 215–17, 224, 227–9, 230–1, 234, 244–6, 248–9, 251, 254–5, 260–4, 270, 273–4, 278–9, 281, 286–90, 292–5, 297–8, 300

gladness 121, 125, 127

gloves 44, 245; *see also* cloths; dress, dresses of children; garments of children

gnomes 225; *see also* dwarves

goblin, goblins 24, 35, 38, 272

godchild 28

godmother, godmothers 27–8
godparent, godparents 27–8, 39, 79
Gospel 41, 43, 48, 59–60, 121, 230
governance 44–6, 132, 137, 144
grammar 82, 207
grandchildren 46
grandfather 26, 37, 214; *see also*
    grandmother; grandparents
grandmother 26–7, 169; *see also*
    grandfather; grandparents
grandparents 87, 192–3, 199; *see also*
    grandfather; grandmother
grief 32, 242, 247–8, 261, 289, 293
Grimm, brothers 256, 260
grotesque 26, 255, 259, 263
growing 1, 5, 9, 11, 61, 100, 115, 118,
    123, 126, 132–3, 168, 175–6, 182,
    186, 192, 200, 227, 277
grownups 209, 212–13
growth 49, 65, 76, 115–16, 123,
    125–7, 178, 190–1, 235
Grundtvig, Nikolaj Frederik Severin 7,
    111–30, 226, 233–4, 236–7
Grundtvigianism 112, 287
guardians 46, 95
guardianship 105
gymnasier 82; *see also* curriculum,
    curricula
gymnasium 141

habit, habits 80, 139–40, 245; *see
    also* custom customs; tradition,
    traditions;
hair, of children 18, 20, 293, 297, 311
hair–pulling 84
handwork 135
handwriting 207
Hansen, Peder 35
happiness 1, 25, 48, 102, 121, 125–6,
    225, 275
happy 19–20, 23, 28–9, 31, 49, 52, 61,
    112, 119, 123, 127–8, 159, 210, 215,
    227, 277, 293, 298
hardship 126, 206, 215–16, 261
harm, harmful 17, 21, 23–4, 28, 35,
    93–4, 102, 114, 125, 139
harmony 29, 176, 248, 300
harvesting 87, 168
Hauge, Hans Nielsen 35–6
Haustafel 56, 62, 74, 79; *see also*
    Household Code
healing, healed 17, 116, 121,
    259, 274

health 1, 13, 17, 92–4, 96, 99, 101,
    170, 215; *see also* illness; sick,
    sickness; symptoms
healthy 28–9, 213, 231, 252, 278, 289
heaven 49–50, 52–3, 59, 65, 75, 115,
    126, 129–30, 226, 247–8, 252, 275
height, of children 63
hepatitis 25; *see also* health; illness;
    sick, sickness; symptoms
herding, by children 80–1, 87, 168–9,
    172, 190
hero, heroine, heroes 210, 216, 223,
    235, 247–8, 256, 260, 283, 293, 300
hierarchy, hierarchies 43, 93, 96,
    248, 250
Hjortberg (family) 66–8
Holck, Hans 242, 244, 251
holiday, holidays 137, 180–2, 186–7,
    211, 222, 234
Holm (family) 71–2
Holst, Elling 284
homes 64, 100, 115, 139, 164,
    181, 199; *see also* house, houses;
    household, households
homesickness 198
homework 140, 159
honest 27, 46, 48, 94, 228, 234, 288–9
honor 5, 22, 43, 45, 63, 117, 126, 128,
    154, 217, 234–5, 246
horror 84, 211, 213, 215, 262–3
horse, horses 23, 81, 167–8, 228; *see
    also* animal, animals
house, houses 20, 23, 25, 32, 34, 41,
    43, 45–6, 51, 54, 61–2, 74, 76, 80,
    93, 95, 140, 158, 165, 167, 211,
    213–14, 217–218, 227, 242, 244,
    249, 253, 275, 294, 296
household, households 6, 8–9, 37– 38,
    40–7, 49–52, 53–5, 57, 61–2, 74,
    78–81, 88, 92–8, 122, 142,144, 164,
    168–70, 177–8, 185, 197; *see also*
    homes; house, houses
Houshold Code 8–9, 40–5, 49–50,
    54–5, 79; *see also* Haustafel
housekeeping 168
humanism 206, 215, 217
humanity 113–16, 119–21, 127–8
humiliation 84, 210
humility 248
humorous 14, 45, 227, 245, 294, 296
hunger, of children 169, 173
hungry 25, 116, 163, 260
hunt, hunting, by children 168

hymn, hymns 3, 10–12, 44–5, 56, 111–13, 115, 123–5, 127–30, 220, 222–3, 225, 228, 230, 233–4, 236, 248

Ibsen, Henrik 226, 232
ideal, ideals 1, 8, 10, 58, 60–1, 64–5, 72–3, 80, 84, 101, 112, 157, 160, 191, 202, 221, 228, 247–8, 256, 274, 297, 300
idealization 62, 288, 297
identity, identities 72, 188, 191–2, 198, 284, 286, 293, 299–300; class identity 9; religious identity 4; ethic identity 13, 202; Sami identity 195, 198, 201–2, 284, 286
ideology, ideologies 42, 44, 91, 251, 277
illegitimate 132, 166
illiteracy 76–7, 84, 152
illness 19, 36, 80, 247–50, 252; *see also* health; sick, sikness; symptoms
imagination 161, 242, 244, 257, 269, 273–4
imaginative 12, 246, 254, 258, 272–3, 276
imitate, imitating 65, 114, 157–8, 160, 250–1
imitation 62, 157, 244
immaturity, immature 101, 285
inability 137, 144, 248, 263
incident, incidents 205, 207, 209–10, 212, 217, 246, 289
independence 36, 148, 192, 209, 211, 217, 224, 266, 287, 299
independent 3, 11, 97, 133, 149, 157, 160, 165, 172, 195, 213, 217, 221, 224, 229, 242, 251, 286, 289, 293, 300–1
indigenous 188–91, 195–7, 203–4 ; *see also* Sami
industrial 85, 99, 146, 163–6, 168–70, 172–3
industrialization 9, 92, 100, 163–4, 166, 169, 269–70
inexperience, of children 285
infancy 6, 75, 93
infant, infants 26–7, 29, 33, 35, 59–61, 66–7, 69–71, 75–6, 94, 112, 115, 125, 166, 190
infanticide 31, 94
inheritance 30, 95, 105, 122, 252
inhuman 26, 29
injuries 242, 261

innocence 61, 72, 277
innocent 63, 101, 246, 285
institutionalized 149–50, 213
instruction 40, 43, 45, 47–9, 54–5, 64, 69–70, 124, 133, 136, 138–9, 143, 147, 188, 193, 195–7; *see also* education
intelligence 28, 262
involvement 1, 36, 96, 98, 100, 103
invulnerable 21

Jesus 22, 24–5, 51–3, 59, 61, 65, 70, 75, 112, 116, 121, 123–7, 230
Johnson, Eyvind 303, 306–8, 313–14, 316
jokes 19
journal, journals 4, 104, 130, 218, 237, 242, 244–5, 250–1; *see also* magazine, magazines; periodical, periodicals
joyful 20, 112, 116, 123, 127, 247, 249, 252
joyous 125
Judaism 96
juvenile 243–5, 249

kidnapping 32, 288
Kierkegaard, Søren 112, 114, 126
kill, killing 4, 26, 29, 35, 142, 206, 213–21, 292
killed 19, 21, 29–30, 94, 214, 218–19, 231, 274
kindergarten 107, 202, 285
kindness 51, 127, 160, 265
king 39, 41, 43, 45–46, 51, 92, 94–7, 106, 126, 137, 139, 143, 162, 198, 221, 231–2, 256, 261, 277, 279
kiss 115, 227
Kivi, Aleksis 77, 84, 89
knowledgeable 36
Krag (family) 66–7
Kristensen, Evald Tang 17, 19, 28

labor 7, 61, 76, 78, 81, 101, 131, 163–5, 167–73, 175–7, 180–3, 185–6, 203, 227, 229–30, 235–7, 299
Lagerlöf, Selma 233, 315
lament, laments 30, 126
land, lands 40, 45, 48, 53, 95, 165, 230, 251, 269, 273–4, 279, 281
Landstad, Magnus B. 17
language, languages 3, 5, 39–40, 49, 55, 62, 66, 69–70, 72, 97, 104, 114,

119, 133, 142, 149–50, 157, 160, 188–93, 195–204, 223, 226, 229–30, 241, 243, 249, 255, 260, 269, 273, 286, 288
Lapp 196–7; *see also* Sami
Latin 4, 82, 118–19, 148–50, 152, 156–62
laugh 115, 123, 226–7, 256, 296
laws 3, 9, 92–5, 101–2, 105–6, 135, 154, 182; *see also* legislation
lazy 84
learn, learning 5, 13, 28, 40, 43, 45–8, 52–5, 62, 64–5, 80, 83, 85, 87, 97, 102, 111–14, 116–20, 122, 133, 135, 141, 147, 150–1, 157–9, 165–8, 173, 189, 194–6, 198–200, 202, 209, 215–16, 222, 228–9, 231, 242, 260, 295
legacy 131, 144, 241
legend, legends 26, 29, 31
legislation 2, 58, 62, 74, 87, 91–3, 95, 97–101, 106, 149, 152, 162, 164–5, 167, 170, 172–3, 175, 182; *see also* laws
legitimate 36, 41, 132, 244
leisure 5, 7, 136, 140, 165, 175, 269
lesson, lessons 48, 97, 143, 222, 242, 246, 255
letter, letters 27, 42, 51, 63–5, 84, 112, 120, 125–6, 129–30, 157, 161, 242, 245, 294
liberalism 144
lifestyle 99, 191–2, 195
Linder (family) 86, 90
Lindgren, Astrid 11, 233, 267–71, 278, 280–1, 283–4
literacy 2, 5–6, 10, 40, 65, 76–7, 79–80, 82–3, 85, 87, 98, 103–4, 107, 152, 244
literate 40, 79, 156
literature 2–3, 6, 9, 11–12, 56, 111–12, 119, 174, 198, 224–5, 239, 242, 244, 250–1, 255, 259, 265–7, 270–2, 275–8, 280–1, 283–7, 289–91, 293, 295, 297, 299–301
liturgy 60; *see also* Eucharist
livelihood 126, 141, 165–6 , 177, 190
Lo–Johansson, Ivar 186, 250, 253
loss 29, 197, 201, 216, 242, 248
lost 21, 27–8, 47, 70, 87, 126, 198, 202, 208, 213, 216–17, 242, 245, 293
love 8, 10, 25, 29, 41, 43, 45–6, 54, 62, 64, 100, 114, 116–17, 119, 124, 127,

154, 192–3, 220–1, 224–9, 235, 243, 248, 259, 263, 271–2
loveable 159
loving 65, 100, 124–5, 256, 274
Luther, Martin 8, 11, 40–1, 43–6, 49–50, 52, 54, 56, 59–62, 64–5, 70, 74–5, 79, 111, 117, 122–4, 126, 130, 152, 154, 161
Lutheran 4–6, 8–11, 13, 35, 40–2, 44, 48, 50–2, 55, 56n13, 58–63, 65, 67, 69–76, 83, 959, 103–4, 111–13, 115, 117, 121, 127–8, 130, 132, 144, 154, 161, 167, 220–1, 223, 225, 228, 230, 244
Lutheranism 6, 8–10, 12, 58, 62, 95, 111, 127

madness 35
magazine, magazines, 87, 204, 242, 244–6, 248, 251–2, 287, 301; *see also* journal, journals
magic, magical 17–18, 23, 32–3, 255, 259
maids 80
male, males 48, 80, 93, 103, 113, 135, 148, 160, 168, 172, 185, 226
maltreatment 101
manners 72–3, 80, 140
marriage 26, 41, 56, 61, 66, 99, 260, 285
Martinson, Harry 303, 308, 310, 312, 314, 316
Martinson, Moa 303, 306, 308, 312, 315–16
masculinity 274
maternal 26, 135
mathematics 142, 149, 160
matrimony 79
maturation 243
mature 81, 141, 209, 300
maturity 93, 151, 247
meal, meals of children 83, 199
medication, for children 247–8, 252
memorization 79, 118, 122, 157, 161
memory, memories 28, 47, 127, 129, 157, 205–8, 210–11, 213–14, 217–18, 220, 235, 290, 297
metaphor, metaphors 74, 246, 250, 252
midwife, midwives 70, 230
migration 100, 134, 164, 177, 190
minor, minors 32, 81, 134, 169, 171–2, 214, 245
minority 4–5, 7, 96, 185, 191, 195, 201
miracle 257

miscarriage 31
misconduct 94
misdeeds 135
Moe, Jørgen 226, 232, 267, 273, 286–8, 290–2, 294
Moe, Moltke 36
molding, of children 115, 155–6, 158, 160, 266
mortality, of children 17, 27, 66, 75–6, 166, 190, 213
mother, mothers 1, 17–21, 23–6, 29–31, 35–7, 43, 45–6, 48, 54, 58–9, 62–3, 66–7, 70, 94–5, 120, 125, 135, 155, 165–6, 168, 170–2, 188–91, 195, 198–9, 201–2, 212, 216, 221, 227–8, 231, 234, 245–8, 252, 263, 268, 289, 296–7
motif, motifs: play 269–70, 272, 275, 290, 299–301; competent 285–7
Munck, Johan Reinhold 84–6
Munthe, Gerhard 294–5
music 3, 10–11, 111, 118, 123, 220, 222–3, 226–7, 232, 235
mystery, mysteries 53, 113, 116–19, 127
mythology, myths 11, 112, 114, 116–17, 119, 121, 129, 245

naming, of children 26–31, 69; *see also* baptism
nanny 289
narrative, narratives 53–4, 104, 145, 160, 189, 206–7, 210, 214, 216, 248–9, 255, 257–8, 263, 268, 271–3, 275–6, 278, 280, 293
nasty 261
nationalism 191–2
nationbuilding 112, 284, 293, 299
naughty 268
needs, of children 2, 6, 9, 14, 91, 100, 127, 141, 151, 168, 243, 298
neglect 12, 76, 80, 94–5, 115, 121, 147, 191
negligence, negligent 32, 135, 228, 245
New Testament 42, 62, 64, 122
newborn 1, 21–4, 26–7, 29–30
newspaper, newspapers 4, 77, 84–5, 90, 155, 169–70, 175, 183–4, 241–4, 249–51; *see also* journal, journals; magazine, magazines
nightingale 254, 256, 259; *see also* bird, birds
nomadic 190–1, 194, 197

norm, norms 36–7, 49, 62, 78, 100, 136, 144, 167–8, 171, 206, 242, 284, 290, 296, 299
normative 58–9, 167–8, 265
Norwegianization 196, 199–202
nourish, nourishing 115, 123–4, 126
novel, novels 3–4, 6, 77, 84–5, 144, 163, 226, 231, 239, 254, 260, 263, 279, 301
nursery 277
nurture, nurturing 1, 8, 43, 51, 122, 145, 243, 247
nutrition 155, 163
nymph, nymphs 23, 25, 29, 35–8

obedience 43–5, 49, 51, 54–5, 61, 65, 93–4, 154, 156, 250
obedient 38, 43, 79, 102, 158–9, 288
obligations, to children 4, 8–9, 14, 43, 51; *see also* duty, duties to children
obstetric 36
offspring 63, 94, 97, 154, 159, 166
Old Testament 56, 158
ombudsman 2, 91, 202, 285
omens 17, 20, 33
oppression, oppressive 30, 265
ordinance, ordinances 44, 48, 98, 134–5, 139–41, 144
organization, organizations 7, 70, 85, 100, 104, 107, 131–2, 134, 137–8, 140–1, 143–4, 176, 178, 254
orphan, orphans 8, 111, 116, 169
orphanages 111

Pade, Johannes 52–4, 57
pagan, paganism 23, 32–5
pain, painful 70, 84, 126–7, 201, 213, 246, 249, 255, 259–62
Palladius, Peder 64–5, 75
papa 278–9; *see also* father, fathers
papistry, papistical 32–3, 35
parent, parents 1, 8, 10–11, 22–3, 25–30, 32, 41–3, 46, 50–2, 54, 59, 61–5, 69–73, 79, 82–3, 86–7, 90, 93–5, 97–9, 101–3, 105, 117–18, 122, 132–41, 144, 150, 153–4, 158–9, 164–73, 175–6, 178, 182, 186, 192–3, 201–3, 207–13, 228, 235, 242–3, 246–9, 251–2, 277, 284–5, 289, 292, 299
parental 93, 135–6, 138, 154, 170, 185
parenthood 51, 62, 70
pastoral 59, 70, 143, 150–1
pasture 168, 298

paterfamilias 41, 43, 45–6, 51, 54, 62
paternal 26, 43, 54
paternity 95
patriarchal 43–6, 54, 93
patriotic 215–16, 223, 228–9, 251
patriotism 206, 215, 223, 226
peasant, peasants 43, 50, 99, 120, 154, 223–4, 226, 231, 275–6
pedagogic, pedagogical 11, 42, 47–8, 62, 64–5, 91, 99, 136, 138, 152, 159–61, 237, 245, 249, 265
pedagogue 48, 90, 193
pedagogy 5, 47, 53–4, 64–5, 103, 141, 285
peer, peers 86, 97
perception, perceptions: of children 3, 100, 103, 189, 243, 266–7, 270–1, 277, 309; of childhood 127, 213, 217, 266, 270
periodical, periodicals 175, 241–4, 245–6, 250–1; *see also* journal, journals; magazine, magazines
persecution 256
Pétursson, Hallgrímur 111
phase, of childhood 17, 23
philanthropy 88, 100, 103, 161
philosophy, philosophical 33, 116, 153, 236, 258, 279
Pietism, Pietistic 5, 10, 20, 45, 59, 83, 91, 98–100, 103–4, 112, 287
piety 62, 65, 71, 74, 247
pious 31, 69, 246
Pippi Longstocking 2, 11, 233, 267–9, 281, 283, 300
play 13, 19, 64–5, 75, 112, 115, 118–19, 140, 176, 220, 222, 225–6, 228, 244–6, 251, 269–76, 280, 286–7, 290–1, 293, 295–6
playful, playfulness 128, 245, 259, 269, 271, 273
playground 185, 263
playing 11, 46, 70, 166, 223, 231, 235, 242, 258, 260, 285–6, 290, 294, 299–300
pleasure, pleasures 46–7, 117, 128, 159, 230, 244, 251, 255, 259, 261–3, 296
poem, poems 2–3, 56, 111–12, 114, 116, 118–21, 123, 128, 224–6, 231, 254, 283
poetry 36, 226, 232
policy, policies 2–3, 13, 91, 93, 101, 104, 111, 131–2, 144, 188–9, 191–2, 195–7, 199–203, 244

polite 159, 228, 294
Pontoppidan, Erik 8, 33, 39, 45–9, 52, 56, 111, 161
poor–relief 98, 132–9, 143–4, 165, 171–2, 174
porridge 199
portrait, portraits 10, 42, 58–9, 62–9, 71–4, 160, 255
potential 98, 100, 143, 192, 201, 244, 279; of children 14, 229, 244, 305
poverty 1, 111, 127, 131–2, 135, 138, 169–70, 256
power, powers 2, 11, 17, 22–4, 28–9, 31–2, 38, 47–8, 55, 85, 92–4, 96, 114–15, 119–21, 123–4, 137, 150–2, 155, 157, 161, 228, 241, 255–6, 258–61, 263, 267–9, 280–1, 286, 296, 298
powerful 24, 29, 44, 54, 113, 123, 150, 188
powerless, powerlessness 201, 285
prayer, prayers 25, 31, 40, 64–5, 70, 72, 79, 122, 126, 234, 247, 252
precept, precepts 27, 43, 121, 157
precious, children as 38
precocious children 259
pregnancy 17–19, 26, 35–6
pregnant 18–20
premature 277
pretty 115, 227, 274
pride 73, 210, 217
procreate 60, 62
procreation 41, 60
prohibition, prohibitions 19, 56, 133–4, 196, 285
property 95, 99, 105, 148, 167, 222, 231, 254
prophecies 20–1
protagonist, protagonists 158, 259, 263, 272–3
protection 1–2, 9, 12–13, 18, 23–4, 36, 91–2, 94, 99–104, 106, 113, 115, 128, 144, 170, 172, 182, 243, 285
protective 23, 25–6, 38, 92, 101
Protestant 3, 8, 40, 44–5, 52, 58–60, 62, 64, 70, 75
Protestantism 59–61, 73
proverbs 49
Prøysen, Alf 229–30
prudent 48, 51, 53
Psalm 40, 61, 75
psychology 201, 260, 271

punish, punishing 32, 51, 65, 44, 93–4, 137, 289

punishment, punishments 1, 20, 51, 65, 93–4, 100, 259–60, 268–9, 285, 290

pupil, pupils 45–6, 48–9, 65, 76, 82–4, 86, 102, 133–5, 137, 140–2, 147–50, 157–61, 171–2, 175, 181, 192–3, 196, 198, 200, 202, 205, 215–16, 235, 285

puppets 228

pure 44, 114, 121

Quintilian 157

racism 75, 196

Rahkonen, Aleksanteri 86

rational 35, 48, 55, 61, 248–9, 277–8

rationalism 50, 98, 112

rationalist 49

reaction 48, 99–100

reading 2, 7, 10, 47–49, 52, 54–6, 62, 65, 77, 79, 82–4, 103, 116, 124, 132, 140, 143, 157–9, 164, 173, 242, 244, 256, 262, 266, 270, 274–5, 280, 287, 293

reality, realities 54–5, 138, 153, 181, 209, 217, 245, 247, 256–9, 266, 271–4, 276, 290; *see also* fiction, fictional

rearing 73, 103, 135, 138

reason 18, 26, 48, 86, 101, 122, 133, 135, 141, 147, 154, 157, 180, 191, 231–2, 248, 266, 272, 278, 289, 294

rebirth 114, 121, 126

recalcitrant 269

reckless 278

recollection, recollections 57, 165, 206–7

recommendations 20, 111, 135, 139, 141

recovery 247

reflection, reflections 4, 13, 114, 216, 255, 260, 272, 277

reflective 49, 249, 258, 285

reform, reforms 42, 48, 52, 54, 76, 86, 96, 98, 102–6, 111–12, 133, 147–8, 152, 155, 160–1, 182, 197, 241

Reformation 3, 6, 8, 33, 40–1, 43–4, 47, 52, 54–5, 58–61, 70, 76, 79, 111, 117

reformer, reformers 41–2, 61, 64, 70, 75, 90

regret 36, 289, 296

regulation, regulations 43, 50–2, 56, 79, 93, 96–7, 100, 102, 136–7,149, 196, 241

reindeer 190, 194, 197, 200; *see also* animal, animals

rejoice, rejoicing 50, 70, 261

relationship, relationships 11, 13, 43, 46, 49–50, 54, 83, 114, 119, 127, 131, 138, 140, 144, 176, 191, 235, 242–3, 249, 257, 262, 266–8, 270, 272, 277, 280–1, 283, 286–7, 297, 299–300

relative, relatives 26–7, 31, 62, 80, 93, 180, 198, 248–50, 283

relaxation 222, 270

religion, religions 13, 17–18, 52, 58, 85, 99, 103, 111, 121–2, 128, 135–6, 159, 220

remedy 19

representation, representations 8, 58, 63, 71, 73–4, 260, 297, 300

reproduction 62, 79

resistance 36, 205–7, 209–10, 213, 216–17, 269

respect 31, 43, 51, 114, 127, 138, 143, 154, 178, 183, 267, 269, 288

responsibility, responsibilities 1, 4–5, 8, 10, 13, 28, 43, 48, 54, 77, 81, 92, 95, 98, 101–3, 136, 138–9, 143, 152, 154–6, 160, 166–7, 188, 194, 210, 213, 217, 249, 266, 269, 285, 287, 291, 299

restless 18, 30, 259

retarded 25

Reventlow, Johan Ludvig 48–53, 55–6, 161

reward 25, 43–4, 159, 210, 245, 293

rhetoric, rhetorical 58, 66, 69, 74, 101, 249

ridicule 61, 85, 296

rights, of children 1–2, 4, 9, 12–14, 91–3, 95–105, 113, 121, 128, 155–6, 265–9, 279–81, 285,

risk, risks 26, 33, 94, 99, 210

ritual, rituals 26, 28, 31, 38

roles: gender roles 9, 13, 234; of children 9, 117, 243, 250; of parents 61–2, 234

Rolfsen, Nordahl 292

Romanticism 6, 11, 101, 112, 128, 192, 236, 269, 271, 277

Rosenius, Carl Olof 111

Rousseau, Jean-Jacques 65, 75, 107, 112, 250, 280
rude 216, 226
rudimentary 148, 157, 193
rudiments 166
rule, rules 3, 17, 19, 21, 26, 38, 44–6, 49, 54–5, 66, 87, 96, 100–1, 120, 136–8, 142, 151, 157, 181, 193, 224, 262–3, 270
running 55, 64, 169, 178, 212, 249, 253, 294, 299
rural 2, 5, 9, 13, 76–9, 80–9, 93–94, 96–7, 99, 102, 112, 163–9, 172–82, 184–7, 192, 214–15, 221, 223, 226–7, 230, 234, 236, 250, 252, 297

sacrament, sacraments 40–1, 61, 65, 80, 122, 124
sacred 33, 62, 73, 122, 257
sadness 118
safe 21, 23, 103, 125, 138, 212, 223, 227, 290, 299–300
safeguard, safeguarding 101–3, 285
safekeeping 124–5
safety 24, 99, 215, 227
saga, sagas 37, 225, 275
salvation 43, 45, 52, 62, 69–72, 95, 98, 125, 252, 259
Sami 7, 188–204
sanctity 60
Sandell, Karolina W. 111
Savior 25, 70, 100, 121, 252, 228
scare, scary 81, 212–13
school, schools: ambulatory schools 77, 83, 88, 161, 167, 177–9, 181–2, 185–7; boarding schools 86, 141, 177–9, 181, 186–7, 188–9, 191–4, 196–203; burgher schools 149; church schools 132, 134, 137, 139–44; commercial schools 141–2; commoners' schools 148–50, 152–4, 156, 158–61; confirmation schools 83, 87, 195; elementary schools 85–8, 139–40, 143, 149, 156, 160–1, 167, 170–2, 180, 199, 216, 228, 232–3; factory schools 170, 172; grammar schools 82; high schools 111–12, 118–20, 123, 141, 220, 233, 237; industrial schools 99, 146; Latin schools 148–50, 152, 156–62; Sami schools 194, 198, 201–3; secondary schools 140–1,

144, 149, 156, 194, 232; Sunday schools 77, 83–4, 88, 136; work school 182–5, 187
schoolbag 210
schoolboys 82
schoolchildren 49–51, 152, 172, 197, 205
schooling 47, 55, 76–9, 83, 86–8, 92, 95–9, 102–4, 112, 114, 118, 132, 136, 140, 142–4, 150–1, 153–5, 159–62, 176–8, 181, 193, 195, 197–9, 201, 285
schoolmaster, schoolmasters 46–7, 52, 57, 82, 155, 178
schoolteachers 137
schoolwork 87
Scripture 98, 154
seaboys 296
secular 41, 44, 48, 54–5, 72, 79, 95, 153–4, 161, 198, 220, 222, 244
security 79, 100, 192
segregation 98, 131, 145, 197
selfishness 121
sensation 260, 262
sense, senses 1, 8, 77, 96, 98, 102, 114, 118, 124, 133, 138, 148, 150–1, 155, 157–8, 190, 217, 227, 257–8, 262–3, 271, 296–7, 301
sensibilities 235
sensible 273
sensitive, sensitivity 195, 271, 273
sentiment, sentiments 85–6, 100, 279
seriousness 44, 268
sermon, sermons 83, 126, 111–12, 123, 130, 287
servant, servants 45–8, 50, 58, 62, 73, 80, 93, 97, 135, 143, 148, 155, 157–8, 164–6, 168, 181, 293
sexes 27, 50, 65
sexism 75
sexual, sexuality 62, 94, 200
Shakespeare, William 254
shame, shameful 84, 290, 296
sheep 5, 19, 66, 175, 177, 181, 184, 186, 190, 215; *see also* animal, animals
shepherd 246
shoe, shoes 169, 254–5, 259–60, 262, 273
sibling, siblings 26, 46, 68–70, 72, 81, 95, 169–72, 208, 273, 284–6, 290–1; *see also* brother, brothers; sister, sisters

sick, sickness 17, 19, 25, 27, 34, 116, 133–4, 142, 208, 213, 242, 248; *see also* health; illness
simplicity 53, 256, 274
sinful, sinfulness 46, 65 121
sing 115, 119, 124–5, 222, 224–5, 228–32, 234
singer 221, 229
singing 10–12, 118, 123, 220–3, 227, 230, 232–3, 235, 248, 257
sins 22, 122, 247
sister, sisters 26, 30, 66, 68, 72, 95, 169, 172, 214, 216, 247–8, 263, 274, 289–290; *see also* sibling, siblings
Sivle, Per 224, 232, 234
Skaktavl (family) 66, 68
skating 228, 290, 300
skills 79–86, 88, 97, 99, 102–3, 132, 135, 143, 150, 153, 155, 157, 167–8, 172–3, 192, 242
sledge, sledging 255, 294, 296, 300
sleep, sleeping 29, 60, 68, 115, 124–5, 193, 233, 224, 249
small 1, 8, 18, 20, 30–2, 36, 38, 40, 44–6, 49, 54, 59, 61–2, 64–5, 74, 77–9, 82, 86, 92, 105, 115, 118–19, 122–4, 126–7, 151, 156, 161, 165, 168, 187, 198, 208, 224–5, 227, 230, 252, 258, 269, 272, 286–7, 289–90, 294, 296–8
smart 295
smile, smiling 61, 115, 210
snowball, snowballs 275–6, 296
socialization 80, 88, 139–40, 193
society, societies 6, 9, 12, 29, 36, 41, 43, 48, 54–5, 58–9, 61–2, 77–9, 85, 87, 92–3, 96–7, 100–2, 104, 117, 119, 134–6, 141, 143, 151, 153–6, 158, 160–1, 163–4, 166–9, 174, 176–7, 180–1, 185–6, 192–4, 198, 201–2, 221, 225, 234, 236, 241, 243–4, 250–1, 265, 269, 283, 285–6, 296–7, 299
song, songs 2, 10–12, 111–15, 117–19, 123, 126, 128–30, 220–37, 252, 257, 259, 283, 287
songbook, songbooks 4, 123, 220–7, 228–35, 237
sons 63, 67–8, 82–3, 112, 114, 126, 168, 171, 208, 252, 296
sorrow, sorrows 124–6, 208, 248, 261
soul, souls 47, 114–15, 118, 123, 125–6, 248, 255, 273

speech, speeches 3, 51–2, 114–15, 150, 268–9
spelling 140, 207
sphere: ecclesiastical 76; humoristic 268; international 266; political 156; private 71, 213, 243, 250; public 58, 71, 73, 241–4, 250
spinning 24, 167, 227, 278
spirits 17, 23, 31–3, 35–7, 114, 127, 278
spiritual 51, 65, 117, 119, 123–7, 259, 287, 290
sports 7, 221, 224–5, 235
stage, stages: of education 140, 149; of life 8, 136, 277
status: adult 243; of children 4, 36, 60–1, 243, 286, 308, 310; of Sami 191, 196, 202; social 167, 202, 312
Struensee, Johann Friedrich 241, 251
stepchildren 46
stepmother 84, 260
stillborn 66–70
story, stories: Biblical 47; for children 2, 6, 11, 118, 242, 245, 254–6, 259–60, 263, 269–71, 278, 280, 283, 286–8, 290, 292, 305, 308–9, 312–13, 315; told by children 206–17
storytelling 118, 255, 296
strategy, strategies, 66, 155, 165, 172–3, 215, 219, 256
student, students 2, 14, 17, 86, 132, 202, 214, 285
stupid, stupidity 25, 256, 298
subjectivity 265–7, 273, 279–80
subordinate, subordinates 41, 43, 45–6, 87, 134–5, 150–1, 249
subordination 61
suckle 115
suffering, sufferings 22–3, 26, 101, 126–7, 163, 249, 253, 255, 259–63
supernatural 17, 21–2, 32, 35–6, 193
superstition 18, 20, 32–6, 38, 150, 222
superstitious 28, 32–3, 48
supervision 135, 139–40, 150, 285–7, 296
supper, of children 199, 208
survival 35, 81, 171, 173, 192, 214
Svenningsen (family) 62–6
swaddling 33, 35
sweet 114–15, 118, 125, 227, 252
sweeties 171
swimming 18, 211, 274
syllabus 99

symbol, symbols 9, 62, 69, 167, 224–5, 235
sympathy 142, 215, 262
symptoms 247–8 ; *see also* illness, ilnesses
Søren Kierkegaard 32, 112, 114, 126, 160

table 61, 64, 72, 297; *see also* eating
tale, tales 57, 158–9, 162, 169, 211, 226, 231, 239, 245, 249, 254–61, 263, 270–3, 281, 287–8, 297
talents, of children 10, 28, 117
tasks 47, 63, 80–1, 87–8, 95, 139, 151, 154, 160, 168, 217, 222, 242
teach 8, 45, 47, 50, 54, 64, 81, 83, 86, 95, 98, 114, 119, 122, 135, 137–9, 143–4, 149, 156, 160, 167–8, 178, 188, 195–6, 199, 201–3, 245, 273, 280, 283, 287, 298, 312
teacher, teachers 36, 40, 43, 47–9, 51–2, 54, 65, 82–6, 97, 103–4, 114, 119, 122, 124, 129, 134, 137–41, 143, 149, 153, 156, 167, 188, 195–7, 199–200, 205, 207, 215–16, 218–19, 221, 232, 277, 290, 296
teaching, teachings 9, 41, 43–4, 46–7, 49–50, 52–5, 64, 76, 78–9, 82–6, 88, 96–7, 99, 103, 122–3, 134, 137, 139–40, 143–4, 150, 153, 161, 188, 194, 196–7, 202, 235, 278
tears 51, 227, 234, 248, 259, 268; *see also* crying
teenagers 81, 181, 183, 235; *see also* adolescent, adolescents; youths
Tegnér, Alice 232
temptation 127–8, 154, 272
tender 61, 66, 115
terror, terrifying 18, 29, 38, 84, 212, 215, 269
textbook, textbooks 52, 54–5, 79, 158–60, 162
theology 61, 130, 275
theory, theories 65, 93, 106, 111, 150–1, 161, 191, 237, 243
thoughtless 242, 245, 248–9
threat, threats 17, 21, 23, 37, 94, 99, 152, 155, 203, 215, 233, 269
tiny 106, 185, 216
tobogganing 294–6
toddlers 69
Topelius, Zacharias 267, 270, 276–8, 280–2

touch, touching 18–19, 23, 28
toys 272
tradition, traditions 10–12, 17–18, 21, 23, 26–7, 29–32, 36, 39, 47, 85, 91, 98, 103–5, 116, 121, 127–8, 144, 162, 180, 199, 220, 222–4, 226, 228, 230, 233–5, 250, 252, 255–6, 260, 267; *see also* custom, customs; habit, habits
traditional 37, 48–52, 55, 85, 92, 136, 142–4, 147–8, 150, 153, 155, 161, 178, 185, 190, 193–4, 230–1, 234, 236, 246, 260
tragedies 242
tragic 27, 247, 293
training 76, 80–1, 85, 88, 103, 134, 157, 165–6, 168, 171, 188, 194–5, 222–4; *see also* education; instruction
Treschow, Niels 153–4, 161
trick, tricks 193, 256
troll, trolls 22–6, 38
trouble, troubles, troublesome 20, 25, 124, 289
trust 1, 70, 131, 145, 168, 211, 225, 229, 231, 234–5, 248
tuition 2, 134, 172
Turi, Johan 198,204
tutelage 93
tutor, tutors 76–7, 83, 112, 118, 160
tutoring 64, 83–4, 86, 149, 161

ugly 18, 25
unable 47, 114, 133, 142, 148, 155, 257
unbaptized 23–4, 27, 30, 69–70; *see also* baptism
unborn 18, 20, 31, 33
uncle 169, 173, 210–11, 294
uncultured 192
underdeveloped 58, 148, 160
undernourishment 163
underworld 17, 24, 32
undisciplined 158
uneducated 135, 150; *see also* unlearned
uniqueness 103, 147, 175, 205
university, universities 31, 56, 61, 67, 74, 82–3, 85, 87, 104, 119, 149, 153, 174, 188, 194, 198, 204, 214, 220
unlearned 41; *see also* uneducated
unruly 249, 288
upbringing 17, 40–1, 43–5, 48, 51, 65, 76–7, 87–8, 92, 101–2, 135, 143,

161, 191–2, 228, 233, 269, 275, 280, 288–90
urban 2, 13, 93–4, 97, 99–102, 132–3, 144, 161, 163–5, 168–70, 172–3, 176–81, 186, 210, 296
Uro (family) 69–70

vacations 137, 139, 176
valuable 10, 59, 136, 147–8, 160, 235, 242, 270
value, values 5–6, 12, 18, 38, 53, 59, 98, 120, 131, 145, 154, 191, 193, 201, 206–7, 217, 223, 232, 235, 243, 255, 260, 263, 277, 283
Viking, Vikings 116, 231, 235, 274–5, 288–90
village, vilages 25, 27, 32, 36, 62, 76–8, 80–4, 86–8, 165–6, 169, 175–81, 185–6, 199, 214
violence 29, 193, 200, 268–9, 281
violent 280, 293
Virgin Mary 40
virtue, virtues 63–5, 141, 283, 291
virtuous 48, 65, 246, 287
vision, visions 35, 101, 116, 118–120, 122, 125, 246, 261, 276
vitality 113–16, 118–19, 123, 127, 218
vocation 8, 10, 41, 50, 54, 61–2, 73, 117, 154, 225
voice, of children 12, 118, 205, 222, 244, 261, 267
vulnerability 114–16
vulnerable 11, 101, 113–14, 116, 120, 127, 138, 165, 250, 285

walk, walking of children 25, 88, 172, 210, 228, 233, 235
Wallin, Olai 85–6
wash, washing by children 293, 297
weak 17, 25, 35, 80, 95, 116, 168, 269, 278
weakness 45, 138
weeping 29–30

welfare 1, 4, 6, 76, 78, 91, 102, 104, 107, 120, 131, 176, 269, 285, 300
Welhaven, Johan Sebastian 226, 231
wellbeing 113, 213
Wergeland, Henrik 225, 231
whipped 25
wicked 32, 162
Wigström, Eva 17, 19, 23, 26
wisdom 114, 118, 150, 227, 277
wise 48, 119, 248, 288–9
witch, witches 211, 260–1
womb 18, 20–1, 31, 70, 121, 155
work, done by children 6, 165–6, 168, 170, 172–3, 175–6, 181–4, 186
worker, workers 85, 138, 156, 164, 169–70, 172–3, 183, 206, 209, 211, 217, 230, 234, 250, 296
workforce 81, 97, 153
worship 46, 59, 122, 130
wounds 93, 123
wrong 19–20, 28, 32, 207, 228, 257
wrongdoing 121

young 6, 20, 23, 29, 46–7, 50–1, 55, 63–4, 77–7, 80–1, 83–6, 95–6, 99, 100–1, 104, 111, 113, 125, 141, 147, 157, 165, 167–70, 173, 176, 181–3, 186, 189, 192, 198, 200, 202, 208–11, 213–16, 227, 230, 241–2, 244, 246–7, 249–50, 252, 254, 259, 261–2, 267–8, 275, 278, 281, 301
youngsters 94
youth 92, 94, 96, 112, 123, 163, 175, 177, 185, 220, 231, 251
youthful 126
youths 142, 175–177, 182–6, 247; *see also* adolescent, adolescents; teenagers

Zweygberg, Fredrik Johan 83
Zwilgmeyer, Dikken 286, 293–5, 297, 300